**Language, Society,
and Paleoculture**

Language, Society, and Paleoculture

Essays by Edgar C. Polomé

Selected and Introduced
by Anwar S. Dil

Stanford University Press, Stanford, California   1982

Language Science and National Development

A Series Sponsored by the
Linguistic Research Group of Pakistan

General Editor: Anwar S. Dil

Stanford University Press
Stanford, California
© 1982 by Edgar C. Polomé
Introduction and compilation © 1982 by the
Board of Trustees of the
Leland Stanford Junior University
Printed in the United States of America
ISBN 0-8047-1149-6
LC 82-80925

H
2-8-85

Contents

Acknowledgments

The Linguistic Research Group of Pakistan and the General Editor of the Language Science and National Development Series are deeply grateful to Professor Edgar C. Polomé for giving us the privilege of presenting his selected writings as the nineteenth volume in our series established in 1970 to commemorate the International Education Year.

We are indebted to the editors and publishers of the following publications. The ready permission on the part of the holders of the copyrights, acknowledged in each case, is a proof of the existing international cooperation and goodwill that gives hope for better collaboration among scholars of all nations for international exchange of knowledge.

Cultural Languages and Contact Vernaculars in the Republic of the Congo. Texas Studies in Literature and Language 4(4). 499-511 (1963), with permission of the University of Texas Press.

The Choice of Official Languages in the Democratic Republic of the Congo. Language Problems of Developing Nations, ed. by Joshua Fishman, Charles Ferguson, and Jyotirindra Das Gupta (New York: Wiley, 1968), pp. 295-312, with permission of the publisher.

The Position of Swahili and Other Bantu Languages in Katanga. Texas Studies in Literature and Language 11(2). 905-13 (1969), with permission of the University of Texas Press.

Multilingualism in an African Urban Center: The Lubumbashi Case. Language Use and Social Change, ed. by W. H. Whiteley

(London: Oxford University Press, 1971), pp. 364-75, with permission of the International African Institute.

Problems and Techniques of a Sociolinguistically Oriented Language Survey: The Case of the Tanzania Survey. Language Surveys in Developing Nations: Papers and Reports on Sociolinguistic Surveys, ed. by Sirarpi Ohannessian, Charles Ferguson, and Edgar Polomé (Arlington, Va.: Center for Applied Linguistics, 1975), pp. 31-50, with permission of the publisher.

Tanzanian Language Policy and Swahili. National Language Planning and Treatment (Word 30, fascicles 1 and 2, 1979; special issue edited by Richard Wood), pp. 160-70, with permission of WORD, the journal of the International Linguistic Association.

Tanzania 1970: A Sociolinguistic Perspective. Language in Tanzania, ed. by E. C. Polomé and P. C. Hill (London: Oxford University Press, 1980), pp. 103-38, with permission of the International African Institute.

Sociolinguistically Oriented Language Surveys: Reflections on the Survey of Language Use and Language Teaching in Eastern Africa. Language in Society 11. 265-83 (1982), with permission of Cambridge University Press.

Swahili in Tanzania. Language in Tanzania, ed. by E. C. Polomé and P. C. Hill (London: Oxford University Press, 1980), pp. 79-100, with permission of the International African Institute.

Lubumbashi Swahili. Journal of African Languages 7(1). 14-25 (1968), with permission of the Center for International Programs, Michigan State University. (This journal was formerly a publication of the African Studies Center.)

Creolization Theory and Linguistic Prehistory. Studies in Diachronic, Synchronic, and Typological Linguistics. Festschrift for Oswald Szemerényi, ed. by Bela Brogyanyi (Amsterdam: John Benjamins, 1970), pp. 679-90, with permission of the publisher.

Arnold Highfield (New York: Academic Press, 1980), pp. 185-202, with permission of the publisher.

Creolization and Language Change. The Social Context of Creolization, ed. by E. Woolford and W. Washabaugh (Ann Arbor, Mich.: Karoma, 1982), pp. 126-36, with permission of the publisher.

Old Norse Religious Terminology in Indo-European Perspective. The Nordic Languages and Modern Linguistics, ed. by K.-H. Dahlstedt (Umeå: Sweden-Kunglige Skytteanska Samfundets Handlingar, 1975), vol. 2(13), pp. 654-65, with permission of the editor.

A Few Thoughts About Reconstructing Indo-European Culture and Religion. Journal of the Department of English (University of Calcutta) 14. 45-62 (1978), with permission of the department.

The Reconstruction of Proto-Bantu Culture from the Lexicon. L'Expansion Bantoue. Actes du Colloque International du CNRS, Viviers (France), 4-16 avril 1977, ed. by Luc Bouquiaux (Paris: SELAF, 1980), vol. 3, pp. 779-91, with permission of the publisher.

Indo-European Culture, with Special Attention to Religion. The Indo-Europeans in the Fourth and Third Millennia, ed. by E. C. Polomé (Ann Arbor, Mich.: Karoma, 1982), pp. 156-72, with permission of the publisher.

Lexical Data and Cultural Contacts: A Critique of the Study of Prehistoric Isoglosses and Borrowings. Logos Semantikos, III, Semantics, ed. by Wolf Dietrich and Horst Geckeler (Berlin: de Gruyter, 1981), pp. 505-13, with permission of the publisher.

EDITOR'S NOTE

These essays have been reprinted from the originals with only minor changes made in the interest of uniformity of style and appearance. In cases where substantive revisions have been made, proper notation has been added. Misprints and mistakes appearing in the originals have been corrected in consultation with the author. In some cases references, notes, and bibliographical entries have been updated. Footnotes marked by asterisks have been added by the Editor.

Introduction

Edgar Charles Polomé was born on July 31, 1920, in
Brussels, Belgium. After graduating from the Athénée Royal de
Koekelberg in Brussels, he attended the Université Libre de Bruxelles, earning the equivalent of a bachelor's degree in Germanic philology in 1940. During the next three years, he did graduate work in
Germanic philology, first at the Université Libre until it was closed
by the German occupation forces, and later at the Université Catho-
lique de Louvain, where he earned the equivalent of a master's degree
and spent an additional year learning Sanskrit and obtaining a teaching
certificate. In 1946 he returned to the Université Libre to work on
his Doctorat en philologie germanique, equivalent to a Ph. D. degree,
which he was awarded in 1949.

From 1942 to 1956 he taught Dutch, English, and German in
the educational system of the city of Brussels, serving also in 1954-
56 as a lecturer in Dutch for the Belgian Broadcasting Corporation.
In 1956, he was appointed professor of linguistics at the newly established Université Officielle du Congo Belge et du Ruanda-Urundi. For
four years he taught courses in general, Indo-European, and African
linguistics and carried on extensive field research on African sociolinguistic problems. In 1961, he came to the United States as Visiting Associate Professor in the Department of Germanic Languages
at the University of Texas at Austin, and since 1962 he has been Professor of Linguistics, Germanic Languages, and Oriental and African
Languages and Literatures at that university. He has also served as
Director of the Center for Asian Studies (1962-72) and as Chairman
of the Department of Oriental and African Languages and Literatures
(1969-76).

Dr. Polomé was a Fulbright Professor at the University of Kiel, Germany, in 1968, and Visiting Research Professor at the University of Dar es Salaam, Tanzania, in 1969-70. He has participated actively in numerous national and international conferences and has edited the proceedings of a number of such conferences, notably Old Norse Literature and Mythology (1969), Language Testing and Criteria for Linguistic Proficiency in South Asian Languages (1973), Man and the Ultimate (1979), and The Indo-Europeans in the Fourth and Third Millennia (1982). He has been a co-editor of the Journal of Indo-European Studies since its establishment in 1972, and is an active member of the editorial committee of Mankind Quarterly.

Polomé's Swahili Language Handbook (1967), sponsored and published by the Center for Applied Linguistics in Washington, D. C., remains a useful introduction to the general linguistic and cultural setting of the Swahili-speaking areas, and offers a readable description of the structure of the standard variety of the language as spoken in Zanzibar and the Mrima coast area.

Polomé's rich knowledge of the Swahili language and culture led to his appointment as Team Director of the Language Survey of Tanzania, part of the five-nation Survey of Language Use and Language Teaching in Eastern Africa, conducted during 1969-71. The resulting volume, Language in Tanzania (1980), co-edited with C. P. Hill, is a landmark in the field. Recommending the book to "all serious scholars and language planners interested in the question of language development," N. A. Kuhanga, Vice-Chancellor of the University of Dar es Salaam, in his Foreword, points out the merit of the survey results in the history and classification of Tanzanian languages, the distribution patterns of the usage of Swahili and other languages in the country, and the assessment of the role of Swahili in education, especially at the primary level.

An important by-product of the five-nation Survey was a 1971 conference held in New York to review the role and function of language surveys in light of the experiences gained. Polomé's excellent paper on the Tanzania Survey (Chapter 5 in this volume) was included in the resulting volume, Language Surveys in Developing Nations (1975), co-edited by Polomé, Charles Ferguson, and Sirarpi Ohannessian.

This selection of Polomé's contributions to sociolinguistics and related areas must inevitably exclude his distinguished work in African linguistics, Indo-European studies, and general linguistics. Although much of that work belongs squarely in the European linguistic tradition represented by Emile Benveniste and Georges Dumézil, among others, the essays in this volume constitute a sort of bridge between the European and American approaches to sociolinguistic research.

What is especially impressive in Polomé's sociolinguistic and paleocultural work is his open-minded outlook and his remarkable breadth, especially now that his classical Indo-European grounding and his African experiences have been supplemented by an increasing interest in the South Asian and Middle Eastern religious and mythological traditions. His careful descriptions of African sociolinguistic phenomena, centering on what happens when the languages of the colonizers and the colonized come in contact, have made him keenly aware of the great complexities involved in studying language as part of the larger framework of human communication and sociocultural change. In his more recent work, he is moving toward a broader synthesis of linguistics and the belief systems of peoples.

It gives me great pleasure to present this collection of Edgar Polomé's essays to readers across the world.

Anwar S. Dil

United States International University
San Diego, California
October 18, 1982

**Language, Society,
and Paleoculture**

Part I. Sociolinguistics

1 | Cultural Languages and Contact Vernaculars in the Republic of the Congo

More than any other new independent state in Africa south of the Sahara the young Republic of the Congo is faced with the complex problem of the linguistic factor in its national development. Though with the choice of French as the official language of the new state it met the immediate need for a "language of wider communication used for national purposes as well as for access to science and international communication, "[1] it actually dodged the question of assigning their proper share to the major local languages in the cultural and social development of the African communities. In spite of considerable efforts to expand the use of French as the medium for education at all levels, only a very small portion of the population has indeed a working knowledge of this language, and the African elite of the Congo practically never uses French at home. This is essentially due to the fact that the education of women has considerably lagged behind for several decades, so that only very few young African wives would be able to resort to French for all practical purposes of communication in their family life. Therefore, in spite of the status of French as the official language of the Republic, there is very little prospect of its ever superseding the established local cultural languages and contact vernaculars, which have become deeply rooted in wide areas of the nation after numerous decades of constantly expanded use.

Though it would be quite erroneous to ascribe the same importance to language as a political factor in Africa as in Europe, it can appear as one of the characteristic features of tribal nationalism, especially when it is backed by a several-centuries-old cultural tradition! Therefore, the fact that the first African political party ever formed in the Congo—President Kasavubu's Abako—was originally an "association of the baKongo for the unification, conservation, and

expansion of kiKongo, " can hardly be considered as merely accidental.
The baKongo tribesmen living in the Lower Congo can indeed boast of
a long tradition in the use of their language for cultural purposes,
since the seventeenth-century Jesuit missions to the Kongo kingdom
of San Salvador published various religious books in it and even compiled a grammar and a dictionary of its southern dialect.[2] Later on,
the European traders along the coast used a basically kiKongo contact
vernacular known as "Fiote. " No actual common literary standard
emerged, however, from these early contacts with Western civilization and at the time of deeper European penetration in the Lower Congo
area, the action of local missions rather tended to emphasize the dialectal split in developing standardized literary forms in definite
regions, e.g. in maYombe, where the keener interest taken by several
missionaries[3] in the language problem in the Kangu area led to an early
normalization of the dialect spoken by the local villagers. As a reaction against this situation young baKongo intellectuals have initiated a
movement to level out the differences between the various dialects and
to create an acceptable common standard, which could be used by the
baKongo of Angola and the Congo Republic (in former French Equatorial
Africa) as well. In a hitherto unpublished tentative grammatical
sketch of "common kiKongo, " one of them states their aim very plainly:
"In spite of their special flavor local differences must not prevail over
our unity. " Unfortunately, while he reproaches the "foreigners" (i.e.
the missionaries) with "deliberately" preserving the dialectal split,
he ignores the fact that the baKongo themselves fail to agree about the
literary dialect which should serve as a basis for the development of
a common standard. As a matter of fact, as early as 1935 a Commission composed of delegates of the three main Catholic "vicariates" of
the Kongo-speaking area started working on the problem of unification,
but without any tangible result.[4] In spite of further efforts connected
with the development of a kiKongo press,[5] various "normalized" dialect forms are still being used by the different missions, e.g. the
maZinga dialect or Central kiKongo, described by K. E. Laman in
his Grammar of the Kongo Language (New York, 1912), or the east-
central dialect of the baMpaangu in the region of Lemfu, described
in Cours de kiKongo of F. L. Dereau (Namur, 1955). This last is
assumed to be "closest to the generally accepted forms" of kiKongo
and is presented as a model grammar to the baKongo trying to unify
their language,[6] though it actually sticks to the dialect variant of the
"vicariate" of Matadi.

Cultural Languages and Contact Vernaculars
in the Republic of the Congo

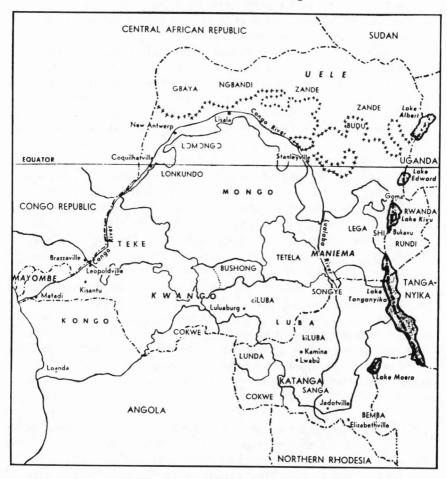

CENTRAL AFRICAN REPUBLIC   SUDAN

U E L E

GBAYA   NGBANDI   ZANDE

ZANDE   Lake Albert

New Antwerp   Lisala   Congo River   BUDU

LƆMƆNGƆ

EQUATOR   Coquilhatville   Stanleyville   UGANDA

LONKUNDO   Lake Edward

M O N G O   Goma

CONGO REPUBLIC   RWANDA Lake Kivu

LEGA   SHI Bukavu

TEKE   RUNDI

Brazzaville   TETELA   MANIEMA

Leopoldville   BUSHONG

MAYOMBE   Kisantu   K W A N G O   ciLUBA   SONGYE   Lake Tanganyika   TANGA-NYIKA

Matadi   Luluaburg

K O N G O   COKWE   L U B A

kiLUBA

Loanda   LUNDA   Kamina   Lwabù   Lake Moero

KATANGA   SANGA

ANGOLA   COKWE   Jadotville

BEMBA   Elizabethville

NORTHERN RHODESIA

•—·—·—·—.   Political Boundary

♦ ♦ ♦ ♦ ♦ ♦   Bantu (South) : Non-Bantu (North)

━━━━━━   Linguistic Boundary

Other languages, though not evidenced at such an early date
as kiKongo, preserve valuable literary material prior to European
penetration through oral transmission, e.g. the Bushong language of
the baKuba, whose tribal chronicle, recited only at enthronement
festivals, contains very archaic forms of language. Trade along the
Congo River upstream from the Stanley Pool led to the development
of a contact vernacular as early as 1890; it is usually assumed to be
based on Bobangi, which was spoken along the riverside from the
Lower Ubangi down to the mouth of the Kasayi,[7] but recent research
by Malcolm Guthrie rather seems to point to Boloki as its source.
It also contains numerous elements from the Lower Congo area as
well as quite a few Swahili loans brought over by the soldiers from
Zanzibar serving the Congo State. With the rapid increase in traffic
on the waterway, this trade language, known as liNgala, spread
more and more inland, e.g. as far as the Uele region in the northeast. This expansion, however, entailed a considerable adulteration
of the language, as it was used mainly by Europeans in their relations
with Africans, showing the most diversified linguistic background,
especially in the Congolese army, whose recruits often came from
non-Bantu speaking areas. As they adopted liNgala as the basic language, however, for their educational and evangelizing activity along
the Congo River, the Catholic missionaries made a deliberate effort
to bring it closer to the form used by the so-called baNgala tribes in
the area between New Antwerp and Lisalá. This consciously standardized liNgala was widely adopted for teaching purposes in the schools
of the capital, Leopoldville, with due reference to the local variants,
though, and most publications in liNgala now keep to this pattern as
well.

In the east, the slave traffic organized by Arab raiders introduced the coastal trade language of their African henchmen: thus,
Tippu Tip, probably the most conspicuous personality in this late
nineteenth-century trade,[8] is directly responsible for the scattering
of Swahili communities in the Lualaba area, mainly in Maniema.[9]
The dialect spoken by these communities is known as kiNgwana, i.e.
language of the waNgwana, "the more civilized people" as opposed
to the waShenzi, "the uncouth savages of the interior." A group of
waSwahili also assisted the muYeke chieftain Msiri in his conquest
of Katanga and discovered the rich copperfield of Kambove.[10] Later
on King Leopold II's Congo State reinforced this first penetration of

Swahili by recruiting most of its soldiers in Zanzibar, and Swahili remained in use for the training of soldiers in Katanga and the Oriental Province until World War I. With the development of the mining industry in the south, the labor shortage led to the systematic transfer of numerous workers from the northeastern areas where an upcountry dialect of Swahili was used as trade language. This gave rise to the development of Katanga Swahili, which has presently become the mother tongue of a growing percentage of the urban population of the Katangese mining district, whereas it is the only suitable means of intertribal communication for the Africans of various origin who have established residence there. Indeed, in a town like Elizabethville, only 16 percent of the population come from the neighboring rural districts and more than half have immigrated from outside the Katanga Province (about a fourth of the inhabitants are baLuba from the Kasayi Province).[11] An inquiry conducted among school children in a suburb of Elizabethville in 1961 showed that about 11 percent did not know any other African language than Katanga Swahili, whereas only very recently arrived children were not fluent in it and did not use it as their second language. The colloquial Swahili spoken in towns like Elizabethville or Jadotville is, however, very different from East Coast Swahili: its phonemic system has been strongly modified under the influence of Luba; though the changes in its morphology run along the same lines as in the upcountry dialects of East Africa, they are usually more marked; as for the vocabulary, numerous Arabic loans are discarded and replaced by Bantu or European (French, English, Portuguese, or Flemish) substitutes. As elsewhere in the eastern part of the Congo, however, whenever Swahili is taught in schools, a conscious effort is made to comply with the grammatical norms of the "classical" literary language as they have been established by the East African Swahili Committee. But this "Swahili ya kitabu," as they call it, is not always readily understood by less educated people in Katanga, so that a substandard written form is often resorted to when addressing a wider audience. This substandard form is not at all so close to the East African literary standard as a superficial inquiry into the written material appearing in the Congo might give the impression it is.[12] There is indeed a great diversity in it: Katanga, published by the St. John's Catholic mission in Elizabethville, is deliberately using a grammatically normalized language which is more remote from the spoken word than the less "improved" Katanga Swahili of Mwana Shaba, the periodical published by the Union

Minière du Haut-Katanga for its own personnel, or the popular weekly
La Semaine. Closer to colloquial speech are the plays performed in
Katanga.[13] It can accordingly be assumed that Swahili appears simultaneously as a cultural language and as a contact vernacular in Katanga, with very different levels of alteration and simplification according
to the sociocultural context in which its local variant is being used.
It is rather striking that a deliberate effort to improve the knowledge
of Swahili in Katanga has been made from the start by the seceding
provincial authorities, especially under the impulse of the late Minister of Education J. Kiwele. The recent publication of the two volumes
of E. Natalis, La langue swahilie: Cours méthodique et Exercices
(Liége, 1960), provides the pedagogical tool to this effect. The
nationalistic implications of this move may, however, lead to unpre-
dictable reactions in case of a reversal of policy in Katanga, so that
here, as elsewhere, the fate of Swahili as a "national" cultural language depends on the "too many emotional currents flowing through
Africa now."[14]

        The rapid development of urban civilization in Central Africa
has thus brought about linguistic situations in which definite languages
are being used at several levels of communication under multifarious
forms, ranging from the literary standard to the oversimplified contact vernacular, within the same area. This is especially the case
with Swahili in the Katangese mining district and with liNgala and
even kiKongo in Leopoldville. The situation is somewhat different
for ciLuba in the Kasayi province: the contact vernacular, to which
Europeans resorted for their relations with Africans in the main
towns there under the colonial rule, is indeed apparently doomed to
disappear with the remainders of the former Belgian administration.
Though it has often been described as a very adulterated form of Luba,
this so-called kiTuba rather seems to be based on an utterly rudimen-
tary form of Kongo, comparable as such to the Kwango contact language of similar origin. The local population never felt the need of
adopting it since the baLuba, as early as the late nineteenth century,
had already developed a colloquial common language for the purpose
of intercommunication. It was mainly based on the speech of the
Bakwa Disho and rapidly raised to the level of a cultural language
after being adopted as the medium for education by the very active
Catholic missions in the area. As practically all educated people
have been taught by them for two generations now, it has acquired a

considerable social prestige as the literary standard in which a few
gifted African writers start expressing their thoughts and feelings in
the scanty available periodicals.[15] In the various areas of the Luba
territory there are of course different levels of practical knowledge
of this standard, and tribal nationalism is often responsible for reluctance to its adoption, as among the strongly independently minded
baSongye; for similar sociocultural reasons even the linguistically
closely related bena Luluwa consciously stick to their dialectal peculiarities. This is evidenced by the use of different morphemes in the
structure of certain verbal forms, as shown here:

the "resultative": Luba pronominal prefix + á· + stem + i
                  (with "contrasting tone")
                Luluwa pronominal prefix + a·kú + stem + á;

the "constatative": Luba pronominal prefix + stem + ilé
                   Luluwa pronominal prefix + a·ká + stem + á.

Besides, in neighboring Katanga, where variously differentiated ki-
Luba dialects are spoken, the local missions have preferred to resort
to a standardized form of kiLuba-Samba for teaching purposes, which
is clearly different again from the Sanga dialect prevailing mainly
further south in the territory still under the rule of Msiri's baYeke
successors. The excellent Dictionnaire kiLuba-Français by F. E.
Van Avermaet, published in the Annales du Musée Royal du Congo
Belge (Sciences de l'Homme, Linguistique, Vol. 7, Tervuren, 1954),
gives clear evidence of the efforts of the Franciscan Fathers to develop
a kiLuba cultural standard based on the language forms of the area
around Lwabù (near Kamina); the Benedictine missions have not gone
as far ahead in standardizing kiSanga, but the work now being done
by A. Coupez may soon provide them with reliable linguistic descriptions to do so.[16] Therefore, the prospects for the expansion of
"literary" ciLuba as a cultural standard all over the Luba-speaking
area seem on the whole much less bright than many of its Catholic
missionary promoters expected a decade or so ago, especially with
regard to the linguistic implications of the present political situation
for northern Katanga.

     In the Kwango-Kwilu area, where Kongo influence had been
prevailing since the sixteenth century, the contact vernacular, which
used to be called Ikeleve or kiLeta under colonial rule, has gradually

developed from a kind of pidgin based on eastern kiKongo with elements
from various trade languages like "Fiote," liNgala, or Congo Swahili,
as well as from local dialects and French, Portuguese, etc. . . . into
a full-fledged cultural language presently used under the name of ki-
Tuba for the translation of the Bible and the production of Christian
literature. Though Catholic missions still sponsor the use of a standardized dialect of kiKongo (essentially kimaNyanga), it apparently
stands no chance against the steadily expanding literary form of ki-
Tuba, whose local variants also tend to become the "main means of
verbal communication in everyday conversation" in urban centers in
the Lower Congo area and along the Brazzaville-Pointe Noire railroad
in the former French Congo, according to recent inquiries by Harold
W. Fehderau.[17]

    In the non-Bantu area of the Northern Equatorial Province,
recent developments seem to involve better prospects for Sango, a
contact vernacular based on Ngbandi, an important Southern Sudanese
language spoken along the Ubangi River; though it has been widely
superseded by liNgala in the former Belgian territories in the last
decades, it is indeed very much alive in the Central African Republic
and enjoys a remarkable social prestige even among Bantu-speaking
tribes in the area.[18] In the long run, Ngbaka, with more than twice
as many speakers, may however threaten to supersede Ngbandi, as
efforts are being made to introduce literary forms of both as cultural
languages in West Ubangi.[19]

    A very remarkable example of development and expansion of
a cultural language for a larger linguistic area under European influence is supplied by the loNkundo dialect of Mongo in the Equatorial
Province, which has become the literary standard of numerous tribes
speaking related dialects far to the east of its own dialectal area
through the efficient action of the missionaries who introduced it into
education all over this territory and compiled remarkable grammatical
descriptions and excellent dictionaries of it, at the same time gathering and editing the best of its rich oral literature.[20] There is hardly
another language in Central Africa for which so much reliable material
has been published and the continuous efforts of the group of Aequatoria
under the leadership of Father G. Hulstaert in Coquilhatville to improve and expand its means of expression by encouraging gifted Africans to communicate in a spontaneous literary form and to record

their tribal traditions in collections of tales, besides producing plays
and current literature for their fellow tribesmen, have undoubtedly
been the decisive factor in its spread and recognition as the Mongo
cultural language.

In other regions efforts have also been made to raise a standardized form of a locally prominent language to the status of cultural
language for a wider area. This has especially been the case with
Zande in the border region bounded by the Republic of the Congo, the
Central African Republic, and the Sudan: under the colonial rule it
was used very extensively in southwest Sudanese schools and numerous works were published in it by Protestant and Catholic missions.
A language conference was held in 1941 in Bangenze for the purpose
of unification of its spelling,[21] but the Belgian and French authorities
did not take any real interest in this initiative, as Zande was taught
neither in the Ubangi province of French Equatorial Africa nor in the
Belgian Congo, although the bulk of the Zande population lived in the
latter.[22] Whether the cultural prestige enjoyed by the aZande and
their political hegemony over lesser tribes, like the Bantu baBudu,
will ultimately lead to a wider acceptance of their language for educational purposes and intertribal communication on a higher level depends very much on the further development of the political situation
in this part of the Republic of the Congo. At any rate, the present
policy of the Sudanese authorities making Arabic the only official language of the country and imposing its use even on the local administrative level in the Zande territory will undoubtedly prove a major
obstacle to eventual further interterritorial efforts to develop a
"unified" Zande common literary standard.

In the Kivu province the situation is by far more complicated,
as Swahili is strongly established there as contact vernacular, especially in Maniema where the only wider dialect cluster, the Lega complex,[23] has not even started developing any form of standardization.
Many people in this area are bilingual, e.g. the baKusu of the Lomami,
through close contact for several decades with the local Swahili-
speaking communities. Some speakers of Lega even fear that Swahili
is ultimately going to supersede their mother tongue.[24] In the east,
however, maShi, spoken mainly west and south of Bukavu in the region
of Kabare and Ngweshe, has already undergone a definite process of
unification and its use for religious education by missionaries in the

neighboring areas where closely related dialects are spoken has
contributed to its spread. In the region southwest of Goma, a language of the same group, kiHunde, is, however, being gradually
superseded by kinyaRwanda as a consequence of increasing immigration from the former Belgian U. N. trust territory of Rwanda.

West of the Lualaba, in the southeast of the Mongo linguistic
area, an entirely different sociocultural setting has led to an independent development of a branch of this language into oTetela, also known
as kiKusu east of the Lomami River. Through uncoordinate action of
Protestant and Catholic missions two strongly divergent spellings had
been introduced, which often made it hard for those trained in the
Wembo-Nyama orthography to read a text printed in the Tshumbe
variant of the written language; but quite recently a conscious effort
has been made to reduce the discrepancies to a minimum by a wider
use of the symbols of the Africa alphabet.[25] Spelling unification is
indeed a measure of pressing necessity in different areas, where
literary standards have been or are being developed because, in spite
of various insistent calls for action, as in 1959, by the Commission
for African Culture and Linguistics at the Department of Education in
Leopoldville,[26] no serious steps have been taken elsewhere to level
out most troublesome discrepancies and inaccuracies in the current
spelling of most of the Congolese languages.

This is but one aspect of the aftermath of the inconsistency
of the language policy of the former Belgian authorities in the Congo,
where, in spite of strenuous efforts by a particularly competent Commission for African Linguistics, practically nothing has been done to
give African languages their due share in education as the only suitable medium for a true understanding of the genuine values of African
cultural traditions.[27] Though at the present time it is difficult to pre-
dict what course of action the government of the Republic of the Congo
may take with regard to this problem, it is at least probable that the
growing consciousness of their cultural past will prompt the younger
generation of Congolese to take more efficient steps to save the little
that can still be preserved of their oral literature and that the necessity to cope with the pressing problem of illiteracy will lead the Congolese rulers to the logical conclusion that a satisfactory solution can
be much more adequately reached by teaching Africans to write and
read an African language closely related to their native dialect than

to impose upon them from the very start the drudgery of learning a
European language.

Though the figures concerning general primary education
in the Congo are very impressive,[28] the training of instructors lagged
behind considerably. A shortage of 15,000 was acknowledged by the
Belgian authorities in 1958, and in spite of all efforts, it was expected
to rise to at least 60,000 if general primary education at the lower
level was to be provided for all African children in the Congo.[29] As
for the interracial schools adopting the Belgian metropolitan curriculum, even with their low figures of attendance[30] the shortage in
experienced European staff was such that the Belgian government had
to resort to sending young Belgian teachers drafted for military service to the Congo to work in the schools. This "tósálisana" operation[31]
was merely patchwork and was of course discontinued on June 30,
1960. After Independence, in spite of all the efforts of the central
and provincial governments and of UNESCO on an international level,
it was impossible even to maintain the preexistent already insufficiently developed school system for lack of adequately trained staff.
Though the situation has gradually improved in recent months, it
stands to reason that the Republic of the Congo will not be able to
recruit a sufficient number of competent French-speaking teachers
to provide satisfactory opportunities for education for the rising
generation. Therefore, even if the use of French as a second language may be considered as an irreversible factual situation in the
Congo, the belated ambition of the Belgian colonial administration to
make it the only medium of education will undoubtedly prove unwork-
able in the near future, in spite of the recommendations of the Yaunde
conference in November 1961 as to the continued use of European languages as the basic medium for education in the former colonial territories. Even with the prestige attached to the language of the ruling
minority, French did not succeed in imposing itself on any group of
Africans as their actual colloquial language at all levels of social
life, and as the former technicians whose overwhelming majority
were Belgians, using exclusively French in their daily relations with
Africans in the larger towns, are gradually replaced by people of
various origins and widely diversified linguistic background, an increasing recourse to the local cultural language, enabling them to
communicate far more adequately with practically all levels of the
African population, is to be expected. This, in turn, will enhance

the African language with a new prestige and contribute to its further
expansion and improved usage, as what has recently happened in the
seceding Katanga province tends to confirm. Before Independence,
French was indeed the only medium of education in the state schools
and no instruction in the state schools and no instruction in African
languages was even offered in the official Teachers Training School
for African instructors of the Province in Elizabethville, but when
the students were given a free hand in organizing a show for their parents and friends as well as for the local population, they adapted the
French medieval play <u>La Farce de Maître Pathelin</u> to the local sociocultural context and performed it in the Katanga substandard form of
literary Swahili. After proclaiming their "independence," one of the
first measures taken by the Katangese authorities was to adopt Swahili,
along with French, as their official languages, and to introduce Swahili courses into the curriculum, taking special care to appoint whatever linguistically trained personnel was still available there to teach
its grammar properly to future instructors.

It is accordingly advisable to follow the evolution of the language situation in the former Belgian Congo very closely in order to
approach its diversity properly when training specialists for service
in any capacity in this country: besides a working knowledge of French,
an introduction to descriptive linguistics concentrating upon the structure of Central African languages should be the basis of further training in the contact vernacular or—better still—in the main cultural language of the area to which they are to be assigned. Stress should
therefore be laid on the preparation of teaching material to give adequate instruction not only in liNgala and Swahili (with due regard to
the Congo variants), but also in kiKongo, loMongo (loNkundo), ciLuba,
and further on as they assert themselves, in the other developing literary standards (oTetela, Zande, [Sango-]Ngbandi, etc.).[32]

NOTES

Revised version of a paper read at the University of Kentucky XVth
Foreign Language Conference on "Foreign Languages in National De-
fense" (27 April 1962). I am deeply indebted to Professor A. E.
Meeussen (Louvain-Tervuren) for most valuable information; to

Professor G. Brausch (Khartoum) and to Dr. J. Knappert (Mombasa) for interesting suggestions and remarks.

[1] Charles A. Ferguson ("The Language Factor in National Development" in Anthropological Linguistics 4 [Jan. 1962]: 26-27) defines the role of the language of the former colonial power in under-developed countries in Asia and Africa.

[2] Cf. C. M. Doke, "Early Bantu Literature—The Age of Brusciotto," in African Studies 18, no. 2 (Johannesburg, 1959): 49-67. Valuable bibliographical data have been collected by G. Van Bulck, S. J., Les Recherches Linguistiques au Congo Belge, Institut Royal Colonial Belge, Sect. des Sciences Morales et Politiques, Mémoires 16 (Brussels, 1948): 334-59.

[3] Cf. F. L. De Clercq, "Grammaire du kiYombe," Bibliothèque Congo 5 (Brussels, 1921), or F. L. Bittremieux, Mayombsch Idioticon, 3 vols. (Ghent-Brussels, 1922-27).

[4] Cf. J. Van Wing, "Nota over de Commissie voor Unificatie van het kiKongo, 1935-1936," in Kongo-Overzee 17 (1951): 38-40.

[5] Cf., e.g., "Manifeste d'un groupe de baKongo: Vers l'Unification de la langue kiKongo," reprinted by F. J. Van Wing in Kongo-Overzee 19 (1953): 178-81.

[6] By Ph. De Witte, in the Preface, pp. 3-4. Unfortunately it can hardly be considered a satisfactory description of the language, as it deliberately dismisses tone as a relevant feature (p. 7).

[7] Cf. J. Knappert, "De bronnen van het liNgala," in Kongo-Overzee 24 (1958): 193-202; G. Hulstaert, "De bronnen van het li-Ngala," in Zaïre 13 (1959): 509-15; a survey of earlier studies is given by G. Van Bulck, Les Recherches Linguistiques au Congo Belge (Brussels, 1948), pp. 610-14.

[8] Cf. his autobiography Maisha ya Hamed bin Muhammed el Murjebi yaani Tippu Tip (kwa maneno yake mwenyewe), republished by W. H. Whiteley, for the East African Swahili Committee (Kampala, 1958-59).

[9] Cf. the historical introduction by A. Smith to the above-mentioned autobiography of Tippu Tip (mainly pp. 12ff).

[10] Cf. F. Grévisse, quoted by G. Van Bulck, Les Recherches Linguistiques au Congo Belge (Brussels, 1948), pp. 277-78, 690; also A. Verbeken, Msiri, roi du Garengaze (Brussels, 1956), pp. 62-65.

[11] Cf. J. Denis, "Le phénomène urbain en Afrique centrale," Académie Royale des Sciences Coloniales, Classe des Sc. Morales et Politiques, Mémoires, n. s., 19: 1 (Brussels, 1958): 132-49.

[12]Such an inappropriate selection of sources to reflect the actual linguistic situation considerably restricts the validity of B. E. Nnunduma's argument in "Written Swahili in the Belgian Congo," in Swahili 29 (Jan. 1959): 24-33, against L. Harries ("Swahili in the Belgian Congo," in Tanganyika Notes and Records, no. 39 [1955], and "Congo Swahili," in the same journal, no. 44 [1956]—both inaccessible to me).

[13]Cf. the sample recently published by C. Makonga and M. Van Spaandonck, "Tumbako ya mu mpua. Een toneelschets in het Potopot-kiNgwana van Katanga," in Kongo-Overzee 25 (1959): 1-16.

[14]A. N. Tucker, "The Present Status of Swahili in Africa," in Indian Linguistics 19 (Turner Jubilee Volume I, Poona, 1958): 375; cf. also W. H. Whiteley, "The Changing Position of Swahili in East Africa," in Africa 26 (Oct. 1956): 343-53. About earlier efforts to make (standard) Swahili the official African cultural language of the former Belgian Congo, cf. mainly J. Tanghe, "Le Swahili, langue de grande expansion," in Institut Royal Colonial Belge, Bulletin des Séances 15 (1944): 1-24; G. Van der Kerken, "Le Swahili, langue de grande expansion," in the same journal, pp. 27-60; V. Gelders, "La langue commune au Congo," in the same journal, pp. 77-104; L. B. De Boeck, "Taalkunde en de talenkwestie in Belgisch-Kongo" (Institut Royal Colonial Belge, Sect. des Sciences Morales et Politiques, Mémoires 17: 1; Brussels, 1949).

[15]Cf. L. Stappers, "Het tshiluba als omgangstaal of unificatie van de Luba-dialekten," in Kongo-Overzee 18 (1952): 59-60. There has even been a plea to make it the "national" cultural language of the former Belgian Congo (cf. E. De Jonghe, "L'Unification des langues congolaises," in Institut Royal Colonial Belge, Bulletin des Séances 15 (1944): 61-71.

[16]The Grammaire de la langue kiSanga by H. Roland (Saint-André lez Bruges, 1957) is a first tentative sketch of the language of the clan of Chief Pande, which will be superseded by the introductory structural description of A. Coupez in his forthcoming edition of F. P. Bourdonnec's dictionary of kiSanga.

[17]Cf. "The Place of the Kituba in Congo," in Congo Mission News (Jan.-March 1962): 9-10.

[18]Cf. B. Lekens, "Nota over het Ngbandi als voertaal in Ubangi," in Kongo-Overzee 17 (1951): 162-64.

[19]Cf. V. Maes, "Het probleem van de cultuurtaal in West-Ubangi" in Handelingen van het 21ste Vlaams Filologencongres (Louvain, 1955), pp. 325-26.

[20]Cf. G. Hulstaert, "Taaleenmaking in het Mongo-gebied," in Kongo-Overzee 16 (1950): 292-98; A. De Rop, "Het loMongo als cultuurtaal," in Handelingen van het 21ste Vlaams Filologencongres (Louvain, 1955): 322-25.

[21]The main conclusions of this conference are elaborated in A. N. Tucker, "Le groupe linguistique Zande" in Annales du Musée Royal du Congo Belge, Sciences de l'Homme, Linguistique 22 (Tervuren, 1959): 82-103.

[22]According to A. N. Tucker and M. A. Bryan (The non-Bantu Languages of North-Eastern Africa, Handbook of African Languages, vol. III [London, 1956], pp. 28-29), about half a million Zande speakers lived in the Belgian Congo, as compared with 181,000 in the Sudan and fewer than 30,000 in French Equatorial Africa. Cf. also B. Dijkman, "Nota over de taalverhoudingen binnen de grenzen van de bestuursgebieden Bondo en Ango: paZande, de taal der aZande," in Kongo-Overzee 17 (1951): 250-57.

[23]Cf. E. Cleire, "Talen en taalunificatie in het Vicariaat Kivu," in Kongo-Overzee 17 (1951): 32-37; A. E. Meeussen, "De talen van Maniema," in Handelingen van het 20ste Vlaams Filologencongres (Antwerp, 1953): 249-51.

[24]Cf. J. R. Kyatangala, "Le kiRega, une langue qui se meurt" in La Voix du Congolais, no. 138 (Sept. 1957), p. 690, quoted in African Abstracts 9 (July 1958): 140.

[25]Cf. J. Jacobs, "Principes généraux de la Nouvelle Orthographe Otetela-Kikusu," in Kongo-Overzee 25 (1959): 145-69; also A. E. Meeussen, "African Reaction to Western Efforts in African Languages" in Papers of the National Conference on the Teaching of African Languages and Area Studies (Georgetown University, 1960), p. 18.

[26]The report of the linguists attending it (A. Burssens, A. De Rop, A. E. Meeussen, E. Polomé) suggested the uniformization of all spelling systems used in the Belgian Congo for African languages on the pattern of a simplified practical "Africa" spelling, along the lines in which it had been suggested for ciLuba by A. De Rop, "L'Orthographe du ciLuba," in Aequatoria 22: 2 (1959): 1-6.

[27]Cf. J. B. Ntahokaja, "La place des langues bantu dans la culture africaine" in Handelingen van het XXIIe Vlaams Filologencongres (Ghent, 1947): 267-72; E. Boelaert, "Taalpolitiek in Belgisch Kongo," in Handelingen van het XXIIIe Vlaams Filologencongres (Brussels, 1959): 251-53; also G. Van Bulck, "Het Taalprobleem in

het Kongolees Universitair Onderwijs, " in Kongo-Overzee 19 (1953): 343-56.

[28]Cf. G. Brausch, Belgian Administration in the Congo (London, 1961), pp. 10-13.

[29]Cf. E. Polomé, Education and Teachers' Training in the Belgian Congo, paper read at the Leverhulme Intercollegiate Conference on the Work of Institutes of Education in Africa, 9 Sept. 1958, Salisbury, S. Rhodesia.

[30] Cf. G. Brausch, op. cit., pp. 26-29, 88.

[31]Named after liNgala tósálisana ("let's help each other").

[32] Interesting suggestions as to the approach to training in African languages were made by various authorities (e.g. W. F. Twaddell) at the 1959 meeting of the Study Group on Asian and African Languages initiated by the NATO Parliamentarians' Conference of 1958. The situation in the Congo was briefly sketched by J. Larochette. Another valuable survey of the language situation in the Congo was published by A. De Rop in Aequatoria 23 (1960): 1-24.

2 | The Choice of Official Languages in the Democratic Republic of the Congo

In the brief outline on the Democratic Republic of the Congo distributed by the Information and Public Relations Service of the Embassy in Washington the language situation in the Congo is described as follows:

> There are more than 200 dialects but only four of the vernacular languages have official status:
> 1. Kiswahili or Kingwana is spoken mostly in the area between Kivu (north), Katanga (south), Lualaba (west), and the Great Lakes (east).
> 2. Tshiluba or Kiluba is spoken in the area between Angola and Lake Mwero.
> 3. Kikongo, the language of Lower Congo and of Kwango.
> 4. Lingala, or language of the river, is spoken in the area between Stanleypool and Ubangi-Uele.
> BUT French remains the Congo's official language.

This statement agrees with the factual situation with regard to the use of languages by the Belgian administration at the end of the colonial regime.

Belgium's linguistic policy in the Congo was, indeed, essentially pragmatic and attuned to the practical purposes pursued by the colonial power in the various areas of its activity. To rule a territory more than 80 times the size of its own, Belgium had to organize an efficient system of local government requiring a limited number of European personnel. This was achieved by integrating the African political institutions—small tribal communities with traditional chiefs —as units of local government into the framework of the colonial

administration. This measure was actually a continuation of the policy
of the pioneers establishing the political power of King Leopold's Congo
Free State by concluding agreements with local chiefs. The chefferies
recognized since 1891 by the Free State administration were too small
and too numerous, and in 1920, the constitution of larger administrative units—secteurs, grouping small rural units—was recommended.
Gradually the number of chefferies was reduced from 6,095 in 1917 to
2,496 in 1935 and 432 in 1955, while the secteurs, first established in
the Oriental Province in 1922, increased in number, from 57 in 1937
to 517 in 1950. By the time of independence, the number of local
government units was about 900 for a rural population of about 10.5
million, each possessing the complete infrastructure of a modern administrative unit. Whereas local business was transacted orally in
the local vernacular, it stands to reason that the keeping of the records
and the maintenance of close relations with the central government
could not be carried out in the more than 200 distinct vernaculars currently used in the country.

Although Article 3 of the Colonial Charter, which served as
the fundamental law of the country during the colonial regime, made the
use of all languages optional, this rule was applied only to direct relationship with the local population, but not to the various levels of government—general, provincial, district, and territorial. The first
paragraph of Article 3 provided for the promulgation of decrees insur-
ing the rights of the Africans with regard to the use of languages in
justice, but since most disputes were settled by customary law before
the tribunal of the chefferie, no major problem ever developed from
the multiplicity of African languages and vernaculars, at least in the
rural areas. In the absence of special legislation, the administration
merely applied the ordinance of May 14, 1886, considering as official
the language sanctioned by tradition. As a consequence, since 1877,
French has been the language of administration and justice in the Congo.
However, during the colonial regime, special provisions were made to
guarantee the linguistic rights of the Flemish-speaking Belgians:
Article 3 of the Charter stipulates: "All decrees and regulations of a
general bearing will be written and published in French and Dutch.
Both texts are official." Moreover, the right of the same Belgians to
be defended and tried in their own language was explicitly recognized
by the tribunal of Elizabethville on January 9, 1952. This decision
was rescinded, however, by a court of appeal which stated that French

was the only legal language in the Congo. A decree issued in 1957
finally settled the question in favor of the use of Dutch, along with
French, in matters of law. But these were matters with political
connotations which did not concern the Africans.

While using French in all its official documents applying to
the African population, the central government and the administration
of the provinces and their subdivisions (districts and territories) were
concerned with finding adequate contact vernaculars to communicate
with their subordinates. In territories with languages of wider expansion such as Mangbetu, which is used in the Uele and Aruwimi basins,
it would have been possible to adopt the language of the area to translate all official documents in the territory under reference. However,
even the number of such languages was too high for an administration
with rather limited resources. Furthermore, if there were many
cases of vast expanses appearing as linguistically coherent areas (such
as that of the Mongo, e.g.), dialect differences within them would be
of such importance that they would have required linguistic unification,
either by choosing a definite dialect as the common standard or by
creating a dialanguage on the basis of the characters shared by the
majority of the dialects. During the difficult period of implantation
of the colonial administration, such an activity was obviously out of
the question. Accordingly, the administration resorted to the immediately available practical solution—the use of the lingua francas.

Typical, in this respect, is the case of the southwest Congo
where the first Bantu language known to Europeans—kiKongo—was
spoken. Early European penetration in this area had led to the development of a simplified trade language, which became known under the
name of Fiote. In the Kwilu-Kwango area, where an extremely complex ethnic and linguistic situation made the use of a contact vernacular unavoidable, the influence and penetration of kiKongo as early as
the sixteenth century entailed the development of a simplified form of
a kiKongo dialect—kiMpaangu, according to Father Swartenbroeck—
whose lexicon was renewed by numerous borrowings from other contact vernaculars. Often called kiKongo ya Leta because of its use by
Belgian civil servants, it soon spread widely throughout the commercial centers of the former province of Leopoldville and beyond the
Congo River in the area of Brazzaville, where it was called Monoku-
tuba. It has now become the main means of communication between

the lower-river tribes speaking primarily dialects of kiKongo and
the up-river Congolese using liNgala. It is currently used under the
name of kiKongo (véhiculaire) by Radio-Kinshasa (formerly Leopoldville) and Radio-Brazzaville, though the missions as well as linguists,
such as H. W. Fehderau and L. B. Swift, prefer to call it kiTuba to
distinguish it from tribal kiKongo. It is now the second language of
about a million and a half people, but has become the first language
of a limited number of young people as a consequence of intertribal
marriage. The present expansion of kiTuba, which is partly responsible for the failure to develop a unified literary kiKongo, illustrates
the far-reaching effects of the choice of a lingua franca by the colonial
power to communicate with its African subjects.

One of the immediate consequences of colonization was the
development of cities in Central Africa, a phenomenon that resulted
in the creation of a type of society previously unknown in this part of
Africa. Flocks of people left their traditional environment to cluster
in the urban centers mushrooming in the vicinity of newly developed
industry. In 1959, this urban population represented 22 percent of
the total population of the Congo. Before 1957, it was organized
either in cités indigènes—"native cities," with a chief and council—
or centres extra-coutumiers—self-contained administrative units not
ruled by customary law. Later, these were replaced by incorporated
municipalities—communes—with wider African participation in political and administrative life. Since the populations of these urban units
were of widely different tribal and linguistic background, the only language suitable for the needs of communication among them was often
the local lingua franca—a situation that, in turn, favored its expansion
and partial creolization.

A typical example of urban development is Lubumbashi
(formerly Elizabethville). This town, situated in the middle of the
wooded savanna, owes its origin and growth to the working of the
mines in the rich copper-ore deposits of Upper Katanga. The building
of the Lubumbashi processing plant and the arrival of the railway linking the community with the big commercial and industrial centers of
South Africa were the decisive steps in its development. Before this,
in April 1910, there were only about 20 Europeans in the area, but
afterwards the town experienced a real boom; by 1912 the resident
population amounted to about 8,000 people, 15 percent European.

Numerous Africans from the neighboring areas flocked to the mushrooming town. They were speaking dialects of Bemba, Luba, Lunda,
and other languages, but for intertribal communication, they resorted
to the simplified Swahili that had already spread in the Garengaze
kingdom of Msiri before the coming of the Europeans. As the copper
production soared, the African personnel of the <u>Union Minière du</u>
<u>Haut-Katanga</u> rose—to 21,107 units by 1928. Though a large portion
of the personnel were transient workers, recruited mainly in Rhodesia,
a considerable number settled in Elizabethville with their families,
while more joined them to work in the smaller industries that were
developing steadily or to perform household tasks for the European
population. Besides, the rural population, which amounted to barely
a few hundred in the area at the beginning of the century, also increased in number as agricultural colonization was organized and as
Africans from various regions were lured by the call for unskilled
labor.

In all these situations Swahili appeared to be the only adequate means of communication between Europeans and Africans as
well as among Africans of different ethnic and tribal backgrounds.
No wonder therefore that the government resorted to this same lingua
franca to communicate with its subjects—the more so since it had
been used as a trade language all over the east of the country since
the penetration of the slavers and elephant hunters from East Africa
in the nineteenth century.

Similar situations occurred elsewhere. Before the arrival
of the Europeans there was already quite an active trade carried on
between the ethnically related tribes living along the Congo River
from Lolango to Mobeka, as well as along the Lower Ubangi and in
the Ngiri marshes. The vernacular used around 1890 for these intertribal contacts seems to have developed on the basis of the local language—boBangi (or rather boLoki?)—with borrowings from the ki-
Kongo dialects of the Lower Congo and the Swahili of the <u>askari</u> of
the Free State. When Leopoldville was established, a considerable
part of the early African population came from the areas where this
trade language was used, and liNgala (as it was called) normally
became the main language of communication in the African township
as well as for contact with the European. It was, accordingly, used
by the administration in its relations with the local population and
became the language of elementary education in the schools as well.

In the meantime, liNgala was spread in modified forms by
the European penetration along the tributaries of the Congo, as far as
the Uele basin. There, as well as in the Equator province, the government resorted to liNgala for its relations with its subjects, and this
situation was practically maintained until Independence in spite of the
strenuous efforts of the missions to have loMongo-loNkundo recognized
as the African language used for administrative purposes in the larger
Mongo area.

In the Kasayi, however, the situation was different, because
there ciLuba had enjoyed considerable prestige among the neighboring
tribes ever since the days of Kalamba Mukenge, when Wissmann
founded Luluaburg (1884). It was currently used by the baKuba, the
baTetela, and others, and was therefore immediately adopted for
teaching purposes when the first Catholic mission was established in
Luba territory in 1892. It has spread ever since as the cultural and
administrative language of the area, though most Europeans never
mastered ciLuba sufficiently to communicate properly with the local
population. Accordingly, in the urban centers of the Kasayi and South-
Senkuru, they resorted for such purpose to a form of kiTuba borrowing
heavily from the ciLuba lexicon.

To sum up, the colonial administration of the early days, being
too much concerned with other urgent problems to devote any attention
to consistent linguistic planning, deliberately resorted to a practical
language policy adapted to the situations which the development of
intertribal trade had created in Central Africa. Taking over the existing lingua francas, it contributed to their expansion. In one case, however, the language of an ethnic group had started imposing itself sufficiently as a language of wider communication over a vast territory to
make the administration adopt it for its own needs. This use of Luba
was also promoted by its own speakers, who proved particularly prone
to serve the interests of the Europeans and who consequently acquired
a rather privileged position in colonial society. This situation was also
brought about by the greater opportunities for education provided to
the baLuba at an early date by the establishment of very active missions on their territory. As a result, the proportion of baLuba in
the civil service, in the teaching profession, and in the economy
exceeded by far their numerical importance.

On the other hand, the limitation of the number of African
languages in administrative usage to four, beside French and Dutch,
advantageously simplified the training of the European personnel.
Future ranking administrators were thoroughly prepared for the complex duties they would have to fulfill in Central Africa in the Institut
Universitaire des Territoires d'Outre-Mer in Antwerp, where they
were taught Swahili and liNgala with a view to achieving an oral command of these languages. Later, courses providing a reading knowledge of ciLuba and kiKongo were added, as well as an introduction to
the structure of Bantu languages. Similarly, other civil servants and
leading administrative personnel in private enterprise were trained in
liNgala and Swahili in a special school at the Ministry of Colonies in
Brussels. However, after the Second World War, more emphasis was
laid on surveying the grammatical features of the main Bantu languages
used in the Congo, giving particular attention to cultural languages
such as ciLuba and loMongo-loNkundo besides the two main lingua
francas, Swahili and liNgala. From the start of the colonial regime,
the mobility of the civil servants prevented them from getting a thorough command of local vernaculars and encouraged them to concentrate on a practical knowledge of the contact vernaculars, which would
be useful to them throughout their career. The limitation of the training of lower-rank civil servants and other personnel to a grammatical
introduction to a set of Bantu languages in the fifties, however, entailed a considerable drop in the command of African languages by
European administrators.[1]

To maintain the armed forces, the Congo Free State initially
recruited mercenaries in various parts of Africa, and such languages
as Hausa and Swahili were used with the troops, especially in the
northeastern territories. Later an effort was made to standardize
the use of languages in the Force Publique, as the army was called.
Until World War I, Swahili was still used as language of instruction
for the troops in the Oriental Province and in Katanga, but it was
eliminated later in favor of liNgala, which became the language of the
armed forces, making the relations between the soldiers recruited all
over the territory of the colony and their African NCO's and Belgian
officers much easier. The use of one language of command was actually consciously imposed as a means of promoting esprit de corps in
the army. Because of the multiple tasks the Force Publique was

called upon to perform in the country, its consistent use of liNgala
also contributed to the spread of this lingua franca.

The problem of the use of languages in education is much
more complex. The policy of the Congo Free State toward the missions
was essentially to grant them the greatest possible freedom of action
in educational matters. As a consequence, the missions resorted to
the local vernaculars for the purpose of teaching as well as evangelizing. This led to the publication of a series of grammars and vocabu-
laries in the 1880s and 1890s. As the missionary penetration went
upstream along the Aruwimi, the Itimbiri, the Ubangi and the Ngiri,
new contacts were established with the riverside tribes and growing
attention was given to the language of the paddlers. As early as 1903,
Rev. W. H. Stapleton of the Baptist Missionary Society established
at Yakusu, near the Stanley Falls, published there his <u>Comparative</u>
<u>Handbook of Congo Languages Spoken Along the Banks of the Congo</u>
<u>River from the West Coast of Africa to Stanley Falls</u> ... and of Swa-
<u>hili, the Lingua Franca, Stretching Thence to the East Coast,</u> together
with his <u>Suggestions pour une Grammaire du Bangala, la "lingua</u>
<u>franca" du Haut-Congo</u>.

The Fathers of Scheut, established in New Antwerp, favored
liNgala, and so did the newly founded <u>vicariats apostoliques</u> in Ubangi
and in Uele-Ituri, so that liNgala was taught even in the heart of Zande
territory until the arrival of the Dominicans. Only kiKongo in the
lower Congo, ciLuba in Kasayi, and loMongo-loNkundo preserved
their position in missionary education, while Swahili was favored in
the East by the White Fathers. Although keeping a lively interest in
the local vernaculars, they indeed adopted Swahili as the language of
evangelization and of instruction, even in the southeast, preventing
the expansion of Luba into this area and probably also preventing the
possible adoption of Bemba as contact-vernacular in the Upper-Katanga
mining district, parallel to its spread in this function in the Zambian
Copperbelt. It appears that the missions initially adopted to a large
extent the contact vernaculars on grounds of expediency, but by doing
so, they definitely favored the expansion and increased the prestige
of the existing lingua francas.

The first State intervention in the problem of the use of languages in education is evidenced by Article 3 of the 1906 convention

between the Congo Free State and the Vatican. It stipulates that "the teaching of the Belgian national languages is an essential part of the curriculum"; but the 1924 report of the Commission established by Minister Franck to coordinate the curricula of the missions stresses that "teaching must be done in a native language. Only the Africans of the urban centers, bound to be living in close contact with the Europeans, will be taught French." The 1926 unified curriculum, based on the conclusions of this report, provided that French should become the language of the curriculum in the upper forms. This curriculum was revised in 1929 and 1938, but the same principle prevailed: "The pupils who will leave junior high school (école moyenne) will usually be called upon to work in contact with Europeans. ... They must accordingly be Europeanized to a degree." To achieve that purpose, French was introduced as a subject in primary schools from the third year on, and in the secondary schools became the language of the curriculum, the formerly used African language being taught as a subject.

In 1948 a new curriculum was made compulsory for the mission schools. In primary education the language of the curriculum was to be the mother tongue or, if possible (and preferably), the lingua franca, which had to be taught as a subject at any rate. In rural schools, no European language was to be taught, but French was optional as a second language in urban centers in lower-grade schools, whereas it was compulsory in schools that provided for continuation beyond the lower grade. French was the language of the curriculum in all secondary schools, but in the écoles de moniteurs, training first-grade teachers mainly for rural schools, the lingua franca remained the language of the curriculum, with French as compulsory second language. In girls' schools, however, the teaching of French as second language was compulsory only from the second grade on in major towns and in the last (sixth) form of primary education elsewhere, as well as in the lower-grade teacher-training schools (écoles de monitrices) and the schools for home economics (écoles ménagères).

A few years later the creation of metropolitan-type schools introduced French as the language of the curriculum from the start and the lingua franca was taught only as a subject on the primary level. This was part of an effort to upgrade education for Africans by establishing a complete equivalence with Belgian metropolitan degrees. All

instruction being given in French, the teaching personnel was entirely
European and submitted to the same requirements with regard to training and qualifications as their colleagues in Belgium. However, since
a great number of these schools were interracial, this entailed compliance with the requirements of the Belgian linguistic policy concerning respect for the rights of the Flemings. Consequently, Dutch was
taught beside French as second language, just as it was in Belgian
bilingual communities like Brussels, though, in a few cases, English
was taught as second language in secondary schools in departure from
this rule.

At the universities, French was the language of the curriculum.
However, in the first year of college, Dutch was a compulsory subject
in the Faculty of Arts at the State University at Elizabethville, where
parallel sections with Dutch as the language of the curriculum existed
in certain fields until independence. Lovanium University and the State
University both organized a comprehensive program in African linguistics, and the curriculum of the School of Education at Elizabethville
included a set of compulsory courses in African linguistics including
the intensive study of an African language.

In 1959, a Commission was established in Leopoldville to
draft a course plan for the study of African culture and linguistics as
part of the curriculum of secondary schools. The submitted proposal
provided for the teaching of an African language in junior high school
to serve as a basis for the teaching of African linguistics in senior high
schools. Furthermore, this language teaching was to be closely coordinated with the part of the course giving an introduction to African
culture. The languages to be taught had to have an adequate literary
form and their choice would depend on local situations. The following
languages were proposed:

1. Bantu: kiKongo, Luba, loMongo, oTetela, liNgombe,
kiNande, loKela, kiLega, Lunda, Ciokwe, ciBemba, maShi.
2. non-Bantu: Zande, Ngbandi, Ngbaka, Mangbetu, Alur,
Lugbara.

The program was to have been introduced in all secondary schools in
September 1959, but owing to strong political pressure, it was never
enacted, so that at the time of independence, African languages had

practically been ousted from all the schools where the future Congolese elite was being trained, and were being maintained only on the
primary level, often merely as a rather poorly treated subject.

        This does not mean that there has never been any deliberate
effort of linguistic planning in the Congo. The most decisive step
taken in this direction by the Belgian authorities probably was the
creation in the late 1940s of the advisory Commission on African linguistics. Eager to coordinate the efforts toward organized linguistic
development in the Congo, this body of specialists tried to promote
the careful study of complex local situations in various parts of the
colony and to evaluate the progress made in the unification of languages of major expansion to be able to give competent advice to the
Minister of Colonies on steps to be taken to solve the pending linguistic problems in Belgian Africa. Its activity resulted in the production
of a series of well-documented reports with many useful suggestions,
which unfortunately appear not to have been followed very often. The
Commission seems to have been essentially in favor of maintaining
linguistic pluralism by promoting the development of African cultural
languages. The success attained in establishing loMongo-loNkundo as
a recognized literary language was indeed a striking example of what
could be achieved through doggedness of purpose and consistent strenuous activity by well-organized groups of devoted educators. However,
the solution of its linguistic situation toward which the Congo appears
to tend is not a pluralism based on the multiplicity of tribal languages.
The latter would imply having, for example, in the vicariate of the
Kivu alone at least three cultural languages—maShi, kiRega, and
kinyaRwanda—other than the Swahili lingua franca, already introduced
in precolonial days and alone able to solve satisfactorily the problems
of intertribal relationship in communities where economic factors had
brought important groups of immigrants.

        For years the question of the advisability of adopting a defin-
ite national language for the whole territory of the Congo has been
brought up by competent authorities. However, the proposed solutions
to this problem have too often been biased. Emphasizing the superiority of Western culture, some people would advocate the exclusive
use of French, unconditionally rejecting all African languages as in-
adequate to express the refined concepts of modern civilization—a
highly prejudiced attitude that has been utterly disproved by recent

developments in languages such as Swahili! Others would insist on
the necessity for giving the Congolese an African national language
they could really consider their own, because it would help preserve
the genuine values of African culture. The question was debated for
the first time in a constructive proposal by E. De Jonghe in his article "Les langues communes du Congo Belge" in the journal Congo in
November 1933, and it was reiterated with further precision and increased conviction in a paper read before the Institut Royal Colonial
Belge and published in its Bulletin des Séances [vol. 6 (1935), pp.
340-51] under the title "Vers une langue nationale congolaise." In
these studies De Jonghe stressed that the multiplicity of languages
was a direct obstacle to the advancement of the African masses. Since
it was a pedagogical heresy to impose a European language, it was
advisable to develop an African language into an adequate tool for the
promotion of cultural and social progress through education throughout the Congo. Since four "common languages" (kiKongo, liNgala,
Swahili, ciLuba) were apparently expanding toward covering the whole
territory of the colony, De Jonghe recommended that the government
encourage their harmonious development as a preparatory step to the
adoption of one of them as the national language, and he decidedly
proposed that ciLuba be chosen for that purpose since it was the only
genuine Congolese language of culture to have become a language of
wider expansion.

   This proposal started a rather lively controversy, especially
because the authority and position of its author—a professor at the
University of Louvain and internationally known ethnologist, director-
general to the Royal Colonial Institute—conferred a special weight on
this pronouncement. Most of those who became involved in the debate
agreed that the efforts of the government had not been successful in
stabilizing liNgala, whose use as mother tongue remained restricted
to an insignificant minority of Africans. It indeed required a thorough
grammatical and lexical unification with a systematic re-Bantuization
to be raised to the level of a genuine cultural language. On the other
hand, many people reproached De Jonghe with leaving aside the Mongo
group, which constituted a coherent ethnic entity covering a continuous
territory stretching from the Lulonga-Lopori in the north to Lake
Leopold II and even beyond the Lukenie into the Kasayi in the south,
reaching the border and the Congo River in the west and even crossing
the Lomami in the east and penetrating into the Sankuru in the south-

west. The linguistic differentiation within this area did not create any difficulty that could not be easily overcome in an effort toward its unification, and the speakers of Mongo dialects ranked at least second in number among the Congolese. Father Hulstaert's argument against the choice of only one national language was particularly conclusive:

1. Education must be given in the mother tongue; trying to substitute a foreign language for the mother tongue, even if this foreign language is Congolese, constitutes a complete reversal of values.

2. Teaching in a language other than the mother tongue will help widen the gap between the elite and the masses (though the situation would probably have been less disturbing with ciLuba than it is with French).

3. Favoring one Congolese cultural language at the expense of the others will undoubtedly entail violent reaction from the elite of the neglected languages, especially among the baKongo and the Mongo, as well as in the large cities, where liNgala and Swahili are solidly established.

4. Will the chosen African language carry enough prestige among the Congolese elite to prevent their being more attracted by the European language used by the administration and the major economic powers in the country?

5. Where will the thousands of instructors required for the introduction of ciLuba as national language be found?

Adding to these points some pertinent remarks about the necessity of preserving the mother tongue as a language of evangelization, Father Hulstaert concluded in favor of pluralism, hoping that the territorial organization of the State and the Church would ultimately be revised to correspond to ethnic and linguistic subdivisions.

Nevertheless, at the eve of the entry of Belgium into World War II, Father Liesenborghs proposed once more to make ciLuba the national language of the Congo, after reexamining the problem of the lingua francas which the government essentially went on using. Fully aware of the involved problems, he brought forward a motion at the Fifteenth Congress of Philologists in Ghent in March 1940 requesting that the government create a commission with the explicit task of studying the linguistic situation in the Congo and drawing up practical proposals in order to regulate by law the use of African languages in administration, justice, and education.

A few months before the Liberation of Belgium, the discussion
was resumed with renewed vigor, when the linguistic problem in the
Congo was put on the agenda of the Royal Colonial Institute. This debate provided the contributors with an opportunity to display their per-
suasiveness in promoting with forcible arguments the language they
particularly favored but, at the same time, betrayed the prejudices
which biased the judgment of the participants. Thus kiKongo, proposed with lukewarm conviction by Mgr. J. Cuvelier, was rejected
by E. De Jonghe because it had "the disadvantage of being the mother
tongue of populations which belonged to three different colonies, "
whereas Swahili, fervently defended by J. Tanghe, G. van der Kerken,
and V. Gelders on account of its international importance, was dis-
missed by the same De Jonghe as "a language which is absolutely foreign to the Congo." He, indeed, decided in favor of ciLuba because
it had "the advantage of being a very widespread language in the Kasayi,
spoken by a solid nucleus of homogenous Congolese populations endowed with a very high vitality. " Though he explicitly denied that any
"imperialistic or exaggerated nationalistic bias" was affecting his
choice, De Jonghe thought that "the colonial government must have
all the control levers at its disposal with regard to the evolution of
the national language, " which would obviously not be the case if Swahili were chosen, since the Congo would then be integrated into a linguistic area stretching far beyond the boundaries artificially established by the colonial powers during the partition of Africa.

As a matter of fact, by that time the debate was purely academic. In spite of the repeated assertion that contact vernaculars
were not cultural languages and the claim that literary forms of languages of wider expansion should be developed, stronger forces than
the limited influence of the promoters of such and such a language
were at work, and even those who, like Father Stappers, devoted the
best of their time and effort to molding ciLuba into a cultural language
with an original living literature, had to acknowledge that, among
other things, it would be necessary to oust Swahili from the large
towns of Katanga to have the slightest chance of success in expanding
the presently developed Luba cultural language outside the Kasayi.
Such a move would indeed encounter tremendous difficulties, in spite
of the sizable emigration of baLuba from the Kasayi to Katanga, in
spite of the presence in northern Katanga of linguistically closely
related Luba populations with whom the Sanga, further south, are also
connected, and even in spite of the fact that a majority of the African

schoolteachers in the Katangese mining district were baLuba from
the Kasayi. A close examination of the facts shows that the evolution
of the linguistic situation in Katanga works in favor of Swahili as the
African language of wider expansion. Its only serious rival is French,
but the prevalence of either of them will depend on the effect the spread
of education has on language usage in urban communities.

An inquiry conducted in June 1963 with a group of 484 students
of the E. Wangermée Secondary School and Teachers' Training College at Katuba, near Elizabethville, shows that out of 174 Luba students, 151 remain loyal to their tribal language in the narrower family circle and 19 claim to use French, and 42 use Swahili as the first
or second language at home. Socially, these young men belong to
families of lower and middle level civil servants and clerks working
in banks and offices of local plants and commercial organizations.
Quite interesting is the fact that the languages they resort to in their
social relations outside the family circle are essentially Swahili (128)
and French (109); only nine state that they address their friends in
Luba. This situation clearly indicates that their social relations are
essentially intertribal, and the relative importance of the use of
French points to their preference for associating with people with the
same level of education. When addressing strangers, only four of
them think it fit to resort to Luba dialects; the vast majority obviously
find it natural to use either Swahili (101) or preferably French (118),
perhaps purposely to display the command they have achieved in this
language of higher prestige. By way of comparison, let us briefly
examine the corresponding figures for a group of 86 Lunda students
from the same school: 63 remain loyal to their tribal language, but
32 use either exclusively Swahili or Swahili in addition to Lunda in
the family circle, whereas only 9 resort to French either as a first or
as a second language at home. With friends, only 6 usually speak
Lunda, whereas the vast majority use either French (63) or Swahili (53);
with strangers, they similarly resort either to French (60) or to Swahili (54). Like their baLuba fellow students, all these Lunda speakers
are actually trilingual.

Considering the composition of the population of Elizabethville/
Lubumbashi, it is probable that this new generation will loosen its ties
with the tribal community to a much larger extent than their parents
ever did, and that intertribal marriages will undoubtedly increase the

number of those whose mother tongue is Katanga Swahili. If this
creolized Swahili is in many respects different from kiUnguja, the
Zanzibar dialect of Swahili adopted as standard language, and shows
several of the features of kiNgwana combined with local pecularities,
essentially due to the influence of Luba and probably also of Bemba,
it is in no way so far from the kiSwahili cha Kitabu taught in the
schools that a child raised in Katanga Swahili would have any more
trouble studying the standard language than a child speaking a rather
divergent dialect of a western language would experience in being
taught that language. Furthermore, except for numerous French
loanwords, the written form of Katanga Swahili as it appears in the
local press, for example, in Uhaki, differs only from the current
language used, for example, in Taifa Leo in Nairobi, by a set of
morphological and syntactic peculiarities that are rather easily identifiable. This is mainly because as far as it is used in education, the
Swahili taught in the schools is essentially the East African standard
language. Considering the prestige now enjoyed by Swahili in Africa,
the Katangese elite can be expected to cling to it, together with
French, and to use it with growing correctness and accuracy, at
least in its written form.

More complex is the situation in Leopoldville/Kinshasa owing
to the tremendous rate at which its population has increased. In 1923,
only 16,701 Africans were living in the capital of the Congo. Thirty
years later there were more than a quarter of a million of them there
and their number increased at a rate of 30,000 a year, reaching over
400,000 inhabitants on the eve of independence. Since then, the flow
of immigrants has only increased and Kinshasa has become the largest
city in Central Africa. If, in the beginning, the majority of the immigrants came from the north and the east along the major waterways of
the Congo and the Kasayi, whereas only notably less would come upstream from the west, the population growth of the capital after 1939
changed this situation. From 1880 until that date, the baKongo formed
only a minority of little influence compared to the masses of immigrants from other regions. The contact vernacular that prevailed in
Leopoldville under the pressure of the circumstances was liNgala,
which was soon also introduced as the language of the curriculum in
African schools, so that even the baKongo who had settled in town had
to resort to liNgala outside their family circle and strictly tribal contacts. Furthermore, the detribalization of many immigrants pro-

duced a generation of townspeople whose mother tongue was liNgala.
At the eve of World War II, liNgala accordingly appeared to stand a
fair chance of becoming the language of Leopoldville. The following
years of prosperity, however, lured tremendous numbers of baKongo
to the booming town right at the border of their tribal territory.
From a minority, they became the majority of the town population,
increasing to the point of 75 percent of the population in the early
1950s, while the speakers of liNgala as first language no longer represented more than 10 percent of the townspeople. Nevertheless,
the government stuck to its policy of imposing liNgala as the language
of the curriculum in primary education, and soon numerous protests
were raised against this improper treatment of the new baKongo majority which prevented them from having their children educated in their
mother tongue.[2] The main objection against the introduction of kiKongo
beside liNgala was the absence of a generally accepted kiKongo standard, as the efforts toward unification of the widely divergent kiKongo
dialects had failed in the 1930s. However, the problem of linguistic
unification was taken up again, but it now appeared to be further complicated by political involvements. The question of the choice of the
language of the curriculum was settled finally by the decision of the
colonial authorities to impose French at all levels, a measure which
became applicable to the whole territory in 1959.

This decision probably constitutes the most radical intervention of the government in matters of linguistic policy. Though practicing linguistic pluralism from a purely practical point of view in its relations with the local population, the colonial government never went
any further than using the contact vernaculars which economic factors
had already started developing and spreading before it moved in. In
the promotion of African cultural languages, its policy was essentially
characterized by a prudent expectant attitude: it gave the missions a
free hand to try and perform this difficult task—sometimes quite suc-
cessfully as in the case of loMongo—but, obviously, except when
strictly practical necessities were involved, the Belgian authorities
carefully abstained from any direct intervention in the touchy matters
of regional planning of definite linguistic policies. The only language
whose expansion they ever actively encouraged through direct use of
their executive powers was French, as is evident when one follows
step by step the growing prevalence of this language in the curriculum
until its eventual use as the only language of education. Their support

of liNgala remained limited and restrained, except in the case of the
Force Publique, where again practical considerations prevailed to
unify the language of command.

The outcome of this policy is the situation described at the
beginning of this paper. To be sure, "there is an urgent need for a
single Congolese language, " as Yvon Nsuka recently pointed out in his
survey of the linguistic problem in the Congo, published in the July
1964 issue of Documents pour l'Action in Leopoldville, but it is probable that for many years to come Article 89 of the Constitution of the
Democratic Republic of the Congo of August 1964: "French is the official language of the Parliament. However, each of the Houses can
also accept other working languages" will remain applicable, not only
to the legislature, but also to the whole administration of the country.

NOTES

[1] This reduced training actually resulted from a lack of motivation to study African languages, because so many Congolese in the
lower administrative ranks, as well as among the current domestic
staff, had acquired a sufficient grasp of French to cope with most situations arising from their contacts with their Belgian bosses.

[2] The protest against liNgala was actually more a matter of
form; the real target was colonial policy. As a matter of fact, the
baKongo of Kinshasa have gone on using liNgala to the present day
when associating with friends and strangers in town.

SELECT BIBLIOGRAPHY

Anon. Belgian Congo, vol. 1. Brussels: Belgian Congo and Ruanda-
       Urundi Information and Public Relations Office, 1959.
_____. Comité Spécial du Katanga, 1900–1950. Brussels: L.
       Cuypers, s.a.
Boelaert, E. 1936. Naar een nationale inlandsche taal in Kongo ?,
       in Kongo-Overzee 2: 240–48.
_____. 1958. Afrikaanse talen in het onderwijs in Belgisch-Kongo.
       In Bulletin des Séances de l'Académie Royale des Sciences 4:

861-76. (Note: pp. 877-945 report the debate which followed the presentation of Boelaert's paper.)

Brausch, G. 1961. Belgian Administration in the Congo. London: Oxford University Press (Institute of Race Relations).

Burssens, A. 1954. Inleiding tot de studie van de Kongolese Bantoetalen. Antwerp: De Sikkel (Kongo-Overzee Bibliotheek, vol. VIII).

Cleire, R. 1951. Talen en Taalunificatie in het Vicariaat Kivu. Kongo-Overzee 17: 32-37.

Cuvelier, J. 1944. Note sur la langue Kongo (kiKongo). Bulletin des Séances de l'Institut Royal Colonial Belge 15: 25-26.

———. 1944. La "lingua franca" du Bas-Congo. Bulletin des Séances de l'Institut Royal Colonial Belge 15: 73-75.

De Boeck, L.-B. 1949. Taalkunde en de Talenkwestie in Belgisch-Kongo. Brussels: G. Van Campenhout (Institut Royal Colonial Belge. Section des Sciences Morales et Politiques. Mémoires. Collection in-8°. vol. 17, part I).

———. 1952. Het Lingala op de weegschaal. Zaïre 6: 115-53.

———. 1953. Taaltoestand te Leopoldstad. Kongo-Overzee 19: 1-7.

De Clercq, A. 1937. Hoe het Tshiluba zich in Kasai verspreidde. Kongo-Overzee 3: 241-44.

De Jonghe, E. 1935. Vers une langue nationale congolaise. Bulletin des Séances de l'Institut Royal Colonial Belge 6: 340-51.

———. 1944. L'unification des langues congolaises. Bulletin des Séances de l'Institut Royal Colonial Belge 15: 61-71.

De Koster, L. 1951. Problèmes linguistiques et culturels au Congo Belge. Problèmes d'Afrique Centrale 1: 7-31.

Denis, J. 1958. Le phénomène urbain en Afrique centrale. Brussels (Académie Royale des Sciences coloniales. Classe des Sciences Morales et Politiques. Mémoires in-8° N.S., vol. 19, part 1).

De Pauw, W. 1957. Het Talenprobleem in het Onderwijs van Belgisch-Kongo. Ghent: Julius Vuylsteke-Fonds.

De Rop, A. 1953. De Bakongo en het Lingala. Kongo-Overzee 19: 170-74.

———. 1960. Les langues du Congo. Aequatoria 23: 1-24.

Fehderau, H. 1962. The place of the Kituba language in Congo. Congo Mission News 196: 9-10.

Gelders, V. 1944. La Langue commune au Congo. Bulletin des Séances de l'Institut Royal Colonial Belge 15: 77-104.

Guilbert, D. 1952. Civilisation occidentale et langage au Congo Belge. Zaïre 6: 899–928.

Harries, L. 1956. Le Swahili au Congo Belge. Kongo–Overzee 22: 395–400.

Heyse, Th. 1952–59. Congo Belge et Ruanda–Urundi. Notes de Droit Public et Commentaires de la Charte Coloniale. 2 vols. Brussels: G. Van Campenhout.

Hulstaert, G. 1937. Het talenvraagstuk in Belgisch–Kongo. Kongo–Overzee 3: 49–68.

———. 1950. Taaleenmaking in het Mongo–gebied. Kongo–Overzee 16: 292–98.

———. 1950. Les langues indigènes peuvent–elles servir dans l'enseignement? Bulletin des Séances de l'Institut Royal Colonial Belge 21: 316–40.

Larochette, J. 1952. Le problème des langues dans l'enseignement aux indigènes du Congo Belge. Problèmes d'Afrique Centrale 2: 72–78.

Lemarchand, R. 1961. The bases of nationalism among the Bakongo. Africa 31: 344–54.

Liesenborghs, O. 1941–42. Beschouwingen over wezen, nut en toekomst der zogenaamde "linguae francae" van Belgisch–Kongo. Kongo–Overzee 7–8: 87–99.

Malengreau, G. 1953. De l'emploi des langues en justice au Congo. Journal des Tribunaux d'Outremer 15: 3–6.

Nsuka, Y. 1964. Le problème linguistique au Congo. Documents pour l'Action 4 (27): 207–16.

Ntahokaja, J. 1957. La place des langues Bantu dans la culture africaine. Kongo–Overzee 23: 232–41.

Polomé, E. 1963. Cultural languages and contact vernaculars in the Republic of the Congo. Texas Studies in Literature and Language 4: 499–511.

Slade, R. 1962. King Leopold's Congo. London: Oxford University Press.

Stappers, L. 1952. Het Tshiluba als omgangstaal, of unificatie van de Luba–dialecten? Kongo–Overzee 18: 50–65.

Tanghe, J. 1930. Le Lingala, la langue du Fleuve. Congo 9: 341–58.

———. 1944. Le Swahili, langue de grande expansion. Bulletin des Séances de l'Institut Royal Colonial Belge 15: 1–24.

Van Bulck, G. 1948. Les Recherches Linguistiques au Congo Belge.

Brussels: G. Van Campenhout (Institut Royal Colonial Belge. Section des Sciences Morales et Politiques. Mémoires. Collection in-8°, vol. 16).

Van Bulck, G. 1950. Le problème linguistique dans les Missions de l'Afrique Centrale. Zaïre 4: 49-65.

_____. 1953. Het taalprobleem in het Kongolees universitair onderwijs. Kongo-Overzee 19: 343-56.

Van Caeneghen, R. 1950. Les langues indigènes dans l'enseignement. Zaïre 4: 707-20.

Van der Kerken, G. 1944. Le Swahili, langue de grande expansion. Bulletin des Séances de l'Institut Royal Colonial Belge 15: 27-60.

Van Wing, J. 1951. Nota over de "Commissie voor unificatie van het Kikongo" (1935-36). Kongo-Overzee 17: 38-40.

_____. 1953. Het Kikongo en het Lingala te Leopoldstad. Kongo-Overzee 19: 175-78.

Vorblicher, A. 1964. Das Sprachenproblem in Kongo (Léo). Neues Afrika 6: 167-69.

3 | The Position of Swahili and Other Bantu Languages in Katanga

On the eve of independence the Katanga Mining District represented one of the most important urban concentrations in Central Africa. Its administrative center, Elisabethville, had a total population of about 175,000 Africans and close to 14,000 Europeans; the other main towns, Jadotville and Kolwezi, totaled about 140,000 African (80,000 in Jadotville and 60,000 in Kolwezi) and more than 8,000 European inhabitants, and less important centers had also developed around rich copper ore deposits like the Prince Léopold mine at Kipushi, with close to 25,000 inhabitants. This situation was due to the tremendous development of the Union Minière du Haut-Katanga in little more than half a century. Indeed, in 1904, the whole area, covering about 5,800 square miles, had a population of hardly 4,000 rather poor villagers, gathered in twenty-five small communities, toiling for mere survival, tilling a mostly arid soil, and trying to escape the raids of slave drivers and rival chiefs.

From the seventeenth century, Katanga had been part of the Lunda empire of the Mwata Yamvo, and local chiefs like Pande-Kilembe, who firmly established his authority over the baSanga in the beginning of the nineteenth century, still owed allegiance to the Lunda Kazembe (governor). The Portuguese pombeiros who visited the governor in 1806 mentioned their trade of malachite and copper with other tribes. This lured Arab traders into the area where they bartered fabrics and beads for ivory and copper; on their way to the East Coast they crossed Unyamwezi, where the baSumbwa, who specialized in elephant hunting, became interested in this distant country rich in ivory as well as copper ore. Soon several groups joined the trading caravans to Katanga and one of the traders, Ngelengwa, later known as Msiri, managed to win the confidence of Pande by helping him in

his struggle against Katanga, the chief of the baLamba. By clever
scheming and ruthless elimination of his opponents he asserted himself, first as ruler of the baLamba at the death of Katanga, then as
follower of Pande, soon controlling the whole area previously under
the rule of the Kazembe. He established his capital in Bunkeya, in the
valley of a tributary of the Lufira. This village became an important
center of slave and copper trade with a multilingual population of
several thousand, where baSanga, baLamba, baUshi, baLunda, ba-
Bemba, and baLuba tribesmen lived side by side with Arab, Nyamwezi, and Swahili traders and immigrants from farther off.

The growing community was divided into several districts
at the head of which Msiri put his bagoli or favorite wives, whose
origin accounts for the influence they brought to bear in this important trading center. One of them came from Angola and spoke Portuguese; she favored the Portuguese traders so much that the Arab
traders brought her rival from the East Coast, whose native language
was Swahili. This illustrates the multilingualism at the court of
Msiri where the ihanga "first wife" was the daughter of a Luba, while
the rest of the harem contained a motley crowd of five to seven hundred women of all possible tribal origins within the sphere of influence of Msiri. Thus, even before European penetration, multilingualism was common in Katanga and outside influences were actively
bearing on the languages of communication used there. The baYeke
went on using their native shiSumbwa dialect of kiNyamwezi, but some
of them, coming from the region of Tabora, still used some dialectal
forms from this area, and also took over the main languages of their
wives and dependents.

This situation has been maintained until the present day,
though the knowledge of kiYeke is deteriorating rather quickly in the
younger generation. Thus my informant Odilon Mwenda, grandson
of chief Kalasa[1] and "queen" Mukunto from the baLunda, born and
bred in Bunkeya in an exclusively Yeke family, usually speaks Swahili and kiSanga at home; he is quite fluent in Bemba, Lamba, and
French (he was for a time a high official connected with foreign relations in the Katanga government), but to give me valuable information
on Yeke he had to consult his relatives, Chief Pande Mulindwa, a
village head who speaks kiYeke and kiAnshi at home, and kiAnshi with
the people of his village and who also uses Sanga and Swahili with

other people from the neighboring areas, and Antoine Munongo, who
became prime minister in the Katanga government, a muYeke of genuine baSumbwa stock, who used kiYeke at home in his youth, now speaks
kiSanga with his wife and French with his children, restricting the use
of Yeke to his private conversations with local chiefs, while addressing
the villagers in kiSanga; he is also fluent in kiBemba and Swahili.

The Yeke used by elderly people is still very similar to the
Nyamwezi dialect from which it originated, as Chief Pande found out
when he visited far-off Tabora some years ago. A comparison of the
lexicostatistic lists of items in both languages shows a perfect correspondence in 95 percent of the cases. KiYeke has indeed renewed its
vocabulary: the older term kuguma 'to appoint' has become obsolete
and is now commonly replaced by kukala; the original kiYeke kubelagula
for 'to squeeze' has been ousted by the dialectal shiRwana non-derived
form kubera; the adjective -elu 'white,' corresponding to Nyamwezi
-elu 'bright,' has been completely replaced by -epe. In many cases
the shiRwana form prevails as with kubera, but the shiSumbwa is still
heard. Thus, 'river' is either mwiga (Sumbwa) or mongo (Rwana), but
the latter is more common in Bunkeya; 'to throw' can be kuvugumizya
(Rwana) or kutela (Sumbwa) and 'to scratch' is either kulahagula (Rwana)
or kushinangula (Sumbwa), the latter corresponding to Nyamwezi (ku)
shinagula. The early Portuguese influence is also perceptible in the
language of the area formerly ruled over by Msiri; the kiSanga word
for butter is manteka, which is also the common substitute of East
Coast Swahili siagi or samli in Katanga Swahili.

But more important by far is the part played by the baYeke in
opening the way for Swahili in Katanga. Most of the young waNyamwezi
took part in Arab raids or trade caravans far inland and were familiar
with the trade language used on the East Coast, so that when they moved
for their own account into the territory of the Kazembe, numerous Swahilis went along with them, and one of them, Mohammed bin Saleh, a
half-breed Arab, got into serious trouble with the Lunda governor when
the baYeke killed the latter's two nephews; his baNgwana 'free men'
joined Msiri's forces, and a note in Livingstone's papers, dated June
1, 1872, even mentions that the latter then became an ally of the famous
Arab slave driver Tippu-Tip, who had asserted himself very strongly
in Maniema. Though Msiri was too exclusive a potentate to allow any-
one else to assert himself within the boundaries of his kingdom—he got

rid of his Swahili allies who discovered the rich copperfield at Kambove for fear of losing the monopoly of the trade of this valuable ore—he nevertheless gave the waSwahili a privileged status in his kingdom, since they were the only ones, besides the baYeke, whom he trusted with guns in his army! As he himself used that language[2] when dealing with foreigners like the leaders of the German expedition, Böhm and Reichard, who visited Bunkeya in 1884, this must have enhanced the prestige of this trade language, whose further spread in Katanga was soon to be favored by the Belgian occupation, after the bloody battle of December 20, 1891, in which Msiri lost his life.

After a few geological expeditions, thorough prospection of the mining district began and in 1906 the Union Minière du Haut-Katanga was created to work the mines in the area, while the Comité Spécial du Katanga, organized a few years before, had pacified the former kingdom of Msiri with its own autonomous police force recruited mainly along the East Coast and using Swahili as lingua franca. One of the first problems the new mining corporation had to cope with was recruiting labor. The local population was too sparse, and also rather reluctant to work in the mines, especially after the way the baSanga and even the baYeke miners had been ill-treated by Msiri's wife Inafumu, who supervised the extraction of the ore under the royal monopoly. Therefore, time and again, recruiting missions had to be sent out to find new manpower, hardly succeeding in compensating for the growing shortage of labor as the industry developed at an increasingly swift pace.

Elisabethville was created in 1909, near the first important mine of the company, and melting works were built on the side of the Lubumbashi River, right in the middle of the bush—full of tsetse flies and mosquitoes. The following year it was linked by train with South Africa, which was an important factor for a growing English influence in the area. As the production of the mines passed from 2,500 tons in 1912 to 112,000 tons in 1928, the African personnel of the Union Minière reached a peak of 21,107—more than four times the population of the Katanga mining district in 1904. The workers came from all the neighboring areas, but mainly from the Kasayi, the northern and western districts of Katanga and Rwanda-Burundi. The latter, with its feudal political organization and obtrusive cattle economy, keeping the bulk of its population in poverty and submission, was a favorite

area for Union Minière recruiters, and between 1949 and 1955 no less
than 4,718 miners were moved from there over twelve hundred miles
of indescribable roads, in overcrowded trucks or trains, with their
families and their scanty belongings, until a permanent airlift for
about 6,000 persons a year was organized. These immigrants would
usually know Swahili if they were familiar at all with any other language but their own; it has been for decades the lingua franca in their
trading centers. The main town in the country, Bujumbura, has an
exclusively Swahili-speaking Muslim township of several thousand
inhabitants.

Another important group of recruited labor used to be supplied
by Rhodesian private firms, which provided the Union Minière with no
less than 56,000 workers between 1921 and 1930; these came from
various rural areas and usually knew no more than a smattering of
English, but they are mainly responsible for the introduction of such
English words as switi 'sweets' (candy), sitampi 'stamp,' hama 'hammer,' wili 'wheel,' motokari 'motor car,' sipani 'wrench' (spanner).
Less organized but even more impressive is the migration of labor
from the Luba-speaking areas. Having enjoyed education of a higher
standard at an earlier stage in the flourishing missions in the Kasayi,
the baLuba secured the best jobs, as clerks and teachers, and lured
more of their clan brothers to Katanga, so that the African middle
class was predominantly Luba there before the tribal conflicts entailed by independence. Usually endowed with greater facilities of
adaptation, they picked up the Swahili lingua franca very fast and
made it their second language, impressing, as it were, their strong
personality upon it.

The development of Katanga Swahili has indeed been directly
influenced by Luba in recent years. This is evidenced, for example,
in its phonology by:

1. The palatalization of [s] and [z] respectively to [š] and [ž]
before [i], e.g. in bushiku 'night,' -epeshi 'quick' versus East Coast
Swahili usiku, -epesi; mbuzi 'goat,' mukazi 'workday' pronounced
['mbuži], [mu'kaži].

2. The co-occurrence of forms with initial nz- versus nj-
[ndž], e.g. nzala 'hunger' alternating with njala (East Coast Swahili
njaa).

Characteristically, Luba is also the less generalized palatalization of [t] to [tš] by Katanga Swahili speakers, e.g. in kichi, plural
bichi, 'chair(s)' alternating with kiti, plural viti.

This trend to bring the phonological system of Katanga Swahili closer to the Luba pattern was favored by the correspondence of
several characteristics of Congo Swahili with typical features of Luba
like the restriction of the occurrence of Luba [g] to postnasal environments paralleled in Katanga Swahili by the neutralization of the contrast between voiced and voiceless velar stops, the phoneme /g/ being
generally reflected by a [k] allophone in words of Bantu origin, except
after nasals, as evidenced by Katanga Swahili ndeke 'bird' versus
East Coast Swahili ndege, beside funga 'close' in both dialects. After
/m/, whose syllabic allophone [m̩] develops into [mu] in Katanga Swahili, the rather technical term muganga 'doctor' preserves [g], which
is not heard in the more common word mukulu 'leg, foot,' corresponding to East Coast Swahili mguu.

Another example would be the replacement of the intervocalic
voiced affricate [dž][3] by the semivowel [j], e.g. in maji 'water,'
often written mayi according to its pronunciation -y- reflecting [j] in
Katanga Swahili, parallel with Luba mâyí. Though various other characteristics of Katanga Swahili reflect the influence of local Bantu dialects, in a number of cases the Luba forms have definitely prevailed.[4]
Unexpected as it may seem, the remarkable impact of Luba on Swahili can be explained in connection with the sociocultural background
of its occurrence.[5]

Until the depression in the 1930's, the policy of the Union
Minière was to recruit transient labor on the basis of short-term contracts; the thousands of Rhodesians who worked in the Katangese mines
came over under such conditions, leaving their families behind to
join them again after gathering enough money to stay home and settle
down in their native villages. They could not, therefore, influence
the lingua franca of the Katangese mining centers significantly, and
in later years, though very large numbers of them still resided in
Elisabethville and Jadotville (10,000 and 3,500 respectively), they
were so outnumbered by migrants from the Kasayi and Luba-speaking
areas of northern Katanga that their influence remained negligible.

In 1955 there were 40,000 inhabitants from the Kasayi in
Elisabethville and 20,000 in Jadotville—about a third of the total
African population of both towns—whereas at least as many came
from Luba-speaking areas in the province (baSanga, baKaonde, Luba-
Hemba, Luba-Samba, baSongye, and others). Being very dynamic,
they soon assumed a prominent position in the communities in which
they settled, acquiring property and getting control of the local ad-
ministration.[6] Among the nineteen teachers of a primary school in
Elisabethville, five are Luba from the Kasayi and three Katangese
Luba; four are benaLulua, members of the linguistically closely
related, but politically strongly antagonistic Lulua tribe in the Kasayi.
There are three baLunda, two Bemba speakers of different dialects
(Lala and Lamba), one muCiokwe, and one muBinji. Accordingly,
two thirds of the instructors who teach the younger generation, using
French and Swahili as a medium, are native Luba-speakers.

An inquiry carried out in 1957 among the students attending
the upper forms of the high school in the Katuba township in Elisabethville led to similar results. Of a total of 180 pupils, 120 spoke the
Kasayi variety of Luba at home and 27 the Katangese dialects of the
same language, whereas the other languages were only represented
by small groups: 15 baLunda, 5 baBemba, 2 baCiokwe, and so forth,
which also shows that the children of the Luba middle class got better
opportunities for higher education than the sons and daughters of the
other ethnic groups in town, with the exception of the affluent baLunda
minority. The same inquiry, by personal interview with the students,
gave also a rather interesting picture of the language situation among
the rising generation. Of 120 speakers of Luba-Kasayi, only 7 pointed
to the fact that their parents used a clearly dialectal form of it (Lulua
or Kanyoka), whereas 113 stressed that they never used their mother
tongue outside their home, but resorted to Swahili when they were
among themselves, even with other younger generation native Luba-
speakers. In five cases Swahili was also used at home in relations
between parents and children; in a few middle-class families, French
was used for that purpose, and 59 at least of the Luba-Kasayi speakers
used it commonly besides Swahili among themselves or with more
educated people.

Similar situations were to be found among the other groups:
altogether 176 of the 180 students used it as their second language,

outside the closer family circle and except for direct relations with
fellow tribesmen, especially those having recently arrived in town.
Ninety would also resort to French in such circumstances, whenever
this language of social prestige proved fit for communication, as in
dealing with more sophisticated people like administration clerks.
Actually, Swahili was the only language used at home in only two cases,
but a more rapid inquiry on the language used in the family circle of
a sampling of 200 primary-school children showed a much higher proportion of younger people having Swahili as their actual mother tongue,
especially in cases of intertribal marriage or "detribalized" townspeople. This was also the case with the two senior high school students I interviewed: one of them was the son of Nganja-speakers who
had come from Rhodesia in the earlier days and only used this language
for private talks among themselves, raising the children in Katanga
Swahili. The other one was the son of the "burgomaster" of one of the
African townships; his father had lived in Kivu and married a woman
from Bukavu, whose dialect he could neither speak nor understand, as
he was a Tetela-speaker. They therefore used Swahili, the lingua
franca of their native districts, all the time, but the boy had also
picked up some kinyaBungo from his mother.[7]

Accordingly, the situation in Katanga urban communities is
rather similar to that of many other towns in Central Africa:

(a) At home, people usually stick to their mother tongue,
except in cases of intertribal marriage, but there is a definite trend
among the younger generation to drift away from it in favor of the
lingua franca, even when associating with people of their age group
with the same tribal background.

(b) In social intercourse, Swahili in its Katangese variety is
commonly used; levels of knowledge vary with education and length of
stay in the urban community (in 1956, only 12 percent of the African
population of Elisabethville had lived there for more than twenty years,
50 percent had been there between two and ten years; in Jadotville,
only 3 percent had settled down more than twenty years ago, whereas
70 percent had been there between two and ten years).

(c) French is the language of prestige, used at all levels in
education and administration, except for public notices and other docu-

ments for general use, which are bilingual (French and Swahili). In
spite of a short revival after the proclamation of Katanga's independence, under the sponsorship of the late Minister of Education Joseph
Kiwele, a native speaker of Swahili from Baudouinville on Lake Tanganyika, the teaching of Swahili seems to be widely discontinued in
towns. However, the local press contains texts in Swahili, comply-
ing rather loosely with the written East Coast standard, but containing tremendous numbers of French words. For religious instruction,
Swahili material is used, mainly by the Protestant missions, who
have partly stuck to this language in education as well. But in current
speech and folk literature like popular plays, only the so-called potopoto-Swahili is resorted to. With the growing number of young people
using it as their first language, it is in the process of becoming a
creole language in Katanga like kiTuba in the Leopoldville province.
It has diverged rather strongly from what is called kiNgwana or Congo
Swahili, which is the language of the Arabized Africans in Maniema
and the northeast, though mutual understanding between a Katanga
Swahili speaker and a Congo Swahili speaker from, for example, Goma
is still satisfactory, but only educated people with some training in
Swahili grammar and idiom will understand without trouble texts in
East Coast Swahili.

The long coexistence of Africans and Europeans in Katanga
has led to wide borrowing as well, not only of technical or even everyday words from French into Swahili, but also of various Swahili words
and expressions into French. It would be worthwhile studying the
semantic areas from which these words were borrowed and the resul-
tant kitchen-Mischsprache[8] that developed under these conditions of
language contact.

NOTES

[1] One of Msiri's sons.
[2] Delcommune, who met him a few years later (in 1891),
also stresses his perfect command of Swahili.
[3] The East Coast Swahili implosive [j] is not heard anywhere
upcountry.
[4] A detailed analysis of the dialectal features of Katanga

Swahili is given in my article "Lubumbashi Swahili, " Journal of African Languages 7, no. 1 (1968): 14-25.

[5] See Bruce Fetter, "Immigrants to Elizabethville: Their Origins and Aims, " in African Urban Notes 3, no. 2 (Aug. 1968): 17-34, and my contribution to the Proceedings of the Ninth International African Seminar on Social Implications of Multilingualism in Africa, "Multilingualism in an African Urban Centre: The Lubumbashi Case, " in Language Use and Social Change, ed. by W. H. Whiteley (London: International African Institute, 1971), pp. 364-75.

[6] In 1957, three of the four African townships of Elisabethville were ruled by "burgomasters" coming from other provinces.

[7] The results of this inquiry can fruitfully be compared with those attained in a more detailed parallel study carried out a few years earlier in the Katanga mining district; see Maria Leblanc, "Evolution linguistique et relations humaines, " in Zaïre 9, no. 8 (1955): 787-99.

[8] Kamata yulu ya planche casserole moya ya kufanya petit pois—or—safisha fenetre na mayi mingi.

4 | Multilingualism in an African Urban Center: The Lubumbashi Case

Multilingualism predates Westernization in Central Africa. In precolonial days intertribal relations had already led to the development of various contact vernaculars which merely spread farther into the country with the European penetration, as they were adopted by the colonizers for economical and administrative purposes. A typical example of a precolonial multilingual community was the capital of the Garenganze kindom of Msiri in the last quarter of the nineteenth century. Its population consisted of several thousand people from all parts of Central Africa: baSanga, baLamba, baUshi, baLunda, ba-Bemba, baLuba, belonging to the areas the muYeke conqueror had cut out of the territory formerly governed by the <u>Kazembe</u> (governor) of the Mwato Yamvo (Lunda emperor) or taken over during his campaigns against the baLuba; Arabs, waNyamwezi, waSwahili traders and immigrants from across Lake Tanganyika, as well as oviMbundu and Luvale from Angola. The town was an important slave market to which many traders came from all directions. At one time Msiri especially encouraged the prosperous commerce in ivory and slaves with the Portuguese on the West Coast; he even took the daughter of a former Portuguese officer in Bihe as his <u>Ihanga</u> ('first wife'), and the Arab traders soon had to strive to neutralize her influence on Msiri. As a result of the constant flow of trade caravans from East and West, Portuguese could be heard in Katanga, beside the more common Swahili from the East Coast, in which Msiri was himself quite proficient. Another important source of revenue for Msiri beside slaves and ivory was copper; all the digging and processing was directly controlled by the Bayeke. This mineral wealth was one of the main sources of the competition of the colonial powers for control of Katanga, which ended with the occupation of the Garenganze kingdom by the Belgians. The center of their administration was, however,

shifted to the South, where the 'Mine de l'Etoile' became one of the
first urban nuclei in the Katanga mining district. In 1906 the Union
Minière du Haut-Katanga was created, one year after the first convoy
of ox-carts brought heavy mining equipment from Benguela on the
West Coast to Katanga. A copper-processing plant was then built
alongside the Lubumbashi River a few miles from the 'Mine d'Etoile.'
Very soon, Emile Wangermée, the head of the Comité Spécial du
Katanga, which was administering the territory, had plans laid out
for building the first colonial town to be founded in Katanga. In September 1909 the Belgian Government approved them and decided to
call the place Elisabethville and to develop it as the administrative
and economic center of Katanga. On 27 September the railroad from
Rhodesia reached the new town and connected it with South Africa and,
somewhat later, with Beira in Mozambique. From then on the city
grew at a tremendous rate due to the immigration of thousands of
Europeans and tens of thousands of Africans, though the process of
growth was not always smooth: the great companies—the Union Minière and the Katanga railway—discouraged their European employees
from staying in Katanga until the depression of the thirties, when
they began hiring Europeans on the spot instead of bringing them over
from Belgium on limited-term contracts; at that time improved public health conditions made it possible for the employees to have their
families stay with them: secondary schools were opened for European
children, and the demographic pattern of the European community
changed drastically, with a considerable increase in the population
under 20 and over 40, as many Belgian residents began to regard
Elisabethville as their home. As a background to this transformation
in the urban picture the successful development of rural enterprises
supplying fresh milk and agricultural produce to the town under the
sponsorship of the Comité Spécial du Katanga was of primary importance. The first cattle and the first colonists arrived in 1911-12 and
experimental farms were established; after the First World War the
whole enterprise was in jeopardy for lack of financial resources and
because the local Africans competed with the settlers in the growing
of vegetables for the urban market. By the thirties the major problems impeding a prosperous development of the agricultural areas
around the town had been solved, and the farms were able to supply
fresh vegetables and dairy products to the steadily growing numbers
of African as well as European inhabitants of the city. Meanwhile,
the settlement of African peasantry in newly cleared land was encour-

aged so that a lively marketing economy between town and country
developed.

Thus, the growth of the mining industry, the development of
the communication system, especially after the establishment of the
railway links with Port-Francqui (1928) and with Lobito in Angola
(1931), and the steady supply of the necessary goods for a modern
city by a growing agricultural belt and the burgeoning of diversified
secondary industries ensured the boom of Elisabethville after the
Depression.

In order to understand its linguistic situation it is necessary
to examine how its population grew. Fortunately, the recent studies
of Bruce Fetter on immigrants to Elisabethville provide us with valuable data on this matter: here again the policies of the Union Minière
determined the pattern of development; until the thirties the Africans
lived in restricted workers' camps, and only those whose employers
could not afford to provide such accommodation stayed in the 'cité
indigène,' where conditions were much worse. In 1931 the colonial
administration constituted this 'cité' as a new political unit called
'Centre extra-coutumier,' placing its inhabitants under a special legal
status independent of traditional African law. Some amount of self-
government was granted to them: they had special urban courts of
law and even a town council under Belgian supervision. This 'Centre
extra-coutumier' became the rallying point of Africans from all parts
of Katanga and beyond and had a very diversified ethnic composition,
in contrast with the camps where the workers came from the various
areas in which the Union Minière had conducted its manpower recruiting campaigns. Until 1925 the population of these camps was merely
transient: thousands of workers were supplied by British companies
from Northern Rhodesia across the Luapula River, but they were
under strict contracts preventing them from settling down in Katanga;
their numbers were more than matched by Congolese recruits who
came mainly from the Haut-Luapula, Lomani, Tanganyika-Moëro,
and Lulua districts of Katanga. Those from the Haut-Luapula were
from the ethnic groups that constituted the core of the old Garenganze
kingdom (baYeke, baLamba, baUshi, baSanga); from the Lomani
came the Luba-Kasai, the Songye, and Kanyoka; the Tanganyika-Moëro
area provided a multitude of tribal groups, among which the largest
were the Luba-Katanga, the Tabwa, the Songye, and the Lunda Kazembe;

the Lulua districts which constituted Western Katanga brought mostly
baLunda and baCokwe. While, at first, the mining company also
applied the non-resident status to them, the labor shortage of the
middle twenties induced the personnel service to try and make experienced workers stay in the city; they were now offered longer contracts
and encouraged to bring their wives and families to live with them.
But even so, the whole Katangese territory within 300 miles of the
city had been practically depleted of available manpower by previous
recruitment, so that new, more distant, recruiting areas had to be
set up in Maniema, the eastern Kasayi, and the trusteeship territories
of Ruanda and Urundi. With the change in policy new services had to
be provided for the African population, especially public health and
social assistance centers and schools, which helped to integrate the
stabilized labor force in the city. In the first half of the thirties the
economic depression stopped this development rather abruptly; recruitment ceased in Rhodesia and was practically never resumed; the
'centre extra-coutumier' lost almost half its population, which declined
from 11,399 in 1929 to 6,282 in 1934. Most of the Africans leaving
town, nevertheless, remained in the area, scratching a living as menial help in rural enterprises in the neighboring villages or settling
down temporarily in close-by chefferies. When the economic life returned to normal they came back to the city, whereas the Union Minière recruited increasing numbers of Kasaians via the Port-Francqui
railway. By 1945 they constituted 60 percent of the Union Minière
camp, but only 29 percent of the population of the 'centre extra-
coutumier.' By then the basis for the further development of Elisabethville had been solidly laid: an increasing proportion of Africans
were firmly settled down there, and the numbers of locally born children grew steadily on school enrollment rosters. In the meantime
the Belgian population had also become more stabilized: after the
Depression Belgian boys born in the Congo outnumbered the foreign-
born by about 2 to 1. A majority of these Belgians working in the
mining industry came from the Walloon part of the country on account
of experience gained in the Belgian mines in that area; the administration was also essentially French-speaking; however, especially after
the Second World War, the percentage of Flemish-speaking Belgians
increased so considerably that special sections with Dutch as the language of the curriculum could be created in the local schools. As
regards the non-Belgian expatriate population, it consisted essentially
of Ashkenazic and Sephardic Jews (from central and eastern Europe

and from the Mediterranean respectively), Italians (mainly from
three villages near Vercelli), and Greeks from the Dodecanese islands. The Jewish community played an extremely important part
in the social and economic life of the city; the rabbi of Elisabethville
had jurisdiction over the whole of Central Africa. The Greeks were
also quite prosperous, and their church was also the main Greek Ortho-
dox religious center for the whole area. British and South Africans
who had been numerous before the Depression mostly moved to the
Zambian Copperbelt during those difficult years, while the other foreigners stayed on. Before Independence a considerable number of
Belgian settlers liquidated their businesses and the European population experienced a sharp drop, from which it only partly recovered
in the middle sixties after the turmoil of the Katanga rebellion. On
the other hand, the African population has considerably increased;
thus in the camps of the Union Minière alone the number of school-
going children has trebled over the last fifteen years.

From the background of this historical sketch of the development of Elisabethville, to which the African name Lubumbashi has
now been restored, it is easier to understand the linguistic situation
prevailing in the town. From the Belgian administration Katanga has
inherited French as the language of all official documents, in keeping
with the Constitution of the Democratic Republic of the Congo. French
is also the language of the curriculum in all the schools of the town,
and the Katanga elite makes it a point of honor to display its command
of the language in public. However, in spite of the prestige position
of French, Swahili is used widely on various occasions: the original
text of documents for the public is composed in French, but when
posted it is always accompanied by a translation in a form of Swahili
which strives to approach the standard written language of the East
Coast, known to the older generation through schooling in the Catholic
and Protestant missions, but which shows definite features of the
local Swahili creole, as well as glaring examples of un-Swahili literal
translations from the French. Official sign plates, e.g. in the Post
Office, are bilingual. While educated people will use French in the
various offices of the public services, the bulk of the population will
resort to the local variety of Swahili to conduct its business there.
In the shops in the center of the town French may often be used as a
starter, but every shopkeeper or craftsman will readily use Swahili
whenever the customer chooses to switch to this language. As a

matter of fact, conversations with constant switching, but prevailing
use of Swahili can often be heard in most places along the central
avenue de l'Etoile. In primary schools, where French is used from
the very start as the language of the curriculum, the teacher will give
explanations in Swahili until the students become proficient enough to
enable him to resort exclusively to French (which usually takes two
to three years). Swahili is currently used in political speeches addressed to the bulk of the population, and political pamphlets were
already written in this language under the colonial regime, e.g. the
appeal of the voters to the Confederation of the Katangese Associations
(CONAKAT), under the leadership of Moise Tshombe before Independence. During the elections to the town council in 1959 the local settlers' association also appealed to the African electorate in Swahili,
and their pamphlets were distributed in three languages: French,
Dutch, and Swahili. The Mouvement National Congolais of Patrice
Lumumba, however, resorted to French in its propaganda, whereas
Jason Sendwe's Balubakat, which appealed more specifically to the
tribal solidarity of the baLuba and their associates used the Katangese
variety of Luba. Swahili is also currently used over the radio, and
programs with local pop singers are extremely popular over the whole
of Central and East Africa. The Swahili Press is, however, very
limited: a weekly paper Uhaki (Truth) is practically the only regular
publication with extensive texts in the language; the Union Minière
used to publish a month paper—Mwana Shaba (The Child of Copper)—
with local information of interest to its workers, which was mainly
written in Swahili, but contained items in other languages commonly
used by its labor force; in the middle sixties it had the widest circulation of any African-language paper in the Congo, with a run of 36,000
copies. The daily Press is exclusively in French. Plays are sometimes performed in Swahili: at the end of the colonial period the governor of the province actually tried to promote original writing as
well as the performance of dramatic works in the language, and some
very interesting texts were produced, e.g. an adaptation of the French
medieval play 'La Farce de Maître Pathelin' to Katangese situations.
As a religious language, Swahili is mainly used in Protestant missions,
where the services are usually conducted in this language.

As regards current conversation, Swahili would be mostly
heard in the African market; it would prevail in the laundry, baby
care, and sewing sections of the 'foyer social,' especially when

Language spoken Tribal origin	No. of students	At home				With friends				With strangers			
		French	Swahili	Tribal language	Other	French	Swahili	Tribal language	Other	French	Swahili	Tribal language	Other
	475												
Luba and Related Language Groups	303												
Luba (Katanga)	19	3	6	15	—	17	9	3	1	11	11	3	1
Luba (Kasayi)	80	7	16	75	—	60	49	4	5	59	44	—	5
Kanyoka	8	—	5	3	—	8	3	—	—	2	5	—	1
Kete	1	1	—	1	—	—	1	—	—	1	1	—	—
Samba (baZela)	10	—	5	6	5	7	5	1	2	7	5	—	1
Sanga	9	—	3	6	—	7	9	—	—	5	4	—	—
Songye	12	2	8	4	—	10	6	—	—	10	6	—	—
Kabinda	13	1	6	8	1	12	7	—	—	6	7	1	2
Hemba	75	7	50	34	—	63	27	1	1	49	39	2	1
(no further specification)	76	9	20	50	—	60	44	5	—	49	46	—	1
Bemba and Related Groups	56												
Lamba	1	—	—	1	—	1	—	—	—	1	1	—	—
Aushi	2	—	—	2	1	1	1	—	—	1	1	—	—
Tabwa	19	—	11	13	—	16	13	—	2	10	11	—	—
Kaonde	1	—	—	1	—	—	1	—	—	1	—	—	—
(no further specification)	33	1	17	25	—	26	18	—	1	18	24	1	1

	105												
Lunda and Related Groups													
Cokwe	12	2	4	10	—	9	6	7	6	7	8	—	—
Ndembo	5	1	1	4	—	4	2	3	—	3	3	—	—
Minungo	2	—	—	2	—	1	2	1	—	1	1	—	—
(no further specification)	86	9	32	64	—	63	53	60	6	60	54	6	9
Lesser Groups	9												
kaBwari	1	1	1	—	—	1	1	1	—	1	—	—	—
baYeke	3	1	1	2	—	3	2	1	—	1	1	—	—
Mambwe	1	1	1	—	—	1	—	—	—	—	1	—	—
Kalanga (Rega)	1	—	—	—	—	1	—	—	—	—	1	—	—
Bangu-Bangu	1	1	—	—	—	1	—	—	—	—	1	—	—
BaNgala	1	—	—	1	—	—	1	1	—	1	—	—	—
WaGenya	1	—	1	1	—	1	1	1	—	1	1	—	—
From Outside the Congo	2												
Ruanda	1	—	—	1	—	1	1	1	—	1	—	—	—
Malawi	1	—	—	1	1	1	1	1	—	1	1	—	—

Notes to the Table of Statistics

1. The higher totals of the languages actually spoken reflect the fact that several students list two or more languages as currently spoken in the social context under reference. Lower totals indicate that some students left one of the questions unanswered.

2. The other language spoken with strangers or friends is usually English, but occasionally also another Congolese language, e.g. liNgala, kiKongo.

expatriates would help the African women in their various activities; the same would be true in the dispensary and the hospital. In general, whenever Lubumbashi town dwellers come into contact with other people in buses, small shops, cafés, and other public places Swahili is the language they naturally resort to, unless they meet fellow tribesmen.

Tribal languages are indeed used essentially within the family group and wider tribal community, but with the growing rate of inter-tribal marriage among the younger generation this situation is changing rapidly, since Lubumbashi townspeople of different tribal origin will normally resort to Swahili or, at a higher level of education, maybe also to French. Accordingly, children born of such marriages will be raised in Swahili or, possibly, partly at least, in French, and will sometimes have no more than a passive knowledge of the respective tribal languages of their parents' family. The statistics on pages 54–55, covering a fairly substantial set of students in a teachers' training college and secondary school in the African suburb of Katuba in 1963, may illustrate the situation in the African community with the rising generation.

However, the Swahili spoken by the Lubumbashi townspeople is not the East Coast Swahili but a creolized form resulting from the adaptation of the Swahili lingua franca introduced in the days of Msiri by the trading caravans from the East, and henceforth as a contact language with the local Africans by the Belgian colonial administration, as well as the foremen in the mining industry. This Swahili shows typical features of a pidginized language: phonological changes under the influence of the prevailing local Bantu languages, mainly Luba and Bemba; simplication of the morphology (especially disruption of the concord system and reduction of the conjugation to a few basic tenses); substantial reduction of the vocabulary. But, having been adopted as first language by a growing number of townsmen, it is being relexical-ized with local Bantu words and borrowing from French. It also bears traces of the various language contacts typical of the area, e.g. a few Portuguese loans like manteka for 'butter' and a considerable number of technical terms from English, due to the influence of Rhodesian labor during the early period of development of the mining industry. The Flemish is extremely limited (e.g. pazopo 'pay attention'), but the influence of French is all-pervasive.

Thus, the linguistic situation in Lubumbashi is a clear reflection of the historical growth of the town under the colonial regime. The agglomeration of considerable masses of Africans of various origins has made the use of a lingua franca imperative: the obvious language for this was Swahili, and as a consequence of progressive detribalization in the urban context, it is gradually becoming the first language of an increasing number of townspeople. The local dialects are, however, still very much alive, and only loss of contact with the family back in the villages and more general intertribal marriage instead of the still prevailing habit of seeking a wife in the home region of the parents will threaten them seriously. The persistence of French as the prestige language may ultimately lead to the formation of a predominantly French-speaking elite, but in view of the frequent association between the various social levels, bilingualism with Swahili as the second language will undoubtedly be maintained by such a group. In view of the ousting of Swahili from the curriculum, it is to be feared that the knowledge of standard Swahili, to which some of the younger generation were at least temporarily exposed in primary schools, may deteriorate even further, in view of the fact that very little literature remains available in the language, and that the means of mass communication do not strive at all to conform systematically with the East Coast standard. A study in more depth of the Lubumbashi situation would, however, be required to assess to what degree the 'mother tongue' regresses among the younger generation, who still, as a rule, identify themselves with the tribe of their father, even if they no longer speak his language. A detailed study would have to be made of the use of the various languages (French, Swahili, tribal languages) according to the age groups, the economic and social background, the personality of the people to whom one speaks, and the circumstances in which the conversation takes place. For Swahili speakers, variations of style would also have to be examined according to the person or persons addressed in private or in public, and the contrast between the spoken and written forms would require careful investigation. Besides, the specific competence of the speakers in the various languages should be measured by adequate testing. With such data, a better assessment of multilingualism in Lubumbashi should be achieved.

BIBLIOGRAPHICAL NOTE

An extensive survey of the sources for the history of Lubumbashi is to be found in the note of Bruce Fetter: 'Elisabethville'— Bibliographical Supplement No. 7, to African Urban Notes (June 1968), 33 pages (mimeographed).

On the history of Elisabethville (Lubumbashi), see especially Bruce S. Fetter, Elisabethville and Lubumbashi: The Segmentary Growth of a Colonial City (PhD dissertation, University of Wisconsin, 1968, 332 pages). Further important sources on the development of the town and the African settlement are: Jacques Denis, Le phénomène urbain en Afrique centrale (Brussels: Académie Royale des Sciences Coloniales, 1958); J. Benoît, La population Africaine à Elisabethville à la fin de 1957 (Elisabethville: Centre d'Etudes des Problèmes Sociaux Indigènes, 1958); Marc Richelle, Aspects psychologiques de l'acculturation (Elisabethville: Centre d'Etude des Problèmes Sociaux Indigènes, 1960); Paul Minon, Katuba. Etude quantitative d'une communauté urbaine africaine (Elisabethville: Centre d'Etude des Problèmes Sociaux Indigènes, 1960); Marcel Anselin, De inlandse middenstand te Elizabethstad (Elisabethville: Centre d'Etude des Problèmes Sociaux Indigènes, 1960); Bruce Fetter, 'Immigrants to Elisabethville: Their Origins and Aims,' in African Urban Notes 3, no. 2 (Aug. 1968): 17-34.

On precolonial and early Katanga, see especially Auguste Verbeken, Msiri. Roi du Garenganze (Bruxelles: Louis Cuypers, 1956); *** Comité Spécial du Katanga, 1900-1950 (Bruxelles: Louis Cuypers, 1950).

On the linguistic situation in Katanga, cf. Maria Leblanc, 'Evolution Linguistique et Relations Humaines,' in Zaïre 9, no. 8 (1954): 787-99; my articles: 'Cultural Languages and Contact Vernaculars in the Republic of the Congo,' in Texas Studies in Literature and Language 4, no. 4 (Winter 1963): 499-511; 'The Choice of an Official Language in the Democratic Republic of the Congo,' in J. A. Fishman, C. A. Ferguson, and J. Das Gupta, eds., Language Problems of Developing Nations (New York: Wiley, 1968), pp. 295-311; 'The Position of Swahili and Other Bantu Languages in Katanga,' in Texas Studies in Literature and Language 11, no. 2 (1969): 905-13; 'Lubumbashi Swahili,' in the Journal of African Languages 7, no. 1 (1968): 14-25.

5 | Problems and Techniques of a Sociolinguistically Oriented Language Survey: The Case of the Tanzania Survey

Any sociolinguistically oriented survey is bound to present problems sui generis as the result of the specific features of the linguistic area surveyed, but the techniques used to collect relevant data must essentially consist of three of the most common approaches to such field work: (a) direct observation of the linguistic situation; (b) interviews with speakers of the various languages of the area; (c) questionnaires geared to the specific groups to be investigated. The detailed organization of the survey and the respective use of different methods of investigation will depend largely upon the more specific aims of the survey. In the case of the Survey of Language Use and Language Teaching in Eastern Africa, gathering research data was only one of the four aims, and special weight was placed on the necessity to stimulate continued research by involving local specialists in the project.[1] The participation of young scholars, specially trained for that purpose, in the data collecting and processing was accordingly an important feature of this survey. The task of "assembling basic data on the major languages in each country, " however, was essentially reserved for each country team. In order to perform this task, it was necessary to analyze the linguistic situation of each country in detail—descriptively, historically, and politically—before examining the impact of linguistic diversity on effective language use as well as on language planning and language policy. The structure of the relevant society had to be probed to determine the correlations between patterns of language use and particular sociocultural factors. The implementation of a national language policy in the educational system required special consideration to study the expected impact of the teaching of specific languages on the better educated upcoming generation—those likely to play a major part in nation building. As a result, three essential sections seemed to impose themselves on the country teams as components of their final report:

● The linguistic situation of the country, describing the linguistic diversity in the area and its historical background, with an attempt at classification of all languages involved and a characterization of the major languages.

● Language use in the country, involving (1) the history of the language policy and development of national languages; (2) the description of the local community and the linguistic correlates of its sociocultural structure; (3) the study of patterns of multilingualism and specific uses of definite languages.

● Language teaching in the country, providing an outline of the structure and historical background of the educational system and a detailed analysis of language teaching at all levels as well as the use of languages in the curriculum.[2]

A systematic survey of the approaches used by the Tanzania team to provide such information may serve as an example of the problems and methods involved in a sociolinguistically oriented survey. Though some features are specific to Tanzania, the work done is essentially representative of current methods in sociolinguistics and may contribute to useful generalizations and fruitful comparisons relevant to the basic issues of the study of language in society.

1. Problems of Organization of the Tanzania Survey

The Tanzania Survey was essentially data-oriented and tried to cope with the type of language problems characterizing developing nations. The study accordingly focused essentially on:

● the degree of multilingualism, with special attention to the measurement of linguistic diversity;

● the social roles played by the various languages involved; vernaculars, national language (Swahili), international language of wider communication (English), with a detailed study of the correlation between the use of these languages and current socioeconomic factors;

● the <u>study of the attitudes</u> of Tanzanians toward the various languages commonly used;

● the <u>national language policy</u> and the degree of success achieved in its implementation, with careful analysis of the role played by Swahili in nation building;

● the <u>language-planning</u> measures taken by the Tanzanian government to make Swahili suitable for adequate use in all social, economic, and cultural activities of the country as well as the coordinated efforts by private and government-sponsored agencies to promote and develop the national language. [3]

The approach to the study of these problems by the Tanzania team[4] was strongly affected by <u>specific local situations</u>. The following pages provide a concise description of these situations.

<u>Language Policy</u>

As a consequence of the irreversible decision of the Tanzanian government to carry through its policy of making Swahili the only commonly used language of the nation, a number of implicit restrictions were imposed upon the survey, namely: (1) the status of Swahili as a national language was not to be questioned; (2) any systematic linguistic study of the local vernaculars was discouraged. This meant, essentially, that extensive studies of attitudes toward Swahili versus English had to be avoided and that linguistic investigation of the vernaculars had to be carried out in correlation with their specifically local role and with the study of interferences between Swahili and Bantu or non-Bantu dialects. The position of the Tanzanian government in this matter was perfectly consistent with its declared policy: it is evident that it could not tolerate the type of yes-or-no questions usually put to students to measure their attitudes toward the language, e.g. "I dread the X language lesson," "Learning the X language is so difficult that I dislike it very much," and "I do not think that there is much value in learning the X language."[5] Such "loaded" questions are indeed likely to confuse the value judgments of Tanzanian students regarding Swahili; an inquiry along these lines a few years ago actually proved most embarrassing to the Tanzanian Ministry of Education.[6] As for the study of vernaculars, it should be pointed out that

the Swahili inspectorate actively encouraged my inquiry on the phonological and grammatical interference of the major Bantu languages of
Tanzania on the local forms of Swahili used by less educated speakers,
since it would help teachers in their effort to improve the standard of
Swahili by identifying mistakes predictable from the ethnic origin of
their students. Moreover, the Ministry of Education sponsored the
research done on vernaculars within the framework of the survey insofar as it was functional and could not be misconstrued by local speakers as enhancing the status of the ethnic languages with respect to
Swahili.

        As a consequence of its systematic effort to ensure the pri-
macy of Swahili, the Tanzanian government was particularly anxious
to circumscribe the actual role of English in Tanzanian society. Many
of the questions the survey was asked to investigate were consequently
centered around this topic, but the Ministry of Education was particularly concerned with the use that students who had to interrupt their
education at the end of primary school would make of English after
leaving school: was it worth the effort and expense involved in teaching them this language if English was not to be used by them efficiently
in their later productive life? In a country like Tanzania, where resources are limited and where the availability of trained teachers of
English has been considerably reduced by the shift from expatriates
to local manpower, the investigation of such a problem is indeed crucial for future government planning. [7]

Research Clearance

        In a socialist country with a strongly hierarchized one-party
organization, the problem of clearing all research activities in close
collaboration with the local academic authorities is essential. It was
therefore a major concern of the Tanzania team to contact all Tanzanian authorities from the Regional Commissioner down to the local officers before proceeding with field work in any area and to obtain their
permission and support as well as the aid of the relevant TANU party
officials. The aims, methods, and expected practical use of the survey were carefully explained to them, and the questionnaires to be
used were submitted for their approval so that any sensitive question
that might cause problems in the present-day Tanzanian sociocultural
framework might be avoided. Although this repetitious and lengthy

procedure was sometimes tedious, it proved most effective, since it
ensured ready access to informants who would otherwise not have
been easily reached or who would have been most reluctant to collaborate. Working through the Ministries of Education, Information, Social
Welfare, and Rural Development, the team involved as many Tanzanians as possible in the research, training university students for field
work, lecturing to groups of teachers and students in Teachers Training Colleges, giving specific instruction to tutors in secondary schools,
and explaining questionnaire techniques to local officials helping in
administering them. The Tanzanians' "feeling of participation" which
resulted from this approach appeared to be a major element in promoting good will and a keen interest in the research and contributed
largely to its success. Nevertheless, aside from the time-consuming
activity it entailed, the approach imposed by the clearance problem
had a considerable number of drawbacks. For example, the lack of
direct contact between the team and the informants (e.g. in the case
of questionnaires administered through rural development or social
work officers) made a control on the validity of certain data impossible,
as insufficient training and misinterpretation of questions entailed
major inaccuracies in the responses. Additionally, working through
administrative channels caused numerous delays and excluded the study
of the essential psycholinguistic problem of attitudes of the informants
versus the languages spoken by them. However, on the whole, the
return of the inquiries conducted through official channels has been
highly satisfactory: more than 90 percent in the case of the secondary
school questionnaires through the Ministry of Education; about 60 percent in the case of the uneducated adult population questionnaires
through the regional Social Welfare Services.

Inaccessibility of Part of the Country

While the team visited practically every part of the country
in which it was allowed to work, certain areas were restricted and
could never be studied directly, namely, the islands of Zanzibar and
Pemba, which were left totally out of the survey, and the southern
regions of Ruvuma and Mtwara and the southern part of Iringa and
Mbeya, about which information was collected from local people
through official channels and from students from these areas residing
elsewhere in the country.

Unavailability of Certain Research Facilities

One of the major drawbacks of working with large samplings in Tanzania was the lack of computer facilities. Only one computer was available at the Treasury Department when the project started, and no computer time could be obtained; moreover, no trained manpower was available for coding, card-punching, and programming. As the original questionnaires had to be left in the country, coding the data with poorly trained help was a major problem and led to subsequent complications when the University of London and the University of Texas computers kept rejecting a considerable number of cards containing obviously erroneous information which had slipped in during the coding procedure and could not be verified against the original. This problem ultimately required numerous months in the adequate computerization of the survey data.

2. The Language Situation in Tanzania

The survey of the languages of Tanzania was intended to give an accurate account of the past and present linguistic situations of the country, dealing with the available data from a descriptive, historical, and political point of view.

Description of the Language Situation

An attempt was made to collect all the available materials on the languages used in Tanzania and to survey the existing literature, to gather identical data on as many languages as possible, to examine and revise their classification, and to provide short structural sketches of the major languages.

Inventory of the languages and available materials. In his linguistic bibliography of East Africa, Whiteley (1958) lists 100 Tanzanian languages, of which 31 are totally undocumented; for many of them, only scarcely accessible short vocabulary or grammatical notes collected rather at random by various local civil servants or missionaries appear to be extant.[8]

More recently, Whiteley (1971, p. 147) identified 114 ethnic-linguistic units in Tanzania (102 Bantu, 7 Highland Nilotic, 4 Eastern Cushitic, and 1 Click language). However, in a footnote, he added the Hadza, a second click-speaking group. He also omitted the Mbugu in his total, which accordingly includes 116 linguistic groups. To these the Tanzania survey would now add 19 ethnic-linguistic units. All the scattered materials on these languages which could be traced in Tanzania have been examined and microfilmed. A copy of these microfilms has been deposited in the Library of the University of Dar es Salaam.[9]

Collection of linguistic data. To provide basic information on the Tanzanian languages, the following data were gathered whenever possible:

• A word list combining the basic vocabulary of the Swadesh expanded list (without the terms irrelevant for East Africa) with the Guthrie and the Meeussen lists for common Bantu lexical items, for a total of slightly more than 1,000 words. The lemmas were given in English and Swahili to avoid confusion in the case of items like bark (Swahili gome, of tree: mbweka, of dog).

• The translation of three sets of Swahili sentences: (1) 75 sentences compiled by D. Lehmann for the comparative study of Bantu languages, containing a lexicon of about 300 root morphemes, presented in coherent contexts with basic syntactic patterns; (2) 36 sentences illustrating the Bantu verbal derivation system, based on W. Whiteley's display of the system of extensions for the root -fung- "close" in Swahili;[10] (3) 75 groups of phrases and short sentences illustrating the main concord and syntactic patterns of Bantu. The target was to obtain the translation of these sets by at least three native speakers of each language. All the translations of the first set were taped, and the linguistic background of the informant was duly recorded. Linguistic information was thus gathered on about 88 Tanzanian languages. Unfortunately, no similar materials could be compiled for the non-Bantu languages.

• A grammatical questionnaire based on the principles of contrastive grammar which endeavored to collect an extensive set of

grammatical data on the class and concord system, the conjugation,
the invariables, and the basic derivation and syntactic patterns of the
major languages as contrasted with Swahili. It followed the outline of
a description of a Bantu language suggested by C. Doke[11] and the plan
of my Swahili Language Handbook (1967).

• A set of questions covering the interferences between major
Tanzanian languages and Swahili on the phonological and grammatical
levels. Samples of interferences were given with their ethnic-linguistic localization:

$$\text{e.g.} \quad p \rightarrow f / \begin{Bmatrix} \# \\ V \end{Bmatrix} - V \text{ in Makua}$$

Additional information was also requested about similar and/or different cases. This questionnaire was addressed to Swahili teachers all
over the country and focused on their observations of the recurrent
"mistakes" of their students of various ethnic backgrounds in their
teaching experience. The aim of the study was to correlate the interferences in Swahili with the linguistic data on the phonology and grammar of the relevant ethnic languages.

Classification of the Tanzanian languages. For the Bantu languages, the prevailing classification is Guthrie's which, through three
revisions, remains essentially the same: large geographical zones,
comprising groups of varying size and closeness of relationship shar-
ing a set of phonological and grammatical features. "To place the
groups in sets ... an arbitrary blend of characteristics is made"
(Guthrie 1948, p. 27), so that the validity of these larger units may be
questioned. The approach is essentially typological, whereas a genetic-
historical method might be more advisable. In his Comparative Bantu
(1967-72), lexical data become the essential basis for comparison and
regrouping, but a rather static interpretation of diachronic semantics
leads to the surprising assumption that definite lexical items whose
meaning has changed through centuries of Bantu linguistic development
may not be counted for comparison purposes or must be referred to
parallel Bantu roots with different basic meanings.[12] In his contribution to the Kenya Survey, J. Sharman has submitted this approach to
a very thorough and constructive criticism. It stands to reason that,
if lexical items are to be used for language classification purposes,
the principles of word geography have to be applied rigorously. An

attempt in this direction was made by André Polomé (1971) on the
basis of the survey data for 50 Northern Tanzanian Bantu languages.
The outcome of the research was thoroughly discrepant with Guthrie's
zones E, F, and G and some of their subdivisions. A further analysis
of approximately 200 isoglosses covering the entire Tanzanian territory is in progress.

On the other hand, the Uganda and Ethiopia surveys have
shown [Ladefoged 1972; Bender, Cooper, and Ferguson 1975] that it
is essential to reexamine the relationship between languages classified in the same unit to determine the degree of variation between
them.

When detailed and reliable linguistic information is lacking,
the use of diagnostic traits favored by Guthrie and Ferguson may be
the only possible solution, but when sufficient data are available, a
better assessment of the situation is undoubtedly possible through a
thorough analysis of phonemic and lexical correspondences. Using
the survey data, Susan Polomé (1971) has studied the synchronic
phonological systems of twelve Chagga dialects to establish a comparative basis for dialect relationships. This has made a redistribution
of the Chagga linguistic territory on the Kilimanjaro in three major
divisions and subdialect areas: (1) Hai: Siha, Musoma, Machame,
Kibosho; (2) Vunjo: Uru, Old Moshi, Vunjo, Kilema, Marangu, Mwika;
(3) Rombo: Mashati, Usseri.[13] Moreover, a comparative study of
present-day reflexes of Proto-Bantu forms for cross-dialectal lexical
items revealed a grouping paralleling what was implied by both geographical data and informants' views. A parallel independent study
carried out in 1972 by D. Nurse of the University of Dar es Salaam
confirmed these results. Perhaps the most significant result of this
inquiry was the confirmation of the reliability of the informants' subjective evaluation of the degree of mutual intelligibility of the various
dialects involved. The same conclusion was reached by B. Heine
(1972, pp. 5-6) in his interviews in the Musama region, which led to
a reclassification of the Bantu languages of that area (Kuria, Kabwa,
and Kerewe, and their subgroup Ngurɪmɪ as well as Zanaki). As
regards the classification of non-Bantu languages, the Tanzania survey will rely essentially on the work of C. Ehret (1968, 1971), with
the recent revisions and additions by B. Heine and B. Blount.

Structural sketches. On the basis of the collected materials,
a structural sketch of the fifteen major Bantu languages of Tanzania
will be given; non-Bantu will be represented by data on Masai, Luo,
Turu, and Sandawe. These structural sketches will cover an inventory of the phonemes of the languages and a survey of their main grammatical features (nominal and pronominal concord system, conjugation,
and basic syntactic patterns).

Historical Development of the Linguistic Situation

To provide an adequate background for the understanding of
the present linguistic situation in Tanzania, three main points have to
be closely examined: (1) the spread of the Bantu and non-Bantu languages in Tanzania; (2) the origin and development of Swahili; (3) the
introduction of English and of Asian languages in Tanzania. Fortunately, a considerable amount of research had been done by historians
on the migrations of Bantu and non-Bantu peoples in the Tanzania area
(Huntingford 1963; Sutton 1968, 1969; Ehret 1968; McIntosh 1968;
Kimambo 1969) so that the basic information on the establishment and
spread of the population speaking languages of various origins is readily available to account for complex local multilingual situations. A
considerable number of special studies on remnant groups, however,
remains to be done.[14]

While the origin of Swahili is still a disputed issue,[15] the
Arabic penetration in East Africa which is responsible for its spread
as a language of wider communication is well documented (Gray 1963;
Smith 1963; Bennett 1968; Alpers 1969; Whiteley 1969, pp. 42-56).
More important for the survey was the diachronic study of colonial
policies which sheds light on the shift in emphasis on definite languages,
e.g. the use of Swahili as a language of wider communication; the introduction of the language of colonial power in administration, education, justice, and other spheres of social life; the emphasis on certain
tribal languages; and the downgrading of other local languages, especially with regard to educational policy (Whiteley 1964, pp. 57-78).
It stands to reason that through the years divergent attitudes of the
colonial power with regard to the language of the curriculum in primary
education can have a considerable impact on the linguistic situation.
In this regard, the study of German archives in Tanzania indicates
how the decisions taken by the German colonial government to sponsor

Swahili have actually been decisive in the role this language has played in education as well as in administration from a very early date, and it can be said that this German decision has been one of the major factors contributing to the ultimate adoption of Swahili as the national language in Tanzania (Brumfit 1971).

Language Policies

The study of the colonial period, especially the British period, provides the background for the present-day situation. Though the available documentation is limited,[16] the materials gathered by Whiteley (1969) and M. Abdulaziz (1971) constitute the basis for a thorough study, presently in preparation by M. Abdulaziz, of the language policies and of the various measures taken by the government in the field of language planning in Tanzania. This study will also devote particular attention to the linguistically oriented societies tending to promote the development of literature in Swahili, such as UKUTA, which played an important part in enhancing the prestige of Swahili as a cultural language and in prompting government action to implement the national policy of using the language as the main language of communication in various fields of everyday activity.[17]

3. Language Use in Tanzania

In order to assess the sociocultural correlates of the patterns of everyday language use, of the degrees of multilingualism and linguistic proficiency, and of the patterns of literacy and reading habits in Tanzania, a thorough study of Tanzanian society was required. This involved a detailed examination of the social stratification on the basis of ethnic, economic, educational, religious, and other cultural criteria.

Special attention was given to the position of the woman in society, since not only are women more conservative in their language usage but the considerable lag in education for girls and their confinement to the home is responsible for a stronger maintenance of the vernacular and, in certain cases, for their lack of knowledge of the languages of wider communication. The contrast between rural and developing urban areas was also emphasized, and all the data obtainable from census surveys and other demographic sources were carefully

compiled. While the survey team was in Tanzania, the government
conducted an extensive survey on family budgets and on other aspects
of the socioeconomic life of the society. The resulting information,
when available, will also be used as background for a study of the
socioeconomic parameters of the linguistic data.

As regards age groups, the generation gap resulting from
different exposure to education was examined in relation to its influence on the position of the individual in society. In traditional societies, older people with less education can enjoy a very high social
status independent of their formal educational background. The role
of such people in society was carefully described and the reason for
their special status analyzed in order to understand the linguistic
correlates of such situations.

A third important point in the preliminary study of the Tanzanian community was the examination of the educational system of the
country with focus on the languages taught in the curriculum in primary
education, the preparation students received for the shift in language
of the curriculum in secondary education, the tests imposed on students
to check their achievement at the end of primary education, and the
average results of these tests.[18] As regards secondary education, the
continued teaching of Swahili as a subject, the contents of the syllabus,
and the available teaching materials were scrutinized with a view
toward assessing the improvement in knowledge of the national language
to be expected from a better educated younger generation. Achievements
in English and its efficiency as a medium were also analyzed in view of
its continued important role in economic, social, and cultural life.
Further attention was given to language problems in other educational
contexts, e.g. by examining what languages were actually used in technical education for teaching and in textbooks, what kind of textbooks
were written or translated into Swahili, etc. At the university as well
as at the Teachers Training College level, an inquiry was made into the
kind of preparation future teachers receive with regard to the teaching
of the national language as well as English or French as foreign languages or of any other language of wider communication.[19]

Another important problem examined by the survey was the
policy with regard to adult education and literacy campaigns: What
kind of international collaboration was there in the literacy campaign?

What was the role of UNESCO? What kind of action was being taken? In what area? At what segment of the population was the program aimed? What kinds of tools were used to implement the policy? How did this fit in with national language policy? In the case of Tanzania, the last question was particularly pertinent since, up to 1961, most of the literacy programs were conducted essentially by the missions in the local major ethnic languages. Since then all programs must be conducted in Swahili, and it is obvious that such a political decision had a considerable impact on the implementation of the literacy program and upon the smooth continuation of prior work.

The extensive work done in the field of education will constitute the third major section of the survey report, edited by C. P. Hill. The study of the background of the current situation was considerably facilitated by the availability of a first-rate survey of the historical development of Tanzanian education: Society, Schools and Progress in Tanzania, by J. Cameron and W. A. Dodd.[20] An abundant and reliable set of source material also aided description of the other aspects of Tanzanian society.[21]

As indicated at the beginning of this paper, the methods used to gather data on language use consisted essentially of questionnaires, interviews, and observation.

Questionnaires

The content of the questionnaires used by the survey was essentially based on three types of data: (1) background on the informant himself; (2) questions illustrating his socioeconomic and educational status; (3) questions illustrating his language competence. The informants were usually reticent to supply their name, and in most cases, it was decided to leave the questionnaire anonymous. The same reluctance was also found with regard to providing personal family information, so this type of information was usually kept to a minimum: the important fact was to be able to trace the ethnic and geographic background of his parents and in certain cases of his grandparents, since mixed marriages are a constant source of language shift or of a shift from the vernacular to Swahili.

Obtaining economic information was also particularly delicate. It was practically impossible to obtain indications as to the salaries of definite persons, but in many cases the scales of salaries were established in such a way that the profession, the level of education, and the rank of the person in his administrative or professional field were sufficient indication of his financial situation. Insistence on obtaining further details on this subject would have created difficulties and generated informant distrust of the interviewer. As has been shown in the Tanzanian Census[22] as well as in other surveys,[23] the economic status of the individual can be measured by certain outward signs in his social context. Possession of a bicycle or of a sewing machine or electronic equipment like a tape recorder, a record player, or a transistor radio are extremely useful indications. The type of roof on the house, the methods used for cooking food, and other such data concerning the house were also found to be extremely useful in measuring the economic position of the informants. This approach involved a preliminary study on the indices of the socioeconomic status in collaboration with University of Dar es Salaam sociologists.[24]

Determining the informant's status with relation to the social stratum to which he belonged was also a delicate problem: age can play an important part as well as clanic and ethnic connections or definite social functions. In non-Western societies, the prestige attached to social functions may be extremely different from that in Western society. In a one-party state like Tanzania, an uneducated, rather poor man who fulfills the function of a block leader for ten houses is a very important man, even though most of the people under his jurisdiction may be economically much better off. It was therefore essential to clearly define the social roles played by individuals. Accordingly, two types of questionnaires were devised—one for the average citizen and another for definite subgroups of society.

In the first case, questions relative to social activities had to be phrased differently depending upon whether they applied to a rural or to an urban population, and in the case of the rural population, a distinction had to be made between men and women. In framing these questions, the extensive preliminary study of Tanzania served as a constant guideline.[25]

Actually, the survey circulated several sets of questionnaires nationwide on general language use:

• The <u>adult questionnaire</u>, which was administered through
various channels, including: (1) local officers of the Ministries of
Information, Rural Development, and Social Welfare, who picked out
a limited, random sample of mostly uneducated adults in rural areas,
after having been briefed by team members on the proper handling of
the questionnaire; (2) students in linguistics and in sociology of the
University of Dar es Salaam who had attended special training sessions
on sociolinguistic research; (3) team members in their field work,
especially in Dar es Salaam and in selected representative communities (a fishing village, a coffee cooperative, an agricultural commune,
etc.) for whom it served more as an interview schedule than as an
actual questionnaire, since it contained, in addition to a common core,
specific questions relevant to urban versus rural communities and
male versus female as well as literate versus nonliterate informants.
In the case of educated informants, only guidance was provided, and
the informants completed the questionnaires on their own, e.g. in the
case of the survey of the Asian urban middle class. The total sampling
covered about 1,200 people from all walks of life.

• The <u>secondary school questionnaire</u>, which was prepared in
collaboration with the Ministry of Education. All the students entering
high school during the school year 1969-70 were submitted to it, with
a total response of 8,333 valid questionnaires. Most of the schools
were visited in advance, and explanations on the administration of the
questionnaire and on the intent of the survey were given to the headmaster and to tutors especially appointed in each school to administer
the questionnaire, so that all the necessary explanations could be given
by them to the students. Guidelines were also sent to the schools when
the questionnaires were sent out. The entire operation was run through
the Ministry of Education to give it the necessary prestige and to ensure return of the forms. The local education officers were also aler-
ted to the fact and made sure that the questionnaires were duly filled
out and sent back to the survey office. This operation proved to be the
most informative and most successful of the project.

• The <u>university questionnaire</u>, to which the students were
submitted on a voluntary basis. About a fourth of the students responded after the survey director gave an hour-and-a-half lecture about
the survey and about the intent of the questionnaire, which contained

various questions covering the specific activities of the best-educated
part of the younger generation, especially their intellectual pursuits.

• The Combined Research Project, set up with the help of the
Institute of Education at the University of Dar es Salaam and the Ministry of Education. It consisted of a study of the lingui stic background
of selected students to measure the impact of the pattern of language
use at home on the school performance of pupils on language subjects.
The project, directed by C. P. Hill, was planned most carefully.
Several months in advance, a four-day workshop was organized in Dar
es Salaam to instruct the Teachers Training College tutors in super-
vising the project and to train them in language research techniques.
Before the students started working on the project, C. P. Hill visited
the relevant Teachers Training Colleges and explained the details of
the administration of the questionnaires to the students involved in the
project. During their teaching practice in rural areas, the teacher
trainees submitted their classes to tests of their knowledge of English
and Swahili to select from among them the best, medium, and worst
pupils in language performance. The parents of the pupils selected
were interviewed according to a schedule corresponding, by and large,
to the adult questionnaire. Results of these interviews were then tabulated by the teacher trainees as part of their final examinations.

In all the general language use questionnaires, the focus was
on the informant's competence and performance in the languages of
which he claimed a certain degree of command. The method used was
essentially that of self-evaluation, since the conditions under which the
questionnaires were administered provided little opportunity for accurate, direct testing of language knowledge.[26] It appeared, however, quite
feasible to measure the degree of knowledge of an informant by listing
a series of situations and asking him whether he was able to handle the
language in those situations. The situations were classified in various
groups: whether he could perform a certain linguistic act like greeting,
asking for directions, discussing everyday life problems, bargaining
when shopping, discussing political problems, talking about his profession, etc., or whether he could understand certain types of discourse,
e.g. greetings, directions, a news item on the radio, a political speech,
a lecture, etc. The contexts were carefully graded and were adequate
for the social context in which they were expected to occur. Another
type of question dealt with the language used in certain activities such

as counting, adding, swearing, cursing, talking to friends, talking to relatives, and talking to strangers. These questions applied to all the languages which the speaker claimed to speak and/or understand. Upon spot-checking, it was found that the way most informants graded themselves was usually honest and accurate. For educated persons, additional questions concerning reading and writing were added as they applied to the person's main vernacular, to Swahili, and to English. Here again, various situations were taken into consideration.[27] Some of these were particularly illustrative of the relative status of languages like the vernacular, the national language—Swahili—or the international language of wider communication—English—in the value scale of the informants, e.g. when schoolboys regularly preferred to resort to English to write love letters to their girlfriends.

Another problem connected with language use also received major attention in the questionnaires, namely, the impact of mass communication on society. The survey team wanted, in particular, to analyze the use of literacy in Tanzania and to measure the impact of the press on the population. In more detailed questionnaires for literate people in towns, information was gained as to the most recent books they had read, asking them to indicate the title and even why they had chosen such a book. This made it possible to connect the motivation for reading with the socioeconomic background of the informant. Along these lines, a special survey of about 1,000 readers was conducted in the various public libraries in Dar es Salaam and elsewhere throughout the country. Besides some basic background information, people were asked very specific questions concerning their reading habits, so that it was possible to list the most read books and to find out how these correlated with the ethnic, educational, and socioeconomic background of the readers. Such information should prove most useful to the government in planning its support of literary development and of the publication of works in the national language. The material available in Swahili is indeed rather limited in Tanzania; it usually does not go beyond the kind of literature read in high school. This explains why so many of the respondents indicated that they were disappointed with the available literature in the national language.[28] On the other hand, the use of urban versus rural informants also provided an interesting check of the correlation between reading practices and the distribution patterns of the local press as obtained from the main publishing houses. It should not be forgotten that, especially in rural areas, one newspaper passes hands very often and that the number of copies available in an area does not at all reflect the actual number of readers, which can be considerably higher. The availability of reading rooms in the various small communities under the sponsorship of the Ministry of Information makes newspapers and journals accessible to a large public. In visits to such reading rooms, it was found that there were always a considerable number of people reading recent periodicals and daily newspapers. Another aspect of the impact of mass communication covered by the questionnaires was the listening pattern of the informants. Certain programs were particularly popular, e.g. information for rural people given immediately after the news in Dar es Salaam every day in the week. The kind of programs that people listened to also provided an indication of what kind of linguistic influence they are exposed to, since the radio network in Tanzania uses Swahili and English exclusively. It will be interesting to ask the same kind of questions when TV becomes available.

The use of language in religion was the subject of a special inquiry both in the Christian and in the Muslim communities. Special attention was given to the differences in use of languages in the liturgy and in direct communication with the congregation, as well as to shifts from the vernacular to Swahili in rural parishes in recent years. The increasing use of the national language in church is indeed a clear sign of the success of Tanzania's linguistic policy.

Interviews

The interview technique was used whenever members of the survey team were able to contact the informants directly and when no extensive sampling was required for research purposes. To begin with, the area where interviews were to take place was carefully canvassed, e.g. the Ilala suburb of Dar es Salaam, in which a block of 200 houses was selected for examination. One person in each house was interviewed for an hour and a half, with informants picked at random with the help of the local TANU representative. However, in view of the status of women in Tanzanian society, the great bulk of the informants were men. The interview was conducted with the help of Tanzanians who could put the interviewee at ease and who could gain his confidence, so that he could answer the questions in a very relaxed

way while the participating linguist listened, filled in the interview
schedule, and, in some cases, taped it. The interviews were conducted in Swahili. Since the community was essentially an urban community, all the interviewees had a sufficient command of the language. The
interview schedule was rather similar to the questionnaire used for the
adult population, but it had been especially framed for the interview
situation.

        A different type of interview was conducted with a limited group
of people—the second-year students of all but one of the Teachers Training Colleges. This sample covered most of the areas of Tanzania and
involved students from all over the country. The students belonged to
the same age group and had the same educational backgrounds and professional aims. They could therefore be considered as a socially cohesive group. The interview was conducted in the schools, and the
students were chosen on a random basis (about 50 per school). The
questions dealt with the students' background and tried to find out: (1)
which languages they used at home, with their friends, and with strangers; (2) what degree of command they had of the vernacular, of Swahili, and of English; and (3) by indirect questions, what kind of attitudes
they, as future teachers of Tanzania, had with regard to the vernaculars.
By asking them whether they would teach their children their own vernacular or would ask their wives to learn their vernacular in cases
where they were from a different ethnic origin, it was possible to
measure their degree of loyalty to the vernacular and to find out why
this loyalty was maintained. In spite of the indoctrination in the National Service and in their school years in favor of the national language,
a large majority remained keenly attached to their tribal language,
which they considered a means of identification. In the case of intertribal marriage, many insisted on their wives learning the language
of their parents, and most of them strongly felt that their children
should study the vernacular so that they could be accepted into the
society of their grandparents. A check was also made on the languages
used in their religious training and in their parishes. This made it
possible to verify some of the data obtained in the inquiry made by
questionnaire to all the parish priests as to the use of language in
church. Another feature revealed by these interviews was their knowledge of vernaculars other than their own and their very keen awareness of the degree of interintelligibility of these vernaculars.

Observation

The technique of observation was applied to various fields, in particular to the use of the language in public life. Though the national policy would prescribe the use of Swahili in most aspects of daily life, there was often a great difference between the wishes of the government and the actual language used when the implementation of the Swahilization of public notices was examined in the signs of public offices, on roads, in hotels, on trains and boats, etc. The remaining predominance of English was particularly obvious at the post office, where practically all forms, except those of the savings bank, were exclusively in English. Similarly, in the banks which had been nationalized for quite a while, all the forms were in English. Accordingly, a careful survey was made of the notices posted in City Hall and in other administration buildings as a source of information for actual language use. Besides this, various inquiries were conducted on the language used in trade, particularly in the marketplace. In the Kenya and Ethiopia surveys, the markets in larger towns as well as smaller communities were examined as to the products being offered for sale and the ethnic background of the people selling them. A number of transactions were observed in order to register the language used for greeting, for advertising the merchandise, for the sale operation itself (including bargaining), for counting at the moment of payment, and for the final greeting. Similarly, some observers watched a number of operations at post offices, in banks, in railway stations, in bus ticket stations, etc., carefully noting the languages used in the transactions. These data are especially valuable for checking the responses of informants in their questionnaires on the use of languages in certain social contacts.

In regard to the judicial system, there is a considerable variation in the language used between the different types of courts in Tanzania. The higher courts of the country still use English, whereas on the lower court level, vernaculars are still currently used as well as the national language. To assess the situation, a Tanzanian researcher, M. Douglas Kavugha, was sent around the country to observe the use of interpreters and the language used by the judge, lawyers, prosecutor, witnesses, the plaintiff, and the accused in a number of cases, in order to establish specific percentages and patterns of usage. The amount of interpretation necessary was quite characteristic. In some cases, vernaculars had to be interpreted into Swahili and then the Swahili in turn translated for the judge. In certain cases, the resident magistrate was indeed an expatriate.

Although the Tanzania survey resorted to the questionnaire method to examine the use of language in the church, on numerous occasions direct observation was also used to determine the language used for the various parts of the service and for preaching. On such occasions, Catholic and Protestant ministers were also asked which language they would use when visiting their parishioners, what language they resorted to in religious education, and what books were available for this purpose, especially the catechism books or the Bibles. Particularly interesting was the change in sale of Bibles. Whereas in Sukumaland most of the Bibles sold until about five years ago were in the local vernacular, a considerable shift to Swahili has taken place quite recently. This might reflect the change in policy on adult education since 1961, as the purchase of the Bible is the first immediate result of the acquisition of literacy among the adult population. In other areas, like Gogoland, the sale of the Bible in the local vernacular has practically been discontinued. Moreover, many parish priests indicated that in recent years shifts have taken place in their preaching habits: whereas ten years ago they preached essentially in the local vernacular, most of the preaching is done in Swahili nowadays, especially for the younger generation, with occasional translation into the local vernacular for the older population. In many cases this was also due to movement in the population which had brought new people to the area as a result of some economic project, such as the construction of a dam or the establishment of a sugar-processing factory.

The technique of observation was also used in many other cases, especially code-switching. Obviously, one of the most difficult problems is to determine what triggers switching in a bilingual person, and only prolonged observation of his linguistic behavior can give hints on this. While it was only possible to pursue such observation on a casual basis, the use of the observers in various offices provided some information, showing, for instance, that the recognition of a person of the same ethnic background would be one of the motives for switching. The shifting to a different style or a reference to some

technical process would also produce switching. Some information
on this was supplied by the linguistic diaries kept by a few volunteers,
indicating quarter-hour by quarter-hour during a whole working day,
and during a whole holiday, what they did, what kinds of subjects they
talked about with whom, and what language they used in each case.
When possible, they also specified their reasons for switching languages. This kind of subjective information provided some valuable
documentation for further study of the motivation for switching in
bilingualism.

Concluding Statement

This short sketch of the methods used in the Tanzania Survey
illustrates its significance as a large-scale, linguistically oriented
survey. None of the approaches described here was really innovative,
but their combination and adaptation to a specific local situation may
provide fruitful hints on their relevance and efficiency for future research in this field.

NOTES

[1] See paper by Prator, p. 145, in Language Surveys in Devel-
oping Nations: Papers and Reports on Sociolinguistic Surveys, ed. by
S. Ohannessian, C. A. Ferguson, and E. C. Polomé (Arlington, Va.:
Center for Applied Linguistics, 1975).

[2] The Ethiopian Survey follows such an outline rather closely;
cf. Fox, p. 8.

[3] An excellent outline of the case of Tanzania was given by
Whiteley 1968.

[4] The Tanzania team was in the field from June 1969 until
August 1970. It was composed of Edgar C. Polomé, Chairman of the
Department of Oriental and African Languages at the University of
Texas at Austin; C. P. Hill, Lecturer at the Institute of Education at
the University of London; and David Barton, graduate student in linguistics at the University of Texas at Austin. Although close team-
work prevailed in the preparation of the major sociolinguistic questionnaires, C. P. Hill took special responsibility for the language

and education aspects of the survey, whereas E. C. Polomé concentrated on the description of the linguistic situation. There was also a major division of work in some special projects: D. Barton devoted a great part of his activity to the thorough sociolinguistic study of the Ilala district of Dar es Salaam; C. P. Hill was entirely responsible for the study of the readers in public libraries; and E. C. Polomé covered the field of language and religion, with the help of a local assistant for Islam.

[5]There is a whole literature on this problem of attitudes (cf., for example, W. Lambert, "A Social Psychology of Bilingualism, " in Journal of Social Issues 23, no. 2 (1967): 91-109). The typical sentences mentioned here were applied to Welsh by W. R. Jones ("Attitudes towards Welsh as a Second Language. A Preliminary Investigation, " in British Journal of Educational Psychology 19 (1949): 44-52).

[6] Cf. Anders Andersson, Multilingualism and Attitudes. An explorative-descriptive study among secondary school students in Ethiopia and Tanzania (Uppsala: Institute of Education, 1967).

[7] Part of the questionnaire given to students entering secondary school contained questions relevant to this subject but applied to third persons (friends of theirs who had not been admitted to secondary schools). The information gathered therefore remains fragmentary and partly questionable, since it comes, essentially, from secondhand sources. A systematic study of selected young school-leavers should be made, and tests should be administered to measure their competence in English. After a number of years, they should be given similar tests to measure the maintenance, improvement, or regression of their language skills in English, and the results should be correlated with their activity in adolescent and adult life. It is hoped that the Institute of Education at the University of Dar es Salaam will conduct such an inquiry in the future, especially since the data of the survey are locally available in the original questionnaires preserved by the Institute of Swahili Research.

[8] A careful check of the libraries in Dar es Salaam and elsewhere in Tanzania indicated, unfortunately, that quite a number of the documents listed by Whiteley have disappeared since 1958.

[9] The survey volume—Language in Tanzania, ed. by E. C. Polomé and C. P. Hill (1980)—provides complete bibliographical data on these sources.

[10]W. H. Whiteley, Some Problems of Transitivity in Swahili

(London: School of Oriental and African Studies, University of London, 1968), pp. 107-10.

[11] C. M. Doke, Outline Grammar of Bantu (Johannesburg: Department of Bantu Studies, University of the Witwatersrand, 1943), pp. 17-65.

[12] Cf. M. Guthrie, "A Two-Stage Method of Comparative Bantu Study, " in African Language Studies 3 (1962): 1-24, esp. 5-11. Thus, Guthrie's Comparative Bantu I, vol. 2 (1970), p. 177, reconstructs P. B. *-dòmò "lip" and *-dòmò "mouth" as separate items, though he admits the primary meaning was probably "lip"—"but it is not possible to determine where the mutation to 'mouth' occurred with any certainty"—hence, the separate listings! Similarly for the feline predator P. B. *-cimbà, he has three entries:

*-cimbà	"wild cat; (leopard)"
*-cimbà	"genet"
*-cimbà	"lion"

The root *-dób-, "to fish with a line, " is considered as not represented in Swahili, although the technical term ndoana, "hook, " reflects a direct derivation from this root.

[13] Cf. Bryan 1959, p. 117: "The Shaka (Chagga) dialects may conveniently be grouped as follows: Dialects of Vunjo administrative division of which that of Marangu may be taken as typical; Moci, of Old Moshi; Shira (own name not known); Dialects of Rombo administrative division; Rwo, on the eastern slopes of Mt. Meru. The Rwo are not administered with the Shaka. Note that MG_3 (i. e. Malcolm Guthrie's third revision of his classification) classes Rwo as a separate language. To these dialects MG_3 adds Hai. "

[14] An excellent example of the kind of research to be done in this field is provided by Isaria N. Kimambo's confirmation through the analysis of oral history (1968) of the original close connection of the Gweno in the Pare mountains with the Chagga, to which the linguistic data clearly point. Similarly, further research on the spread of the Southern Nilotic groups would shed light on a complex problem like that of the background of the Mbugu language in the Usambara area (cf. M. Goodman, "The Strange Case of Mbugu, " in Dell Hymes, ed., Pidginization and Creolization of Languages (Cambridge University Press, 1971), pp. 243-54. It would also explain the survival of some isolated Nilotic groups in the Kilimanjaro area.

[15] See among others F. Johnson, Zamani mpaka siku hizi

(London, 1930); G. W. Broomfield, "The Development of the Swahili Language, " in Africa 3: 4 (1930): 516-22 (continued in "The Re-Bantu-ization of the Swahili Language, " in Africa 4: 1 (1931): 77-85); B. Krumm, Wörter und Wortformen orientalischen Ursprungs in Suaheli (Hamburg: Frederichsen-De Gruyter & Co., 1932), pp. 19-22; R. Reusch, "How the Swahili People and Language Came into Existence, " in Tanganyika Notes and Records 34 (1953): 20.

[16] It is often difficult to find traces of the decision-making. Our experience was that the file on language policy at the Ministry of Education in Dar es Salaam contained only a circular, published by one of the last British administrators at the time of Independence and indicating how Swahili should be emphasized. Only public declarations of ministers and circulars giving instructions to the schools as regards the language policy in the classes shed some light on the facts, for it was impossible to find clear documentation on the work of specific committees involved in decision-making. Very often, decision-making appears to have been based on action outside the immediate govern-ment circles. One of the main moving forces was undoubtedly the National Swahili Council, appointed by the President. It worked rather independently and made recommendations to the administration, which would implement them in various ways in the various departments. At an earlier date, the colonial administration established an Inter-Territorial Committee to regularize the spelling of Swahili and to determine which type of Swahili could be considered correct for text-books (Whiteley 1969, pp. 79-96). The archives of such committees are extremely valuable since the discussions which took place over the years in connection with this direct action on the language contain invaluable hints on the social-linguistic background of decision-making. Unfortunately, most of them remained inaccessible to the survey team.

[17] Cf. Whiteley 1969, pp. 110-12. For the parallel role played by linguistically oriented societies in India, cf. J. Das Gupta, Lan-guage Conflict and National Development. Group Politics and National Policy in India (Berkeley-Los Angeles: University of California Press, 1970), pp. 98-126 and 197-224.

[18] In Tanzania, Swahili is used as a medium and is taught as a subject in primary schools. English is taught as a subject only in primary schools but is used as a medium in secondary school. The achievement test in English at the end of primary education is there-fore of vital importance to screen candidates for secondary education.

[19] In keeping with the aims of the survey as defined by the

Ford Foundation (Fox, p. 20), the team director, E. Polomé, gave
a series of lectures at the university on the role of Swahili in nation
building, on the problems of multilingualism, on the methods of sociolinguistic research, and on other questions relevant to the study of
the Tanzanian linguistic situation. He also actively participated in
the drafting of the syllabus for the new program in Swahili on the B. A.
level.

[20]Oxford-New York: Pergamon Press, 1970.

[21] E.g. J. S. R. Cole and W. N. Denison, Tanganyika. The
Development of Its Laws and Constitution (London: Stevens & Sons,
1964); W. T. W. Morgan, East Africa: Its People and Resources
(Nairobi-London: Oxford University Press, 1969); _____, Tanzania
Today: A Portrait of the United Republic (Nairobi: University Press
of Africa, 1968); A. B. Herrick, S. A. Harrison, H. J. John, S.
MacKnight, and B. Skapa, Area Handbook for Tanzania (Washington,
D. C. : U.S. Government Printing Office, 1968); K. E. Svendsen and
M. Zeisen, Self Reliant Tanzania (Dar es Salaam: Tanzania Publish-
ing House, 1969); etc.

[22] The 1967 Census concentrated on housing conditions. Is
the house permanent, semipermanent, or not? How many rooms are
there (excluding the kitchen)? Is there piped water, a bath or shower,
a water toilet on the premises? Is there electricity? The Household
Budget Survey of 1968-1969 asked much more specific questions about
the foundations, the floor, floor and wall materials, the roof frame,
the drinking water supply, and the toilet system.

[23] E.g. the Philippine Language Policy Survey questionnaire,
in which information about the type of family dwelling and the ownership of such items as a car, a tape recorder, a washing machine, a
TV set, a vacuum cleaner, etc. are asked. Similarly, the Kenya
Survey inquired about the material the roof of the family dwelling was
made of.

[24] This was done with particular care in the case of the Ilala
study (cf. Barton 1972, esp. chap. 1). The existence of two basic
studies on Dar es Salaam—one by a geographer (Harm J. de Blij, Dar
es Salaam. A Study of Urban Geography Evanston, Ill.: Northwestern
University Press, 1963), the other by a sociologist (J. A. K. Leslie,
A Survey of Dar es Salaam; London-New York: Oxford University
Press, 1963)—as well as a set of informative articles on "Dar es
Salaam, City, Port and Region" in a special issue of Tanzania Notes
and Records 71(1970) were especially helpful in providing further
background information on the only major urban area in Tanzania.

[25] E. g. the place where men would meet friends would be different from the place where women would do so. (One of the most common places for women's friendly conversation or gossip would be the well or the spot along the water for washing clothes; whereas men would tend to socialize in bars or clubs.)

[26] Only in the case of the Combined Research Project could some easy tests of language knowledge be introduced for the national language and for English: the method used consisted of omitting every fifth word in a coherent text. The informant was then asked to fill in the word which he thought most adequate in the context. This rather crude procedure gave at least a hint of the degree of comprehension of the text and the mastery of the language in the field of the lexicon.

[27] The model provided by Joan Rubin's study of bilingual usage in Paraguay (1968, esp. pp. 518-20) was followed and adapted to Tanzanian situations.

[28] The questionnaire actually encouraged the readers to indicate explicitly what kind of books they would like to have in Swahili, so that the result of the inquiry may have a direct bearing on the framing of the local publication policy.

BIBLIOGRAPHY

Abdulaziz, M. H. Tanzania's national language policy and the rise of Swahili political culture. In W. H. Whiteley, ed. , 1971, pp. 160-78.

Alpers, Edward A. The coast and the development of the caravan trade. In I. N. Kimambo and A. J. Temu, eds., 1969, pp. 35-56.

Barton, David. Study of language use in Ilala. Ph. D. dissertation, University of Texas at Austin, August 1972.

Bender, M. L. , R. L. Cooper, and C. A. Ferguson. 1975. Language in Ethiopia: Implications of a survey for sociolinguistic theory and method. In S. Ohannessian, C. A. Ferguson, and E. C. Polomé, eds. , Language surveys in developing nations: Papers and reports on sociolinguistic surveys. Arlington, Va. : Center for Applied Linguistics, pp. 191-208.

Bennett, N. R. The Arab impact. In B. A. Ogot and J. A. Kieran, eds. , 1968, pp. 216-37.

Brumfit, Anne. The development of a language policy in German East Africa. In Journal of the Language Association of Eastern Africa 2: 1 (1971): 1-9.

Bryan, Margaret. The Bantu languages of Africa. London: Oxford University Press, 1959.

Ehret, Christopher. Cushites and the Highland and Plains Nilots. In B. A. Ogot and J. A. Kieran, eds., 1968, pp. 158-76.

———. Southern Nilotic history. Evanston, Ill.: Northwestern University Press, 1971.

Fishman, Joshua, Charles A. Ferguson, and Jyotirinda Das Gupta, eds. Language problems of developing nations. New York: Wiley, 1968.

Fox, Melvin J. Ford Foundation grants in language fields. Unpublished report, Sept. 1971.

Gray, Sir John. Zanzibar and the coastal belt, 1840-84. In R. Oliver and G. Mathew, eds., 1963, pp. 212-51.

Guthrie, Malcolm. The classification of the Bantu languages. London: Oxford University Press, 1948.

———. Comparative Bantu. An introduction to the comparative linguistics and prehistory of the Bantu languages. 4 vols. Farnborough: Gregg Press, 1967-72.

Heine, Bernd. Knowledge and use of second languages in Musama Region—A quantitative survey. Unpublished manuscript, May 1972.

Huntingford, G. W. B. The peopling of the interior of East Africa by its modern inhabitants. In R. Oliver and G. Mathew, eds., 1963, pp. 58-93.

Kavugha, Douglas. The language of the law courts. Unpublished manuscript, August 1970.

Kimambo, Isaria N. A political history of the Pare of Tanzania c. 1500-1900. Nairobi: East African Publishing House, 1969.

Kimambo, I. N., and A. J. Temu, eds. A history of Tanzania. Nairobi: East African Publishing House, 1969.

Ladefoged, Peter. The languages of Uganda. In P. Ladefoged, R. Glick, and C. Criper, eds., Language in Uganda, 1972, pp. 31-84. London: Oxford University Press.

McIntosh, B. G. The Eastern Bantu peoples. In B. A. Ogot and J. A. Kieran, eds., 1968, pp. 198-215.

Ogot, B. A., and J. A. Kieran, eds. Zamani. A survey of East African history. Nairobi: East African Publishing House, 1968.

Oliver, Roland, and Gervase Mathew, eds. History of East Africa.
    Vol. I. Oxford: Clarendon Press, 1963.
Polomé, André R. The classification of the languages of Northern
    Tanzania. M. A. thesis, University of Texas at Austin,
    August 1971.
Polomé, Edgar C. Swahili language handbook. Washington, D. C.:
    Center for Applied Linguistics, 1967.
Polomé, Susan E. A phonological survey of the Chagga dialects of
    Tanzania. M. A. thesis, University of Texas at Austin,
    August 1971.
Prator, Clifford H. 1975. The survey of language use and language
    teaching in Eastern Africa in retrospect. In S. Ohannessian,
    C. A. Ferguson, and E. C. Polomé, eds., Language surveys
    in developing nations: Papers and reports on sociolinguistic
    surveys. Arlington, Va.: Center for Applied Linguistics,
    pp. 145-58.
Rubin, Joan. A sociolinguistic typology for describing national multi-
    lingualism. In Joshua A. Fishman, ed., Readings in the
    sociology of language. The Hague: Mouton, 1968, pp. 512-
    30.
Rubin, Joan, and Bjorn H. Jernudd, eds. Can language be planned?
    Sociolinguistic theory and practice for developing nations.
    Honolulu: University of Hawaii Press, 1971.
Smith, Alison. The southern section of the interior, 1840-84. In R.
    Oliver and G. Mathew, eds., 1963, pp. 253-96.
Sutton, J. E. G. The settlement of Africa. In B. A. Ogot and J. A.
    Kieran, eds., 1968, pp. 69-99.
_____. The peopling of Tanzania. In I. N. Kimambo and A. J. Temu,
    eds., 1969, pp. 1-13.
Whiteley, Wilfred H. A linguistic bibliography of East Africa. Rev.
    ed. Kampala: East African Swahili Committee, 1958.
_____. Ideal and reality in national language policy: A case study
    from Tanzania. In J. Fishman, C. Ferguson, and J. Das
    Gupta, eds., 1968, pp. 327-44.
_____. Swahili. The rise of a national language. London: Methuen,
    1969.
Whiteley, Wilfred H., ed. Language use and social change. Problems
    of multilingualism with special reference to Eastern Africa.
    London: International African Institute, 1971.
_____. Some factors influencing language policies in Eastern Africa.
    In J. Rubin and B. Jernudd, eds., 1971, pp. 141-58.

6 | Tanzanian Language Policy and Swahili

More than any other sociocultural agent, language functions as a binding, integrative, and solidarity-producing factor within and between groups. A common language serves as an effective means of identifying a society and as a potent symbol of the social unity and solidarity of those who speak it.

When it became independent in the sixties, the former Tanganyika Territory encompassed a large area of East Africa within boundaries traced arbitrarily on the map by the colonial powers in the nineteenth century. These boundaries cut through ethnic, linguistic, and cultural entities; and as a result, the territory covering roughly 340,000 square miles which they delineated had neither ethnic, nor cultural, nor linguistic unity. The ten largest ethnolinguistic units constituted less than half of the population.[1] The rest of the population was split into more than a hundred tribal groups, each with its own language—more than a third of them numbering less than 10,000 people. Among the 52 administrative districts established by the colonial administration, only one-fifth had one dominant language, whereas in 46 percent of the cases the major language was spoken by less than half of the population. Moreover, there was a sharp contrast between the various parts of the country as regards economic development, with more than half of the population living in less than one-sixth of the territory—with great concentrations in the Lake Region and highland areas of the Kilimanjaro and Meru, and the Makonde plateau.[2]

It stands to reason that, under these circumstances, any social factor likely to contribute to the development of nationhood would be consciously manipulated for that purpose. Language plan-

ning with a view to promote and expand the use of Swahili accordingly
became one of the major concerns of the Tanganyika government.
Three types of reasons —historical, pragmatic, and political—motivated this line of action.

Historically, Swahili had been used since German times[3]
for administrative purposes, for example, for communication with
the local chiefs all over the territory—a procedure that had been
made possible by the early penetration of Swahili inland along the old
Arabic caravan routes across the country through Tabora to Ujiji on
Lake Tanganyika, to the north toward Mwanza on Lake Victoria, and
to the south toward Lake Nyasa. This had given the coastal language
a major new role inland as lingua franca. None of the major tribal
groups had indeed constituted states around which language loyalties
might have focused; and the few who had established more cohesive
states, like the Hehe, had been crushed by the Germans. Numerically
important groups like the Chagga in the Kilimanjaro region were not
even politically centralized. On the other hand, the penetration of
Islam along the trade routes led to Muslim settlements which became
nuclei of Swahili (i. e. coastal) culture as far inland as the great lakes.
These, in turn, contributed to the further spread of Swahili—whereas,
closer to the coast, large majorities of major tribes like the Sambaa,
the Pogoro, and the Luguru were Islamized and became, to a large
extent, bilingual.

From a pragmatic point of view, Swahili being the only language of wider communication currently used by the bulk of the population, and since only a limited, mostly urban "elite" had a sufficient
command of English to communicate effectively, Swahili was the language destined to be used for the lower levels of administration and
education; indeed it was used for that purpose by the Germans and the
British. Early missionary activities had provided Swahili with a
romanized orthography, which eliminated the puzzling ambiguity of
the Arabic spelling—which, for example, had not distinguished properly
such forms as yangu 'mine' and yako 'yours.'[4] In the thirties, the
East African Inter-Territorial Language Committee contributed
largely to the standardization of the written Swahili. The East African Literature Bureau started publishing a substantial amount of
reading material in the language, so that the "standard" language

could be used as language of the curriculum in the primary schools
and as a subject itself in the secondary schools.

Politically, Swahili has many advantages: being a Bantu language, it is genuinely African; having been downgraded by the English
during the colonial regime when its speakers were restricted to the
local baraza,[5] it is not tainted with colonialism or neo-colonialism;
being the language of wider communication for the masses, it is truly
the average citizen's common language—the language of the wananchi;
having played an important role in the struggle for independence,
Swahili has acquired additional prestige through its function as major
means of political communication; the leaders of the trade unions
have employed it since the establishment of their professional associations—Swahili now includes the necessary technical jargon to deal
with their socioeconomic and political problems;[6] and the national
party, TANU (Tanganyika African National Union), identified its use
with the striving for national unity.

As a consequence, it was a logical step for the TANU government of the new Tanganyika Republic to adopt Swahili as the
"national" language. The timeliness of this step was made manifest
by the subsequent establishment of the United Republic of Tanzania
through the union with Zanzibar, where Swahili had always been the
major language of administration, education, and culture, except for
the use of English in very specific fields such as, for instance, secondary education.

However, the concept of "national language," as used by the
Tanzanians, needs further clarification: it means in particular "the
language to be used on national occasions and whenever the image of
the nation is on display." It should however be kept in mind that in
the more westernized urban communities, such as Dar es Salaam,
the upper levels of African society are essentially trifocal in their
linguistic behavior:[7] since marriage is still by and large within the
tribe, the tribal language is maintained at home and in the close-knit
network of tribal relationships where it serves as an identifier—a
sign of recognition of ethnic origin. Swahili is used with various
degrees of proficiency outside the tribal context, in everyday life, in
the market, with friends, in offices, and so on. English is restricted
to relations with expatriates and to higher levels of economic and

intellectual life. Currently one of the major efforts of the government
is to substitute Swahili for English in a variety of settings, especially
those conspicuous to the average citizen. Thus, the whole gamut of
political life is conducted in Swahili: it is the language of the Bunge
(the National Assembly), and the language in which the meetings of
town councils, party sections, and all kinds of administrative working
committees are conducted. In 1969, I was invited by the Regional
Commissioner in Bukoba to attend a meeting of his council for national
development. I was greeted in Swahili and asked to address the meeting
in the same language, though, on other occasions, in this distant region of Uhaya, a rapid switch from Swahili to kiHaya often took place
in public debate (e.g. in the TANU Women's League meetings).

    Similarly, in public offices, on the roads, in the public trans-
portation system, Swahili was progressively substituted for English:
monolingual English inscriptions were gradually replaced by bilingual
ones, usually with Swahili first; and more and more signs exclusively
in Swahili appeared. In the early seventies, this was done most unob-
trusively. In the public services, apparently, when the old stock of
English forms was exhausted, a new bilingual or monolingual Swahili
was printed. In 1973, the Dar es Salaam post office still used monolingual English forms, except for the savings service, but practically
all transactions were carried out in Swahili. At the National Bank of
Commerce in 1973, business forms were still in English only, but the
transactions were conducted in Swahili or in English—especially in the
case of the numerous Asians still involved in the retail trade and
other economic activities. In 1974, a drastic change occurred when
Vice-President Kawawa, translating the impatience of Tanzanian
policy-makers about the slowness of the process of shifting to Swahili,
decreed that "from August first, all correspondence, forms and sign
posts in all parastatal and public organizations must be in Swahili. "[8]
To meet the deadline, special committees had to be set up to find adequate Swahili equivalents of the English terms to be translated: at the
University of Dar es Salaam, the National Swahili Council appointed
a subcommittee under the Chairmanship of Mr. G. Mhina, Director
of the Institute of Swahili Research, to establish a list of Swahili terms
covering all aspects of University activities. New signs with the Swahili nomenclature of titles and subjects appeared on office doors by
June 30, e.g.: "Chancellor, " Mkuu wa Chuo, "Bursar, " Msarifu,
"Botany Department, " Idara ya Elimumimea, "Lecture Room, "

Chumba cha Mihadhara, and "Foreign Languages and Linguistics,"
Lugha za Kigeni na Isimu. Additionally, notice boards warned the
public in Swahili, e.g.: Asiyeruhusiwa asiingie, "No Unauthorized
Person" (lit. 'who is not allowed, should not enter'); Magari yasie-
geshwe hapa, "No Parking" (lit. 'cars should not be "moored" here'),
and Simama barabara kuu mbele!, "Stop, main road ahead!"[9]

In the field of education, where primary education had been
in Swahili since the pre-Independence period, the Teachers Training
Colleges (now called Chuo cha Taifa, 'National Colleges') are switching from English to Swahili as the language of the curriculum, except
for the courses in which expatriates are still teaching. There was a
plan to switch to Swahili as the medium of instruction in the first two
years of secondary schools by 1973, but it could not be implemented.[10]
The main reasons were: (a) the lack of adequate Swahili teaching
materials; (b) the limitations in manpower—the population of secondary
schools had considerably increased and the training of Tanzanian instructors by the University of Dar es Salaam, even with the additional
help from returnees trained overseas, was insufficient to compensate
for the growing scarcity of expatriate teachers. At the University
level, where reliance on a large proportion of non-Tanzanian faculty
is still imperative, English remains the language of instruction, but
a strong Department of Swahili has been developed, in close collaboration with the Institute of Education. A major role is also played by
the Institute of Swahili Research (Taasisi ya Uchunguzi wa Kiswahili),
which, since 1964, has taken over the role of the Inter-Territorial
Swahili Committee as regulator of the language. The activity is focused on various fields which contribute to the promotion of Swahili
and enhance its status as a language of culture and a diversified means
of literary expression:

1. In the field of lexicography, the Institute has been compil-
ing for about two decades a new major dictionary of Swahili which
would incorporate all the materials from Sacleux that do not appear in
Johnson's standard dictionary, as well as the new terms coined in
recent decades, some of which already appear in dictionaries like
Höftmann's or Rechenbach's.[11]

2. In view of the needs of Swahili linguistic studies, the Institute is also sponsoring work on a comprehensive reference grammar,

a simplified version of which could be used for pedagogical purposes.
Moreover, it has been planning a dialect survey.

3. In the domain of literature, it encourages the study of
traditional poetry, the more so since the Institute is the repository
of a wealth of manuscripts collected over the years by interested
scholars like J. Allen. It occasionally publishes works under its
direct sponsorship.

The main publishing activity of the Institute is, however,
concentrated on its journals:

1. Kiswahili—a respectable scientific journal dealing with
lexicography, linguistics and sociolinguistics, and literature, and
the main vehicle through which the Institute publicizes its lists of
new terms in various fields (mathematics, natural science, and so
on). It is published in English and Swahili.

2. Mulika—a journal for the Swahili intellectuals in Tanzania,
containing literary articles, studies on Swahili grammar, reproduc-
tions of related Swahili articles from Kiswahili, papers on the Swahili
language and its position, and so on—altogether an excellent tool to
promote the language among teachers and educated readers.

While the Institute of Swahili Research thus performs modest-
ly the functions of a Swahili academy, other bodies are actively involved in the promotion of Swahili in public and cultural life. Particularly important is the National Swahili Council, which tries to ad-
vise on language use, especially in the administration where it initiated the use of Swahili in official nomenclatures of public functions.
Its journal, Lugha Yetu ('Our Language'), published as early as 1969
a list of translations for the English names of the highest offices in
the State, e.g.: Makamu-Rais wa Kwanza—First Vice-President;
Katibu Mkuu—Principal Secretary; Mkurugenzi wa Mafunzo na Kuajiri
—Director of Training and Recruitment; and Mshauri wa Mipango ya
Watumishi—Staff Development Advisor.[12]

The National Swahili Council also encourages young writers
by giving prizes for the best novel. The Council intervenes actively
to promote the use of Swahili in all sectors of Tanzanian life. An

outstanding result of the action in this field is the remarkable growth
of literature in Swahili outside the narrow scope of the schoolbooks
to which it was largely confined until the late fifties. A major publication achievement was that of the fourteen volumes of the complete
works of the national poet from Tanga, Shaaban bin Robert. Publication of new Swahili reading material was also facilitated through the
establishment of a national enterprise, the Tanzania Publishing House,
which complemented the older publishing outfits, mostly centered in
Nairobi, such as the East African Publishing House, and (belonging
to foreign interests) the Oxford University Press, Evans Brothers
Ltd., Longman, Thomas Nelson, Heinemann—the latter all are British firms interested mainly in large volume sale to schools, though
awareness of the development of a new readers' market led some of
them outside the pedagogical field. Indeed, the Oxford University
Press helped the University of Dar es Salaam in its efforts to develop
new forms of literature by experimenting (e.g. in the theatrical arts),
when it published Kinjeketile, the work of a young dramatist, Ebrahim
N. Hussein, both in the original Swahili and in an English version in
its series "New Drama from Africa" in 1969. Similarly, Heinemann
is now publishing from Nairobi a series of Swahili translations of
novels of some of the best African writers (e.g. Chinua Achebe).[13]

Poetry is also encouraged by voluntary associations which
continue a rich tradition in Swahili cultural life. The composition of
poems is a craft that many a reader of the Swahili press diligently
practices, to judge from the numerous contributions sent to the papers.
The best poems appear in the press and are often collected in book
form (e.g. the poetry produced in the prominent association UKUTA).
Many manuscripts from previous generations are carefully preserved
by families as precious heirlooms, though the Institute of Swahili
Research now tries to collect and preserve them for later publication.

There are two Swahili daily newspapers, Uhuru and Ngurumo.
Though their combined circulation runs only in the tens of thousands
in a country of more than 15,600,000 people, it should be kept in mind
that transportation problems, levels of literacy, as well as economic
factors, tend to restrict the diffusion of the newspapers upcountry.
Nevertheless, wherever they are available, they are passed on from
reader to reader, made accessible to the public in Ministry of Information offices or other reading rooms, and so on—so that the actual

readership amounts to several times the number of copies in circulation. Moreover, there are a number of periodicals catering to special interests: the most popular is the publication of the Ministry of
Agriculture and Cooperatives, Ukulima wa Kisasa ("Present-day
agriculture"). Also important are the official weekly of the trade
unions Mfanya Kazi ("Worker") and the monthly bulletin of the cooperative union Ushirika ("Common Interest"). There are, furthermore,
special journals for definite economic interests (e.g. sisal marketing)
or for members of specific denominations (e.g. the Pentecostal
Church or the Evangelical Lutheran Church). All of them have an
extensive all-Swahili readership.

In the other major field of mass communication, the radio,
Tanzania has its major program in Swahili. Additional cultural and
educational programs are beamed out to the schools. The language
employed, in this case, depends on the subject and the level: civics,
for example, is always in Swahili, while science in high schools is
in English. There are both English and Swahili language courses.
The Swahili program is geared toward the various interests of the
Tanzanian population: emphasis on national news; informative discussions on problems of agriculture and animal husbandry; radio plays
and popular feuilletons; light music; and so on.

In the field of justice, the lower courts have been partly
Swahilized, but interpreters are often necessary, sometimes because
the resident magistrate is not a Tanzanian, but mainly because the
older local people do not have a sufficient command of Swahili.[14]
Some typical attitudes toward the language also tend to appear: often
people who speak Swahili rather fluently claim not to know it properly,
partly because they feel they can explain themselves more accurately
in their tribal language, but also because the time spent in translation
gives them more pause for thought between responses in court. Furthermore, it affords them, when necessary, the opportunity to modify
a statement after claiming as an excuse "misinterpretation." The
higher courts continue to use exclusively English because a number
of higher magistrates are not Tanzanians and the translation of the
laws from English into Swahili is still in progress. As a matter of
fact, a special commission had to be established to coin an adequate
legal terminology in Swahili; the first results of its work have appeared
in the form of an authoritative list of Swahili-English legal terms.[15]

Church policies used to differ substantially according to denominations and regions of the country, the aim of missionary work being to communicate adequately with the local people converted to Christianity. However, in various parts of the country, a considerable number of churches have now switched over from the local vernacular to Swahili. This is ascribable to a combination of factors: (a) governmental pressure (since 1961, all adult literacy programs—an activity mostly sponsored by the Churches—have to be conducted in Swahili, which has drastically reduced the sale of vernacular Bibles in many areas, with Swahili becoming more widely used); (b) movements of population—the resettlement in ujamaa villages,[18] the development of new economic units, hence bringing together of people of different tribal backgrounds, as well as the frequent transfers of civil servants outside their home territory—all factors that make the use of Swahili for communication imperative; and (c) education—a substantial portion of the younger generation prefers to use Swahili in all social and public activities (also, as a result of the repeated transfers of their parents, their command of their tribal mother tongue may often be rather limited). Nevertheless, in isolated rural areas, preaching, singing hymns, and other church activities are still conducted in the vernaculars (e.g. in the villages in the Pare mountains, where some books in Chasu (kiPare) printed before World War I in Germany are still in use). Also, there might be some services in the vernacular for the older generation whose command of Swahili is more limited.

In the army, Swahili is the language of command. Swahili experts, like Shabaan Farsi, have been commissioned to translate the basic British manuals into the language. The police also draws up its reports in Swahili; but, while some forms like the printed applications for a driver's license were still in English in 1970, the situation has changed with the 1974 ordinance which implemented total Swahilization of the administration.

So, in every field of human endeavor Swahili progresses steadily, but at an increasing pace. The government moves very carefully, putting pressure where it pays off, without disrupting the sociocultural, economic, or educational framework. But that does not exclude drastic steps when impatience grows as a result of the slackness in the implementation of certain rulings, as with the almost

overnight removal of English language signs and their replacement
by Swahili equivalents in 1974.

The choice of Swahili as national language represented a
significant gesture of independence from colonialism and a recognition of the role that the language played in achieving Independence.
With the Arusha Declaration[17] in 1967 and the establishment of African socialism, Swahili has become a major tool in the anti-elitist
character of education of the masses. Its use has been strengthened
by the new institutions established by the regime, be it the National
Service for the Tanzanian youth or the ujamaa villages for the resettlement of adults. These institutions, serving popular needs and
interests, have not only increased the attachment to the system, but
have served as major instruments in nation-building through self-
reliance. The fact that the use of Swahili is so closely linked to such
institutions illustrates its prominent role in making the Tanzanian
wananchi ('citizens,' literally 'sons of the country') feel that they belong to a new culture characterized by Swahili and symbolized by Tanzanian nationhood.

NOTES

[1] According to the 1957 census (the last one providing information on 'tribal languages'), the ten most important ethnic groups
speaking Bantu languages were:

Sukuma	1,093,767	Gogo	299,417
Nyamwezi	363,258	Ha	289,792
Makonde	333,897	Hehe	251,624
Haya	325,539	Nyakyusa	219,678
Chag(g)a	318,167	Luguru	202,297

(Total population of Tanganyika [without Zanzibar]: 8,609,661.)
[2] On the spread and density of the population, see the Atlas
of Tanganyika [East Africa] (Dar es Salaam: Department of Lands
and Surveys, 1956, ed ed.), map 13; L. Berry, Tanzania in Maps
(London: University of London Press, 1971), maps 5-6, pp. 18-23.
[3] An exhaustive study of German linguistic policy in East
Africa was prepared by Anne Brumfit for the Survey of Language Use
and Language Teaching in Dar es Salaam in 1970. An extract of her

work appeared under the title "The Development of a Language Policy in German East Africa," in the Journal of the Language Association of East Africa 2: 1 (1971): 1-9. See also Marcia Wright, "Swahili Language Policy, 1890-1940," Swahili 35: 1 (1965): 40-48 (esp. 41-46).

[4] A thorough study of the history of Swahili orthographies and the standardization of the written form of the language was presented in the master's thesis of Rachel Angogo, "Standard Swahili: Its History and Development" (Department of Linguistics, University of Texas at Austin, 1978), chaps. 2 and 3. See also Whiteley, Swahili—The Rise of a National Language (London: Methuen, 1964), pp. 79-96.

[5] Place where public meetings are held.

[6] On the use of Swahili for political purposes, see Wilfred H. Whiteley, "Political Concepts and Connotations on the Use of Some Political Terms in Swahili," St. Antony's Papers 10: African Affairs 1 (1961): 7-21; Wilfred H. Whiteley, "Problems of a Lingua Franca: Swahili and the Trade-Unions," Journal of African Languages 3 (1964): 215-25; Carol M. Scotton, "Some Swahili Political Concepts," Journal of Modern African Studies 3: 4 (1965): 525-42; Harold A. Goldklang, "Current Swahili Newspaper Terminology," Swahili 37: 2 (1967): 194-208; Gerard Philippson, "Etude de quelques concepts politiques swahili dans les oeuvres de J. K. Nyerere," Cahiers d'Etudes Africaines 10 (1970): 530-45; Canute W. Temu, "The Development of Political Vocabulary in Swahili," KiSwahili 41: 2 (1971): 3-17; Rajmund Ohly, "The Conception of State Through Swahili," KiSwahili 45: 1 (1975): 25-35.

[7] M. H. Abdulaziz-Mkilifi, "Triglossia and Swahili-English Bilingualism in Tanzania," Language in Society 1 (1972): 173-213; Edgar C. Polomé, "Tanzania 1970: A Sociolinguistic Perspective," in Language in Tanzania, Edgar Polomé, ed. (London: International African Institute, 1980).

[8] See K. Legère, "Zum Verhältnis zwischen dem Swahili und anderen tanzanischen Sprachen," Zeitschrift für Sprachwissenschaft und Kommunikationsforschung 28 (1975): 343-48 (esp. p. 346).

[9] See M. M. R. Alidina, "The Switch-over to Swahili," KiSwahili 45: 1 (1975): 51-54; Siegmund Brauner, "Swahili an der Universität Dar es Salaam," Zeitschrift für Sprachwissenschaft und Kommunikationsforschung 28 (1975): 331-42.

[10] This was apparently correlated with the decision to limit the English-medium primary education to the number required for the children of expatriates working in Tanzania and to offer the pri-

mary school leaving examination in Swahili only, as from 1974, for previously English-medium schools. See J. Cameron and W. A. Todd, Society, Schools and Progress in Tanzania (Oxford: Pergamon Press, 1970), p. 192.

[11] Though compiled at the beginning of this century, and completed by the end of World War I, the two-volume Dictionnaire Swahili-Français by Ch. Sacleux (Paris: Institut d'Ethnologie, Musée de l'Homme, 1939-41) remains the most complete and reliable Swahili dictionary, with an abundance of dialectal material, ethnographical detail, and proverbs and saws, unparalleled by any other Swahili dictionary. These other Swahili dictionaries, such as Hildegarde Höftmann's Suaheli-Deutsches Wörterbuch (Leipzig: Enzyklopädie Verlag, 1963) and Charles W. Rechenbach's Swahili-English Dictionary (Washington, D. C.: The Catholic University of America, 1967) ultimately derive from the original collections of Krapf (1882), Madan (1903), and Johnson (1934), and badly need to be updated, though Höftmann (on which Rechenbach depends rather heavily) made a considerable effort to include new words from the Swahili press and current daily usage.

[12] Translations suggested by the National Swahili Council [Baraza la Taifa la Lugha ya Kiswahili], Lugha Yetu 1: 2 (Sept. 1969): 24.

[13] The Heinemann African Writers series in Swahili [Waandishi wa KiAfrika] already lists 17 titles, including an anthology of Swahili poetry; the two latest volumes are translations of Chinua Achebe, e. g. Mwakilishi wa Watu [A Man of the People] by Douglas F. Kavugha, a collaborator of the Tanzania Survey, a Ph. D. student at the University of Texas at Austin.

[14] An extensive study of language in the courts in Tanzania has been prepared by Don Bobb and Douglas F. Kavugha for the volume Language in Tanzania, edited by Edgar Polomé (London: International African Institute, 1980), on the basis of field work done by D. Kavugha in 1970.

[15] See A. B. Weston, "Law in Swahili—Problems in Developing the National Language," Swahili 35: 2 (1965): 2-13; A. B. Weston and Sheikh Mohamed Ali, Swahili Legal Terms (Dar es Salaam: The Legal Research Centre, Faculty of Law, University College, 1968).

[16] These resulted from African socialism applied to rural development through pilot settlement schemes. The pattern of living is based on three assumptions: personal involvement of individuals

in community with mutual respect and loyalty; acceptance that all basic goods are held in common and should be shared; obligation to work. See Julius K. Nyerere, "Socialism and Rural Development," in Nyerere, Uhuru na Ujamaa [Freedom and Socialism] (Dar es Salaam: Oxford University Press, 1968), pp. 337-66 (especially pp. 337-39).

[17] Document accepted on 29 January 1967 by the National Executive Committee of TANU in Arusha, which marked a turning point in Tanzanian politics. It made the ideology of the country explicit: socialism and self-reliance, and introduced a series of deliberately socialist policy initiatives such as measures for public ownership, culminating in an article in the Sunday News of 12 February 1967, elaborating on the future position of private enterprise in Tanzania (see J. Nyerere, Uhuru na Ujamaa [Freedom and Socialism], see n. 16 above, esp. pp. 231-56).

7 | Tanzania 1970: A Sociolinguistic Perspective

1.0 Society in Transition

Tanzania in the late sixties and early seventies was a society in transition. Step by step, the old social order inherited from the colonial period was being replaced by the new socioeconomic framework defined in the Arusha Declaration (19 January 1967). On this programmatic statement, President Nyerere had pointed out that one of the major policies of his socialist government was to place the instruments of production and exchange under the control and ownership of the people of Tanzania. The list included:

> land; forests; minerals; water; oil and electricity; news media; communications; banks, insurance, import and export trade, wholesale trade; iron and steel, machine tool, arms, motor-car, cement, fertilizer, and textile industries; and any big factory on which a large section of the people depend for their living, or which provide essential components of other industries; large plantations, and especially those which provide raw materials essential to important industry. (Nyerere 1968b: 234)

Implementation followed very quickly, though a private sector remained operative under specific provisions (Nyerere 1968b: 251-56). As early as February 6, 1967, all banks in Tanzania had been nationalized, and the Bank of Tanzania notes became the only legal tender in the country after September 1967. The National Development Corporation, created in 1962, became the agent through which the Government acquired controlling interest in the major enterprises. Since February 1968, the National Insurance Corporation controls practically all insurance business. The State Trading Corporation, after

taking over control of all the external trade, was progressively completing the nationalization of the wholesale trade in 1969-70. These
decisions entailed important socioeconomic consequences for the
Asian community in Tanzania, as it had played a leading role in the
wholesale trade and the distribution network for import products;
moreover, Africanization which followed nationalization had a serious
impact on job opportunities for Asians in the banking and insurance
business (Ghai 1969: 95-100).

Sweeping changes were also taking place in rural development
with the application of socialist principles: in a policy statement issued in September 1967, President Nyerere (1968b: 337-66) outlined
the objectives of the new policy of ujamaa agriculture based on economic and social communities where rural people would live together
and work together for the good of all.

As a result of the step-by-step transformation advocated by
the President, ujamaa villages were established in various parts of
the country, partly in order to mobilize underutilized labor for agricultural development, but in spite of sustained government and political pressure, the socialist agricultural communities were only partly
successful, depending on the commitment of the participants and their
experience in farming and related activities, and on the competence
and the sense of organization and leadership of the officials in charge.

1.1 Education
In the field of education, Tanzania, following the lead of
President Nyerere (1968a: 267-90), had embarked upon a reorganization of the school system and curriculum to inculcate socialist values
and "encourage the development of a proud, independent, and free
citizenry which relies upon itself for its own development." New
courses in civics were instituted, and new examinations syllabi drafted; schools started schemes intended to emphasize service to the
community and self-reliance, students helping toward the upkeep of
their school. As enrollment increased (in 1968, there were five times
as many students taking the Higher School Certificate exam as in 1961),
the need for teachers became more acute. In 1963, there were only
12 African teachers holding University degrees out of a total of 677
in Tanganyika. For this reason the supply of secondary school teachers was largely dependent on recruitment from outside the country.

In the years following Independence, the main source of teachers was
a cooperative venture of the Agency for International Development
(AID) and the British Department of Technical Corporation with the
governments of East Africa—the Teachers for East Africa Scheme.
In 1964, 120 of them worked in Tanzania, and additional help was provided by the Peace Corps. In the late sixties, Anglo-American assistance was being phased out. There was a dire need, therefore, to
produce local teachers in large numbers in the teachers training colleges and at the University of Dar es Salaam. The Government
planned to increase the total number of secondary school places
(forms I to IV) to 43,000 by 1973, and to bring the enrollment in
forms V and VI up to 4,000. To achieve this a total of 1,900 teachers
were needed, most of them Tanzanian, since the recruitment of expatriates (e.g. Dutch, Scandinavian, Canadian) able to teach in English was limited. Simultaneously, the replacement of English by
Swahili as the medium of instruction was being completed in primary
education and planned for secondary education (in the first two forms
to start with, where Swahilization was expected to be achieved by
1973). The target year for total self-sufficiency in manpower in Tanzania education was 1980 (Resnick 1968: 124). The training of graduate secondary school teachers was entrusted to the University College
of Dar es Salaam, where academic study was combined in a three-
year degree course from which about 280 were to graduate in 1970
(Cameron-Dodd 1970: 215).

1.2 Society

Tanzania society in 1970 was also deeply affected by the
changes in its foreign policy: as a result of the economic agreement
with China and of the building of the Tanzania-Zambia railway, a considerable amount of Chinese technical and professional aid was being
provided. However, the Chinese socialized very little outside their
professional activities, so that they had little impact on social life as
such. As for the internal relationship within the Tanzanian federa-
tion, there were considerable restrictions to the circulation of persons and goods between continental Tanzania (former Tanganyika) and
the islands of Zanzibar and Pemba, whose administration (including
the police) remained distinct and separate from that of the mainland
under the direct control of the first Vice-President A. A. Karume
and his Revolutionary Committee.

1.3 Language

1.3.1 Language in Government

As regards the use of language, the Tanzanian government promoted the total Swahilization of the administration. At all levels, Swahili was being used internally for oral communication and as far as possible for all written messages and outside activities. Similarly, inside the ruling party, Swahili was the language of political life at all levels. The National Swahili Council played an important role in the promotion of language in official and public life. Nevertheless, there were still a large number of inscriptions and official papers in English, and mixed usage prevailed in many cases.[1] Apparently, a large number of forms printed under the colonial regime had merely been reproduced with a new heading for lack of available Swahili translation.[2] Mostly English were, however, the documents likely to be used by foreigners or Tanzanians involved in relations with foreign countries, such as import and export licenses, customs and currency control declarations, etc. In other cases, old painted boards or other public notices had just not yet been replaced, e.g. notices on public transportation and in government-controlled buildings, road signs, etc.[3]

1.3.2 Language in the Law

In the field of justice beyond the level of the primary courts, Swahilization was hampered or slowed down by various factors: though legal terminology had been developed, the transfer into Swahili of the complex body of laws including Bantu customary law, Islamic law, and English common law was progressing at a slower pace than expected; a number of resident magistrates and judges in the High Court were still non-Tanzanian legal experts who had no sufficient command of Swahili. Moreover, in a large number of cases, interpreters had to be used to help older citizens from rural areas who spoke only tribal languages and were unable to present their argument in Swahili.[4]

1.3.3 Language in the Media

As for the press, in 1970 there were only four daily newspapers, two in English—The Nationalist and The Standard—and two in Swahili—Uhuru and Ngurumo—their total circulation averaging less than 68,000 copies. There were a considerable number of weeklies,

fortnightlies, and monthlies, some published by governmental services, some by religious institutions, some by private groups. Most
important were Nchi Yetu ('Our Country') published by the Ministry
of Information and Broadcasting, and Ukulima wa Kisasa ('Present-day
Agriculture'), a joint endeavor of the Ministry of Agriculture and Cooperatives and the Lint and Seed Marketing Board, with a circulation
of 32,000. These, as well as a number of other publications in Swahili, such as Mfanya Kazi ('Worker') the trade unions official weekly,
or Ushirika ('Common Interest'), the monthly bulletin of the Cooperative Union (34,000 copies circulated), were directly aimed at definite sections of the Tanzania population and were widely read, even
at the village level. The Catholic presses at Peramiho published a
number of Swahili periodicals: Mwenge (12,500 copies), Mtima (4,000
copies), Mlezi (2,600 copies). The circulation of the fortnightly
Kiongozi ('Guide') owned by the Tanzania Episcopal Conference was
also rather wide (23,000 copies), as was that of the Pentecostal Church
publication Habari Maalum—ya Uzima Tele ('Famous News—of Abundant Life') with 20,000 copies. The Evangelical Lutheran Church put
out a couple of monthlies, including Uhuru na Amani ('Freedom and
Peace'—12,000 copies). The relative small number of copies available in comparison with the population of the country (estimated at
13,273,000 in 1970) is, however, misleading in judging the number of
readers: papers were passed on from person to person to a rather
considerable extent; numerous readers would come and read them in
the facilities provided by the Ministry of Information all over the country for this purpose, so that, ultimately, the impact of the press was
much wider than actual circulation figures would tend to suggest.[5]

As for the radio, it appeared to play a growing role in Tanzanian sociocultural life as radio ownership increased dramatically
among the Tanzanian population in the late sixties.[6] Between 1964
and 1969, 253,399 radio sets were imported for sale in Tanzania, and
in 1967, the Philips factory in Arusha started production, so that by
the end of 1969, 24,751 locally manufactured radios were also available for sale. With a total of 288,150 new radios in five years, it is
easy to understand the shift that was taking place in the relative importance of the sources of news information: among persons with
middle-grade position in Tanzania society, 54 percent relied on radio
for daily news, whereas 37 percent still considered the newspapers in
Swahili and English as their best source of information.[7] The news

was indeed on top of the preference list of a sampling of listeners
taken in September 1969 (Dodds 1970: 3), immediately before "music."[8]
Programs focusing on political information were also highly favored
by male respondents, but figures were significantly lower for female
listeners, who would tune in to such programs 37.5 percent of the
time only (as against 65.2 percent for the men). Similar results were
obtained for farming information and religous programs: respectively,
26.1 and 30.4 frequency of listening for male respondents, and 18.7
in both cases for female respondents. As a source of entertainment,
women enjoyed music, but seemed to favor "stories" much more than
men (31.2 frequency of listening, versus 17.4 for male respondents).
The educational programs of high quality which the Tanzania Broadcasting Corporation was producing were also highly appreciated:
male respondents would listen to them 36.4 percent of the time, and
female respondents 31.2 percent, but here a considerable difference
appeared according to the age group: people over 40 would tune in
50 percent of the time, whereas people between 30 and 39 would do so
only 33.3 percent of the time. Differences connected with age groups
were even more conspicuous for other programs, e.g.

	People 20-29	People 30-39	People over 40
Farming information	12.5%	33.3%	50.0%
Religious programs	16.4%	37.0%	33.3%
Stories	33.3%	10.8%	16.7%

With two regular Swahili programs, the Tanzania radio stations tried
to meet the wishes of their listeners, while serving the national interest in providing educative programs for adults, valuable information
on farming and related activities, special programs for the schools.
These school broadcasts begun in 1954 are of a particularly high standard and cover almost all subjects of the upper primary and secondary
schools. For the primary schools (Monday through Friday, from
2:30 till 3:55 p.m.), the medium is Swahili; for the secondary schools
(Monday through Friday, from 4:00 till 5:55 p.m.), it is mostly English, but there are 'Beginning French' and 'Advanced Swahili' les-
sons, and civics (Uraia) is taught in Swahili. As for the other programs, in the late sixties there were (a) the National Program in
Swahili, broadcasting 13 hours a day and including news, commentar-

ies, music, magazine and children's programs; (b) the Second Program in English, transmitting 5 hours a day and relying mainly on taped material and outside sources such as the BBC but with an emphasis on the news on Tanzania from a national point of view; (c) the Third Program only broadcast for one and a half hours from Monday to Friday on such subjects as advanced language courses in French and Swahili, music from various countries, cultural material (e.g. art and drama critiques, classical music). Swahili feature programs produced over the National Program are sent out again, e.g. Ulimwengu Siku Hizi ('The World Today'); (d) and the Commercial Service, using predominantly Swahili, and started in October 1965, was devoted essentially to light music, news, and advertising for about 10 hours a day (Widstrand 1966: 2-5; Tanzania Today 1968: 108-9). Nevertheless, the majority of respondents did not seem totally satisfied with their own broadcasting system and many of them, mainly the older ones, often tuned in to foreign stations.[9] However, one of the major reasons was also the poor reception of the National Program in certain areas distant from Dar es Salaam.

1.3.4 Entertainment and Sport
        Besides the radio, the main source of entertainment was the cinema, but here, on the contrary, Swahili material hardly ever appeared on the screens, which were shared by the slightly outdated British and American productions and the current products of the Indian film industry, with occasional Russian and East European or Japanese films in their English version. There was little theatrical activity, except for the experimental group in the Faculty of Arts at the University, who staged a few plays in Swahili and started Ebrahim N. Hussein on his dramatic career with Kinjeketile (1969), and for the non-professional group at the Little Theatre, which performed such musicals as South Pacific or modern English plays.

        Swahili pop music was very popular, especially the type produced in the Congo at that time, but records were hard to come by. Jukeboxes often contained mostly Indian film music which African teenagers would sing along in Hindi or whatever without understanding the words.

        The greatest form of entertainment was soccer, and the big games would draw capacity crowds to the stadiums. The language there was definitely Swahili to encourage one's favorite player or to blast him if he fumbled.

1.3.5 Language in Advertising

All around Dar es Salaam, advertising showed the transitional stage in which the society was: expensive sky signs or neon signs were almost all in English, as were the older big boards on the roadside, but in the shops, on the buses, in the gas stations, on the side of vehicles more and more advertisements appeared in Swahili. Churches had notice boards in both languages, but big construction enterprises still listed all their contractors in English, and sales were announced in the same language. Packaged goods, electricity bills, and other everyday things were increasingly labeled in the two languages. [10]

1.3.6 Reading

Another interesting clue to the actual use of Swahili in some aspects of Tanzanian sociocultural life was supplied by the survey of the reading habits of the more educated part of the population. A study of the use of public libraries and of their visitors is included in Chapter 8; * it also provides a list of the books most frequently read as well as a list of some of the books taken out by the sampling used in the survey; these lists are particularly indicative of the use made of literacy, of the concerns and interests of the readership, and of the limitation of the choice of materials available in Swahili.

2.0 Multilingualism

2.1 Patterns of Multilingualism

If we turn our attention to Tanzanians themselves and their use of languages, various patterns emerge, reflecting various degrees of multilingualism. The studies of Henry Barton on Ilala and selected locations outside Dar es Salaam illustrate the situation in a number of African households in urban and semi-rural communities. But they do not show the linguistic behavior of individuals in the day-to-day running of their active life. An effort to document this was made

---

* Language in Tanzania, ed. by Edgar C. Polomé and C. P. Hill (London: Oxford University Press, 1980).

through the keeping of diaries by about 25 persons, whose linguistic
activity was recorded on a full workday and a holiday. The sampling
represented people of both sexes with various professional, religious,
and ethnic backgrounds; one-third of them had received no formal education; another third had gone to primary school (at most up to standard 8 of upper primary); the rest had attended secondary school and
some had gone to university. For all of them Swahili was used more
frequently than their own language in proportions that varied from a
high of 15:1 to a low of 3:2.[11] With highly educated people, English
only appeared once with a higher frequency than Swahili, namely 42
percent versus 34 percent (with 20 percent Chaga and 4 percent Meru).
Usually, however, the proportion of use of English versus Swahili
varies between 7:1 and 3:2. Non-Africans would, of course, show
completely different patterns of usage, e.g. an Asian would use English 26 percent of the time versus Kachi 52 percent and Gujrati 14.5
percent, with Swahili only 7.3 percent. Hezekiah Mlay and David
Mkindi, who conducted this investigation in August 1970, also examined the amount of switching done by the respondents, noticing that
switching from English or a vernacular into Swahili was far more frequent than the reverse, and trying to determine the circumstances
that triggered the change of language: in 44 percent of the cases, it
seemed to result from an arbitrary personal choice; 23 percent were
ascribed to a desire by the speaker to express himself in a more effective way; 11 percent were due to the need to resort to a language understood by a third party entering the conversation. Furthermore, in 10
percent of the cases, the switching was initiated by the other party,
forcing as it were the speaker to use the same language for the listener's convenience. Switching to vernaculars was connected with kinship, relationship, and familiarity of the parties, recognition of belonging to the same area, etc. and accounted for 8 percent of the
cases.

        All this tended to show that Tanzanians in all aspects of their
social activities played various roles for which various linguistic codes
were being used with a definite amount of discrimination. But Tanzanian society, though less diversified than that of a developed industrial
country, presents typical features in the complexity of its multilingual
sociolinguistic patterning. Let us illustrate this by briefly examining
some of the most characteristic types of Tanzanians and their linguistic behavior:

2.1.1 The Farmer

"Farming is the way of life to most people in Tanzania, either on the large estates or small holdings run by a single family" (Tanzania Today 1968: 111). Traditional agriculture is based on a system of land tenure regulated by customary law; it is characterized by subsistence farming and shifting cultivation as a result of soil deterioration. With the activity of the Department of Agriculture, the social and political changes of recent years were having an impact on land use, and semi-permanent and permanent cropping with smallholder farming became the dominant pattern in some areas more favored by nature and with better access to markets (Ruthenberg 1968). Cooperatives, encouraged at an early date by the British administration, have also helped the smallholders market their cash crops, e.g. of cotton around Lake Victoria, or of coffee in the foothills of Mount Kilimanjaro. A new pattern has developed with the establishment of the ujamaa village and its experiments in collectivization, with far-reaching social implications.[12]

Traditionally, farmers would live in essentially monolingual areas and most of their activities would be confined to their village environment where they would speak their own language constantly. Language continuity would be ensured by the family pattern, which practically excluded marriage outside the local community. At the marketplace, the vernacular would be commonly used by local people, but Swahili would be resorted to with outsiders. Thus, farmers might be expected to have a fair to poor command of Swahili, depending on the area. Swahili would also be the language of the radio programs beamed to rural areas and specially designed for farmers. In the field of politics, larger meetings would be conducted in Swahili, but smaller village meetings would be more frequently run in the local vernacular (e.g. Sukuma or Nyamwezi).[13]

In church, the local language is also likely to prevail, but if a Sukuma cotton farmer goes and sells his crop in the cooperative he may have to use Swahili depending on the official he deals with; similarly, when a cattle buyer comes around, though the latter may know Sukuma (or Maasai, as the case may be) and tend to bargain in the local language. When a Chaga coffee grower delivers his beans to the cooperative, the transaction usually occurs in Chaga, as it will be when he goes shopping in the dukas run by Africans in his area. In

Sukumaland, though, the shopkeeper is more likely to be an Asian, who will use Swahili, possibly pidginized, but some Asians may have a sufficient command of the vernacular to conduct their business in it as well.

Farmers' children have access to rural primary education, but barely 50 percent of the younger generation takes advantage of this opportunity. There they receive at least four years' instruction in Swahili and are taught some amount of English, which, however, rapidly deteriorates if they neither go beyond standard IV nor have an opportunity for practice of the language. Few children from rural areas enter secondary education and the lack of job opportunities as karani ('clerk') in the towns has reduced the attraction of the cities as a motivation factor.

In certain areas, farmers also have contact with the neighboring languages, which accounts for partial bilingualism, e.g. along the outskirts of Sukumaland, where the Jita often also speak Sukuma. Nomadic pastoral tribes like the Maasai will also pick up the dominant languages on their regular migration route: thus, those who serve as cattle drivers for the Tanganyika Meat Packers Corporation through the Uluguru mountains have acquired a sufficient knowledge of Luguru besides Swahili to conduct their trade in it.

2.1.2 The Shopkeeper

Many shopkeepers in Tanzania are of Asian descent and accordingly speak Kachi (a Sindhi dialect), Gujrati, or some other Indo-Aryan language. They are to a large extent trilingual, having a reasonable command of English and being fluent in duka-Swahili, i.e. a substandard upcountry pidginized form of the language. In many cases, they may also be quadrilingual, if they have acquired a working knowledge of the vernacular.

In the marketplace, the vendors are more likely to be Africans who will use either Swahili or the vernacular, and since Independence there has been a growing number of African shopkeepers as well, who are actively bilingual, using the dominant language of the area with local people besides Swahili, and knowing some English as well.

2.1.3 The Craftsman (Fundi)

The majority of the craftsmen were Indians, especially Sikhs, but the number of skilled African craftsmen having gone through technical colleges was increasing steadily. Both groups were trilingual, and at work Swahili seemed to be the dominant language, while at home Punjabi would prevail for the Sikhs, and their own vernacular for the Africans; the third language, resulting from their education, was English, but upcountry it would be of little use, e.g. to a duka tailor, who would more likely be trilingual in Swahili and more than one vernacular.

2.1.4 The Unskilled Laborer

Wage earners tend to show a limited bilingualism: besides their own vernacular, they have acquired Swahili as a result of their migrant status. Actually, some may even have picked up other vernaculars on the way, e.g. while working on sisal plantations or tea estates, where some of them married women from the surrounding area, thus becoming trilingual: Swahili + their own vernacular + their wife's language.

2.1.5 The Clerk (Karani)

Clerks are basically trilingual—Swahili, English, and their own vernacular—but often actually quadrilingual (or even more multilingual) as a result of their migration from one urban center to another. They mostly work outside their own area and pick up the vernacular of their new location, e.g. non-Sukuma in the Mwanza area learn enough Sukuma for greetings and bargaining when handling shamba cotton at the marketplace.

2.1.6 The Professional

Professionals are as a rule trilingual, with English prevailing mostly over Swahili; depending on their ethnic background, they will also speak an African language or an Asian language. Even expatriates will show enough knowledge of Swahili to meet their professional as well as practical needs; in the case of doctors, thorough command of a lot of medically oriented Swahili vocabulary will be necessary, but lawyers can operate at certain levels of the judicial system without any Swahili at all.[14]

2.1.7 <u>The Manager/Administrator</u>

Africans in positions of responsibility are at least trilingual, with a ready command of their own vernacular, Swahili and English. They frequently switch languages, even within one sentence.[15] In the course of their career, they are often moved from one part of the country to another and while in residence there they usually learn at least a smattering of the local vernaculars with which their profession brings them in contact. This situation has direct consequences on the education of their children, whom it loosens even more from the traditional influences and encourages to use Swahili in most of their verbal communication.

2.1.8 <u>The Teacher</u>

Tanzanian teachers are trilingual and often quadrilingual. Primary teachers use Swahili as the medium and teach English as a subject, and are trained accordingly (with Radio Tanzania offering help with its school programs). Besides their own vernacular, as they are often appointed to schools outside their original home area, they have to acquire a sufficient working knowledge of the local vernacular to teach in Standard I, where the children coming in from rural areas often have only a rather limited knowledge of Swahili.[16]

Secondary school teachers would be fluent in Swahili, English, and their own vernacular. The dominant language at school in the early seventies was still English, except for the Swahili teacher and the teacher of civics. In the course of his training and of his career, the teacher had had the opportunity to acquire a limited knowledge of vernaculars other than his own, e.g. a Zalamo teacher could reach a certain degree of competence in Sukuma or Chaga, for example, depending on his contact with his fellow students in college or with the local population if stationed, for example, in the Mwanza or Marangu area. In the staff room, with his colleagues, he would presumably speak English, as several of them would be expatriates, but with fellow Tanzanians a lot of switching to and fro with Swahili was to be expected.

2.2 <u>Urban v. Rural Patterns of Multilingualism</u>

In a different perspective, if we examine the use of languages in a situational dimension in a rural versus an urban context, the following picture obtains:

URBAN	RURAL

I. At work:

Swahili   Vernacular

Special situations:

(1) An industrial worker will use the vernacular with fellow laborers if they belong to the same area but this is usually not the case.

(1) If agricultural advisors or government officers visit the fields, Swahili is likely to be used. Farmers and rural laborers will try to deal with all officials in Swahili unless they are from the same area.

(2) White and/or blue-collar workers will resort to English with their superiors and with the public, e.g. in a bank, but with equals Swahili will prevail, as well as with such part of the public which they identify as 'lower class.' If they recognize people from the same area, they will switch to the vernacular. Asians will similarly address fellow Asians in the relevant Indian language, e.g. Gujrati.

(2) If farmers go to market, they will use either Swahili or vernacular depending on circumstances and their own competence.

II. Shopping:

(1) Market: Swahili and local vernacular. In Dar es Salaam, Kariako merchants also use English as a number of expatriates shop there.

(1) Market: Swahili and local vernacular.

(2) Shops: Swahili, especially if kept by Asians. In some cases, multilingual notices, e.g. prices chalked on board in Arabic, English, Gujrati, and Swahili in Dar es Salaam duka.

(2) Shops: Swahili and local vernacular.

III. Recreation:

(1) Bar: Discussions carried on in Swahili and vernacular.

(1) Bar: Discussions carried on in local vernacular; Swahili used sometimes when outsiders received as visitors.

(2) Sports events: Comments in Swahili, but the local team may be encouraged in the local language during soccer games.

(2) Sports: The language of the prevailing sport—soccer—is Swahili, with typical English loans, e.g. (piga) goli '(shoot) a goal'; shouting is in Swahili as in town, though vernacular is also used.

(3) Playing cards: Always done in Swahili, as well as the accompanying gossip, except for the Asians, who use mostly Gujrati.

(3) Playing cards: Done in the vernacular, but with the Swahili technical terminology (the gossip is exclusively in the vernacular).

(4) Radio: Listening to Swahili programs.

(4) Radio: Listening to Swahili programs.

(5) Dances:

   (a) Ngoma: Traditional dancing, organized on an area basis and therefore strongly emphasizing local songs.

   (b) Western style: Taking place in regular dance halls, they give the 'clerk-playboys' the opportunity to show off their English, but, for the major part, Swahili pop music prevails.

(5) Dances: More of the traditional type and with prevailing use of the vernacular. If mixed groups are formed, as is often the case, even in the smallest trading centers, which are usually multiracial, Swahili tends to be used. However, in conservative areas, like Uhaya, only the local vernacular would be used; this would also apply to Ha in remote rural areas.

(6) Cinema: All films are either in English or in Indian languages, except for a few Russian films with English subtitles.

(6) Cinema: Only rarely does a mobile cinema unit of the Ministry of Information come through to show documentary/propaganda films in Swahili.

IV. Health:

Hospital and dispensary services are available in town, and the language of communication between patient and doctor is Swahili as a rule, except for the rare cases when they are from the same community and will converse in their own vernacular.	Where medical care is available in mission hospitals and dispensaries, like Dr. Taylor's at Mvumi, the local vernacular prevails (in the case in question, Gogo).

2.3 The Church and Multilingualism

As for other dimensions of social life, the situation of the churches is examined elsewhere (Polomé 1982); the shift to Swahili is practically complete in African urban communities and taking place progressively in rural areas, even in conservative territories like Uhaya: there is obviously a generation gap, some parish priests and ministers preaching in vernacular for the older people, and the old hymn books dating back to pre-World War I German missionary action are still being used in the Pare Mountain for speakers of Chasu or Pare. However, decline in the sale of vernacular Bibles indicates the change that has taken place (Polomé 1975: 45).

2.4 Politics and Multilingualism

In political life, as already mentioned, the Tanganyika African National Union (TANU), the party controlling the country since Independence, has promoted the use of Swahili at every level of its organization and activities, but even at the village level, extensive use of vernaculars may often still be required to achieve adequate communication in some parts of the country. The Union of Women of Tanzania—Umoja wa Wanawake wa Tanzania—an affiliate of TANU, is predominantly urban; its language is officially Swahili, and though Swahili mostly prevails, the local vernacular may often be used in some regions like Uhaya. But in the small villages all women still meet going to the well, and their conversation is entirely in vernacular. The National Union of Tanganyika Workers (NUTW), constituted in 1964, encompasses all types of labor force activities and trade union functions, and its members accordingly constitute a quite heterogenous set of people, for whom the use of Swahili necessarily follows.

Occasionally, shop stewards and definite members may use vernaculars, but all operations at the level of union and employers as well
as with Labor Ministry officers are conducted in Swahili.

2.5 Labor and Management
With growing Africanization, the language barrier between
labor and management tends to disappear, as Swahili prevails as language of communication, for example, in the nationalized hotel industry between menial and managing personnel; in state-run factories
between workers and managers. However, in 1969-70, this Africanization had not eliminated the contrast in language use (English versus
Swahili) between the lower echelons and the upper-level officials in
parastatal enterprises where the people in authority would often be
Asians as well as Africans or even expatriates and had constant contacts with foreign technicians. Similarly, in the nationalized banks,
most positions of higher responsibility were still occupied by Asians,
especially Goans, whereas the common clerks were usually Africans;
here again, the role of the banks in the transitional economic life
explains the continued prevalence of English in the higher echelons.

2.6 The Army and Police
The language of command in the army was Swahili, and the
Government was having the basic British training manuals translated
into Swahili by experts from Zanzibar like S. Farsi.

The police wrote its reports in Swahili, but used English in
cases when expatriates were involved. In dealing with the public,
the usual language of communication was Swahili, but when necessary,
the local vernacular was used.

2.7 Multilingualism and Language Skills
This short survey of sociocultural situations in Tanzania
illustrates the multilingual pattern of the society. If multilingualism
is defined as a speaker's competence and performance in a number
of languages in multiple social settings, it is obviously necessary to
determine which language or languages are actually used in each
specific context and what degree of proficiency the user demonstrates
in any particular context. A distinction also needs to be made between
the various language skills: understanding, speaking, reading, and

writing—keeping in mind that though there are no detailed national
statistics on literacy, in the late sixties, hardly 45 percent of the
children went to school. With wastage and dropouts, the percentage
of those becoming actually literate was even lower: 80 percent of the
adult male and 89 percent of the female population was illiterate; however, illiteracy was spread unevenly, reaching up to 95 percent in
some areas, and being as low as 40-50 percent in others.

2.7.1 Oral Competence

In the case of oral performance, the competence of a person
in a language can be measured on the basis of his or her ability to
understand and respond in the following situations:

(1) exchanging greetings;
(2) understanding and/or giving directions;
(3) selling and/or buying things at the market and bargaining about
the price of goods;
(4) carrying on a simple conversation;
(5) talking about health, farming, the weather, etc.;
(6) talking about mechanical things, e.g. repairing a bicycle;
(7) talking about one's work (in non-technical terms);
(8) listening to a political speech and discussing it;
(9) making a speech on a specific occasion;
(10) understanding jokes or telling funny stories (e.g. with puns);
(11) understanding baby talk;
(12) discussion complex technical problems (including, e.g., mathematical calculations);
(13) understanding songs and rapid speech on the radio, etc.

Though such a sampling of situations may not be adequately
graded for certain linguistic contexts, it definitely implies different
levels of competence in the relevant language.[17] The "first" language
of an individual could be defined as the language he resorts to automatically in the absence of outside pressure to use any specific language:
asking the respondent to count aloud, for example, usually provides
an efficient means of identification.

2.7.2 Literate Competence

As far as literate people are concerned, the use of literacy
is an important clue to their linguistic competence: for many Tanzan-

ians, lack of practice leads to loss through regression of the limited
amount of English learned in primary school, though some of it may
still be known passively.[18] Literacy in the vernaculars would be expected to be largely on the wane, since all adult literacy programs
had switched to Swahili and the religious publications in other languages
had become fewer after Independence. However, literacy in Swahili
seemed to enable most Bantu language speakers to write their own
vernacular, using the orthographical conventions of Swahili and disregarding phonemic differences for which Swahili did not provide graphemic representation.[19] As regards Swahili and English, the degree of
competence of respondents in these languages could be partly measured on the basis of their ability to read road and shop signs; maga-
zines or newspapers; religious, educational, or technical books; materials for pastime or pleasure; or more serious materials requiring a
higher intellectual acumen. Similarly, involvement in writing could
range from personal or business letters to the composition of essays,
prose fiction, and poetry, or the redaction of legal documents.

2.8 Choice of Language

An equally important factor in determining the degree of
multilingualism of an individual is the choice of language he makes in
definite social settings. As in other societies, home work, social and
cultural activities, and official functions are determining factors in
this evaluation in Tanzania. Verbal communication at home is generally monolingual, except in the case of mixed marriages, which are
more common these days, even in the rural areas.[20] A bilingual
home will be characterized by constant switching between two vernaculars, but in the coastal area and among the literate population, bilingualism is also common with spouses with the same mother tongue,
the languages used being their common mother tongue and Swahili.
Also reflecting the process of change in the country is the generation
gap in language use: parents with the same mother tongue use it when
talking to each other, but resort to Swahili when addressing their
children.[21] As regards the use of languages in the various aspects of
socioeconomic life, the subject has already been discussed at some
length, so that we can summarize it as follows:

(a) though English is on the wane as a result of nationalization and
    Africanization of a considerable number of enterprises (banks,

import and export trade, wholesale distribution to retail dealers,
etc.), it is still used on a wide scale in the upper levels of economic life;

(b) in industry, Swahili prevails as the labor force is recruited from
various parts of the country, and it is indispensable as a lingua
franca;

(c) in government, Swahili is strongly promoted officially and except
for certain specific cases, all transactions are in this language;
public services are assumed to run in Swahili, but as many forms
are still in English, local people have to rely on friendly bilingual
employees to help them or take along a child who has studied Swahili and some English at school.[22]

On the basis of such situations, a set of questions is asked to respondents to evaluate their use of a language in correlation with their competence in it, namely: 'What language do you use when

(1) conversing with your father ?
(2) conversing with your mother ?
(3) conversing with your father's parents ?
(4) conversing with your mother's parents ?
(5) conversing with your brothers and sisters ?
(6) conversing with close friends ?
(7) conversing with strangers (of your home area; of Tanzanian
origin; from other African countries; of non-African origin)?
(8) conversing with an inferior at work?
(9) conversing with a superior at work?
(10) discussing technical matters at work?
(11) at the post office (and other public services, e.g. the bank, the
town hall, etc.)?
(12) describing an accident at the place where it occurred ?
(13) reporting something that happened at a police station?'—etc.'[23]

Using the informants' ability to operate in different languages in a
number of situations as a basis, tentative ratings can be established
for his degree of proficiency in each language under consideration.
Thus, on the basis of the Tanzania adult survey questionnaires (Polomé 1975: 40), the following scales were used for respondents from
rural areas:

(a) understanding: 0-13;
(b) speaking: 0-12;
(c) reading: 0-6;
(d) writing: 0-6.[24]

Similarly, their actual use of the language in definite social contexts was rated as follows:

(a) at home: 0-13;
(b) in social life: 0-14;
(c) in professional life: 0-12 for men; 0-5 for women.

In such an analysis of the data, the first language will always reach high or even maximal scores, but only _real_ bilinguals will score high on the "second" language, whether it be Swahili or any vernacular. The scores in English tend to be lower, except for people whose professional and related social activities entail the extensive use of that language. In the case of vernaculars, the third language very seldom scores high, whereas the fourth and following ones will seldom rise above 10 as regards the level of proficiency (maximum: 37) and will also be very low in occurrence in definite social contexts (0-5 out of maximum of 39 or 32, depending on the sex of the respondent). Swahili is vigorously expanding in all aspects of Tanzanian life. The history of Swahili in Tanzania has been described in detail from its very beginnings (Polomé 1980, chap. 4) to its prominent role in nation-building since the foundation of TANU and the independence of Tanganyika (Abdulaziz in Polomé 1980, chap. 6). Its use in education, in the mass media, and in government, the establishment of a regulating body (the National Swahili Council) to ensure its promotion, the development of adequate technical terminology in all fields are so many assets that have contributed to its spread. Other important social factors are geographical mobility and upward mobility: the former is a result of a deliberate policy of the Tanzanian government to assign officers outside their area of origin and to increase their experience by acquainting them with various parts of the country; to ensure that a large percentage of the student population in secondary schools and teachers training colleges comes from other regions of the country and to increase the "melting pot" effect of education by enlisting students in the National Service, where all activities are conducted in Swahili, during their vacation period; to transfer people of various regional backgrounds

to resettlement schemes (ujamaa villages) in government estates, e.g.
sisal plantations, or semi-industrial projects, e.g. the Kilombero
sugar estate, in various parts of Tanzania. As for upward mobility,
children of farmers and low-level employees like messengers obtain
better positions through better education and identify themselves with
their new social status by shifting to Swahili as the language of their
sociocultural life as well as of their professional activity.

Nevertheless, the Swahilization of Tanzanian society is slowed
down by two major factors:

(a) the still very strong linguistic loyalty to the vernaculars, especially in those areas where the people have preserved strong traditional cultures, since the language remains one of the basic
means to identify with the tradition;
(b) the insufficient development of the educational system, which in
1970 was still unable to provide basic primary education to about
half the children of school age in rural areas, and whose secondary schools are too few[26] and remain concentrated in a few
urban areas.

2.9 Typology of Multilingualism

It is possible to establish a tentative typology of multilingualism in Tanzania on the basis of the considerations made in connection
with the Tanzania Survey. If we use the signs 'S' for Swahili, 'E' for
English, 'V' for vernacular, and 'A' for Arabic, the tabulation in
Table 1 can be made (leaving out the Asian minority).

By providing each symbol with indices indicating the scores
of a respondent in both scales—degree of proficiency (maximum: 37)
and amount of use in specific social environments (maximum: 39 [for
men] or 32 [for women])—it is possible to evaluate his or her command of the languages he or she claims to know and the extent to
which he or she uses them, e.g. a 26-year-old Muslim clerk, whose
"first" language is Swahili and mother tongue Rufiji, but who also
claims to know English and Arabic, scores: V9/20 S37/28 E21/3 A1/0,
which means that he has total command of Swahili, though he may not
use it in some social contexts, like talking to an expatriate or a relative of his wife, in which case he uses, respectively, English or Rufiji. His knowledge of English is more limited; he uses it more for

Table 1.   Typology of Multilingualism

1. Monolingual	2. Bilingual	3. Trilingual
(a) V	(a) VS or SV	(a) VSE
(b) S	(b) SE	(b) VSA
	(c) SA	(c) VVS
	(d) VV	(d) VVV

4. Quadrilingual	5. Plurilingual	Key
(a) VSEA	(a) VV(V..)SEA	V vernacular
(b) VVSA	(b) VVV(V...)SE	S Swahili
(c) VVSE	(c) VVV(V...)SA	E English
(d) VVVS	(d) VVVV(V...)S	A Arabic

reading than for talking; he never speaks it at home, and practically
never uses it at work. His use of Arabic is strictly limited to prayer.
His knowledge and use of Rufiji is limited to domestic matters and he
does not claim any literacy in this language, which he does not use in
his social activities outside the family circle, since he is living in a
Zigula-speaking area.

2.9.1 Rural Areas

An examination of the Tanzanian evidence shows the following patterns prevail in the rural areas:

(a) V (mainly inland
(b) S (mainly in the coastal area)
(c) VS (mainly in the coastal area; sometimes the vernacular will be
    the mother tongue, sometimes Swahili)
(d) VV (only inland)
(e) VVS
(f) VSA (Muslims)

Though knowledge of English is found among educated people in rural
areas, these will be essentially government agents, teachers, medical assistants, etc.—not farmers. The trifocal type VSE, described

by Abdulaziz (1972), prevails in towns; the other plurilingual types
show considerable discrepancies in their level of command of the
respective languages they claim to know, and which usually reflect
the mobility of the speaker.[26]

Using the responses to the secondary school survey (Polomé
1975: 41) and analyzing a random sampling of about 1,550 respondents,
statistical data were compiled to illustrate the degree of proficiency
of the informants in a selected set of languages and to determine the
relative frequency with which these languages were used by them in
various contexts. The languages chosen were:

(a) Swahili and English;
(b) Hindi, Gujrati, Kachi (for Asians);
(c) the 15 Tanzanian vernaculars with the highest number of speakers,
    namely Sukuma, Nyamwezi, Makonde, Haya, Chaga, Gogo, Ha,
    Hehe, Nyakyusa, Lugulu, Bena, Nyatura, Shambala, Zalamo,
    Nilyamba;
(d) a selection of non-Bantu languages, namely Sandawe, Maasai,
    Iraqw, Luo;
(e) a set of smaller Tanzanian Bantu linguistic-ethnic units, Zanaki,
    Tongwe, Pogolu, Matumbi, Makua, Matengo, Fipa, Safwa,
    Kerewe.[27]

C. P. Hill did a graphic analysis of the data which illustrates
a number of interesting facts: proficiency profiles dip as the type of
linguistic accomplishment gets more complex, and for the vernaculars
they sink particularly low as far as question 14 (Do you ever think out
what to say in this language before you speak in another?) is concerned,
indicating that none of the respondents apparently tries to think out
what he is going to say in English, for instance, in his mother tongue
first. The frequent recourse to vernacular in greetings is also illustrated by the peaks in questions 1 (Do you understand greetings in this
language?) and 6 (Can you greet people in this language?). Profile
analyses of language use in various situations yield quantitative data
for frequent, occasional, and rare use of the same set of languages by
the informants and illustrate a number of interesting facts: the prevalence of English and Swahili for writing and reading; apart from Hindi
and Gujrati, only very few vernaculars score significantly as regards
the written language or the printed word; Haya shows the highest figures,

which is in keeping with the strong language loyalty of the area and the
continued use of the language in some publications, for example Rumuli,
published twice a month by the Diocese of Bukoba in Haya and Swahili
(3,000 copies in 1970-71). Languages of people with strong ethnic traditions, like the Sukuma, the Nyamwezi, the Chaga, and the Nyakyusa,
also seem to have maintained a relatively high level of literacy in the
vernacular, presumably also under the influence of the availability
and still fairly widespread use of a rather extensive religious literature in the language. Such is no longer the case with other important
people like the Gogo or with those living closer to the coast like the
Sambaa or Zalamo. Remarkable also is the scarcity of the use of the
vernacular in oral communication in a large number of situations, for
example, in shops, at home, or when selling produce at the market.
It is more understandable that Swahili should be used in places like
the railway station or the post office, where the officials may not be
local people. More complex are situations with political implications
like 'self-help schemes': evidently, the deliberate use of Swahili is
expected to be high, but the incidence of the vernaculars can be quite
significant, as in Haya, or even in Chaga, whereas in other cases,
languages like Sukuma or Nyamwezi are only used occasionally or just
rarely. Striking are the low scores of the vernaculars in the case of
playing games like football or bao: again the Haya and the Chaga are
the only ones who use their language frequently in this context; the
scores in Sukuma definitely point to a scarcer use of the vernacular,
and in Gogo or Hehe, the language seems to be resorted to even less
frequently. Thus the statistical data confirm the growing importance
of Swahili in every field of social life.

If we try to determine regional differences in the degree to
which the impact of Swahili on sociocultural activities can be felt, it
is obvious that a number of factors are going to affect the results of
any inquiries, such as (a) historical factors, like the degree of Swahilization due to pre-colonial contacts along the caravan routes and the
lines of penetration of Islam;[28] (b) change in attitude due to political
motivations, in particular in the period leading up to the Arusha
Declaration (1967).[29]

Two inquiries done in the second part of the sixties illustrate
this shift in attitude: one, conducted by Anders Andersson, of the Institute of Education of the University of Uppsala (Sweden), revealed

Table 2. Language Attitudes

Area	Dialect losing		Dialect 'nicer'		Prefer vernacular		Prefer Swahili	
	1965	1967	1965	1967	1965	1967	1965	1967
West	67	35	90	65	64	42.5	36	57.5
North	93	58	86	58	36	39	64	61
East	75	58	100	52.6	33	42.1	67	57.9
South [a]	79	34.2	80	41	50.9	31	49.1	62
Center	83	42.1	96	57.9	61	26.3	39	73.7

Note: The West includes West Lake, Mwanza, and Kigoma. The North includes Kilimanjaro. The East includes the Coast Region, Tanga, and Morogoro. The South includes Ruvuma, Mtwara, Iringa, and Mbeya. The Center includes Tabora, Singida, Dodoma, Shinyanga, and Mara.
[a] In 1967, 7% of the respondents showed no language preference.

that the main factors determining students' attitudes toward Swahili
were their 'home language,' i.e. whether they spoke a vernacular or
Swahili at home, and their family background, i.e. their father's occupation and their coming from a rural or an urban area. The inquiry
showed that students from more "educated" homes display a less favor-
able attitude toward Swahili. Sex and religion, according to Andersson's corpus of data, played no specific role (Andersson 1967: 17, 39).
However, his aim was to measure how secondary school students in
Tanzania responded to English versus Swahili as a language and as a
medium, and, therefore, his results were definitely lopsided and in-
adequate to reflect upon the major problem of the position of Swahili
versus the vernaculars.[30] The other study was a more modest project
directed by J. Mittelmeyer with the students of the Morogoro Teachers
College from 1965 to 1967. Dividing continental Tanzania (former
Tanganyika) in five major areas, it tried to establish whether the vernaculars were losing ground or not in these territories, what the feelings of the speakers were toward their own language and toward Swahili, and whether aesthetic connotations in the vernacular were partly
responsible for those feelings.

The results of the inquiry were rather complex to interpret,
as can be seen from Table 2. The reason why these figures cannot be
interpreted at face value is that between 1965 and 1967, the regional
spread in the recruitment of students in Morogoro college changed considerably, as the following figures may show:

	South	Lake area	Center	Kilimanjaro	Coast/Tanga Morogoro
1965	38.5%	27.3%	16.1%	9.8%	8.3%
1967	16%	22.1%	20.9%	20.5%	20.5%

This shift in distribution may partly account for the fluctuation in the
responses about the situation of the vernacular: while the number of
students from the more conservative areas in the west and the center
(Uhaya, Usukuma, Uha, etc.) has not changed dramatically, the doubling of the enrollment from the Chaga-speaking area and the even
sharper increase from the coastal regions, including Tanga (and, further inland, Morogoro), with the concomitant drastic cut of the flow of
students from the south must necessarily have influenced the results

Table 3. Language in the Home

Area	Year	Parents speaking				Students speaking in town/village	
		With each other		With children			
		Vernacular only	Vernacular + Swahili	Vernacular only	Vernacular + Swahili	Vernacular only	Vernacular + Swahili
West	1965	90	10	87	13	72	28
	1967	92.5	7.5	60	40	17.5	82.5
North	1965	(no data)		86	14	50	50
	1967	80	20	47	53	19	81
East	1965	92	8	25	75	8	92
	1967	21	79	10.5	89.5	2.6	97.4
South	1965	94.2	5.8	58.2	41.8	30.9	69.1
	1967	48.2	50	27	73	13.7	86.3
Center	1965	91	9	87	13	48	52
	1967	65.8	34.2	44.7	55.3	13.2	86.8

Note: The West includes West Lake, Mwanza, and Kigoma. The North includes Kilimanjaro. The East includes the Coast Region, Tanga, and Morogoro. The South includes Ruvuma, Mtwara, Iringa, and Mbeya. The Center includes Tabora, Singida, Dodoma, Shinyanga, and Mara.

of the survey, since it accounts for 38.7 percent of the parents speaking only vernacular to their children. But this strong hold of the vernacular on the family circle is not the main reason for the change in
percentages of those who think "dialects are losing ground to Swahili":
in the middle sixties there was a strong action to promote Swahili, and
the younger generation was also motivated by patriotic feelings to prefer
the national language over the vernacular, which appeared as a feature
of the divisions which the vigorous efforts to build a new nation wanted
to eliminate. Hence, the shift in preference: in 1965, 53 percent of
the students preferred their vernacular over Swahili; in 1967, 62.4
percent gave Swahili the preference over the vernacular. In the meantime, the aims of the Tanzanian national policy had become well defined after the Arusha declaration; Swahili and the traditional languages
had their respective places and functions in the new society, and a
better-balanced judgment on the aesthetic values of the vernacular was
given, as it was no longer felt it was threatened with disappearance,
and as growing awareness of Swahili literary achievements and rich
modes of expression changed the views on the assumed limitations of
this language.[31]

A project directed by J. Mittelmeyer and his students at the
Morogoro Teachers Training College (1965-67) considered the question of the language spoken at home: percentages are provided for the
five major areas considered for two sets of situations:

(a) parents speaking with each other,
(b) parents speaking with children,

as well as for the use by the respondent of Swahili or the vernacular—
or—exclusively of the local tribal language in a town or village. The
results (i.e. percentages) can be tabulated as found in Table 3. The
table provides clear evidence of the generation gap in the use of Swahili in certain parts of Tanzania: in the large areas of the west, the
north, and (partly) the center, the Haya, the Ha, the Sukuma, the
Chaga, and others continue to use their own languages at home, but
as their children are educated in Swahili in primary school, they try
to use this language as well when talking to them, though usually much
less frequently when speaking to each other. For many, indeed, Swahili presents a number of problems, even on the phonological level,
and sound substitutions like the Chaga use of [s] for the dental frica-

tives [θ] and [ð] are not uncommon. Being exposed to a considerable amount of Swahili through the mass media, the governmental services, the political action of TANU and, recently, also the Church (though vernaculars were still widely in use in the late sixties, including the Bible and religious literature), the older generation gradually improves its knowledge of Swahili and uses it more with the younger people. The differences between the 1965 and 1967 figures are quite impressive in this regard and dramatize the success of the campaign for the shift to Swahili among the upcoming generation of Tanzanians. In talk with peers, young Chagas who, two years before, would still be 50 percent dialect users only in their familiar surroundings use Swahili as well in a proportion of 4 to 1 in 1967.

The most dramatic change is presumably to be found in the data from the eastern part of the country, but they are rather misleading: the 1965 students come mostly from rural backgrounds, hence the high percentage of use of their own language by their parents at home (92 percent). Actually, Swahili had a very high frequency of use besides the vernaculars in this area, as shown by the percentages in the village (1965: 92 percent; 1967: 97.4 percent). This is due to a number of reasons:

(a) the majority of the population is Muslim:

	Muslims	Christians	Other
Tanga	71.9%	19.8%	7.3%
Dar es Salaam	75.0%	16.1%	8.4%

(b) there is considerable influence from Zanzibar (the coast used to be controlled by the Sultan, who still appointed liwalis in the colonial period);
(c) the missionaries mostly neglected the vernaculars in recent years and shifted to Swahili;
(d) there are numerous marriages between people of different language background.

Even so, there is a considerable difference between the coast and the inland territories, e.g. the percentages for preference of vernaculars in 1966 are: 0 for the Coastal Region; 10 for Tanga; but 42.9 for Morogoro.

In non-Bantu areas like the territory of the Iraqw in the north, there is little interest in speaking Swahili, except in the semi-urban center, Babati, where there are a hospital, a bus station, dukas, etc. When children enter school, no knowledge of Swahili can be assumed for any practical purposes, but Swahili becomes more effective from Standard II on.

Studies such as these provide more depth and perspective to our knowledge of the language situation of which we tried to capture one phase of change at the turn of the sixties. In 1974 new decisive steps were taken to speed up the process of Swahilization: 'From August 1, all correspondence, forms and sign posts in all parastatal and public organizations must be in Swahili' (Legère 1975: 346).[32] Thus, the implementation of the program of making Swahili the national language of Tanzania at all levels of public and sociocultural life moves ahead, and future research will be able to measure Tanzania's progress to the achievement of its goals in the field of language use and nation building.[33]

NOTES

[1] An examination of documents in public buildings in Dar es Salaam in the Spring of 1970 yielded the following results:

Town Council. At City Hall, of 26 notices on a board, twelve were in English and 14 in Swahili (they involved advertisements for the sale of a vehicle, announcements about vacant posts, etc.). On the wall, such indications as 'City Engineer's Office'/'Fundi Mkuu wa Jiji' were bilingual, but the main listing of offices was in Swahili.

As regards licenses issued by the town council like the 'license to hawk,' the application was in Swahili, but the license in English; for retail trading, the applications were available both in Swahili and English, but the licenses were in English, whereas the Internal Revenue Office had bilingual Swahili/English retail licenses. For a number of other licenses (liquor licenses, auctioneer's licenses, petrol installation permits, etc.), both applications and licenses were in English. At the Accounts Department, the ledgers, the notations on payments and receipts, estimates, schedules of payments, final accounts, etc. were all in English (for the Councilors' benefit, authorizations for payments were in Swahili). However, the minutes of the Town Council meetings were in Swahili and English, and the language

used in correspondence depended on the addressee: letters to all
ministries were usually in Swahili, except when they dealt with very
technical matters; letters of appointment of staff, promotion and transfer were in English—mainly because the relevant rules and regulations
had not yet been officially translated into Swahili; letters to traders
and various enterprises were consistently in English or Swahili.
Written communication between the heads of departments was in English, except with the Town Clerk (because of the mixed origin of the
staff including Asians and non-Tanzanians). Verbal contact with the
public was mostly in Swahili; verbal instructions to the staff were
nearly always in Swahili.

     Department of Health. Most of the correspondence was con-
ducted in Swahili, since most of the complaints recorded, e.g., came
from Africans and were transacted in Swahili, but when appropriate,
English was used. Reports for and from Health Officers were in Swahili. Interstaff communication was also in Swahili, at least at the
junior staff level; if the senior staff consisted of expatriates, English
would be used. Seventy percent of the verbal contacts took place in
Swahili, but with foreigners, e.g. embassy staff, English was used—
also in all correspondence. Vaccination forms, Infant Welfare Clinic
forms, and such documents were still in English; health reports, licenses, etc. were in both English and Swahili.

    [2] This was particularly obvious in public places like the post
office or the banks. Thus, in 1970, practically all the forms of the
East African Posts and Telecommunications in Dar es Salaam, such as
a list of registered postal packets, a dispatch note, a requisition for
a money order, a telegram, were still monolingual in English. The
only exception was the Postal Savings Service, whose forms were
also in Swahili.

    [3] To illustrate this the situation on the ships on Lake Victoria
could be mentioned: on the M. V. "Victoria," all public notices were
bilingual, with the Swahili text first, e.g. Hakuna ruhusa ya kupita
hapa/No Admittance; only the bulletin board was in English only, except for navigation notices—but on the S. S. "Usoga," all notices were
still in English only, except for the obviously later addition of Hakuna
ruhusa ya kupita hapa in one case. Similarly, on the train from Dar
es Salaam to Tabora and Kigoma all notices were in English, and all
tickets, vouchers, receipts, etc. as well. In the Tanzania Railway
hotels, the situation varied; in Tabora, all notices, except on the staff
notice board, were only in English; in Dodoma, they were in Swahili

and English, e.g. Chumba cha chakula/Dining room; Msalani/Toilets,
etc. Elsewhere, e.g. in Mwanza, one hotel had all its notices in
Swahili, and another all in English, except for the indication in Swahili of the time at which the room should be vacated.
    [4] For examples, see chap. 9 [in Language in Tanzania, ed.
by E. C. Polomé and C. P. Hill (London: Oxford University Press,
1980)] on 'The Use of Language in the Law-Courts' by D. Kavugha
and D. Bobb.
    [5] Nevertheless, transportation problems are responsible for
the fact that more than half of the newspapers are sold in Dar es
Salaam and that the news is stale by the time it reaches places like
Songea which have only limited air service, so that the papers have
to go by bus. A table for the main distribution centers for the four
dailies is given below with the respective percentages:

	Uhuru	Ngurumo	Nationalist	Standard
Arusha	250 (1.4%)	1,800(15.0%)	139 (1.6%)	900 (4.7%)
Coast (less Dar es Salaam)	130 (0.7%)	50 (0.41%)	34 (0.39%)	500 (2.6%)
Dodoma	285 (1.5%)	300 (2.5%)	134 (1.5%)	390 (2%)
Iringa	304 (1.6%)	280 (2.3%)	136 (1.5%)	493 (2.6%)
Kigoma	120 (0.65%)	500 (4.1%)	75 (0.87%)	125 (0.6%
Kilimanjaro	200 (1.1%)	400 (3.3%)	190 (2.2%)	795 (4.2%)
Mara	133 (0.73%)	—	59 (0.78%)	190 (1.0%)
Mbeya	216 (1.2%)	100 (0.82%)	140 (1.6%)	315 (1.6%)
Morogoro	495 (2.7%)	750 (6.2%)	155 (1.8%)	685 (3.6%)
Mtwara	437 (2.4%)	100 (0.82%)	189 (2.2%)	210 (1.1%)
Mwanza	750 (4.1%)	200 (1.6%)	180 (2.1%)	845 (4.4%)
Ruvuma	79 (0.43%)	50 (0.41%)	60 (0.69%)	130 (0.68%)
Shinyanga	580 (3.1%)	50 (0.41%)	20 (0.23%)	185 (0.97%)
Singida	15 (0.08%)	—	5 (0.06%)	130 (0.68%)
Tabora	240 (1.3%)	250 (2.1%)	100 (1.2%)	339 (1.8%)
Tanga	1,781 (9.7%)	1,300 (11.0%)	290 (3.4%)	1,345 (7%)
West Lake	190 (1.0%)	20 (0.16%)	90 (1.0%)	240 (1.3%)
Dar es Salaam	11,573(63.0%)	6,000(49.0%)	4,327(50.0%)	10,365(54.0%)
Outside Tanzania	163 (0.88%)	—	755 (8.7%)	125 (0.65%)

The consequences of this distribution pattern are obvious when one
looks at the frequency of reading in some locations assessed, e.g.,
by the survey conducted by Graham L. Mytton, of the University of

Manchester (U. K.), in 1967–68: in Dar es Salaam 44.2 percent of
the newspaper readers would read them every day; another 11.6 percent four to five times a week, and 26.3 percent more than two to
three times a week; in the Kilimanjaro urban centers—Arusha and
Moshi—reached by air every day, the corresponding percentages are
33.3, 3.7, and 33.3, but here 29.6 percent of the readers read the
newspapers only <u>once</u> a week, whereas in Dar es Salaam only 11.1
did so, and in the rural area of the Kilimanjaro this percentage climbs
up steeply to 60 percent.   Kigoma which gets the newspapers with two
or three days' delay by train from Tabora, to where they are flown in
from Dar es Salaam, shows the following percentages: 8.3 percent
read the papers every day; 41.7 percent two or three times per week;
25 percent once a week, but in the neighboring rural areas these percentages drop to 7.7, 15.4, and 15.4 respectively, 53.8 percent of
readers getting to see a newspaper less than once every two weeks.
This time lapse is particularly evident when respondents are asked
when they last read a newspaper: in Dar es Salaam 59.5 percent answer 'today' or 'yesterday'; in Kigoma, the majority (66.7 percent)
says 'within the last week'; in the Kilimanjaro area, 39 percent reply
'today' or 'yesterday, ' but 55.6 percent 'within the last week. ' And
the gap in communication between the urban and rural areas is even
greater (e.g. in Kigoma rural area, 23.1 percent 'within the last week, '
but 38.5 percent 'more than a week ago').

     [6] In 1960, there were only 72,232 radio sets in Tanganyika,
of which 41,144 were owned by Africans: 31,195 in rural communities;7,449 in urban areas; 2,500 in schools, clubs, and other institutions (TBC Survey 1960: 3).

     [7] Widstrand (1966: 7) points out that only 13 percent buy their
own paper daily; 23 percent read the paper daily, 42 percent about
once a week.   On the other hand, the Tanzania National Radio news
program—<u>Taarifa ya Habari</u>—is preferred by 87 percent of the respondents, though 32 percent also listened to the Voice of Kenya and 20
percent to the BBC.

     [8] The sampling discussed in Tony Dodds' report covered a
wide geographical area in Northern Tanzania, including the districts
of Bukoba, Arusha, Kilimanjaro, Pare, Tanga, Lushoto, Chunya,
Morogoro, and Dar es Salaam.   As it was conducted by University
students during their home vacation time, it was strongly biased
toward the environment of the students' family: it included 36 percent
of professional people (teachers, magistrates, government officers),

17 percent of clerical or secretarial staff, 14 percent of skilled
workers and craftsmen, 12 percent of unskilled labor, 12 percent of
farmers, and 9 percent of businessmen, and there was a strong im-
balance between urban and rural participants as well as between both
sexes (only 28 percent of the sampling were female). Eighty-two percent of the respondents were between the ages of 20 and 39; 78 percent
had a higher than Standard V educational background, and 35 percent
actually attended secondary school (6 percent continuing their education beyond Form IV).

[9] Only 60 percent of the people under 20 listen to foreign
broadcasts, compared to 87 percent for the 20-29 age-group, 96.4
percent for the 30-39 age-group, and 100 percent for those over 40
(Dodds 1970: 5).

Among the foreign stations most listened to were the following, with the assumed percentage of those listening according to two
surveys in the late sixties:

	According to Mytton (1968: 12)	According to Dodds (1970: 15)
The Voice of Kenya	63.0%	61%
BBC	17.3%	32%
Voice of America	3.9%	23%
Deutsche Welle (West Germany)	4.3%	23%
Radio Uganda	7.5%	21%
Radio Voice of the Gospel (Ethiopia)	7.1%	18%
Radiodiffusion Congo (Lubumbashi mainly)	9.1%	13%
Radio Burundi	10.6%	13%
Radio Rwanda	7.5%	11%

Though the coverage of the two surveys was not the same (Mytton
interviewed 838 persons in 1967-68 in the districts of Mzizima, Kisa-
rawe, Kigoma, Mwanza, and Kilimanjaro, besides the Dar es Salaam
area, choosing representatives of every age-group, social and professional status, and educational background, in urban as well as
rural contexts as far as possible), the data are significantly indicating a trend to the increased listening to broadcasting stations; particularly dramatic is the increase in the case of the Voice of America
and the Deutsche Welle, especially since the latter had installed its

powerful relay station in Kigali. On the other hand, the sharp drop
registered by the All India Radio (Mytton, 10.2 percent; Dodds, 2
percent) and Radio Pakistan (Mytton, 6.7 percent; not even mentioned
by Dodds) is also indicative of a shift of interest among the Asian
population. Interest for such stations as Radio Moscow or Peking
remains rather limited (together with East Germany, less than 4 percent in Mytton; 3 percent for Moscow and 2 percent for China Radio
in Dodds). Radio Zanzibar (Sauti ya Unguja) which continued its independent programming and operation after the establishment of the
United Republic in 1964, remained a favorite among continental listeners (it drew 11.8 percent of them in 1967-68 according to Mytton).
      [10] On Dar es Salaam buses, e.g. Philips (radios) and Suzuki
(motor bikes) advertised in Swahili, but Shell/Afrigas in English. All
the National Milling Corporation products, e.g. Nguvu flour, were
labeled in Swahili and English. As regards posters, English and Swahili were found: the Saba Saba advertisements and the National Lottery
posters were in Swahili, but a Ngoma (dance) of TANU Women's Union
and a Yugoslavia exhibition were announced in English. The inscriptions on all official vehicles were in Swahili, as were those on the
vans of the power company (Tanesco), including Kwa maisha bora
tumia umeme 'Use electricity for better living.' Breweries (Chituku,
Tusker, Kilimanjaro) would also use Swahili, but other industries
(Leyland paints, Tasini fabrics, etc.) would prefer English; even the
TANU Youth League would have its name in English painted on its
vehicles. Coca-Cola had its truck with Swahili inscriptions, but its
billboards (Coca-Cola, Sprite, and Fanta) were in English only. Tanzania cigarette brands like Sportsman advertised mostly in Swahili,
as did Embassy Shirts, and Cafenol.
      In this context, it might be worth mentioning that English-
language advertising would often appear in Swahili-language papers
and periodicals like Uhuru and Mfanya Kazi, covering respectively
up to 8 percent and 14 percent of an issue in July/August 1970.
      [11] The usual pattern of difference in frequency of use is, how-
ever, less aberrant: (a) for people who use Swahili and one vernacular, it may rise to 5:1 in favor of Swahili, but is usually around 4:1
or even much less (e.g. Swahili 72 percent, Yao 28 percent; Swahili
66 percent, Bondei 34 percent); (b) for people who use Swahili plus
more than one vernacular, we find percentages like 59.6 percent Swahili, 35 percent Chaga, 5.2 percent Zalamo; (c) for people who speak
English as well as Swahili besides vernacular, the vernacular often

shows the lowest level of use, e.g. Swahili 59.4 percent, English 28.8 percent, Chaga 11.7 percent; but the reverse occurs almost as frequently, English being less used than the vernacular (this may depend very much on the contacts and context of conversation on the days of the survey), e.g. Swahili 56.8 percent, Nyakusa 23.5 percent, English 19.6 percent—sometimes even on a par with the second vernacular, e.g. English 8.3 percent = Nyakyusa 8.3 percent versus Kinga 33.3 percent and Swahili 50 percent.

[12] Two major traditional structural components of village life —the patrilinear extended family and the hierarchical organization of the community as a 'chiefdom' are done away with. In two important papers, C. R. Hatfield (1972a and b) has given a penetrating analysis of the strains that result from this reorganization of socioeconomic life in the village and shown how these stresses affect a major livestock development project in Sukumaland.

[13] Cf. Hatfield (1972a: 20), who points out that "at local meetings initial discussion always centered around whether Kiswahili or the local language was to be used. Arguments for the former were strong: it is progressive to use Kiswahili, primitive to use the local dialect; do you want our government to think we are not conscious of our responsibilities. The problem is that few local individuals understand Kiswahili well enough to be effective listeners, and even fewer have facility in using the language to make their opinion known (for rhetoric and metaphor are extremely important in public speaking and the Sukuma and Nyamwezi pride themselves on their abilities in speaking elegantly) ... Meetings conducted ... in Kisukuma or Nyamwezi involved greater discussion, greater local rhetoric, but I think greater mutual information flow."

[14] Thus, in 1970, the Resident Magistrate in Moshi was a non-Tanzanian who did not know any Swahili at all.

[15] Abdulaziz 1972: 207-10. Personal observation in the offices of high officials in Tanzanian ministries confirmed Abdulaziz' results: in the course of a Swahili telephone conversation with a Regional Director, the Principal Secretary of the Education Ministry, for instance, switched several times to English phrases and back to Swahili, using expressions like 'claim per diem' in a Swahili context.

[16] As has been demonstrated by W. M. Shedu Chamungwa (1971), when showing school-entering children a set of culturally adequate, easily identifiable pictures, for which a correct interpretation in their own vernacular does not appear to create any major problem,

the response in Swahili, on the contrary, varies considerably, depending on the part of the country: thus, in rural areas in the south, where
Nyakyusa prevails, the correct answers in Swahili amount to 44–56
percent and the response in vernacular instead of Swahili to 32–25 percent (the rest of the answers being invalid); similarly, in Muganza,
near Lake Tanganyika, the scores are respectively 33. 3 percent and
31. 9 percent, and in Bukandwe, near Lake Victoria, 40. 2 percent
and 37. 3 percent. As soon as an area shows a strong Muslim influence, is urbanized, and has lost a marked identity (e.g. Kipampa
and Uvinza, near Lake Tanganyika) or gathers many different groups
in an urban center or rural community (e.g. Magomeni Nursery, in
Dar es Salaam; Bunda, near Lake Victoria), the percentages change
dramatically:

Kipampa	Swahili 95. 6%	Vernacular	0%
Uvinza	Swahili 88. 8%	Vernacular	0. 4%
Magomeni Nursery	Swahili 88. 5%	Vernacular	0%
Bunda	Swahili 87. 7%	Vernacular	3. 3%

Distance from the coast is also an important factor as is demonstrated
by the scores of Mwakidila (suburb of Tanga), Lusanga (22 miles from
Tanga), Mgombezi (further inland), and Lushoto (in the Usambara
mountains, 100 miles from the coast):

Mwakidila	Swahili 97. 9%	Vernacular	0%
Lusanga	Swahili 91. 0%	Vernacular	1. 0%
Mgombezi	Swahili 86. 4%	Vernacular	1. 9%
Lushoto	Swahili 67. 9%	Vernacular 17. 7%

[17] Further indices of command of a language would be "spon-
taneously thinking or dreaming" in this language, but this criterion
can be contextually restricted, e.g. a Chaga informant indicated
that he dreamt about his girlfriend in his mother tongue, but his
nightly concerns about his job came up in Swahili. Other forms of oral
performance, such as singing and praying, can point to a different
type of familiarity with the language, e.g. a Muslim will pray in
Arabic, even if his knowledge of that language is minimal, because
he memorized the text of the relevant prayer in Quranic school.
[18] A medical assistant in the Gogo-speaking area near Dodoma,
who never used English either in his professional or in his social activities, indicated that, in his dreams, English sentences would occasionally flash through his mind.

[19]Seven-vowel languages would, for example, blur the contrast between /ɛ/ and /e/, and /ɔ/ and /o/; such sounds as [ʊ] would be reproduced either as < b > or < v >. For the mother-tongue speaker, these orthographic approximations or loss of phonemes in the transliteration never seemed to constitute a serious obstacle to comprehension.

[20]This will occur particularly where smaller, not necessarily related groups come in contact. More complex links can even develop along these lines, e.g. a Sandawe farmer married a Maasai woman and, later, gave in turn his daughter in marriage to a Maasai, both families, his own and his daughter's, being perfectly bilingual in Sandawe and Maasai and using both languages at home.

[21]There are actually considerable differences in attitude: besides this progressive attitude geared to serve the national purpose in making Swahili the first language of the upcoming generation, there is a whole gamut of diverging positions. About four-fifths of the last-year students in the teachers training colleges interviewed on a person-to-person basis in 1970 declared that they would make their children learn their mother tongue as well as Swahili, though they would give the national language priority. The motivation was most often self-identification, the vernacular being the genuine bearer of traditions; important also was the need for the child to be able to communicate adequately with his/her grandparents, whose knowledge of Swahili may have been limited. One high government official actually complained about his teenage children's practical ignorance of their vernacular and traditions and felt that a very important part of their heritage was getting lost.

[22]This situation also occurs frequently in dispensaries, where a young boy will accompany his grandfather to the medical assistant's office to explain the older man's ailments in Swahili.

[23]A complete study of language use would also imply the examination of linguistic behavior under emotional stress, e.g. what language does the respondent use when involved in a heated argument; when insulting or cursing someone; when teasing a girl or flirting with her. But coping with such situations within the framework of a survey would be a rather complex and delicate matter.

[24]Standard ratings on lexical and grammatical levels, like those of the Foreign Service Institute in Washington, could not be readily used in surveying Tanzanian multilingualism, but a five-point scale was used to measure the degree of intercommunication between

two languages or dialects from a mother-tongue speaker's point of
view. The method used was to ask a speaker of language A: "If a
story is told to you in language B, can you:

(a) understand every single word and meaning?" (positive answer
    = rated 5)
(b) understand almost everything, though you might miss the mean-
    ing of a few words here and there?" (positive answer = rated 4)
(c) understand the general meaning of the story, though you miss
    quite a few words and phrases?" (positive answer = rated 3)
(d) understand only a few phrases here and there, without being able
    to follow the whole story properly?" (positive answer = rated 2)
(e) catch only a few isolated words, without being able to make any
    sense out of the text?" (positive answer = rated 1).

[25] Less than 5 percent of the children entering primary
schools will make it into secondary schools. Regional distribution
of the students is not too much affected by the location of the latter,
since most of them are boarding schools.
    [26] A sampling of cases may illustrate the situations described:

(a) farmers: Respondent A: scores $V^1 24/25$ $V^2 11/4$; 21-year-old
    Protestant woman, whose first language is Nyambo (the language
    of Karagwe where she has lived all her life), but who also knows
    Haya, the neighboring, closely related language. She was illit-
    erate and unmarried, and she occasionally switched to Haya
    when talking to her parents; otherwise her use of Haya was re-
    stricted to church and socialization at the market.
        Respondent B: scores $V27/23$ $S37/19$; young Catholic woman,
    whose first language is Sabi, though she has a thorough command
    of Swahili and has acquired literacy in it through four years in
    primary school. The pattern indicates a shift to almost exclus-
    ive use of Swahili outside the family circle (she read a lot, in-
    cluding the Swahili-language daily paper Uhuru).
        Respondent C: scores $V^1 13/10$ $V^2 10/2$ $V^3 10/0$ $S32/31$; 38-
    year-old Muslim man, from a bilingual family, using Hehe (V^1),
    which he still speaks with his father and father-in-law, and Swa-
    hili, which was the language of his mother's family. His wife is
    a mother-tongue speaker of Gogo (V^2), but at home she speaks
    only Swahili with her husband and children. Since they live in a
    Kaguru (V^3)-speaking area, this language is also used by him at
    the market and with the people in his neighborhood.

(b) shopkeeper: Respondent's scores: $V^1 26/12$ $V^2 27/11$ $(V^3 7/5$
$V^4 6/3$ $V^5 5/1)$ $S33/13$; 38-year-old Protestant man, from the
Gogo-speaking area; his father was, however, a Hehe. He has
moved around quite a bit in the area and picked up some knowledge of the languages, of which he takes advantage for his trade,
though he is essentially trilingual: Swahili, Hehe (V^1) and Gogo
(V^2); the other languages are Kinga (V^3), Maasai (V^4), and
Nyakyusa (V^5).

(c) village executive officer: Respondent's scores: $V^1 37/27$ $V^2 37/6$
$V^3 37/7$ $V^4 37/6$ $S37/24$; 34-year-old Protestant man from a mixed
marriage (father, Gogo; mother, Hehe). Involved in village matters with Gogo (V^1), Hehe (V^2), Kaguru (V^3), and Nyambwa (V^4),
he has acquired a very thorough command of these languages,
enabling him to translate from Swahili into these vernaculars.
He has only a limited reading knowledge of English (E2).

[27] The data were computerized at the University of London,
and C. P. Hill took care of the graphic representation of the results.
It was planned to include Hadza and Mbugu in the limited analysis,
but the data on these languages proved to be insufficient for this purpose.

[28] Struck (1921) has given a comprehensive survey of the language situation found by the Germans in Tanganyika, with a very useful map of the extent to which Swahili was used, known, or understood
in those days.

[29] Cf., for example, the comments of Lyndon Harries (1969).

[30] The study of Andersson was essentially a group-factor
statistical analysis based on questionnaires listing a set of statements
whose 'truth' was investigated. These questionnaires contained 'negative' statements such as: 'I think that it takes so long to learn Swahili that the attempt is not worth while,' or 'I wish that we had very
little Swahili in school,' or 'I wish that no schoolbooks were written
in Swahili.' Though the same questions were asked about English and
'positive' statements like: 'I think that everyone should be taught Swahili,' or 'I try to do something every day to improve my Swahili vocabulary,' or 'When I think of Swahili I become happy,' it appears that
the Tanzanian authorities were rather displeased with the inquiry and
its focus on the confrontation of English and Swahili at a time when
they were trying their utmost to upgrade Swahili teaching and to give
the language additional prestige and value as a tool of nation-building,

while planning to substitute it gradually for English in secondary education. As a result of their discontent, the team of the Tanzanian
Survey was specifically advised not to conduct research in attitudes
versus languages in the country, especially in the schools.

[31] There is a considerable amount of diversity in the motivation that the younger generation was given for its linguistic behavior
in the late sixties.

In the western part of the country where the Sukuma, Ha,
and Haya continued to find their vernacular 'nicer' than Swahili, they
emphasized the national role of Swahili, its role as means of inter-
groups communication, the possibility to use it in a wider field (e.g.
for writing letters) thanks to education; some even claimed an insufficient knowledge of their own language in 1967 to explain their preference
of Swahili.

In the north, the Chaga, after feeling their language was losing out as a result of the strong action in favor of the national language
in 1966, realized that, ultimately, things were evening out: Swahili
and Chaga each have their area of wider use for communication—the
former, e.g. in the public services; the latter, especially, at home,
in tribal functions, etc. Compulsory education was a decisive factor
for the spread of Swahili, and many youngsters did no longer understand a number of vernacular words used by the older generation.
Some of the younger people remained very attached to their home language, as they were fluent in it and could talk to older people and
understand their interesting tales about traditions.

In the non-Bantu Mbulu-speaking section, Swahili was promoted by education, politics, religion, and the medical service, the
younger people encouraging the older to participate in the Swahili adult
literacy program, but both generations would lapse again into the vernacular at home.

In the east, the older people in Usambara and Uluguru would
use practically only their vernacular, but Muslims would use Swahili.
There again the spread of Swahili depended essentially on education,
with compulsory primary schooling for the younger generation and
literacy programs for the older people. The Christian churches still
used the vernaculars to a large extent, whereas Islam used Swahili
(besides Arabic). The language of politics was basically Swahili. In
1965, when most of the students from this part of the country in Morogoro came from rural areas, they considered their vernacular as the
'nicest' language, but felt it was threatened. In 1967, with a shift to

more urban representatives, a better-balanced view of the situation
is reflected by the data: there is still a high level of language loyalty
to the vernacular in Usambara and Uluguru, and even the younger
generation feels more at ease with friends and older people speaking
its own language, like the majority of the villagers; they will only
shift to Swahili when they feel quite confident in their command of the
language, but may still use the vernacular as a kind of 'secret language' with kinsmen versus outsiders.

In the south, the younger generation is motivated by the following factors in its choice of languages:

Vernacular	Swahili
Ethnic pride: loyalty to vernacular as means of ethnic identification	Nationalism: avoidance of vernacular to prevent identification with specific ethnic group
Village language: famil- iar, more homely	Wider communication: used with people from all parts of the country

After completing primary school, where Swahili is the medium, students tend to use Swahili among themselves, as the population of secondary schools and teacher colleges is linguistically very mixed; this
accounts for their vernacular being largely forgotten by the younger
educated generation.

In the central regions, education, politics, and religion are
major factors in the attitudes versus Swahili and the vernaculars—
the churches shifting rapidly to Swahili. Important also is the rise
of the ethnic group, since members of small groups are usually able
to speak the language of the neighboring larger group or Swahili besides their own vernacular, even if it is non-Bantu, e.g. Sandawe.
Nevertheless, a strong feeling for the place of the ethnic language
remains obvious, though the 1967 figures presumably provide a more
realistic picture of the situation: many feel they can express themselves better in their vernacular (up to 61 percent in 1965), but the
role of Swahili as a uniting factor stressed by TANU slogans and the
influence of multiethnic urban situations strongly favor Swahili. With
a majority of students from rural areas, vernaculars prevail in 1965
(61 percent), but with shift in recruitment to the urban areas and a
change of attitude in 1967, Swahili is preferred by 73.7 percent.
This assessment based on the work of S. Kamatta (West),

S. Shayo and F. Tlemu (North), M. Sempombe (East), G. Haule
(South), and P. Warrantse (Central), valuable as it is, has to be
judged in the right perspective: it elaborates on the personal statements of teachers college students and does not result from field
work covering a random sampling of the Tanzania population. The
data reflect the personal background of these students, but provide
hardly any information on the status of their family and the level of
education of their parents, which are major factors conditioning their
language use. Within these constraints, they are, however, quite
useful, as an illustration of the crisis of linguistic identity that
gripped younger Tanzanians in the late sixties.

[32] On the implementation of this measure at the University
of Dar es Salaam, cf. Brauner 1975: 332-38.

[33] A complete examination of the linguistic situation should
include a special chapter on the Asian minority. For lack of space,
only a short note can be devoted to this important subject (the information recorded here being based mainly on A. O. Kassam's report
on the Asian community in Tanzania (1971), sponsored by the Tanzania
Survey). According to the 1967 census, there were 85,000 Asians living in Tanzania. They speak five different Indian languages or dialects, all of them Indo-Aryan: (1) Kachi (a dialect of Sindhi); (2) Konkani; (3) Gujrati; (4) Punjabi; and (5) Urdu.

The subgroups of the Asian community are not based on linguistic, but on religious differences:

(1) The largest group are the Ismailis—followers of the Aga Khan—
who use mainly Kachi, but many of whom also speak Gujrati and
some Hindi (a number of them migrated in 1964 from Zanzibar
and are mainly using Swahili; otherwise, Swahili, in which they
are most fluent, is not used at home); they used to have an excellent education system and their command of English is usually
excellent.

(2) Among the Muslims, four subgroups are further to be distinguished:
(a) the Ithnaasheries (Sunni Muslims) who are mostly bilingual—
Gujrati and Swahili (30 percent of them migrated from Zanzibar)—and use Kachi and read Quranic Arabic, besides having
some Persian, Hindi, and Urdu, and often a fair reading knowledge of English;
(b) the Bohoras, native speakers of Gujrati, with a fair knowledge
of English and a lesser command of Swahili;

(c) the Kachi-speaking Sunnis, 40 percent of whom are literate in
   Gujrati, whereas all can read Quranic Arabic and their level
   of competence in English depends on education;
(d) the Urdu-speaking Sunnis, showing the same proficiency in
   reading Quranic Arabic and command of English determined by
   educational background, and mostly able to read and write Urdu.
(3) Gujrati is also the language of the Parsees and the Hindus:
   (a) the Parsees are Indian Zoroastrians, whose sacred writings are
      still in Avestan, but in Gujrati or English script; their command
      of English is usually excellent, but they have hardly any know-
      ledge of Swahili;
   (b) the Hindus are essentially Vaishnavites, whose community
      association—the Arya Samaj—runs classes in Hindi, Gujrati,
      and Sanskrit so that some of them can read the Bhagavadgita
      in the original text and many speak Hindi besides Gujrati;
      a subgroup—the Bhattias (Lohanas)—speaks Kachi. The Hindus
      are usually able to speak English fluently, but they hardly read
      it; Swahili is neglected.
(4) The Sikhs constitute a separate group with their own beliefs; their
   mother tongue is Punjabi, but they have an excellent command of
   Swahili, and many have become fluent and literate in English as
   well. Those more recently arrived from India also know Urdu,
   which they studied at school there.
(5) The Goans are Roman Catholic; though they still speak the Konkan-
   ese of their original homeland, English is their mother tongue for
   all practical purposes. Many also know Portuguese.

Until 1961, Asian education was separate from African education
(Cameron and Dodd 1970: 125), and social contacts between Africans
and Asians were minimal: the various closely knit Asian groups were
very community-minded and intermarriage did not occur. In their
professional activities, the level and depth of contact with Africans
was the greatest for the Ithnaasheries, the Sunnis, and the Sikhs; it
was lesser with the Ismailis and the Bohoras, and even more with the
Hindus. The Goans kept quite aloof from the Africans, and the Parsees had practically no relation with them.

   In the new Tanzanian society many forces are at work to
break the barriers to interracial social mingling, but will this lead in
the long run to genuine social integration of the Asians? (Ghai 1969:
103-6) A first consequence would certainly be an improved knowledge
of Swahili, which in many cases now appears as a mixed language of

Kuchi verbal stems with Swahili morphemes, as in the following examples:

'we will meet'	tutamale	(Kuchi male 'meet')
'to understand'	kusamje	(Kuchi samje 'understand')
'you will come'	utaache	(Kuchi ache 'come')
'it will do'	itahale	(Kuchi hale 'do')

REFERENCES

Andersson, Anders. 1967. Multilingualism and attitudes. An explorative-descriptive study among secondary school students in Ethiopia and Tanzania. Uppsala: Institute of Education, University of Uppsala. [mimeo.]

Angogo, Rachel. 1978. Issues in the use of standard Swahili. Paper presented at the 9th Annual Conference on African Linguistics at East Lansing, Michigan.

Berry, L. 1971. Tanzania in maps. London: University of London Press.

Brauner, Siegmund. 1975. Swahili an der Universität Dar es Salaam. Zeitschrift für Phonetik, Sprachwissenschaft und Kommunikationsforschung 28: 3/4, 331-42.

Cameron, J., and W. A. Dodd. 1970. Society, schools and progress in Tanzania. Oxford: Pergamon Press.

Chamungwana, W. M. Shedu. 1971. Primary school entrants' knowledge and use of Swahili. Research paper submitted to the Tanzania Survey at University of Dar es Salaam. Stenciled [with pictograms].

Cliffe, Lionel, ed. 1967. One party democracy. The 1965 Tanzania General Elections. Nairobi: East African Publishing House.

Dodds, Tony. 1970. Report of a survey of radio ownership and listening habits in Tanzania. Report submitted to the Institute of Adult Education, University of Dar es Salaam. Manuscript (typewritten).

Dryden, Stanley. 1968. Local administration in Tanzania. Nairobi: East African Publishing House.

Ghai, D. P., ed. 1965. Portrait of a minority. The Asians in East Africa. Nairobi: Oxford University Press.

Ghai, Dharam, and Yash Ghai. 1969. Asians in Tanzania: problems
and prospects. In Knud Erik Svendsen and Merete Teisen,
eds., Self-reliant Tanzania. Dar es Salaam: Tanzania Publishing House, pp. 91-110. Published previously in Journal
of Modern African Studies 3:1 (1965): 35-51.
Harries, Lyndon. 1969. Language policy in Tanzania. Africa 39:
275-79.
Hatfield, C. R. 1972a. The agent of change. The agent of conflict.
Paper presented at the Third World Congress for Rural Sociology, Louisiana State University, Baton Rouge.
_____. 1972b. Livestock development in Sukumaland: the constitu-
ents of communication. I. Interface structuring and the development process. Paper presented at the Third World Con-
gress for Rural Sociology, Louisiana State University, Baton
Rouge.
Herrick, Allison Butler, et al. 1968. Area handbook for Tanzania.
Washington, D. C.: U. S. Government Printing Office.
Hyden, Göran. 1969. Political development in rural Tanzania.
TANU yajenga nchi. Nairobi: East African Publishing House
[focuses on Uhaya].
Ingle, Clyde R. 1972. From village to state in Tanzania. The poli-
tics of rural development. Ithaca, N. Y.: Cornell University
Press.
Ishige, Naomichi. 1969. On Swahilization. Kyoto University African
Studies 3: 93-108.
Kassam, A. O. 1971. The linguistic system within the Asian commun-
ity in Tanzania (with particular reference to Dar es Salaam).
Report submitted to the Tanzania Survey. Manuscript [mimeo.].
Kurtz, Laura S. 1972. An African education. The social revolution
in Tanzania. Brooklyn, N. Y.: Poseidon Ltd.
Legère, Karsten. 1975. Zum Verhältnis zwischen dem Swahili und
anderen tanzanischen Sprachen. Zeitschrift für Phonetik,
Sprachwissenschaft und Kommunikationsforschung 28: 3/4:
343-48.
Liebenow, J. Gus. 1971. Colonial rule and political development in
Tanzania. The case of the Makonde. Nairobi: East African
Publishing House.
MacDonald, Alexander. 1966. Tanzania: Young nation in a hurry.
New York: Hawthorn Books.

Maguire, G. Andrew. 1969. Toward 'Uhuru' in Tanzania. The poli-
     tics of participation. Cambridge: University Press [focuses
     on Sukumaland].
Mbilinyi, Marjorie J. 1969. The education of girls in Tanzania. A
     study of attitudes of Tanzanian girls and their fathers towards
     education. Dar es Salaam: Institute of Education, University
     College.
Mittelmeyer, J., et al. 1967. Growth of Swahili. Language situation
     and attitudes towards dialects and Swahili, 1965-1967. Moro-
     goro: Teachers' College, Linguistics Department [unpublished
     typewritten manuscript].
Mlay, Hezekiah, and David Mkindi. 1970. An investigation into the
     pattern of language use of a number of multilinguals in Tan-
     zania through keeping of linguistic diaries. Report submitted
     to the Tanzania Survey. Manuscript [stenciled].
Molnos, Angela. 1969. Language problems in Africa. A bibliography
     (1946-1967) and summary of the present situation with spec-
     ial reference to Kenya, Tanzania, and Uganda. (EARIC In-
     formation Circular No. 2.) Nairobi: East African Research
     Information Centre, The East African Academy.
Mytton, Graham L. 1969. Tanzania: A mass media audience survey.
     Some preliminary results and observations. Manuscript
     (typewritten).
_____. 1970. Tanzania: The problems of mass media development,
     pp. 89-100 [xerox].
Ntemo, Finehas D. 1964. The language situation in Tanganyika.
     Report submitted to the Institute of Education, University of
     Exeter (Great Britain). Manuscript [stenciled].
Nyerere, Julius K. 1967. Freedom and unity. Uhuru na Umoja. A
     selection from writings and speeches, 1952-1965. Dar es
     Salaam: Oxford University Press.
_____. 1968a. Ujamaa. Essays on socialism. Dar es Salaam:
     Oxford University Press.
_____. 1968b. Freedom and socialism. Uhuru na Ujamaa. A selec-
     tion from writings and speeches, 1965-1967. Dar es Salaam:
     Oxford University Press.
_____. 1974. Man and development. Binadamu na Maendeleo.
     London/New York: Oxford University Press.
O'Barr, William M., and Jean F. O'Barr. 1976. Language and pol-

itics. (Contributions to the Sociology of Language, vol. 10.)
The Hague: Mouton.

Polomé, Edgar C. 1973. Sociolinguistic problems in Tanzania and
Zaire. The Conch 4, no. 2 (Sept. 1972): 64-83. (Edited as
separate volume by Sunday O. Anozie under the title: Language systems in Africa.)

_____. 1975. Problems and techniques of a sociolinguistically
oriented language survey: The case of the Tanzania Survey.
In S. Ohannessian, C. Ferguson, and E. Polomé, eds.,
Language surveys in developing nations. Arlington, Va.:
Center for Applied Linguistics, pp. 31-50.

_____. 1980. Swahili in Tanzania. In E. C. Polomé and C. P.
Hill, eds., Language in Tanzania. London: International
African Institute/Oxford University Press, pp. 79-100.

_____. (forthcoming) Rural versus urban multilingualism in Tan-
zania. An outline.

Polomé, Edgar C., André R. Polomé, and Ali Abdullah. 1982. Language and religion in Tanzania. Orbis 32 (forthcoming).

Resnick, Idrian N. 1968. Educational barriers to Tanzania's development. In Idrian N. Resnick, ed., Tanzania: Revolution
by education. Arusha: Longmans of Tanzania, 1968, pp.
123-34.

Rigby, Peter. 1969. Cattle and kinship among the Gogo. A semi-
pastoral society of central Tanzania. Ithaca, N.Y.: Cornell University Press.

Ruthenberg, Hans, ed. 1968. Smallholder farming and smallholder
development in Tanzania. Ten case studies. (IFO-Institut
für Wirtschaftsforschung München-Afrika Studien, vol. 24).
Munich: Weltforum Verlag.

Rweyamamu, E., ed. 1970. Nation-building in Tanzania. Nairobi:
East African Publishing House.

Struck, B. 1921. Die Einheitssprache Deutsch-Ostafrikas. Kolon-
iale Rundschau 1921: 4, 164-96 [with map].

Svendsen, Knud Eric, and Merete Teisen, eds. 1969. Self-reliant
Tanzania. Dar es Salaam: Tanzania Publishing House.

Tordoff, William. 1967. Government and politics in Tanzania.
Nairobi: East African Publishing House.

Widstrand, C. G. 1966a. Radio and adult education in Tanzania:
Some considerations. (Adult Education Studies, No. 1.)

Dar es Salaam: Institute of Adult Education, University
College.

Widstrand, C. G. 1966b. Development by exhortation. A study of
nation-building over the radio in Tanzania. Paper given at
the Social Science Council Conference organized by the University of East Africa in Nairobi. Typescript draft.

Yoneyama, Toshinao. 1969. The life and society of the Iraqw—
Introductory remarks. Kyoto University African Studies,
pp. 77-114.

1960. Listener Research Survey—Tanganyika Broadcasting Corporation. Dar es Salaam: Market Research Company (MARCO)
of East Africa.

1968. Tanzania today. Nairobi: University Press of Africa (for the
Ministry of Tourism, United Republic of Tanzania).

1969. 1967 Population Census. Vol. 1, Statistics for enumeration
areas. Dar es Salaam: Central Statistical Bureau, Ministry
of Economic Affairs and Development Planning.

1969. Quotations from President Julius K. Nyerere. Morogoro:
Teachers' College.

1970. The Economic Survey and Annual Plan, 1970-71. The United
Republic of Tanzania. Dar es Salaam: The Government
Printer.

1970/71. Press Directory. United Republic of Tanzania. Dar es
Salaam: Information Services Division.

1971. Ostafrika: Sprachraum des Suaheli. (Special number of the
Zeitschrift für Kulturaustausch, with contributions of E.
Dammann [language and religion], W. Küper [on education],
H. Helmschrott [on economic development], etc.) Stutt-
gart: Institut für Auslandsbeziehungen.

8 | Sociolinguistically Oriented Language Surveys: Reflections on the Survey of Language Use and Language Teaching in Eastern Africa

1. A Few Preliminary Remarks

Though a number of sociolinguistically oriented language surveys have been conducted elsewhere in the world—from the Philippines to Belize—none is comparable in size, scope, impact, financial support, and manpower input to the Survey of Language Use and Language Teaching in Eastern Africa conducted in 1968-71 with a generous grant from the Ford Foundation under the sponsorship of the African institutions of higher learning in the countries surveyed: Ethiopia, Kenya, Tanzania, Uganda, and Zambia. The complex administrative procedures, which included preliminary meetings of an Advisory Committee, the establishment of a central office in Nairobi with a Field Director and staff, regular meetings of a Survey Council with representatives of the various countries involved, backstopping operations by the University of California at Los Angeles and the Center for Applied Linguistics, need not be discussed in this context.[1] More important are the aims assigned to the Survey and the methods used to attain them, since they throw a particular light on the theoretical background of the techniques of sociolinguistic surveys and may allow certain interesting generalizations.

Actually, the aims of the Survey of Language Use and Language Teaching in Eastern Africa, as agreed upon by representatives of the Universities of Ethiopia, Kenya, Tanzania, Uganda, and Zambia, went far beyond the collection and adequate presentation of data: it was expected to act as a catalyst to stimulate linguistic, sociolinguistic, and pedagogical work in the five countries under consideration and to create links between scholars in Africa, across national and disciplinary boundaries, while contributing to the development of the manpower

resources of each country in the field of language study. While such
results would normally be the practical outcome of the collaboration
of the research teams with the local language specialists and educational authorities, they were pursued as a major goal in the Eastern
African Survey, and Clifford Prator, the first Field Director—himself
a specialist in the Teaching of English as a Second Language—considers (1975: 147) that this strengthening of local resources may well
turn out to have been more significant than the gathering of research
data.

Obviously, the first task of a country language survey is, as
Ferguson (1975: 2) puts it: 'to determine which are the major languages of the country and to assemble the basic sociolinguistic information about them.' This includes, in particular, the attitudes of the
people on language use—a major factor in the effectiveness of any language policy. And in Africa, where linguistic diversity is a problem
practically every developing country has to cope with, it would stand
to reason that it is essential to know the actual linguistic situation
before formulating a meaningful language policy. However, the matter of language choice is not always decided on a purely rational basis:
strong emotional undercurrents may motivate a policy decision, and
a total awareness of the situation is important to understand the language planning and its implementation as reflected, for example, in
the educational policies of the country. Thus, when Swahili is confronted with the tribal languages and with English, the use of each
language does not only become functional in a specific social domain:
each language is emotionally associated with that domain, and with
its new symbolic value it can serve political ends; if Swahili is associated with independence and nation building, English is to be rejected
as the language of the 'colonialists' and the local languages smack of
tribalism, but if the true spirit of Africanness is emphasized, the
tribal language can best express it—Swahili is alien to the local culture,
and English just serves the purpose of efficiency in conducting trade
and government business. The educational system is then geared to
whatever solution has been chosen, and all the techniques of language
engineering locally available and applicable are put to work to implement the policy chosen. But, as Whiteley (1974: 2) pointed out, there
is a limit to the extent to which government may control language use
through the educational system, by passing edicts, or by setting examples: 'if the choice of language runs counter to prevailing patterns of

language use, then the language will only be used in those contexts
where some degree of enforcement can be assured. ... The use of
language in a community, therefore, is likely to be surrounded with
many and conflicting emotions, and to serve as an expression of tensions in social life for which no alternative outlet is available.'

These premises set forth some basic prerequisites to a
sociolinguistically oriented survey: to study language in its social
context on a country-wide scale, it is necessary to have a comprehensive knowledge and understanding of the country and its people, of its
economy, of the fabric of the nation, of the historical development of
its policies and government administration, as well as of its education
system. Perhaps one of the best presentations of such basic information available for a subsaharan African country is the first part of
Cameron and Dodd's study of the development of education in Tanzania
(1970). William Labov (1972: 110-11) has always stressed his indebt-
edness to prior sociological studies for the elaboration of his studies
on the Lower East Side of New York City, which illustrate the close
relation between linguistic features and extralinguistic social factors.
One of the first tasks of the scholar involved in a sociolinguistic survey is accordingly to familiarize himself thoroughly with all the aspects
of the sociocultural, political, economical, and religious life of the
speech community he is about to investigate, and to probe into its
past, when necessary to account for present-day situations.

2. Basic Research in the Eastern Africa Survey

The structure of the country surveys in correlation with the
first aim of the Eastern Africa Language Survey, i.e. 'to gather and
disseminate basic information on the use and teaching of languages,'
consisted essentially of three parts: (1) a description of the linguistic
situation in the country; (2) a study of language use; (3) an examination
of the role of language in education. Though each team in the field
resorted to some specific techniques geared to the special situations
they encountered in their respective countries, their approach was by
and large governed by the same basic principles, partly as a result
of the methodological and theoretical discussion of the Advisory Committee prior to the beginning of the Survey, partly as a consequence
of the similar background and training in descriptive linguistics, sociolinguistics, and applied linguistics of the participants.[2]

Table 1. Percent Words in Common Among Ugandan Bantu Languages

	Lumasaba	Lunyole	Lusamia	Lugwe	Lugwere	Lukenyi	Lusoga	Luganda	Ruruli	Runyoro	Rutooro	Ruhororo	Rutagwenda	Runyankore	Rukiga	Lubwisi	Runyarwanda	Rukonjo	Rugungu	Rwamba	Mean
Lumasaba	—	54	70	74	74	64	55	54	49	48	50	49	49	49	49	44	46	38	34	21	51
Lunyole	54	—	80	82	64	76	70	66	58	55	59	56	55	56	56	50	49	44	51	22	58
Lusamia	70	80	—	92	60	62	64	61	52	54	56	55	55	57	55	47	50	44	45	22	56
Lugwe	74	82	92	—	60	63	65	62	56	54	56	55	55	57	55	48	49	45	48	22	58
Lugwere	74	64	60	60	—	76	70	66	66	56	60	54	54	51	54	49	47	54	54	23	57
Lukenyi	64	76	62	63	76	—	81	74	66	61	60	60	59	57	61	51	48	49	55	23	60
Lusoga	55	70	64	65	70	81	—	86	62	68	64	66	64	64	67	56	53	53	55	27	63
Luganda	54	66	61	62	66	74	86	—	62	65	64	66	63	63	68	54	50	51	54	24	61
Ruruli	49	58	52	56	66	65	65	62	—	71	69	67	67	65	68	58	54	54	60	31	59
Runyoro	48	55	54	54	56	61	68	65	71	—	93	86	90	86	87	72	62	64	64	33	67
Rutooro	50	59	56	56	60	60	64	64	69	93	—	84	91	86	85	73	60	63	65	32	66
Ruhororo	49	56	55	55	54	60	66	66	67	86	84	—	91	96	96	67	63	61	56	30	66
Rutagwenda	49	55	55	55	54	59	64	63	67	90	91	91	—	93	90	70	60	64	60	31	66
Runyankore	49	56	57	57	51	57	64	63	65	86	86	96	93	—	94	67	65	62	54	30	67
Rukiga	49	56	55	55	54	61	67	68	68	87	85	96	90	94	—	68	64	63	59	31	66
Lubwisi	44	50	47	48	49	51	56	54	58	72	73	67	60	67	68	—	55	57	49	31	57
Runyarwanda	46	49	50	49	47	48	53	50	54	62	60	63	60	65	64	55	—	64	54	38	53
Rukonjo	38	44	44	45	54	49	53	51	54	64	63	61	64	62	63	57	64	—	52	34	53
Rugungu	34	51	45	48	54	55	55	54	60	64	65	56	60	54	59	49	54	52	—	29	53
Rwamba	21	22	22	22	23	23	27	24	31	33	32	30	31	30	31	31	38	34	29	—	28

Source: Ladefoged et al. 1972, Table 2.11.

2.1. The Language Situation

Traditionally, such a section would contain:

(a) a listing of the languages with their dialects and location, and the latest census figures available;
(b) an attempt at classification (with a family tree) and the relevant historical comments;
(c) short descriptions of selected characteristic languages of the major subgroups.

The first part of the Ethiopia volume (Bender et al. 1976: 1-180) at first sight appears to fit that pattern, but upon closer examination it is obvious that there is much more to it which is also characteristic of other volumes of the Survey, i.e. a new technique of classification based on feature distribution and shared basic vocabulary. It was initiated by Peter Ladefoged in the Uganda volume (1972: 51-84) as part of a method to establish statistically significant differences between languages. As it had appeared that subjective answers to questions on mutual intelligibility provided only quantitatively unreliable data,[3] Ladefoged compared lists of words, measuring 'the degree of likeness between two languages by taking a list of meanings and counting the number of similar words which have the same area of meaning in the two languages.' By pairing all the languages of an area and measuring their percentage of shared vocabulary, it is possible to map out the degree of similarity between any two languages on a two-dimensional chart, as shown in Table 1. The method was applied in great detail in an attempt to improve the classification of the languages of Ethiopia by Marvin L. Bender (1971; 1976: 53-58); it was used by Mubanga Kashoki and Michael Mann to sketch the relationship between 25 Zambian languages and/or dialects (1978: 50-60), and Gerard Philippson and Derek Nurse refined it further when they applied it to the study of the classification of the Bantu languages of Tanzania (1980: 26-67).

Though the method provides data that correspond satisfactorily to the geographical distribution of the languages and to the degree of comprehension of the target language relative to the informant's first language, when subjects are tested on their understanding of recordings of stories, it shows some major weaknesses:

Table 2. The Classification of the Places of Articulation
Required for the Description of Ugandan Bantu Languages

Example	Phonetic term	Characteristic Features		
		anterior	alveolar	coronal
b	labial	+	−	−
d+	dental	+	−	+
d	alveolar	+	+	+
d−	postalveolar	−	+	+
j	palatal	−	−	+
g	velar	−	−	−

Table 3. The Classification of Some Manners of Articulation
Required for the Description of Ugandan Bantu Languages

Example	Phonetic term	Characteristic Features		
		nasal	stop	fricative
n	nasal	+	−	−
nz	nasal compound fricative	+	−	+
nd	nasal compound stop	+	+	−
d	stop	−	+	−
j	affricate	−	+	+
z	fricative	−	−	+
l/r	approximant	−	−	−

Table 4. The Degree of Similarity Between Some Consonant
Segments in Ugandan Bantu Languages

	d+	d	d−	j	g	dy	dw	dd	dz	z	nz	l	r	h	s	sh	sy	shy
b	9	8	7	7	9	7	7	7	7	6	5	7	6	7	5	4	4	3
d+		9	8	8	8	8	8	8	8	7	6	8	7	6	6	5	5	4
d			9	7	7	9	9	9	9	8	7	9	8	5	7	6	6	5
d−				8	8	8	8	8	7	6	8	7	6	6	7	5	6	
j					8	6	6	6	8	7	6	6	7	6	6	7	5	6
g						6	6	6	6	5	4	6	7	8	4	5	3	4
dy							8	8	8	7	6	8	7	4	6	5	7	6
dw								8	7	6	8	7	4	6	5	5	4	
dd									8	7	6	8	7	4	6	5	5	4
dz										9	8	8	7	4	8	7	7	6
z											9	9	8	5	9	8	8	7
nz												8	7	4	8	7	7	6
l													9	6	8	7	7	6
r														7	7	8	6	7
h															6	7	5	6
s																9	9	8
sh																	8	9
sy																		9

Sources for Tables 2-4: Ladefoged et al. 1972, Tables
2.6, 2.7, 2.8.

(1) though the basic vocabulary is theoretically more resistant to change through contact, experience has shown that even the Swadesh list is in many respects culture-bound and therefore less reliable than often assumed for historical relationships;

(2) lexical correspondences may be due to borrowing instead of historical relationship: if it is fairly easy to recognize recent Swahili loans, what about possible interdialectal borrowing ?[4]

Another method resorted to by Ladefoged (1970; 1972: 62-65, 77-78) is using the measure of the degree of phonetic similarity. To do so, he carefully charted the features of articulation characteristic of the Bantu languages of Uganda and determined the total number of features shared by each set of two phonemes in these languages. For the consonants, the resulting tabulation appeared as shown in Tables 2-4—which enabled Ladefoged (1972: 78) to chart the relationship between the Ugandan Bantu languages according to the matrix shown in Table 5. Though Robert Hetzron and Marvin L. Bender briefly examine the possibility of classifying the Ethio-Semitic languages on the basis of phonological correspondences (Bender et al. 1976: 30-33), they do not follow Ladefoged's model. Similarly, Whiteley's feature analysis of the characteristics of the Kenya language groups (1974: 14-26) follows another model, namely Guthrie's, who uses phonological, morphological, and syntactic features for comparison. Particularly interesting is the fact that using such diagnostic features as criteria in the same way as Murray Emeneau had done it for India (1956), Charles Ferguson defines Ethiopia as a language area characterized by eight phonological features and 18 grammatical features (1976).[5]

More sociolinguistically oriented is the approach of Whiteley (1974: 26-54), when he tackles the problem of size, distribution, and homogeneity of the linguistic groups in Kenya. It is based on a set of premises assumed to determine the incidence of monolingualism versus multilingualism:

High monolingualism	High multilingualism
Linguistically homogeneous community	Linguistically heterogeneous community
Access to education limited in duration and availability	Unlimited and protracted access to education

Table 5. The Degree of Phonetic Similarity Between Some Ugandan Bantu Languages

	Lumasaba (S)	Lumasaba (N)	Lunyole	Lusamia	Lugwe	Lugwere	Lukenyi	Lusoga	Luganda	Ruruli	Runyoro	Rutooro	Ruhororo	Runyankore	Rukiga	Lubwisi	Runyarwanda	Rukonjo	Rugungu	Rwamba	Mean
Lumasaba (S)	—	85	76	78	81	73	79	76	74	73	71	77	72	73	69	69	68	69	60	47	73
Lumasaba (N)	85	—	82	78	80	78	83	81	79	74	77	80	77	82	83	71	75	68	68	52	76
Lunyole	76	82	—	88	87	76	81	85	80	71	73	77	70	73	75	67	73	65	63	46	74
Lusamia	78	78	88	—	97	75	80	83	80	71	72	75	71	71	76	67	73	65	62	48	74
Lugwe	81	80	87	97	—	74	82	81	79	71	72	75	72	74	77	68	75	66	62	48	75
Lugwere	73	78	76	75	74	—	81	75	75	80	73	76	71	77	74	74	71	65	63	48	72
Lukenyi	79	83	81	80	82	81	—	85	84	78	79	82	77	81	83	71	75	70	67	50	77
Lusoga	76	81	85	83	81	75	85	—	82	75	74	77	74	78	77	70	74	68	65	50	75
Luganda	74	79	80	80	79	75	84	82	—	72	80	82	78	78	81	70	65	67	61	46	74
Ruruli	73	74	71	71	71	80	78	75	72	—	77	76	71	77	71	74	66	67	65	52	72
Runyoro	71	77	73	72	72	73	79	74	80	77	—	93	87	88	86	76	75	70	70	46	76
Rutooro	77	80	77	75	75	76	82	77	82	76	93	—	88	90	88	77	76	71	67	47	77
Ruhororo	72	77	70	71	72	71	77	74	78	71	87	88	—	90	87	70	75	71	64	46	77
Runyankore	73	82	73	71	74	77	81	78	78	77	88	90	90	—	86	77	75	74	66	52	77
Rukiga	69	83	75	76	77	74	83	77	81	71	86	88	87	86	—	74	80	69	68	50	74
Lubwisi	69	71	67	67	68	74	71	70	70	74	76	77	70	77	74	—	69	66	67	55	70
Runyarwanda	68	75	73	73	75	71	75	74	65	66	75	76	75	75	80	69	—	70	67	48	71
Rukonjo	69	68	65	65	66	65	70	68	67	67	70	71	71	74	69	66	70	—	64	48	67
Rugungu	60	68	63	62	62	63	67	65	61	65	70	67	64	66	68	67	67	64	—	44	63
Rwamba	47	52	46	48	48	48	50	50	46	52	46	47	46	52	50	55	48	48	44	—	48

Source: Ladefoged et al. 1972, Table 2.14.

High monolingualism (cont.)   High multilingualism (cont.)

Poor communications and little   Good communications and various
  incentive to use them   incentives to use them
Low personal mobility   High personal mobility
Strong constraints against   Strong encouragement to speak a par-
  using other languages   ticular language, e.g. the official
                                       language of the country

Using five point scales, Whiteley then tried to assess the rate of competence and the frequency of use of each language spoken by his informants.[8] He then tabulated the claimed competence in the various languages for 20 samples of households in core dialectal areas and three
in border areas according to their particular levels and patterns of
competence,[7] obtaining the diagram, shown in Figure 1, of the language
situation in rural Kenya as a result (Whiteley 1974: 54).

As regards the historical background of the language situation,
the Eastern Africa Language Survey made some minor contributions in
providing brief historical notes, e.g. on the peoples of Zambia (Kashoki 1978: 9-15). In the case of Tanzania, two questions received special attention: the earliest attestations of Swahili (Polomé 1978) and
the language policy of the German colonial administration (Brumfit
1971).[8] The problem of Bantu migrations for which J. C. Sharman
ventured a new hypothesis in the Kenya volume (1974) is briefly tackled

Level of language competence   Particular pattern of competence

Monolingual   L1
                            (Luo, Meru (a), Kipsigis, Kuria)

Bilingual   L1 + Eng.   L1 + L2   L1 + Sw.
              (Luo, Gusii border) (Kamba, borders) (Pokomo, Gusii)

Trilingual   L1 + L2 + Eng.   L1 + L2 + L3   L1 + L2 + Sw.
              (Luo, Gusii border) (Logoli, borders) (Luyia (Khayo),
                                                       Pokomo (Zubaki))

Quadrilingual   L1 + L2 + Eng. + Sw.
                                (Embu, Kamba (Kambai),
                                 Luyia/Luo border,
                                 Luyia (Logoli))

Fig. 1. Language situation in rural Kenya (Whiteley 1974: 54).

by E. Polomé (1980: 19-21) in the Tanzania volume, after being discussed in detail elsewhere (1975a, 1977).

2.2. Language Use

As Donald Bowen (1975: 15) points out, the 'consumer' has
a legitimate role to play in focusing the research on matters of interest to him, so that he may obtain relevant information to help him
make and carry out decisions relating to language use in the community. The sociolinguist is also expected to provide the 'consumer' with
relevant alternative courses of action, but to carefully avoid trying
to guide policy.

In order to make such reliable sociolinguistic information
available, the sociolinguist has to analyze the various facets of linguistic activity within the community. Discussing the ways the information provided by sociolinguistic surveys can be used by a society
or a government, Sirarpi Ohannessian and Gilbert Ansre (1975: 52-
54) show how they 'provide insights into attitudes, trends of thought,
and directions of social and other change,' which 'make it possible to
influence opinion for the benefit of the nation.' Among the important
indices of attitudes, the pattern of behavior toward a variety of language in multilingual settings is particularly instructive: how do
people 'feel' about the standard language versus substandard varieties
(social dialects, creole, pidgin, lingua franca); about the 'national
language' versus their mother tongue, etc. How much does change in
social setting affect their language loyalty? Such a question also
points to language affiliation as a correlate of group identity, the degree of adherence and integration being measured by the rejection of
former patterns of linguistic behavior. As a case in point, Ohannessian and Ansre (1975: 53) stress the frequent occurrence of significantly different language use in religious communities.

Studies covering this type of linguistic behavior would belong
to the field of macro-sociolinguistics, which encompasses numerically sizable communities, such as ethnic groups, or, in the case of the
Eastern Africa Language Survey, whole nations, and tries to provide
extensive quantifiable data on their broader characteristics, such as
percentages of mother-tongue speakers claiming various numbers of
second languages or self-assessed degrees of proficiency in various

languages in a definite set of social contexts (Polomé 1975b: 40-42).
There are, however, other domains of language behavior that need to
be examined carefully in a sociolinguistic survey, namely the 'specific
sets of role-relations which are culturally designated as belonging to
a particular sphere of activities' (Parkin 1974a: 134). These studies
in social interaction which involve detailed analyses of language use
in role relations at home, at school, at church, at the work place, in
the neighborhood, in public places, etc. are described as <u>micro-socio-
linguistics</u>. Analyzing multilingual settings to recognize the variables
that determine <u>who</u> speaks <u>what</u> to <u>whom</u> and <u>when</u> in speech communities characterized by widespread and relatively stable multilingualism,
Joshua Fishman (1972b) attempted to reconcile the macro- and micro-
sociolinguistic approaches, producing Cooper's diagram (see Fig. 2)
as a model for research and analysis (Fishman 1972b: 452; Parkin
1974a: 134).

Correlating the anthropological view of speaking as the utili-
zation of a speech community's cultural resources with the studies
linking language style to social status and mobility, Parkin (1974a:
137-40) maps sociolinguistic research as follows:

A. Language <u>shift</u>:
    (a) language <u>adding</u>   ⎱ converse: language <u>stability</u>
    (b) language <u>substitution</u> ⎰
B. Language/dialect/code <u>switches</u>, i.e. small group/dyadic transactional speech patterns seen in <u>parole</u>.
C. Socially determined <u>linguistic changes</u>, i.e. specific lexical, syntactic, and phonological alterations in <u>langue</u>.

Having defined the two major organizing principles of social life in
Nairobi as 'ethnic affiliation' and 'membership of a status-group,' he
can then show how socioeconomic status factors are crucial in language
adding, with little regard for the ethnic variable in the Bahati housing
estate in Nairobi (Parkin 1974b), whereas an interplay of ethnic and
status variables determines language adding (and the limited language
'substitution') in the ethnically mixed and socioeconomically more
heterogeneous speech community of Kaloleni (Parkin 1974c).

In Ethiopia, the Survey team focused its attention on the impact of migration and urbanization on language shift and on comparing

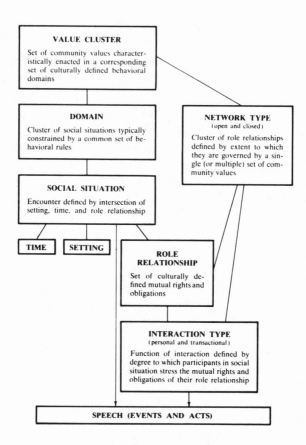

Fig. 2. Relationships among some constructs employed in sociolinguistic analysis (Cooper 1968). Source: Fishman 1972b, Fig. 15.1.

the language situations of town and countryside. In conclusion of a statistical analysis of percentages of mother-tongue groups in 188 towns and in the capital, Addis Ababa, compared with the national percentages, Robert L. Cooper and Ronald J. Howath stated (Bender et al. 1976: 212): 'Whether or not language shift eventually occurs among the country's non-Amharic groups ..., the process of urbanization is likely to act as an agent for the spread of Amharic as a second language, i.e. a language which people speak in addition to their mother-tongue.'

In a further pilot study of towns and the neighboring rural areas in Kefa and Arusi province, R. L. Cooper, B. N. Singh, and A. Ghermazion (Bender et al. 1976: 213-43) provided an eloquent illustration of the contrast between the linguistically homogeneous, largely Galla-speaking countryside, marked by monolingualism, and the linguistically diverse towns, marked by bilingualism, with Amharic playing a prominent role as first and second language. The outcome of this inquiry was that, while Amharic mother-tongue speakers would be more likely to know Galla if they lived in the countryside, and Galla mother-tongue speakers would mostly acquire Amharic as a second language if they lived in towns, Amharic appeared to exert a greater pressure than Galla, as Amharic was the prestige language as the country's official language, with the backing of the numerically largest and politically most influential group as well as a long written tradition.

The problem of switching falls directly within the scope of ethnography of communication: the kinds of situations involved have been illustrated by numerous studies in recent years (Gumperz and Hymes 1964; 1972; Baumann and Sherzer 1974; etc.). In the case of Nairobi, D. J. Parkin (Whiteley 1974: 189-215) analyzed a set of transactional and non-transactional conversations, which involve:

(a) joking about ethnic and status differences as a technique to cope with the particular sensitivities attached to group loyalties and prestige competitions;
(b) highlighting ethnic group affiliation and personal socioeconomic status ties.[9]

Use of the vernacular will enhance ethnic identification; Swahili and English are more likely to symbolize specific individual interests. The necessity of studying 'switches' in the wider frame of code choice and code mixing in multilingual settings is illustrated by M. H. Abdulaziz-Mkilifi's exploratory examinations of the Tanzania situation (1972).

Various techniques were applied to analyze micro-sociolinguistic situations: in the Tanzania survey, linguistic diaries were kept, reporting all activities during workdays and holidays and the language used in each case, providing specific data on any motivation for switching when possible, but the results did not throw any new light on the sociopsychological conditions that triggered switching in the Tanzanian context (Polomé 1980: 109).

Another favorite approach was market surveys: the technique was elaborated by Robert L. Cooper and Susan Carpenter (Bender et al. 1976: 244-55) and consisted in observing a number of market transactions in various languages on a specific market day, tallying the languages used with the commodities sold and/or the services performed. The results were extremely interesting:

(a) apparently no specific language (Amharic or Arabic) served as trade language;

(b) handicrafts and trades being along ethnic lines in Ethiopia, buyer and seller transact their business in a common language, because the seller, as a rule, accommodates himself to the buyer by speaking his (first) language.

From a more general point of view, this study indicates that heterogeneous market settings do not necessarily entail the development of a lingua franca (Bender et al. 1972: 227).

It is a standing feature of sociolinguistic surveys to study multilingualism in various contexts: public places, courts of law, factories, churches, educational institutions, etc. (Polomé 1975: 44-45). The Tanzania Survey went in great detail into court procedures at all levels of the judiciary system and observed language use in the various phases of trials, e.g. complaint of plaintiff, interrogation of defendant, deposition of witnesses, indictment, pleas, sentencing, taking careful notice of the respective use of English and Swahili, and of the intervention of interpreters to translate statements from or into the vernaculars. The picture that emerges is that of a rather fluid situation in which Swahili still has a long way to go to prevail above the level of the district court.[10] The Ethiopian Survey is the only one which addressed the problem of language and factory workers directly (Robert L. Cooper and B. N. Singh, in Bender et al. 1976: 264-72), though it might have been instructive to examine the language situation in the Zambian Copperbelt in the same way as it has been studied in the Shaba province of Zaire (Polomé 1969; Heine 1970: 88-89; Polomé 1971; Heine 1979: 85-86).[11]

As for language and religion, considerable attention was devoted to the topic by different survey teams, though their approach was in many respects different: Janet Bujra (in Whiteley 1974: 217-52) is

interested in assessing the influence of adherence to Islam on language
loyalties in the predominantly Muslim estate of Pumwani in Nairobi,
and she examines to what extent Swahili is ousting the tribal languages
as a medium of communication not only between different ethnic groups
but within the same ethnic group. Arabic has an aura of religious prestige and power, but is obviously little known except for prayers and
Quranic lines learned by rote. Swahili, then, appears as a cultural
marker: it symbolizes the Islamic community in its shared cultural
values despite its extremely diverse ethnic make-up. David Aoko (in
Whiteley 1974: 253-62) looks at the African Independent Churches which
mushroomed in Nairobi by breaking away from established Christian
churches: he lists 17 of them, with a total membership of 2, 345, distributed over 44 congregations; language use varies considerably depending on the ethnic background of the adherents of the sects, e.g.
Luo in the Nomiya Church founded by the 'prophet' Johana Owalo, or
essentially Swahili in the African Israel Church Ninevah, except when
they claim to 'speak in tongues.' The Tanzania Survey tried to provide
information on the languages used for catechization, for communication
with parishioners, in the liturgy and every other situation relating to
the church; it also focused attention on the minister's ability to cope
with the language situation in his parish and on the cases of shift to
Swahili, investigating the motivation for the change and determining
the time at which it occurred (Polomé 1975b: 44-45). The data clearly
showed a progressive Swahilization of the churches, the pace varying
regionally, depending on population mobility and economic development,
language loyalty of ethnic groups, and such factors, but also strongly
affected by the high prestige given to Swahili by the national government
and by the impact of education in Swahili on the younger generations
(A. Polomé 1982).

Parallel to the study of language use in definite sociocultural
contexts, the surveys have considered the language situation in specific
socioculturally differentiated communities, like the Asians in East
Africa: Barbara Neale (in Whiteley 1974: 262-317) has very carefully
analyzed the Kenya Asian community, its socioeconomic and cultural
pursuits and its religious orientations, and correlated these with their
language use at home, at play, at work, at school, and in their place
of religion. The picture that emerged was one of utter complexity:
the Asian population normally has a working command of four languages,
e.g. speakers of Gujarati will also use Hindi, Swahili, and English,

Table 6. Language Used in Church Work in Kenya

(a)

Language used	Protestant Liturgy	Protestant No. of cases Baptism	Protestant Marriage	Catholic Liturgy	Catholic No. of cases Baptism	Catholic Marriage
Vernacular only	17 45.9%	18 48.7%	17 45.9%	73 44.0%	91 54.9%	90 54.2%
Swahili only	1 2.7%	3 8.1%	4 10.8%	33 19.9%	33 19.9%	35 21.0%
Swahili and English	2 5.4%	2 5.4%	1 2.7%	7 4.2%	6 3.6%	7 4.2%
Vernacular and Swahili	7 18.9%	7 18.9%	7 18.9%	12 7.2%	12 7.2%	10 6.1%
Vernacular and English	2 5.4%	1 2.7%	3 8.1%	5 3.0%	2 1.2%	5 3.0%
English only	0 —	1 2.7%	1 2.7%	0 —	0 —	0 —
V. (inc. Sw.)+Latin				26 15.7%	13 7.8%	10 6.1%
Other combinations and possibilities	4 10.8%	4 10.8%	3 8.1%	9 5.4%	8 4.8%	8 4.8%
Not clear/No answer	3 8.1%	1 2.7%	1 2.7%	1 0.6%	1 0.6%	1 0.6%

(b)

Language used	Protestant Preaching	Protestant Benediction/Bible	Protestant Safari	Catholic Preaching	Catholic Benediction/Bible	Catholic Safari
Vernacular only	13 35.3%	14 37.8%	13 35.3%	100 60.3%	77 46.5%	94 56.6%
Swahili only	2 5.4%	3 8.1%	2 5.4%	27 16.3%	30 18.0%	31 18.7%
Swahili and English	2 5.4%	1 2.7%	2 5.4%	8 4.8%	4 2.4%	2 1.2%
Vernacular and Swahili	10 27.1%	10 27.1%	12 32.5%	15 9.0%	5 3.0%	22 13.3%
Vernacular and English	1 2.7%	1 2.7%	1 2.7%	6 3.6%	1 0.6%	4 2.4%
English only	3 8.1%	2 5.4%	1 2.7%	0 —	0 —	0 —
V. (inc. Sw.)+Latin	0 —	0 —	0 —		21 12.6%	
Other combinations and possibilities	6 16.2%	5 13.5%	5 13.5%	9 5.4%	18 10.8%	7 4.2%
Not clear/No answer	0 —	1 2.7%	1 2.7%	1 0.6%	10 6.1%	6 3.6%

Points arising from these two tables:

1. The Catholics use more vernacular than the Protestants, most particularly in preaching and on safari work. There is also a greater percentage who use Swahili only—possibly because of the greater proportion of Catholics who were working on the coast (respondents, that is); in other words there may be as many Protestant missions on the coast as Catholic missions, but fewer of the former answered questionnaires.

2. Only the Catholics use Latin, of course. Curiously, it was only amongst the Protestants that English alone was used in services.

3. The figures for 'preaching' are perhaps the most significant, since here are the results of two tendencies. First, it is most important that here the actual *meaning* of the words gets across to the congregation. This is the explanation, I think, for the high percentage of vernacular used by the Catholics in this sphere, and the lack of use of Latin. Preaching, however, is also a task which is probably done by the most senior official—in most cases the respondent. It probably cannot be easily delegated. Thus the respondents are thrown back on their own language abilities—and in the case of some of the Protestants may have to use English (the rate for the use of the vernacular is at its lowest here for Protestants, highest for Catholics).

4. Many Protestants also added that English was used in education, in colleges, in Sunday school training and wherever wider groups were dealt with.

Source: Whiteley 1974: 337.

and traders and professional people often know enough of other languages to meet their needs in their business or other specific activities. However, no generalization can be made about the language use
of the Asians as a group: they enjoyed a rather autonomous status in
pre-Independence days, and their current language use reflects the
diversity of the patterns of adaptation developed then.[12]

Such studies lead us back to the macro-sociolinguistic approach which focuses, among other things, on patterns of language
use: each survey has been involved in this type of research which combines the questionnaire with the interview technique (Polomé 1975: 39-
44). Whiteley (1974: 319-50) examined the relative percentages of use
of Swahili, English, and vernacular in rural areas in Kenya in a number of social contexts: at home, talking with friends, acquaintances,
or strangers in the market, at church, at work, in public services, in
political meetings, etc. The confrontation of his statistics with those
of Tanzania as regards the use of Swahili in religious activities is particularly eloquent, as seen in Tables 6-9.

Even if the percentages for Swahili are too high in view of the
respondents' vague statements, the difference with Kenya is obvious
and shows the considerable impact of the Tanzania language policy in
promoting the shift to Swahili in every sphere of the country's life.

Both the Ethiopian and the Zambian Surveys examined language
use among the university students: the freshmen were asked to fill in
questionnaires reporting which languages they used with whom; this
included the frequency of use of the mother tongue, e.g. with their parents, with older relatives, with young relatives, with close friends,
for letter writing, etc. There were also some questions that involved
the respondents' attitude versus the language, e.g. which language
would they like their children to learn[13]—or—which language did they
find the 'most beautiful or pleasant to hear.' (Strangely enough, only
11 percent gave their mother tongue as the answer to this second question [Robert L. Cooper and Michael King, in Bender et al. 1976: 277].)

Such questionnaires were used on a larger scale by the Tanzania team (Polomé 1975: 39-43): combined with the household survey
technique (also used by the Ethiopian Survey; cf. Bender et al. 1972:
224-25), and with personal interviews they led to the study in depth of

Table 7. Language or Languages Used for the Mass and Sermons
in the Catholic Church in Tanzania

Dioceses	Percent Swahili[a]	Percent vernacular	Percent both
Arusha	100		
Bukoba		Haya	100
Dar-es-Salaam	100		
Dodoma	100		
Iringa	100		
Karema	100		
Kigoma	50	Ha 50	
Mahenge	100		
Mbeya	95	Nyakyusa 5	
Mbulu	100		
Morogoro	100		
Moshi	100		
Musoma	40	Luo 45; Kuria 15	
Mwanza	30	Sukuma 40	30
Nachingwea	100		
Ndanda	100		
Peramiho	90	10 (Bena ~ Ngoni ~ Mpoto)	
Rulenge	30	60 (Haya ~ Hangaza ~ Zinza)	10
Same	90	Luo	10
Shinyanga	5	Sukuma 5	90
Tabora	60	Nyamwezi	40
Tanga	100		

Source: A. Polomé 1982, Chart 1.

[a] The percentages represent estimates based on the answers
provided by priests who usually used expressions like "mainly,"
"mostly," etc.

(Table 8 notes continued from facing page.)
[c] The various vernaculars are used in different parishes
according to the geographical distribution of the parishes.
[d] The percentage varies from parish to parish.
[e] In the Lumbiji Parish, 30 percent of the parish uses only
Kaguru for informal transactions.

Table 8. Language or Languages Used by Catholics for Confession
and Informal Meeting with Priest[a] in Tanzania

Dioceses	Percent Swahili[b]	Percent vernacular
Arusha	80	20 Masai~ Kikuyu~ Kamba
Bukoba		100 Haya~ Ha
Dar-es-Salaam	100	
Dodoma	80	20 Sandawe~ Gogo
Iringa	90	10 Hehe~ Bena
Karema	50	50 Nyamwanga~ Fipa~ Mambwe~ Rungu [c]
Kigoma	10~25	75~90 Ha[d]
Mahenge	98	2 Pogoro
Mbeya	75~90	10~25 Nyakyusa~Nyika~Fipa~Nyamwanga
Mbulu	95	5 Kilimi (= Rimi)
Morogoro	100	
Moshi[e]	90	10 Chaga (various dialects)
Musoma	40~50	50~60 Kwaya~ Ngoreme~ Kuria~Luo~ Jita~Ruri~Zanaki[c]
Mwanza	10~10	80~90 Sukuma~Kerewe~Jita~Haya~Zinza
Nachingwea	90~100	5 Makua~5 Makonde (in the Nanjota parish)
Ndanda	100	
Peramiho	90~100	10 Bena~Kinga~Pangwa~Nyakyusa~ Mpoto~Ngoni
Rulenge	0~5	95~100 Haya~Rundi~Subi~Zinza
Same	95~100	5 Pare
Shinyanga	5~25	75~95 Sukuma
Tabora	10~25	75~90 Nyamwezi
Tanga	100	

Source: A. Polomé 1982, Chart 2.

[a] Generally confession is conducted in the vernacular language with women and older men. School children and males less
than 35 years old generally prefer to use Swahili. This is repeatedly
accounted for in the data by pointing out that Swahili is a prestigious
language and also the language of uhuru and unity.

[b] These percentages represent estimates of usage because
the answers provided were often expressed in the form of statements
like "mainly, " "mostly, " etc.

(Table 8 notes continued at bottom of preceding page.)

Table 9. Language or Languages Used in the Catholic Church
for Various Parts of the Liturgy in Tanzania

Part of liturgy	No. of parishes using vernacular[a] only	Percent	No. with Swahili only	Percent	No. with both	Percent
Hymns	7	2.2	243	77.2	65	20.6
Baptism	42	13.3	237	75.3	36	11.4
Marriage	41	13.0	241	76.6	33	10.4
Funerals	41	13.0	252	80.0	22	7.0

Source: A. Polomé 1982, Chart 3.

[a] The vernacular being the language or languages spoken
natively in the particular parishes.

multilingualism and language use in the Ilala section of Dar es Salaam
by David Barton (1972), which he further compared with the linguistic
situation in selected communities in the Tanzania volume. The kind
of information provided by the questionnaires lends itself to some tentative measurement of the degree of multilingualism, since it indicates
how the respondent claims to perform in the four language skills:
speaking, understanding, writing, reading, in a graded set of situations of increasing complexity or level of abstraction. It is not sufficient, indeed, to establish a typology of multilingualism, as Whiteley
(1974: 37-54) has done, merely tabulating percentages of claimed competence in the various languages spoken by the respondent. It takes
different degrees of command of a language to perform in the following
social contexts: (a) greeting people; (b) giving someone directions
about the way to go; (c) buying things in the market; (d) carrying on an
everyday conversation; (e) making a speech; (f) talking about politics;
(g) talking about health and farming; (h) talking about mechanical things;
(i) talking about one's work; (j) doing mathematical calculations. Thus,
a Tanzanian university student in civil engineering, who comes from
a village in the Ntombe district in Iringa Region, will have no major
problem doing all those things both in English and Swahili, but when
it comes to using his mother tongue—Bena—making speeches, discuss-

ing politics, mechanical gadgets, or mathematical problems do not even come into consideration; however, he dreams, sings, and prays in Bena as well as in Swahili, but not in English (except for an occasional prayer). Therefore, in the Tanzania survey, the language competence typology was supplemented by scoring the performance of the respondents on two scales: (self-assessed) degree of proficiency in the languages claimed to be known, and amount of use in specific social contexts. Thus, a bilingual Catholic woman, whose 'first' language is kiSubi (T), though she has a thorough command of Swahili (S) and has acquired literacy in it through four years in primary school, would score $T27/23$ $S37/19$ (the maximum for the first score, i.e. ability to operate in the language, is 37; for the second score, reflecting the actual use of the language in definite social contexts, is 32). The pattern indicates a shift to almost exclusive use of Swahili outside the family circle (she reads a lot, including the Swahili-language TANU daily paper Uhuru) (Polomé 1974; 1980). The ideal solution would be to test the respondents on their actual knowledge of the languages they claim to be able to use: applying the technique developed by Ladefoged (1972: 65-68) and Bender and Cooper (1971), Mubanga E. Kashoki (in Ohannessian and Kashoki 1978: 123-43) focuses on between-languages communication in Zambia, since the assumption that the seven Zambian Bantu languages officially recognized as media of communication and of instruction—Bemba, Kaonde, Lunda, Luvale, Lozi, Nyanja, Tonga —are mutually unintelligible is essential to the assessment of multilingualism in Zambia. Though the tests were not conducted in optimal conditions (Kashoki, loc. cit. pp. 140-41), the correspondences between Bemba, Nyanja, and Tonga in basic vocabulary and morphemic structure correlate most interestingly with the comprehension scores of the respondents, as shown by Tables 10 and 11.

The high Nyanja-Bemba scores were also paralleled by the better scores of Bemba speakers in the comprehension of Nyanja in Lusaka, though a number of other factors are involved (e.g. the predominant ethnic group in the residential area; Serpell 1978: 164-77). An important factor is also that both Nyanja and Bemba in their urban varieties are linguae francae (Heine 1970: 56-70), and where there is a high concentration of town-Bemba speakers in Lusaka, as in the Libala section, their language contains a sizable number of borrowed Nyanja vocabulary items which do not occur in the Copperbelt variety of town-Bemba. As Serpell indicates (1978: 153), native speakers of

Table 10. Average Listening Comprehension Scores of
Four Groups in Bemba, Lozi, Nyanja, and Tonga

Mother-tongue group	Number of respondents	Average percentage correct				
		Bemba	Lozi	Nyanja	Tonga	Average
Bemba	88	–	20	42	27	30
Lozi	93	16	–	26	28	23
Nyanja	57	25	13	–	21	20
Tonga	48	25	18	58	–	35
Average		22	17	42	25	27

Table 11. Percentages of Basic Vocabulary Shared Among
Bemba, Lozi, Nyanja, and Tonga

	Percentage				
Language	Bemba	Lozi	Nyanja	Tonga	Average
Bemba	–	30	47	57	45
Lozi	30	–	28	32	30
Nyanja	47	28	–	46	40
Tonga	57	32	46	–	45

Sources for Tables 10-11: Kashoki 1978: 123-43, Tables
4.4 and 4.6.

Bemba often cannot decide whether a particular Nyanja word they
have used is an accepted loan or a purely occasional switch.

        In general, the problem of linguae francae has not received
focal attention from the Survey teams in Eastern Africa. In Uganda,
the deliberate anti-Swahili position of the government, which since
1952 does not recognize Swahili as a vernacular to be taught in the
schools except those for the police and their children (Ladefoged et
al. 1972: 22, 91), led to negative attitudes toward the language, which
were not even offset by the unpopularity of LuGanda as a national language outside Buganda (Ladefoged et al. 1972: 28-29).[14] For Kenya,
extremely valuable but unfortunately rather limited data on the Swahili used by Asians were provided by Barbara Neale (in Whiteley
1974: 73-79), but the problem of pidginization and creolization of
Swahili was completely neglected.[15] The Ethiopian survey documented the existence of a pidginized variety of Italian, which reduced the

verb system to two forms: the past participle, referring to the past, and the infinitive, used for all other tenses (Bender et al. 1972: 230-32; Habte-Mariam Marcos, in Bender et al. 1976: 170-80).

3. Language in Education

As Donald Bowen put it (1975: 20), in developing nations 'research is the handmaiden of national policy.' Faced with the problems of implementing the language policy they have formulated in a political decision, the governments of these countries need a large amount of sociolinguistic information providing insight into the actual linguistic situation in order to take the most effective steps to develop their educational system. The choice of the medium of instruction is crucial and may be determined by political issues or socioeconomic needs instead of reflecting the pattern of language use in the country (Ohannessian and Ansre 1972: 55-57). The language used as medium of instruction may also be purposely changed during the years of schooling, e.g. resorting to the child's mother tongue or an African national language for the early primary grades and shifting to an international language—as a rule, the West European language of the former colonial power, or a world language like English (e.g. in government secondary schools in Ethiopia). Therefore, the various Survey teams have devoted a considerable part of their activities to investigating:

(a) the patterns of language use among school children;[16]
(b) the development of the language policy in the country they surveyed;[17]
(c) the use of languages in the educational system; at the university level; in literacy programs;
(d) the use of the media as auxiliaries for the implementation of the language policy.[18]

Particular attention was given to problems of manpower, teaching materials, and aspects of the economics of education in developing countries.

4. Practical Issues

Evaluating the preliminary results of the Survey of Language
Use and Language Teaching in Eastern Africa, Clifford Prator (1975:
151-52) stressed the stimulating effect this linguistic activity had had
on language and education research in Africa, with the establishment
of the Language Association of Eastern Africa and the publication of
its Journal, with the involvement of many local scholars, teachers,
and students in the research process and their exposure to new techniques and new ideas in their field, with the development of linguistics
and language teaching at the universities of the various countries in
which the Survey operated.

Did it accomplish what it set out to accomplish?

Obviously, any answer to this question will have to be qualified, since, as Prator also points out (1975: 154), 'it has often been
argued that the Survey attempted to do too much in too short a time
and that it would have been better to concentrate on a smaller geographical area.' Actually, the scope of the Survey provided for the collection of the kind of data that would illustrate a variety of linguistic situations in contiguous countries and remain nevertheless comparable because of parallel gathering and similar processing. This breadth of
investigation did not prevent specialized research in specific areas,
but helped maintain a sound balance between purely academic interests
and more practically oriented inquiries. The volumes produced by the
Survey teams bear witness of these facts, but they do not tell the whole
story: a number of specific Zambian language descriptions are being
published separately in Lusaka; several contributions to the Tanzania
Survey appeared elsewhere, e.g. the description of 14 Bantu languages of Tanzania by Derek Nurse and Gerard Philippson, published as a supplement to the linguistic journal of the International
African Institute in London; other materials are contained in articles,
papers, theses, and dissertations,[19] and a special number of the International Journal of the Sociology of Language, edited by E. Polomé
and devoted to urban versus rural multilingualism contains contributions by Mohammed Abdulaziz, Mubanga Kashoki, Carol Scotton, and
Edgar Polomé relevant to the Eastern African problems studied by
the Survey.

By and large, the Survey has been quite successful in mapping out language usage and throwing new light on the problems of multilingualism and the choice of a national language or a language as a medium in the education system. Maybe some governmental officials would have expected specific recommendations to be made by the Survey teams, but being mostly expatriates, they carefully and wisely abstained from any participation in the decision-making process, only providing the relevant data on controversial issues. Sometimes the questions asked by the Government were unanswerable, though quite understandable: thus, in Tanzania, the education authorities, confronted with the high cost of teaching English in all primary schools and aware of the rapid regression of the knowledge of English of primary school leavers to practically nil, wondered if the Tanzania team could not build into its secondary school questionnaire administered to students entering the schools in 1969-70 some questions about students who failed to qualify, in order to assess the impact of their language background, use, and proficiency on their results. It was obvious that such information obtained from secondary sources was highly unreliable and practically unusable, and that no response could be given to the Tanzanian Ministry's wish along those lines. This extreme case underscores the inherent weaknesses of the questionnaire technique:

(a) while it may appear advantageous to use school children as informants, because their services are readily available and they constitute a captive audience to whom the questionnaire can be administered under proper supervision, they may easily misinterpret the questions, and, in view of their age group, they cannot provide any information on a large number of social situations and lack the maturity to answer properly when matters pertaining to ethnic, sociocultural, or religious subjects are concerned;
(b) if the questionnaire is not administered under the control of the investigator, errors in presentation or comments by inadequately trained assistant surveyors may easily lead to incorrect responses from unsophisticated school children.

Only large-scale inquiries with repeated sampling for personal interviews when feasible can effectively offset these disadvantages, and personal observation should then check the validity of the self-assessed measures of performance and competence.

Questionnaires should also be prepared with processing in mind: multiple-choice questions can only be included insofar as they can be adequately programmed for computer processing, which implies the avoidance of open-ended questions which often create complex encoding problems.

In working in subsaharan Africa, some general considerations also need to be kept in mind:

(a) to be able to assess and to understand the function of language in various social contexts and contacts, the help of a sociologist or social anthropologist is necessary: he should indicate how to determine the societal structure of the linguistic community to be surveyed—in other words: a social typology has to be established prior to the measurement of multilingualism (cf. Polomé 1980).

(b) is the Survey feasible in the country for which it is planned? — This depends on a number of factors, such as (1) the Government's attitude toward research which will determine the degree of accessibility of the sources of information, e.g. will the survey have to rely exclusively on self-evaluation, or will it be able to observe people in social interaction, or will it be allowed to test language proficiency and competence in the vernaculars as well as in the national language? Will it be permissible to study marginal subgroups in detail to determine their linguistic and cultural idiosyncrasies and their place in society? and (2) a sufficient pool of local manpower and availability of data-processing facilities: the survey will have:

A. to collaborate with local scholars—is there an interest among them for sociolinguistic research?

B. to recruit local help: secretarial staff—assistant surveyors—interviewers (preferably students trained in sociology or anthropology), etc.

C. to have typewriters, stencil and xerox machines, and similar office equipment at its disposal;

D. to have access to a computer and the personnel to prepare its data for processing (encoding, programming, typing in memory bank).

The necessity of complete processing on the spot is crucial as most African countries require scholars to leave behind their raw data (questionnaires, etc.).

(c) Time is a key factor of success, and provision should be made to allow sufficient time to test all survey research materials before using the field, especially to give the questionnaires a dry run.

Careful planning is paying dividends, as Donald Bowen (1975: 26) said, but not every detail of the research can be anticipated: 'any sociolinguistically oriented survey is bound to present problems sui generis' (Polomé 1975: 31).

NOTES

This paper was prepared for publication in Voprosy Jazykoznanija and appears in Russian translation by D. B. V. Zhurkovskij of the Linguistic Institute of the Academy of Sciences of the USSR in Moscow in this journal in 1982; a shortened English text also appeared in Language in Society 11. 265–83 (1982).

[1] On the organization of the Survey, see especially Prator 1972: 1–7; 1975: 145–49. Some of the motivations for the administrative complexity are discussed by Bowen 1975.

[2] The teams were constituted as follows:

1. Uganda: Professor Peter Ladefoged (UCLA, experimental phonetics); Dr. Ruth Glick (UCLA, comparative education); Dr. Clive Criper (Edinburgh, sociolinguistics);
2. Kenya: Professor Wilfred H. Whiteley (London, SOAS, linguistics); Dr. David Parkin (London, SOAS, social anthropology); Ms. Barbara Neale (U. T. Austin, sociolinguistics);
3. Ethiopia: Professor Charles A. Ferguson (Stanford, linguistics); Dr. Robert Cooper (Yeshiva, sociolinguistics); Dr. Marvin Bender (U. T. Austin, linguistics);
4. Tanzania: Professor Edgar Polomé (U. T. Austin, sociolinguistics); Mr. Peter Hill (London, Institute of Education, TESL); Mr. Henry Barton (U. T. Austin, linguistics);
5. Zambia: Ms. Sirarpi Ohannessian (Washington, D. C., Center for Applied Linguistics, TESL); Dr. Mubanga E. Kashoki (Lusaka, linguistics).

[3] Ladefoged (1972: 53) tried to get people to answer questions like: 'How much can people around here understand of such and such language?' and to rate their understanding according to a five-point

scale: (1) none; (2) only a few words; (3) about half a conversation; (4) most that was said; (5) everything.

[4] Ladefoged (1972: 54) points to this danger when he indicates that the list ought to 'be balanced so that it does not reflect one aspect of the culture unduly. It would be unwise for it to consist entirely of a list of wild animal names; an agricultural people might have borrowed these and almost no others from their hunting neighbors. ' However, borrowing does not bother him, since he only wants to assess 'relative similarity' without drawing conclusions on genetic relationship.

[5] In an evaluation of the Ethiopian survey, Bender, Cooper, and Ferguson (1972) stress the importance of their use of the technique of selected diagnostic traits for linguistic classification and emphasize the new insights gained by their use as the basis of a measure of linguistic difference, pointing specifically to Ferguson's suggestion of an Ethiopian language area; the classification of the Ethio-Semitic languages, and the study of the Amharic dialects.

It should be noted that these techniques have also been applied to in-depth study of definite areas, e.g. in Dorothy Lehmann's study of the languages of the Kafue Basin in Zambia (in Ohannessian et al. 1978: 101-20); in Derek Nurse's study on Chaga dialects (1979), which corroborates the findings of Susan Polomé in her M.A. thesis: A Phonological Survey of the Chagga Dialects of Tanzania (U. T. Austin, 1971), and the data on mutual intelligibility. Quantitative studies on the basis of diagnostic features and basic cognate frequencies underlie the pioneering work of Marvin L. Bender on Omotic (1975).

A tentative word-geographical study of lexical items in the Bantu languages of Tanzania was presented in the Ph.D. dissertation of André Polomé (1975), whose findings corresponded, by and large, with the mapping resulting from Nurse's analysis of basic cognate frequencies in the same languages (Derek Nurse used a word list based on Swadesh's 100-word list, whereas André Polomé derived his information from words in context in a set of 75 sentences devised by Dorothy Lehmann for the study of the Bantu languages in Zambia).

[6] Competence was measured as follows:

5 = fluency, i.e. ability to talk on any topic;
4 = 'enough for most conversations';
3 = 'quite a lot';
2 = 'enough for simple conversation';
1 = 'very little. '

Since the informant was asked to rate his own performance (Whiteley 1974: 37), it stands to reason that subjective bias could not be avoided in this rating system. As for frequency, it was based on the following scale:

> 5 = regularly, every day;
> 4 = at least once a day;
> 3 = several times a week (= 'quite often');
> 2 = once a week (= 'from time to time');
> 1 = once a month (= 'very little').

[7] This sampling was tabulated as shown in Table 12 (Whiteley 1974: 38). Examples of Whiteley's percentage tables are shown in Tables 13 and 14.

[8] A revised version of Polomé's article is included in the Tanzania volume. The complete text of A. Brumfit's study appeared in Vol. 2 of Sprache und Geschichte in Afrika (Cologne, 1980: 219-329).

[9] A particularly instructive approach to the linguistic correlates of relative social status among the Amhara is presented in Susan J. Hoben's paper on 'The meaning of the 2nd person pronouns in Amharic' (Bender et al. 1976: 281-88), in which she illustrates how the power and solidarity semantics are operative in the Amharic deference use of the pronouns—a feature of interaction between linguistic and non-linguistic social behavior that raises a number of interesting questions about, e.g., 'semantic universals' (Bender et al. 1972: 230).

[10] The Ethiopian Survey pointed out the complexity of language use in Ethiopian courts with respect to interpretation of written law and to court proceedings, and to the prospect of greater standardization and uniformity in legal interpretation and use of Amharic throughout the country's juridical system (Robert L. Cooper and Fasil Nahum, in Bender et al. 1972: 256-63).

[11] On Town-Bemba, cf. especially Mubanga E. Kashoki, 'Town-Bemba: A sketch of its main characteristics,' (African) Social Research 13 [June 1972] : 161-68); on its development, cf. Heine 1970: 56-58.

[12] Quite different is the situation of the Zambian Asians who are usually Gujarati speakers; their second language is generally Hindi, and their knowledge of English depends very much on the age group (the younger generation has mostly been educated in English-medium schools). Except for those living in rural areas, there is no effort to acquire a high standard of proficiency in a Zambian language. All they know is enough of the local lingua franca, e.g. town-Bemba

Table 12. Samples of Rural Communities
(See note 7; Whiteley 1974, Table 1.7)

	Total in sample	% Homogeneity	Men % Overall total	Men 15–29	Men 30+	Women % Overall total	Women 15–29	Women 30+	Total % 15–29	Total % 30+	(Kenya 1962) Differential* Age 15–29	% Groups 30+	Edu Men 15–29	Edu Men 30+	Edu Women 15–29	Edu Women 30+
Luo (*Oyugis*) (a)	110	99	55	21	34	45	25	20	46	54		+5.4	7	2	4	nil
(Gusii border) (b)	43	77[1]	79	42	37	21	14	7	56	44		+5.4	7	5	7	3
Gusii (*Manga*)	97	100	74	22	52	26	10	16	32	68		+0.45	6	4	5	nil
Kuria (*Kihancha*)	28	93	54	29	25	46	25	21	54	46		+0.45	8	4	4	2
Luyia (Bukusu) (a)	80	99	67	45	22	33	21	12	66	34		+0.45	7	2	5	nil
(Idakho) (b)	131	100[2]	62	40	22	38	22	16	62	38		+0.45	5	2	3	1
(Logoli) (c)	35	100[3]	60	11	49	40	26	14	37	63		+0.45	5	3	4	—
(Khayo) (d)	78	72[4]	47	3	34	53	6	35	12	88		+1.37	8	3	1	1
Kipsigis (Lugumek s/l)	197	100	50	18	32	50	25	25	43	57		+2.65	6	nil	6	nil
Taita (*Wundanyi*) (a)	36	100	36	22	14	64	31	33	53	47		+2.65	6	4	6	4
Pokomo (Salama) (a)	88	95	73	16	57	27	16	17	32	68		+2.65	8	3	3	2
(Gwano) (b)	88	98	42	19	23	58	31	27	50	50		+2.65	6	2	1	nil
(Zubaki) (c)	93	100	63	10	53	37	3	34	13	87		+3.67	6	6	10	1
Kikuyu (Karatina) (a)	24	100	67	54	13	33	25	8	79	21		+3.67	10	6	9	5
(Kirimukuyu) (b)	26	100	77	42	35	23	15	8	57	43		+3.67	6	8	9	5
(Kiambaa) (c)	43	91	86	81	5	14	14	—	95	5		+3.67	10[5]	8	8	6
Embu (*Runyenje's*)	36	95	53	22	31	47	36	11	58	42		+3.67	9	2	4	nil
Meru (Katheri s/l) (a)	162	100	47	29	18	53	33	20	62	38		+3.67	6	3	6	1
(Ntima) (b)	149	98	54	32	22	46	26	20	48	66		+3.67	8	3	6	nil
Kamba (Mbitini) (a)	29	100	76	59	17	24	14	10	73	27		+3.67	9	4	10	4
(Kambai) (b)	44	95	61	13	48	39	19	20	32	68		+3.67	7	2	3	5
Kips./Luo/Gusii (*Sondu*)	80	Luo 39 / Kips. 34 / Gusii 26 / Nub. 1	85	19	66	15	9	6	28	72			4	4	5	
Luo/Luyia (*Maseno*)	51	Luo 53 / Luyia 47	73	24	49	27	18	9	42	58		nil	7	4	7	nil

* Abstraction from figures in table V.4 of *Kenya Population Census* (1962) vol. III, Ministry of Economic Planning and Development, Nairobi, 1966, p. 38. The figures represent the percentage difference between the two age groups.

1 Included 5 Gujarati, 2 A abs, 1 Kuria, 1 Logoli, 1 Gusii. The sample is anomalous in that it contains no farmers, 86% being semi-skilled, skilled artisans or professionals, including 30% teachers.

2 The sample is 100% homogeneous Luyia but at most only 89% homogeneous Idakho.

3 The sample is 100% homogeneous Luyia but at most only 94% homogeneous Logoli.

4 Includes 28% Teso.

5 Educational figures largely estimated due to failure to answer questions.

Note: Samples are identified by their geographical location, in locational or sub-locational terms. In some cases the nearest settlement has been used to identify the sample e.g. where more than one sub-location is involved. In these cases the reference is italicized.

Table 13. Percentage Claiming Monolingual Competence
(See note 7; Whiteley 1974, Table 1.8)

	% of sample	% Constituents				Average years' education	
		Men		Women		Men	Women
		−30	30+	−30	30+		
Luo (*Oyugis*)	49	5	43	15	37	1	1
Meru (*Katheri*)	39	2	17	32	49	nil	nil
Kipsigis (*Lugumek s/1*)	37	2	7	38	53	nil	nil
Gusii/Kips./Luo border. Luo	23	14	43	29	14	nil	4
Kuria (*Kihancha*)	21	—	33	—	67	nil	nil
Taita (*Wundanyi*)	17	—	15	—	100	—	nil
Meru (*Ntima*)	17	4	40	4	77	nil	nil
Pokomo (*Zubaki*)	16	—	—	—	60	nil	nil
Luyia (*Idakho*)	14	10	25	16	74	2	1
Luyia (*Lozoli*)	11	—	—	—	75	—	nil
Kamba (*Mbitini*)	10	—	10	—	100	nil	2
Gusii	9	—	—	50	90	—	—
Luo (Gusii border)	5	—	100	—	50	1	—
Kikuyu (*Karatina*)	4	—	—	—	—	—	—
Luo/Luyia border. Luo	4	—	—	—	100	nil	—
Embu (*Runyenje's*)	—	—	—	—	—	—	—
Kikuyu (*Kiambaa*) (Kirimukuyu)	—	—	—	—	—	—	—
Kamba (Kambai s/L)	—	—	—	—	—	—	—
Pokomo (Salama) (Gwano)	—	—	—	—	—	—	—
Luyia (Bukusu) (Khayo)	—	—	—	—	—	—	—
Gusii/Kips./Luo border. Kipsigis Gusii	—	—	—	—	—	—	—
Luo/Luyia border. Luyia	—	—	—	—	—	—	—

Table 14. Percentage Claiming Trilingual (L1 + L2 + Sw.) Competence
(See note 7; Whiteley 1974, Table 1.12)

	% of sample	Men		Women		Average years' education		L2
		−30	30+	−30	30+	Men	Women	
Luyia (Khayo)	37	—	38	4	58	1	—	Teso dominant here
Gusii/Kips./Luo border. Kipsigis	26	—	100	—	—	1	—	6 Luo
Luo/Luyia border. Luyia	25	5	83	17	—	1	4	
Pokomo (Zubaki).	23	—	71	—	24	1	1	Galla as L2
Gusii/Kips./Luo border. Gusii	20	—	75	25	—	2	2	3 Gusii; 2 Kipsigis
Luo	16	—	—	—	—	2	—	4 Luo
Pokomo (Gwano)	16	21	100	—	22	2	nil	8 Sanye; 2 Galla
Kipsigis (Lugumek s/1)	14	—	57	8	11	—	—	Maasai (10); Kikuyu (6); Kamba (1)
Pokomo (Salama)	7	—	81	—	—	nil	—	Galla as L2
Meru (Ntima)	6	23	100	33	33	2	5	9 Kikuyu
Luyia (Idakho)	6	13	11	25	12	2	1	5 Kikuyu; 3 Nandi
Gusii	5	—	50	—	—	2	—	
Luo/Luyia border. Luo	4	—	100	—	—	nil	—	
Kamba (Kambai)	4	—	100	—	—	nil	—	
(Mbitini)	3	100	50	—	50	4	1	
Taita (*Wumdanyi*)	3	—	100	—	—	nil	—	
Luo (Gusii border)	2	—	100	—	—	5	—	
(*Oyugis*)	2	—	50	50	—	nil	nil	
Kikuyu (Kiambaa)	2	—	100	—	—	8	—	Gusii (1)
Kuria (*Kihancha*)	—	—	—	—	—	—	—	
Embu (*Runyenje's*)	—	—	—	—	—	—	—	
Kikuyu (*Karatina*)	—	—	—	—	—	—	—	
(*Kirimukuyu*)	—	—	—	—	—	—	—	
Meru (Katheri)	—	—	—	—	—	—	—	
Luyia (Bukusu)	—	—	—	—	—	—	—	
(Logoli)	—	—	—	—	—	—	—	

in the Copperbelt, Chilapalapa (or Fanagalo) elsewhere, to carry on their trade. Important is the reinforcement of their Asian mother tongue by (a) the broadcasts from the South Asian subcontinent (All India Radio and Radio Pakistan); (b) very popular Indian films, mostly in Hindi; (c) private schools teaching Gujarati; (d) contacts with India and/or Pakistan and expatriates from South Asia (Ansu K. Datta, 'Languages used by Zambian Asians,' in Ohannessian and Kashoki 1978: 244-67).

[13] The context in which Moses Musonda ('A Study of language use among local students at the University of Zambia,' in Ohannessian and Kashoki 1978: 228-43) asks this question was bound to produce the high percentages for English (96.8 percent) versus the middle-of-the-range percentages for the most common Zambian urban languages—Bemba (51.6 percent) and Nyanja (49.5 percent): (a) the respondents are students whose complete education has been conducted through the medium of English from grade 1 to their final year at the University; (b) as the official language of Zambia, English enjoys the highest prestige, and the best jobs go to those who have a perfect command of it. In a different setting, students in teachers' training colleges in Tanzania, while fully recognizing the primacy of Swahili as the national language and its role as a major instrument of nation building, insisted that their children should learn their own tribal language 'to know who I am,' i.e. for the purpose of ethnic identification, language loyalty being equated to adherence to the cultural heritage.

[14] On the actual position of Swahili in Uganda, see Scotton 1972.

[15] For an extensive study of Kenya pidgin Swahili, see Heine 1973: 69-118.

[16] For Kenya, T. P. Gorman (in Whiteley 1974: 351-93) broadened the inquiry to obtain a profile of language use by the children's parents, because of the impact that parental patterns of language use could have on the children, especially if their mothers knew Swahili. He also investigated attitudes as part of the children's motivation to acquire languages other than their mother tongue, and found interesting indications of shift in the direction of increased use of English in Nairobi and of Swahili in Mombasa.

[17] Uganda: Ladefoged et al. 1972: 87-99. Kenya: T. P. Gorman, 'The development of language policy in Kenya with particular reference to the educational system,' in Whiteley 1974: 397-453. Ethiopia: Richard K. P. Pankhurst, 'Historical background of educa-

tion in Ethiopia,' in Bender et al. 1976: 305-23.   Zambia: Ohannessian and Kashoki 1978: 271-91.   Tanzania: Cameron and Todd 1970; Douglas Kavugha, 'Language in education in Tanzania,' in Polomé and Hill 1980; Brumfit 1971, 1980.

[18] More extensive analyses of the use of languages and the media were conducted by Graham L. Mytton in Tanzania and Zambia (cf. his contribution to Ohannessian and Kashoki 1978: 207-27, and his studies on the press and the radio in Tanzania, discussed in Polomé 1980: 128-29).   Abdu Mozayen focuses more specifically on the use of mass media in language teaching in Ethiopia (in Bender et al. 1976: 505-19).

[19] For an earlier list, see Prator 1975: 156-58.   An updated list has been compiled by Charles Ferguson in 1977.

BIBLIOGRAPHY

Abdulaziz-Mkilifi, M. H.   1972.   Triglossia and Swahili-English bilingualism in Tanzania.   Language in Society 1.2: 197-213.

Barton, David.   1972.   Study of language use in Ilala.   Austin: University of Texas, Ph.D. dissertation.

Baumann, Richard, and Joel Scherzer, eds.   1974.   Explorations in the ethnography of speaking.   London: Cambridge University Press.

Bender, Marvin L.   1971.   The languages of Ethiopia.   A new lexico-statistic classification and some problems of diffusion. Anthropological Linguistics 13.5: 165-288.

_____.   1975.   Omotic: A new Afroasiatic language family.   (University Museum Studies—Research Records, No. 3.)   Carbondale: University Museum, Southern Illinois University.

Bender, Marvin L., and Robert L. Cooper.   1971.   Mutual intelligibility within Sidamo.   Lingua 27.1: 32-52.

Bender, Marvin L., R. L. Cooper, and Charles A. Ferguson.   1972. Language in Ethiopia: Implications of a survey for sociolinguistic theory and method.   Language in Society 1.2: 215-33.

Bender, M. L., J. D. Bowen, R. L. Cooper, and C. A. Ferguson. 1976.   Language in Ethiopia.   London: Oxford University Press.

Blount, Ben G., and Mary Sanches, eds. 1977. Sociocultural dimen-
sions of language change. (Language, Thought, and Culture.
Advances in the Study of Cognition.) New York: Academic
Press.
Bowen, J. Donald. 1975. Organizing international research in socio-
linguistically oriented language surveys. In Sirarpi Ohannes-
sian, Charles A. Ferguson, and Edgar C. Polomé, eds.,
Language surveys in developing nations. Papers and reports
on sociolinguistic surveys. Arlington, Va.: Center for
Applied Linguistics, pp. 11-29.
Brumfit, Anne. 1971. The development of a language policy in
German East Africa. Journal of the Language Association
of Eastern Africa 2.1: 1-9.
_____. 1980. The development of a language policy in Tanzania.
Sprache und Geschichte in Afrika 2: 219-329.
Cameron, J., and W. A. Dodd. 1970. Society, schools and progress
in Tanzania. Oxford: Pergamon Press.
Emeneau, Murray B. 1956. India as a linguistic area. Language
32.1: 3-16.
Ferguson, Charles A. 1975. On sociolinguistically oriented language
surveys. In Sirarpi Ohannessian, Charles A. Ferguson, and
Edgar C. Polomé, eds., Language surveys in developing
nations. Papers and reports on sociolinguistic surveys.
Arlington, Va.: Center for Applied Linguistics, pp. 1-5.
_____. 1976. The Ethiopian language area. In M. L. Bender, J. D.
Bowen, R. L. Cooper, and C. A. Ferguson, eds., Language
in Ethiopia. London: Oxford University Press, pp. 63-76.
Fishman, Joshua A., ed. Advances in the sociology of language.
2 vols. The Hague: Mouton.
      1971. Basic concepts, theories and problems: Alterna-
tive approaches.
      1972a. Selected studies and applications.
Fishman, Joshua. 1972b. Domains and the relationship between
micro- and macro-sociolinguistics. In John J. Gumperz and
Dell Hymes, eds., Directions in sociolinguistics. The eth-
nography of communication. New York: Holt, Rinehart &
Winston, pp. 435-53.
Fishman, Joshua A., ed. 1974. Advances in language planning.
The Hague: Mouton.

Gumperz, John J., and D. Hymes, eds. 1964. The ethnography of communication [= American Anthropologist 66.6, Part II]. Washington, D. C.: American Anthropological Association.

———. 1972. Directions in sociolinguistics. The ethnography of communication. New York: Holt, Rinehart & Winston.

Heine, Bernd. 1970. Status and use of African lingua francas. (IFO —Institut für Wirtschaftsforschung München-Afrika-Studienstelle—Afrika-Studien No. 49.) München: Weltforum Verlag.

———. 1973. Pidgin-Sprachen im Bantu-Bereich. (Kölner Beiträge zur Afrikanistik, vol. 3.) Berlin: Dietrich Reimer.

———. 1979. Sprache, Gesellschaft und Kommunikation in Afrika. (IFO—Institut für Wirtschaftsforschung München—Abteilung Entwicklungsländer. Afrika-Studienstelle—Afrika Studien No. 103.) München: Weltforum Verlag.

Hymes, Dell. 1974. Foundations in sociolinguistics. An ethnographic approach. Philadelphia: University of Pennsylvania Press.

Kashoki, Mubanga E. 1978. The language situation in Zambia. In Sirarpi Ohannessian and Mubanga Kashoki, eds., Language in Zambia. London: International African Institute, pp. 9–46.

Kashoki, Mubanga E., and Michael Mann. 1978. A general sketch of the Bantu languages of Zambia. In Sirarpi Ohannessian and Mubanga E. Kashoki, Language in Zambia. London: International African Institute, pp. 47–100.

Labov, William. 1972. Sociolinguistic patterns. (Conduct and Communication, No. 4.) Philadelphia: University of Pennsylvania Press.

Ladefoged, Peter. 1970. The measurement of phonetic similarity. Statistic Methods in Linguistics 6: 23–32.

Ladefoged, Peter, Ruth Glick, and Clive Criper. 1972. Language in Uganda. London: Oxford University Press.

Nurse, Derek. 1979. Classification of the Chaga dialects. Language and history on Kilimanjaro, the Taita Hills, and the Pare Mountains. Hamburg: Helmut Buske.

Ohannessian, Sirarpi, and Gilbert Ansre. 1975. Some reflections on the uses of sociolinguistic surveys. In Sirarpi Ohannessian, Charles A. Ferguson, and Edgar C. Polomé, Language surveys in developing nations. Arlington, Va.: Center for Applied Linguistics, pp. 51–69.

Ohannessian, Sirarpi, and Mubanga E. Kashoki. 1978. Language in Zambia. London: International African Institute.

Parkin, D. J. Four articles in Wilfred H. Whiteley, ed., Language
in Kenya. Nairobi: Oxford University Press, pp. 131-216.
1974a. Nairobi: Problems and methods.
1974b. Status factors in language adding: Bahati housing estate in Nairobi.
1974c. Language shift and ethnicity in Nairobi: The
speech community of Kaloleni.
1974d. Language switching in Nairobi.
Philippson, Gérard, and Derek Nurse. 1980. Classification of the
Bantu languages of Tanzania. In Edgar C. Polomé and Peter
C. Hill, eds., Language in Tanzania. London: International
African Institute, pp. 26-67.
Polomé, André R. 1975. Classification of the Bantu languages of
Tanzania. Austin: University of Texas, Ph.D. dissertation.
_____. 1982. Analysis of the language situation in the major churches
of Tanzania. In Edgar C. Polomé, André R. Polomé, and
Ali Abdullah, Language and religion in Tanzania. To appear
in Orbis 32.
Polomé, Edgar C. 1969. The position of Swahili and other Bantu
languages in Katanga. Texas Studies in Literature and Language 11.2: 905-13.
_____. 1971. Multilingualism in an African urban center: The
Lubumbashi case. In Wilfred H. Whiteley, ed., Language
use and social change. London: International African Institute, pp. 364-75.
_____. 1974. Rural versus urban multilingualism in Tanzania: An
outline. Paper read on August 21, 1974, at the 8th World
Congress of Sociology, Toronto, Canada. Revised version
to appear in the International Journal of the Sociology of
Language, 1982.
_____. 1975a. The reconstruction of Proto-Bantu culture from the
lexicon. In Working Papers in Linguistics 19 (ed. by Robert
K. Herbert). Columbus, O.: Department of Linguistics. Reproduced in L'Expansion Bantoue. Colloques Internationaux du
Centre National de la Recherche Scientifique—Sciences Humaines
—Viviers (France), 1977. Paris: SELAF, 1980, pp. 779-91.
_____. 1975b. Problems and techniques of a sociolinguistically
oriented language survey: The case of the Tanzania Survey.
In Sirarpi Ohannessian, Charles A. Ferguson, and Edgar C.

Polomé, Language surveys in developing nations. Arlington, Va.: Center for Applied Linguistics, pp. 31-50.

Polomé, Edgar C. 1977. Le vocabulaire proto-bantou et ses implications culturelles. In Paleontologia Linguistica. Atti del VI. Convegno Internazionale di Linguisti (Instituto Lombardo—Accademia de Scienze e Lettere), pp. 181-201. Brescia: Paideia.

_____. 1978. The earliest attestation of Swahili. In memory of Professor P. B. Pandit. Indian Linguistics. Journal of the Linguistic Society of India 30: 165-73.

_____. 1980. Tanzania 1970—A sociolinguistic perspective. In Edgar C. Polomé and Peter C. Hill, eds., Language in Tanzania. London: International African Institute, pp. 102-38.

Polomé, Edgar C., and Peter C. Hill, eds. 1980. Language in Tanzania. London: International African Institute.

Prator, Clifford H. 1972. Introduction. In Peter Ladefoged, Ruth Glick, and Clive Criper, Language in Uganda. London: Oxford University Press, pp. 1-15.

_____. 1975. The survey of language use and language teaching in Eastern Africa in retrospect. In Sirarpi Ohannessian, Charles A. Ferguson, and Edgar C. Polomé, eds., Language surveys in developing nations. Papers and reports on sociolinguistic surveys. Arlington, Va.: Center for Applied Linguistics, pp. 144-58.

Sanches, Mary, and Ben G. Blount, eds. 1975. Sociocultural dimensions of language use. (Language, Thought, and Culture. Advances in the Study of Cognition.) New York: Academic Press.

Scotton, Carol Myers. 1972. Choosing a lingua franca in an African capital. Edmonton/Champaign: Linguistic Research Inc.

Serpell, Robert. 1978. Comprehension of Nyanja by Lusaka schoolchildren. In Sirarpi Ohannession and Mubanga E. Kashoki, Language in Zambia. London: International African Institute, pp. 144-81.

Sharman, J. C. 1974. Some uses of common Bantu. In Wilfred H. Whiteley, ed., Language in Kenya. Nairobi: Oxford University Press, pp. 115-27.

Sudnow, David, ed. 1972. Studies in social interaction. New York: The Free Press.

Whiteley, W. H., ed. 1974. Language in Kenya. Nairobi: Oxford University Press.

Part II. Swahili

9 | Swahili in Tanzania

1.0 The Earliest Attestations of Swahili[1]

1.1 Origin of Swahili

The term 'Swahili' is derived from the plural form sawāhil of Arabic sāhil 'coast' and accordingly refers to the language used in the coastal trade between the Arabs and local population. The question of the origin of Swahili has given rise to a number of hypotheses: F. Johnson (1930) considered it as 'mixed language' resulting from intermarriage between Arab immigrants and Bantu women in Lamu; G. W. Broomfield (1931) expanded this view to include the various Bantu languages with which the Arabs came into contact, considering Swahili rather as a diasystem to which both these Bantu languages and Arabic contributed. Since a careful perusal of the grammatical structure of Swahili indicates that the influence of Arabic on its morphology and syntax has at best been minimal, and that the impact of Arabic phonology on its phonemic system has not affected the regularity of the correspondences of the terms of Bantu origin with their cognates in other Bantu languages, it is obvious that Swahili does not result from a language mixture. As B. Krumm (1932: 19) recognized, the Arab traders adopted the Bantu language of the coastal population and introduced a number of loanwords relevant to their commercial activity into it: the main linguistic consequence of this extensive borrowing from Arabic was presumably the establishment of a subsystem covering the unfamiliar phones of the borrowed terms. The problem of the location of the area where Swahili was originally spoken remained to be solved: F. Johnson and B. Krumm thought it must have been Lamu and the neighboring islands. R. Reusch (1953: 24) preferred to assume it developed at various places along the coast between Mombasa and Mogadishu in the eighth century. Recently B. Heine (1970: 81-83),

reviewing all the previous hypotheses, considered the view of B.
Struck (1921: 178) that Swahili originated around the Tana River estu-
ary as the most plausible. This location would put it closer to the
Pokomo area than to the Nyika dialects, in particular Giriyama, with
which Swahili is assumed to have 'marked affinities' (Bryan 1959:
129). T. Hinnebusch (1976) has, however, confirmed, after careful
study of the linguistic evidence, that Swahili is clearly connected with
Pokomo and Mijikenda (i.e. the Sabaki subgroup of Northeast Coastal
Bantu). Not only do they share phonological innovations, but lexicostatistical comparisons confirm their relationship.[2]

2.0 History of the Spread of Swahili

2.1 Spread to the South
          If Swahili has originated on the coast of the Indian Ocean near
the mouth of the Tana River, its spread to the south is undoubtedly a
result of the trading activity of the Arabs and Persians along the coast.
Unfortunately, there is little documentation available on this process
of expansion: both João de Barros (1552) and the Arabic History of
Kisimani (ca. 1520) date the penetration of Islam southward and the
opening of the gold trade with Sofala (in southern Mozambique) back
to the middle of the tenth century; this is traditionally assumed to have
led to the foundation of Kilwa by 'Alī ibn al-Ḥusain ibn 'Alī, about 957
(Freeman-Grenville 1962a: 66; Mathew 1963: 103). The situation
there at his arrival appeared to be rather complex: on the one hand,
the island was ruled by an African chief; on the other hand, it had already been partly Islamized, since a mosque had already been erected
and the newcomers called upon a local Muslim, Muriri wa Bari (obviously a Bantu name), to serve as 'interpreter.' No indication is given
about the language used in the negotiations with the African chief, from
whom the island was purchased under the bizarre condition that the
newcomer should encircle it with colored clothing—hence the nickname
nguo nyingi 'many clothes' given to 'Alī. One obviously wonders how
apocryphal this story may be, though it is often quoted as evidence for
the early presence of Swahili in the area: de Barros merely mentions
'Alī bought the island for some pieces of cloth! The other alleged Swahili nicknames of the early rulers of Kilwa according to Freeman-
Grenville (1962a: 83, 117): mkoma watu for 'Alī's son, Muhammad,
and hasha hazifiki for Ṭālūt ibn al-Husain (second half of the fourteenth
century) are disputable (Whiteley 1969: 34-35). The former can hardly

mean 'Borassus Palm of the People' as Freeman-Grenville claimed: mkoma watu must be a compound of the type mvunja mawe 'stone cutter' from the verb -koma, presumably in the meaning 'kill,' with watu as direct object, the meaning being 'the killer of men,' a nickname for which the text of the History of Kilwa Kisimani, unfortunately, does not provide any factual justification. As for Freeman-Grenville's reading (h)asha (h)azifiki it is only one among several possibilities of vocalization of the Arabic consonant sequence sh-z-f-k. Anyhow, it refers to a much later period, about thirty years after Ibn Baṭṭūta visited Kilwa. Though the latter specifically mentions the 'land of the Swahili,' the location remains vague: Mombasa is at least two days' journey from there. It is, however, obvious that, in spite of Freeman-Grenville's suggestion (1962a: 105), this 'land of the Swahili' cannot be the dominions of Kilwa: Ibn Baṭṭūta quite explicitly states that Kilwa is 'in the land of Zanj'; the people of the town, mostly 'Zanj of very black complexion,' are 'engaged in a holy war, for their country lies beside that of pagan Zanj' (Freeman-Grenville 1962b: 31). Accordingly, his testimony does not supply any information as to the linguistic situation in his time.[3]

Moreover, the alleged tenth-century Swahili nickname may also be spurious, since it now appears from the research of H. N. Chittick (1965) that it was not until the end of the twelfth century that Kilwa became an important trading center, and that 'Alī ibn al-Ḥasan, the founder of the local dynasty, may have ruled from Kisimani Mafia (cf. also Sutton 1966: 10; Chittick 1968: 111; Kimambo 1969: 36).

There is, however, evidence of permanent settlement and trading in Kilwa since the ninth century, but in those early days Unguja Ukuu on Zanzibar was flourishing: about 915 al-Mas'ūdī visited the area and in his description of the 'land of Zanj' he quoted three terms in the local language: (a) flīmī, plural waklīmī, designating the local 'kings'; (b) maliknajlu 'god'; (c) kalari, 'an edible plant' (Freeman-Grenville 1959: 11-12; 1962a: 40). The first word has been identified with the current Swahili word for 'king': mfalme, plural wafalme, and the second has been considered a modification of mkulu-ngulu, akin to the Zulu name of 'god' U-nkulu-nkulu; in both cases, the phonetic changes implied make the interpretations most disputable, though no satisfactory substitute solution has been offered.[4] As for the third word—kalārī—Freeman-Grenville's identification of the plant with 'the tough

leathery sheath of the coconut-flower stem (Swahili <u>karana</u>) is unconvincing, since it is supposed to be pulled out of the earth like truffles.'
However, Jan Knappert's suggestion that it designates the 'sweet po-
tato' (Swahili ki[l]azi) is not phonetically plausible, though Whiteley's
doubts about the cultivation of yams in East Africa at that time (1969:
33) are unjustified (cf. Wrigley 1970: 68–69).[5]

   Al-Mas'ūdī also mentions <u>Kanbalū</u> as the main island center
of Muslim trade in the land of Zanj in his day; this has been equated
with Madagascar (Freeman-Grenville 1962a: 40, n. 43) but can be
more plausibly identified with Pemba (Freeman-Grenville 1962b: 14)
or Zanzibar (Mathew 1963: 106).[6] This island was mentioned as a
major trading center by al-Idrīsi in the <u>Kitāb Rujār</u>, the first Western
notice of East Africa (twelfth century); he indicates that 'the principal
town is called Unguja in the language of Zanzibar' and that the people
of the coastal islands of Zanj go there to trade their goods 'for they
understand each other's language.' He also quotes the local names
of five types of bananas, namely <u>kundi, filī</u> (weighing up to 12 oz.),
<u>'omānī, muriyāni,</u> and <u>sukarī.</u> These terms do not provide very val-
uable clues; only <u>kundi</u> and <u>sukarī</u> correspond to two Swahili varieties
of bananas: <u>kikonde</u> (round, rather thick, sometimes granulose) and
<u>kisukari</u> (very sweet); the former is related with Swahili <u>ukonde</u> 'small
kernel';' the latter is obviously an Arabic loan, as are the other three,
which do not occur in present-day Swahili. However, <u>filī</u>, from Arabic
<u>fil</u> 'elephant,' corresponds to Swahili <u>mkono wa tembo</u> (literally 'ele-
phant trunk'), applying to large-size cooking bananas.

   The unreliability of the alleged Swahili material in the early
documents does not, however, preclude the use of Swahili as a lingua
franca in the trade centers along the coast down to Sofala,[8] but it has
to be remembered that until the end of the thirteenth century, the
Arabic settlements are essentially limited to the islands; the East
African coast, according to contemporary Arab geographers, is 'in-
habited by black people who were idolaters' (Ingham 1962: 2). The
majority of the inhabitants of the towns were also black, as well as
most of their rulers, undoubtedly as a result of intermarriage with
African women.[9] Piously devout Muslims, they must have maintained
Arabic at least as a language of prestige, since ibn Baṭṭuṭa does not
seem to have had problems in communicating with the sultan and the
high court officials at Kilwa. However, they must have used a lan-

guage of Bantu origin when dealing with their African subjects; the
question is whether, at this early date, the town language was already
Swahili?[10]

The only original text that has come down to us from this
time is the Kufic inscription in the mosque on Kizimkazi on the east
side of Zanzibar stating that Shaikh al-Sayyid Abi Amran al-Ḥasan
ibn Muḥammad ordered its building on the first day of the month Khul-
Qada in the year 500 A.H. (27 July 1107). Apart from confirming the
presence of Muslim rulers on the island at that time, it does not throw
any light on our problem.

2.2 Middle Period
More important seems the fact that a series of smaller settlements were established along the Tanzanian coast between the thirteenth century and the fifteenth century: Tongoni, in the Mtang'ata
chiefdom south of Tanga; Utondwe, south of the Wami River; Kaole,
south of Bagamoyo; Kunduchi, north of Dar es Salaam; Ras Malibe,
close to Mbwamaji, and Kisiju, halfway between Dar es Salaam and
the Rufiji River (Kimambo 1969: 39). Increased contact down the
coast and closer links with major centers like Zanzibar and Kilwa must
have promoted the use of a lingua franca in this period.

The first Portuguese who visited the area in the late fifteenth
and early sixteenth centuries do not provide any positive clue on the
linguistic situation at that time: Vasco de Gama (1498), who mistakes
the vegetarian Indians in Mombasa and Malindi for Christians, is aware
of their using a different language but points out their ability to communicate with the Arabs, because they picked up some of their language in years of mutual contact (Freeman-Grenville 1962b: 55). Similarly, Cabral (1500) uses an interpreter who speaks Arabic to nego-
tiate with the 'king' of Malindi, as he probably also did in Kilwa
though it is not indicated specifically there (Freeman-Grenville 1962b:
60-62). During his second trip, Vasco de Gama (1502) has an interpreter address the 'king' of Kilwa, his court, and even the women of
the city in the 'language of the country,' so that they might understand
his command (Freeman-Grenville 1962b: 69). Wherever the language
of the 'Moors,' as the Portuguese call the Muslims of the East African
towns, is specified, it is Arabic; describing Sofala, Duarte Barbosa
(1517-18) states (Freeman-Grenville 1962b: 127): 'The Moors of this

place speak Arabic' and he contrasts these Muslim merchants with
the 'Heathen of the kingdom of Benametapa' (Monomotapa), indicating
that 'some of them speak Arabic, but the more part use the language
of the country.' Similarly, the 'Moors' of Kilwa 'speak Arabic and
follow the creed of the African' being very pious (Freeman-Grenville
1962b: 131)—another reason for them to maintain Arabic, besides
their continued commercial links with the Arabic peninsula.

Perhaps N. Chittick (1968: 117) may have best summarized
the sociolinguistic profile of the cities along the Tanzanian coast:

> Their society was primarily Islamic, and their way of life
> mercantile. This does not mean to say it was Arab; the im-
> migrants were few in number, and intermarrying with Afri-
> can women and those already of mixed blood, their stock was
> rapidly integrated with the local people. Probably by the
> second or third generation they would have abandoned their
> spoken language for Swahili or the local language, though re-
> taining Arabic for writing.

However, his statement about Arabic might be somewhat qualified in
view of its use with foreign visitors and, undoubtedly, also in prayer
and other religious activities.

At the time of the first Portuguese intervention in the sixteenth century, the coastal towns constituted a strong of largely independent city-states under the control of often feuding 'Shirazi' ruling
families. Kilwa was the only major settlement in the south, but at
the time of its sack in 1505, the island and the town had a population
of only 4,000 people according to an eyewitness account (Freeman-
Grenville 1962b: 106); the central Tanzanian coast was more sparsely
settled; there were a series of small sultanates in the north, e.g. in
Mtang'ata (Tongoni) and Vumba. The disruptive impact of the Portuguese on the coastal settlements was increased by migrations of small
Bantu clans and tribes starting around the middle of the sixteenth century and moving mostly from north to south along the hill ranges fring-
ing the coast of Kenya and northern Tanzania. The situation was only
stabilized about 1700, at a time when the Portuguese had practically
established their supremacy over the Shirazi city-states for more than
a century (Berg 1968: 120-22).

Particularly important in this context is the migration and resettlement of inhabitants of Swahili settlements on the north coast of Kenya: some of the refugees went to Pemba, and "most of the Twelve Tribes, which comprise the present Swahili population of Mombasa occupied the island in this period." Further southward, many of the small Swahili towns along the Mrima coast in Tanzania may have been founded as a result of this movement of population (Berg 1968: 129). One wonders how much of an impact this migration from the north may have had on the old southern settlements like Kilwa, if the comment made by M. H. Abdulaziz about the language of the fourteen letters from Kilwa dating back to 1711-28 found in the Goan archives—"that the Swahili in which they were written is not too dissimilar from his own kiMvita" (Whiteley 1968: 38)—proves correct.

Anyhow, by the seventeenth century, we seem to have some direct evidence of a dialect related to Swahili spoken in the Comoro Islands: the short list of local terms compiled by Walter Payton, who visited 'Johanna' (Anjuani) includes five types of words (Gray 1950: 96):

(a) unidentifiable words, like seivoya 'cocker nuts' or quename 'pine';
(b) Portuguese loan words, like surra (kind of drink) and figo 'plantains,' reflecting Port. sura 'first juice of palm tree' and figo 'fig,' presumably applying to what Sacleux (1949: 314) calls 'figue banane' and renders by Swahili ndizi;
(c) Arabic loan words, like soutan (Swahili sultani < Arabic sultan) and cartassa (Swahili karatasi < Arabic qartas);
(d) Bantu terms shared by a number of East Coast languages, namely gombey 'bullock' < Bantu [C. S. 849] *gòmbè 'cattle' (Guthrie 3.225); coquo 'hen' < Bantu [C.S. 1203] *kúku (Guthrie 1.123-4 [§74.11-14; topogram 24]; 3.310); buze 'goat' < Bantu [C.S. 185] *búdì (Guthrie 3.61)—as regards coastal Bantu languages the change d → z/—i occurs essentially in southern Kenya and northern Tanzania, whereas devoicing to s takes place in southern Tanzania; in the Comoro form (Ngazija dialect) dz would be expected.
(e) terms with close Swahili correspondents, namely sinzano 'needle' = Swahili sindano;
arembo 'bracelet' = Swahili urembo 'ornaments' (from -remba 'adorn, decorate');
tundah 'oranges' = Swahili tunda (plural matunda) 'fruit' (< -tunda 'pluck') with a rather surprising specialization of the meaning,

since oranges are definitely not the characteristic fruit crop of
the Comoro Islands;

mage 'water' = Swahili maji—a very valuable sample if the graph-
eme <g> has the phonetic value [dʒ] of English -g- in image, since
this would be the normal reflex of Bantu *j in the Ngazija dialect
of the Comoro Islands (as the display of the forms under C.S. 937
*jí and C.S. 943 *jí [Guthrie 3.248,250] shows, the reflexes are
also affricates—dz or ts—in Kenya, but fricatives in Tanzanian
coastal dialects: z in the north and s [occasionally ð] in the south).

2.3 Eighteenth-Nineteenth Century

From the eighteenth century on, evidence for the use of Swahili becomes abundant: the oldest preserved manuscript is dated
1728 and contains an epic poem Utendi wa Tambuka written in Pate
(Harries 1972: 5; Knappert 1967: 3, 143-44); the oldest known poet
Aidarusi bin Athumani seems to have been active in the same town at
the end of the seventeenth century though the oldest manuscript of his,
al-Hamziyah, an interlinear version of the Arabic poem Umm al-Qura,
is dated 1749 (Knappert 1968: 55). The northern Kenya coast is indeed
the center of Swahili literary activity and Swahili poetry will only
start flourishing further south in Mombasa with Muyaka bin Haji in the
first decades of the nineteenth century, though earlier poems from
this town already found their way as far south as Anjuani in the Comoro Islands in the last quarter of the eighteenth century (Knappert
1969: 1-2).

As to Tanzania, literature began in Zanzibar toward the middle of the nineteenth century and the Mrima coast produced religious
poetry like the Kiyama in the second half of the nineteenth century.
Anyhow, written Swahili literature was essentially didactic and em-
bedded in an entirely Islamic sphere of life until the advent of the
German administration in 1884 (Knappert 1971: 4-5, 13).

3.0 The Present Situation

3.1 Swahili Dialects along the Tanzanian Coast

The linguistic situation along the Tanzanian coast is characterized by much less dialectal differentiation than in Kenya; from
Vanga to the Rufiji River, facing Mafia Island, Mrima is used, especially in towns like Tanga, Bagamoyo, and Dar es Salaam; it is very

similar to the main Zanzibar dialect—kiUnguja; south of the Rufiji a
subdialect known as Mgao has its main center in Kilwa (Sacleux 1909:
ix). As characteristic features of Mrima, Stigand (1915: 16-25)
mentions:

(1) l for r, e.g. balua for barua 'letter';
(2) s for sh, e.g. sauri for shauri 'plan, council';
(3) occasional devoicing of g, e.g. kiza for giza 'darkness';
(4) occasional palatalization of k to ch [tʃ] before front vowels [i],
    [e], e.g. kucheti for kuketi 'stay, sit';
(5) trend to realize [m̩] as [mu] and insertion of u after m before
    consonants, e.g. mutu for mtu 'person,' amuri for amri 'order';
(6) insertion of l or r in various sequences of two vowels, e.g. njara
    for njaa 'hunger';
(7) use of ya instead of la-concords with the 5th class, e.g. soka ya
    kuni 'axe for firewood'; jiko yake 'his kitchen.'

Many of these features are shared by Mgao, where they usually appear on a larger scale, in particular:

(1) confusion between r and l, e.g. asari for asali 'honey,' kuludi
    for kurudi 'return';
(4) palatalization of k to ch before i, e.g. chichwa for kichwa 'head';
(5) mu for [m̩] and insertion of u between m and consonant, e.g.
    muti for mti 'tree,' kuamuka for kuamka 'awake';
(6) insertion of l or r in sequences of two vowels (also in ia and ea
    where it does not occur in Mrima), e.g. kugwira for (kiMrima)
    kugwia 'seize,' kumera for kumea 'grow.'

Both Mrima and Mgao also show specific grammatical and lexical
peculiarities. Typical Mrima words are kugwia (kugwira) for kuka-
mata 'seize'; kitumba for kanda 'fisherman's basket'; machufuko for
fitina 'disorders'; a typical archaism in an outlying territory is the
old Swahili verb kuima for kisimama 'stand' preserved in Mgao.[11]

        The Mrima coast dialects have close links with the island
dialects; there are, for example, noticeable lexical correspondences
between Mtang'ata (south of Tanga)[12] and Pemba (Whiteley 1956: 6).
A closer relation between Vumba, Mtang'ata, Hadimu, Tumbatu,
and the northeastern and southeastern Pemba dialects, including

further connections with the Comoro dialects, has been assumed
(Whiteley 1959: 42).

In the islands, Pemba, spoken on Pemba island, shows four
local varieties: (1) kiPemba cha kusini; (2) kiPemba cha kivintongoji
(Mvumoni); (3) kiChake-Chake (Chake-Chake), and (4) kiMsuka (Chal-
eni), according to Sacleux (1909: ix). In the late fifties, when W. H.
Whiteley visited the islands, Zanzibar Swahili had apparently replaced
the local dialects in the western half of the island owing to the influx
of migrant workers from Zanzibar and the mainland in the above plantations. Distinctive Pemba dialects still survived in the Micheweni-
Wingwi peninsula of the northeast, on Kojani island in the east, and
the Matela-Kiuyu area south of Kojani (Whiteley 1958: 8). No detailed
description of these dialects is available, which Whiteley[13] divides
roughly into three groups, with a set of local variations: (1) northern:
Konde, Tumbe, Micheweni; (2) central: Kowani, Matele, Ndagoni,
Ngwachani, Kiuyu, Kambini; (3) southern: Chokocho. The differences
are essentially lexical, though there is also some variation in the demonstratives and the affixes in the verbal complex. Pemba in general
has two sets of subject prefixes in the singular of the affirmative
forms—a feature it shares with Vumba (on the Kenya-Tanzania border),
Hadimu (in southern Zanzibar), and Mtang'ata (on the Mrima coast);
one of them, however, is as a rule restricted to the -li- and -me-
tenses (Whiteley 1958: 12-15).

3.2 Zanzibar and the Coast
        On Zanzibar, three distinct dialects coexist: (a) Unguja,
which has become the basis of standard Swahili, and is originally the
language of Zanzibar town and the central part of the island; (b) Hadimu, also called Kae, is the dialect of the east and south of the island;
(c) Tumbatu is a subdialect spoken on the small Tumbatu island and
in Mkokotoni Bay in the northwest of Zanzibar island.

Both Hadimu and Tumbatu share a number of features with
Pemba; some of them point to the preservation of older forms where
Unguja innovates, e.g. in the case of the development of fy- (from Bantu
*pi-) before back vowel [u, o] to s-, as illustrated by Bantu *píú 'knife'
(C.S. 1544)> Pemba, Tumbatu, Hadimu kifyu, Zanzibar kisu (Ingrams
1924: 542).[14] Similarly, the three dialects maintain vy- as the reflex
of Bantu *bj- before vowel, where the cluster developed into z- in

Unguja, e.g. Bantu *bịád- 'bear (a child)' (C.S. 136) > Pemba, Tumbatu, Hadimu vyaa: Zanzibar zaa (Ingrams 1924: 536; Lambert 1962:
66). Also characteristic is Pemba, Tumbatu, Hadimus s versus Zanzibar sh [ʃ] as reflex of Bantu *ki, e.g. Bantu *kịŋgò 'neck' (C.S.
1086) > singo in the three dialects, but shingo in standard Swahili;
Bantu *yókị 'smoke' (C.S. 2114) > mosi in the three dialects, but
moshi in standard Swahili.

In other cases, however, Pemba goes its own way as opposed to the dialects of Zanzibar island, e.g. in the treatment of
Bantu *c, which is reflected by [ʃ] < sh > in Pemba versus [tʃ]
< ch > in the Zanzibar dialects, e.g. Bantu *càŋgà 'sand' (C.S.
288) > Pemba mshanga: Unguja mchanga; Bantu *cúpà '(calabash)
bottle; jar' (C.S. 425/6) > Pemba shupa: Tumbatu, Unguja chupa;
Bantu *cí 'country' (C.S. 331) > Pemba shi: Tumbatu muchi, Hadimu
chi, Unguja nchi. An important morphophonemic distinction is the
preservation of the prefix ki- before vowel-initial stems, e.g. Pemba
kiuma 'iron,' kielezo 'float (of fish net),' kiakwe 'his,' kiangu 'my':
Unguja chuma, chelezo, chake (Tumbatu chakwe), changu.

As for the Zanzibar island dialects, Tumbatu appears to
have preserved the Bantu prefix *di- of class 5 in a number of cases,
e.g. dyipu 'abscess' (versus Pemba and Hadimu ipu with zero prefix
and standard Swahili jipu), dicho 'eye' (: standard Swahili jicho).[16]
Prevocalic root-initial and intervocalic -l- (from Bantu *d) appears
as -y-, e.g. in yaya 'sleep' (: standard Swahili lala < Bantu *dáád-
[C.S. 456]), vuya 'rain' (: standard Swahili mvua, in which l → ∅
in /V - V/; Bantu *bụdà [C.S. 225]).

Characteristic features of Hadimu are: (a) the "lenition" of
/p/ to the voiced bilabial fricative [β] represented by < ʋ > (Lambert
1962: 51; Polomé 1967: 24), e.g. mọisi 'cook' (: Sw. mpishi); -ʋita
'pass' (: Sw. -pata); yaʋo 'there' (: Sw. hapo); (b) future: kachakufwa
= Sw. atakufa 'he will die'; akaga kuchamuwapa = Sw. akipotea utam-
tafula 'if he is lost, you will look for him.'

In Hadimu, loss of initial l- occurs in class 3/4 nouns like
mwango, plural miango 'door(s)' (: standard Swahili mlango); mwomo
'mouth,' plural miyomo 'lip(s)' (: standard Swahili mdomo, with [ɗ]!).
While Ingrams (1924: 540) recorded Tumbatu and Pemba mliango, he

also found mwango in Comoran (Ngazija); as for mwomo, this is also
the form occurring in the northern Tikuu dialect (cf. Guthrie 1970:
177, s.v. P.B. *-dòmò [C.S. 652]).[16] Similarly, Hadimu shares the
shift of l to u in the environment /a-m/ in the reflexes of Swahili
mfalme 'chief' with Ngazija, but it also occurs in Tumbatu with the
development of a glide between a and u: Hadimu/Ngazija mfaume:[17]
Tumbatu mfayume (Ingrams 1924: 538).

3.3 Regional Variation inside Tanzania

The dialects briefly described represent the primary regional
differentiation within the Swahili linguistic area. As the language
spreads through education, administrative and political use, economic
and cultural activities, and especially through the media which now
reach even the remotest corners of the country, new varieties are
likely to develop. These will be characterized by specific phonological
and grammatical features, by semantic shifts and by particular lexical
items. Thus, F. Madoshi noted a number of changes in meaning in
Swahili words in the Mwanza area (1971: 88), e.g. kalua (sect of Indian
fishermen) applying to a big boat,[18] mseto (literally: 'mash, mixture,'
applying in politics to a 'coalition' [Goldklang 1967: 198; Temu 1971:
12] or a 'multiracial government' [serikali ya mseto; Whiteley 1961:
13]) referring specifically to the 'opposition.' In some cases, however, rather than a semantic shift, direct borrowing seems to have
taken place: thus, mtumba 'container for snuff or powdered medicine,'
which Madoshi equates with coastal Swahili mtumba 'bale, load' (also
meaning 'book-casing' in Mvita and Amu according to Sacleux [1941:
617]), is presumably a loan from Sukuma tumba (class 3/4) 'snuffbox.'
So are a number of local Swahili terms listed by Madoshi (1971: 85-
88), for example:

Mwanza Swahili	Sukuma
palika 'be polygamous'	palika 'take a second wife'
udaga 'dried cassava'	budaga 'dried or powdered manioc'
(= Swahili makopa)	
sesa 'cut the grass before the real cultivation'	sesa 'hoe on the surface, remove the grass before cultivating a field'
sato (a general name for tilapia)	sato (fish of the carp family)
soga (rather small type of fish)	soga (fish variety)

gunguli 'village' (usually with
   natural boundaries in form of
   a valley, hills, and streams)
mlamji 'subchief'
nsumba ntare 'assistant
   headmaster'

gunguli 'village' (with locative
   prefix, also 'on the hill')

lamuji (class 1/2) 'judge'
nsumba 'junior' (literally 'young
   man') + ntale 'superior, notable,
   elder, authority'

It stands to reason that as Swahili takes firmer hold as first language of a large section of the population in many parts of Tanzania, it will expand its lexicon in this way, especially to denote local features and ecological realities, like the typical fish of Lake Victoria, the traditional dances of the area, or the plants and trees that are essentially found in the Lake region.

     Studies on lexical distribution in the primary dialects of Swahili are few: Ingrams (1924) merely provides a comparative word list; the model analysis of a set of verbal stems and their extensions by Carol Eastman (1969) covers essentially the dialects of the Kenya coast with Vumba in the south reaching into Tanzania (139); my own outline of the problem in 1968 remains sketchy, but cases like the term for 'refrigerator' indicate how new regional differentiations tend to develop; as I concluded on the basis of field notes collected in 1963:

> a pure Swahilization rifrijeratani in the locative is not un-
> common, though the abbreviated form friji is more currently
> used in Zanzibar; more conservative people on the Mrima
> coast and in rural Zanzibar will resort to phrases like mash-
> ini ya barafu,[19] joko la barafu (literally 'oven of ice'), san-
> duku la barafu, or the vaguer mtambo wa barafu, dude la
> barafu; nevertheless, a typical insular word rifu has emerged
> and is spreading all over Zanzibar and Pemba (Polomé 1968a:
> 610).

     Another field of incipient dialectal differentiation is revealed by the repeatedly reported "mispronunciations" of Swahili which local teachers point out. They reflect the well-known phonic interferences characteristic of bilinguals (Weinreich 1953: 14-28). A few examples based on the observations of Mr. Mhaiki, an experienced Tanzanian teacher, are given in Table 1.

Table 1. Examples of Variation in Pronunciation of Swahili[20]

	Sampling	Language area
(a) <u>devoicing</u>: [+ voice] → [- voice]		
(1) b → p	<u>parua</u> 'letter,' <u>paraparani</u> 'on the road'	Makua
(2) v → f	<u>fiatu</u> 'shoes,' <u>ufumbuzi</u> 'discovery,' <u>fyofyote</u> 'whatever'	Matengo, Nyakyusa, Bena, Ndendeule
(b) <u>strengthening</u>:[21]		
(1) fricative → stop [+ continuant] → [-continuant] f → p	<u>piga kopi</u> 'slap,' <u>kopia</u> 'cap,' <u>nina kipu</u> 'I am scared'	Makua, Ndendeule, Matengo, Mavia
(2) fricative → affricate (introduction of the feature [delayed release]) (I) s → ch[t∫]	<u>chacha</u> 'now,' <u>chokoni</u> 'at the market,' <u>chamaki</u> 'fish'	Mavia
(II) z → j [dʒ] <u>after nasal</u>	<u>njima</u> 'alive, sound,' <u>njungu</u> 'European'	Mavia
(III) z → ch [t∫] <u>with devoicing</u>	<u>checha</u> 'play,' <u>chamani</u> '(ancient) time(s),' <u>chawadi</u> 'present'	Mavia
(c) <u>'weakening'</u>:		
(1) affricate → fricative [dʒ] < j > → [z]/C$_{[+ nasal]}$ —	<u>nzaa</u> 'hunger,' <u>nzia</u> 'path,' <u>kunzua</u> 'spread open,' <u>mzane</u> 'widow,' <u>mzinga</u> 'simpleton, idiot'	Sukuma, Kerewe, Kinga
(2) d → l	<u>leni</u> 'debt,' <u>lobi</u> 'washerman,' <u>lukani</u> 'in the shop'	Matengo, Haya
(3) j → y	<u>kuya</u> 'come,' <u>yana</u> 'yesterday,' <u>yumapili</u> 'Sunday'	Matumbi

4.0 Language and National Development

As a society grows in complexity, the lexicon which expresses the various aspects of its activities expands, using various devices provided by the language to create new lexical items.

4.1 Semantic Development

The use of terms in a new context entails an expansion of their semantic field, and as cultural changes affected the Swahili-speaking community, numerous examples of such expanded semantic content appeared, e.g. in the vocabulary of law:

	Original meaning	New specialized meaning
kura	lot(s)	ballot
utoto	childhood	minority
majaribio	(plural of jaribio 'test')	probation
-thibitisha	secure, prove	probate
msamaha	pardon	amnesty

Similarly, in the field of mechanical engineering, kombo 'crank' applied originally to anything crooked, hook-shaped, for instance a small curved tool; chemua 'exhaust' meant originally 'sneeze'; etc.—but often the extended meaning is also linked with a new set of derivations, e.g. sharabu 'absorb'—literally: 'suck up'—and the related nominals kisharabio 'absorbent,' usharabu 'absorption'; chapuza 'accelerate'—causative of chapua 'speed up'—and the nominals kichapushio 'accelerator,' mchapuko 'acceleration,' etc.

The use of the prefix of class 14—Swahili u- (< Proto-Bantu *bu-)—creates new 'abstracts,' e.g. in the political terminology:

ubwanyenye	'exploitation'	(: bwanyenye 'bourgeoisie');
ubeberu	'imperialism'	(: beberu 'strong man,' also used for 'colonialist');
ukabila	'tribalism'	(: kabila 'tribe');
utaifa	'nationalism'	(: taifa 'nation'); etc.

4.2 Derivation and Composition

As in the majority of the Bantu languages, the flexibility of the derivational processes of Swahili greatly simplifies the task of

creating a technical terminology: with a semantically adequate combination of suffixes and the assignment of the nominals to the proper
classes the same root can produce a set of relevant specific terms,
e.g. from the verbal root tum- 'send' the following nouns can be derived:

(cl. 3/4)	mtume 'prophet'(applying to Mohammed),
	mtumo 'employment,'
(cl. 5/6)	tumo 'paid servant,'
(cl. 9/10)	tume 'messenger,'
(cl. 14)	utumo/utumi 'employment,'
	utume 'status of one sent.'

The passive form -tumwa 'be sent'—serves as a basis for the nouns
mtumwa 'slave' (literally: 'one sent'), utumwa 'slavery'; mtumwaji
'one regularly employed,' kitumwa '(diminutive) 'one who is employed
or sent.' Further derivations are based on tumisha/tumiza 'send off,
dispatch,' e.g. mtumishi 'paid servant,' matumishi 'service,' matu-
mizi 'employment,' utumishi/utumizi 'act of service, employment'
(Trager 1973: 45).[22]

There are some very striking examples of new terms coined
by such procedures, e.g. kutoingiliana 'non-intervention,' a negative
infinitive of the reciprocal of the applicative—ingilia ('enter with a
purpose, pry into') of -ingia 'go into' (Goldklang 1967: 203)—or President J. Nyerere's kujitegemea 'self-reliance,' the reflexive infinitive
of -tegemea 'rely upon' (Besha 1972: 34).

Composition serves similar purposes, e.g. on the pattern of
terms like mwanafunzi 'pupil,' a large number of new compounds with
mwana as first element were introduced: mwanamaji 'sailor,' mwana
sheria 'lawyer,' mwananchi 'citizen,'[23] etc. Some compounds are particularly descriptive, especially in engineering and the sciences, e.g.
kibadilimwendo 'cam,' containing badili 'change' and mwendo 'course';
nusukipenyo 'radius,' consisting of nusu 'half' and kipenyo 'axis.' Pur-
istic efforts to avoid loanwords will lead to such formations as, e.g.
gendameme, instead of dainamo 'dynamo'—literally 'fastening up electricity' from (-ganda 'coagulate' + (u)meme 'lightning')—or kizaameme,
instead of jenereta 'generator'—literally '[thing] engendering electricity'
(from -zaa 'give birth'). Some elements like da- from dawa 'drug'
function as affixes, e.g. in the biological terms:

dakuvu   'fungicide' (: kuvu 'mold'),
dabuibui   'arachnicide' (: buibui 'spider'),
dadudu   'insecticide' (: dudu '[large] insect'),
danyungu   'nematicide' (: nyungunyungu '[kind of] worm'),
dakono   'moluscicide' (: konokono 'snail'),
dagugu   'herbicide' (: gugu 'weed').

Similarly, -mea (the root of the verb 'grow,' applying to plant and
animal life) has practically become a suffix in nyungumea 'nematode,'
kungumea 'bugs,' kupemea 'scale insects' (Gurnah 1974: 43).

Often, however, phrases are used to render foreign concepts,
e.g. kuandika kwa ufupi 'stenography' (lit. 'writing with brevity'); njia
ya ugunduzi kwa lijulikanalo 'deductive method' (lit. 'way to cause what
is knowable to be discovered'); usomaji wa mchanganyiko 'co-education'
(lit. 'education of mixing together').

Compounds and periphrastic expressions are quite common
in the case of loan translations—a device frequently resorted to in
order to expand the specialized vocabulary, e.g. in the religious terminology: habari njema 'good news' for 'gospel' (instead of the loan
injili); chuo cha sala 'prayer book'; jamii ya utawa 'religious community'; etc. Similarly, in other fields, 'horsepower' is rendered by
nguvu farasi, 'hexagon' by pembesita ('six angles'), 'television' by
kionambali (lit. 'see far off'), etc.

4.3 Borrowing

As regards loans, previously hardly ever occurring Arabic
terms like thaura 'revolution' have become more commonly used, also
entering in compounds like mpingathaura 'counterrevolutionary' (the
first element belonging to the verbal root ping- 'oppose' [Temu 1971:
4]). New fields of application have been found for terms like gharadhi
('aim, intention, wish' → 'everyday goods') or irabu (vowel sign in
Arabic script → 'vowel'). However, the main source of loans in
English, not only in the field of technical development, but also in all
aspects of social and cultural life, though a conscious effort appears
to have been made in recent years to limit the borrowing of lexical
items as much as possible and to encourage Swahilization. In fact,
the number of English loans in the legal terminology compiled by A.
B. Weston and Sheik Mohamed Ali (1968) is remarkably small: prac-

tically, only the so-called 'stabilized anglicizations' (Weston 1965: 9),
like <u>kesi</u> 'case,' <u>ripoti</u> 'report,' <u>korti</u> 'court,' have been maintained,
but just as the Tanzanian administration replaced <u>rejinoo kamishna</u>
'regional commissioner' by <u>mkuu wa mkoa,</u> <u>siti konseli</u> 'city council'
by <u>baraza la jiji,</u> or <u>direkta</u> 'director' by <u>mkurugenzi,</u> the older Swahili <u>mahakama</u> 'place of judgment' (related with the Arabic loan <u>hukumu</u>
'pass sentence') may eventually replace <u>korti.</u>

Efforts to Swahilize the religious terminology are also illustrated by the successive publication of revised lists[24] containing increased number of Swahili equivalents, e.g. <u>papa</u> 'pope' → <u>baba mta-
katifu</u> 'holy father';

<u>retriti</u> 'retreat' → <u>mafungo</u> (: <u>funga</u> 'shut in');
<u>konsekrasyo</u> 'consecration' → <u>mageuzo</u> (: <u>geuza</u> 'cause to change');
<u>epistola</u> 'epistle' → <u>waraka</u> 'letter';
<u>epifania</u> 'Epiphany' → <u>tokeo la Bwana</u> 'apparition of the Lord'; etc.

This includes the use of specific Islamic terminology with a new Christian content, e.g. <u>tabishi</u> for the 'rosary,' <u>haji</u> for a pilgrimage to
Rome or Jerusalem, <u>nabii</u> 'prophet' (versus <u>mtume</u> 'apostle'), etc.
Swahilization efforts also include the technical terminology of mechan-
ics, for instance, as the following samples may show:

<u>breki</u> 'brake' → <u>zuio,</u> from –<u>zuia</u> 'cause to stop';
<u>klachi</u> 'clutch' → <u>mfumbato,</u> from –<u>fumbata</u> 'make come into contact.'

Sometimes, there even seems to be a choice between an English loan,
a Hindi loan, and a Swahili term, as in the case of the constellation of
the Charioteer (<u>Auriga</u>) for which the names <u>derava</u> (< E. <u>driver</u>),
<u>gariwala</u> (Hindi derivation with –<u>wala,</u> indicating the operator of a
vehicle—<u>gari</u>) and <u>mwendashaji</u> (Swahili for 'driver') are in competition (Rupper 1965: 75).

Nevertheless, the number of English loans in general remains
large. Mostly they have been adapted to the phonological structure of
Swahili by elimination of the phonemes not occurring in Swahili and
reshaping the pattern of syllabification in compliance with Swahili restrictions as regards consonant clustering. Thus, an epenthetic vowel
has been added to English words ending in consonants, e.g. <u>cheki</u>

'check,' kuponi 'coupon,' chati 'chart,' magrovu 'gloves,' lokapu
'look up,' etc.[26] Final -er is rendered by -a, e.g. silinda 'cylinder,'
poda 'powder,' jampa 'jumper,' pasenja 'passenger,' supa 'super,'
etc. Reshaping English words according to the Bantu syllable pattern
accounts for (li)kurutu 'recruit,' landirova 'Land Rover' (type of car),
sarakasi 'circus,' sitoo 'store,' etc. Sometimes, this may entail syllable loss as in (mu)enjilisti 'evangelist,' but usually the Swahili rendering is fairly close to the actual phonetic realization of the English
loan by local Bantu speakers, e.g. in fenicha 'furniture,' spea pati
'spare parts,' injinia 'engineer,' etc.

Whatever device is resorted to, it is obvious that a language
that can coin from its own resources such terms as kichungi 'filter
tip (of cigarette)' (from changa 'sift' [i.e. separate fine from coarse
particles]), papasio 'antenna (of insect)' (from -papasa 'grope about'
[i.e. feel one's way in the dark with the hands stretched out]), or
kigongaufizi 'flap (in descriptive phonetics)' (from -gonga 'knock' and
ufizi 'gum'), is undoubtedly well equipped to meet the needs of the
modern technological world.

NOTES

[1] A first version of sections 1 and 2 appears under the title
The earliest attestations of Swahili in a volume in memoriam of Professor P. Pandit (Delhi) published by the Linguistic Society of India
(Polomé 1978).
[2] In Hinnebusch's subgrouping (1976: 99), Swahili would be
placed as follows:
Sabaki-Seuta subgroup (connecting itself further up with Ruvu)
    A. Sabaki
        1. Pokomo-Mijikenda
          a. Pokomo
          b. Mijikenda (Giryama ... Digo)
    B. Seuta
        1. Zigula-Ngulu
        2. Bondei-Shambala
A typical Sabaki feature is the treatment of the class 5 prefix */di/
as dzi- (Giryama dzino 'tooth') or ji (Swahili jino 'tooth'). Seuta has
zi- (103). Swahili appears, consequently, as 'coastal Sabaki' (104).

[3] Tolmacheva (1975: 21-22), however, points to the use of the term jammun for a fruit in Mombasa—apparently Eugenia jambos 'rose-apple' ('It has a nut like an olive, but its taste is very sweet.' —Free-man-Grenville 1962b: 31). Known as mpera wa kuzungu, the plant actually originated in the South Asian subcontinent, where it is known as jambú- (Sanskrit > Punjabi jammū, Hindi jām, Gujrati jām, jā̃bu, etc.). The term jammun, mentioned by Ibn Baṭṭuṭa, however, is an Indic loan word reflecting the derived form *jambūna- (Turner 1966: 283) appearing with -mb- > -mm- (-m-) in a number of Indo-Aryan languages, e.g. Punjabi jammūn 'Syzygium jambolanum,' Maithili jāmun (a tree with a bitter purple fruit), Bhojpuri jāmun(i) 'edible blackberry,' Hindi jāmun 'Eugenia jambolena, Syzygium jambolanum.' Swahili mzambarao, designating the Java plum tree ('Syzygium jambo-lanum') reflects Indic jambula- which appears in Konkani as zāmbal 'Eugenia jambola' and may have been introduced by the Portuguese from Goa.

[4] Whiteley (1969: 33) quotes Knappert's alternate suggestions: (a) flĭmĭ/waklĭmĭ would reflect iqlimi 'district head,' but this term can hardly be considered as Swahili. Sacleux (1941) does not even list it under the sporadically attested Arabic loans; moreover, as Tolmacheva (1975: 21) indicates, the term is derived from the Greek loan iqlim 'area, district' in Arabic (< Gk. kluma—originally 'slope'), which does not apply to administrative divisions and would hardly be applied to themselves by the Bantu inhabitants of Zanj. (b) maklandjalou in-stead of maliknajlu (in the French translation of al-Mas'ūdī) is to be read mukulu ijulu 'the great one above.' Whiteley himself wonders whether wa in waklĭmĭ is not the 'possessive' and the kl- cluster related with Swahili kulu 'great,' since the Arab geographer claims the term means 'son of the great Lord.' As for the second term, Whiteley sug-gests a connection with the Arabic root m-l-k 'dominion.'

Ohly (1973: 17) compares Mas'ūdī's flĭmĭ (to be read [falimi]) with Shela mfaulume 'king' (= Amu, Pate, Mrima mfaume) and points to the derived meaning 'one who is violent, oppressive' in Nyika. In the absence of a properly documented modern edition of al-Mas'ūdī, with a critical examination of the variant readings of the manuscripts, all this remains highly speculative.

[5] Tolmacheva (1975: 20) assumes a basic meaning 'edible ground plant,' referring to the use of the same term in various Bantu languages, respectively for 'sweet potatoes,' 'cassava,' and 'ground nuts.'

[6]Tolmacheva (1975: 22) identifies Qanbalo in Al-Jahiz with Mkumbuu, an ancient port in Pemba, and wants to recognize a distorted form of Unguja in Lanjuya in the same author.

[7]Not derived from konde 'cultivated field,' as Whiteley (1969: 29) assumes; cf. Sacleux 1939: 371; 1941: 945.

[8]Additional material was adduced by the Leningrad scholars V. V. Malveyev and L. E. Kubbel, who examined the early Arabic sources. Thus, al-Biruni provides the name of the 'tamarind' under the plural form makuaju—Swahili mkwaju (: Nyika mukuaju; Ohly 1973: 17)—and the name of the 'rhinoceros': impila, which Tolmacheva (1975: 20) compares with Nyamwezi mpala/pera, without taking into account the Swahili dialectal form pe(r)a (with initial $[p^h]$) found in Mvita and Amu according to Sacleux (1941: 738-39).

[9]According to tradition, the first ruler of Kilwa, 'Alī ibn al-Husain, was the son of a Shirazi sultan and an 'Ethiopian' (Freeman-Grenville 1962a: 66, 75). Actually, the term Shirazi need not point to direct Persian origin: as Freeman-Grenville indicates (1962a: 78-79), it may apply to some African group along the coast in whom a few original traders from Persia (Shiraz) would have completely merged. More specifically, this seems to have been the case with the 'Shirazi' merchant rulers of Kilwa and Kisimani Mafia who set out from the Banadir coast in the Bantu-speaking area of southern Somalia to control the sea route to Sofala and the gold supplies from Monomotapa (Chittick 1968: 110-12).

[10]After surveying the sociological, linguistic, historical, archaeological, and literary data, R. Ohly (1973: 23) came to the conclusion that the Swahili language originated before the tenth century, but his position was questioned by M. Tolmacheva (1975: 24), who rightly points out: "... the available information ... proves that the basic ... phonetics and grammar had been established in the Zanj language by the 9th century and that native literacy was probably being shaped into a literary culture. The question remains whether we may call the language Swahili. ... the dialects of which Kiswahili is composed are still in the process of convergence into a united linguistic entity."

[11]Also occurring in Hadimu (Kae); see Lambert (1962-63: 56).

[12]The study of Mtang'ata—rapidly disappearing dialect of the Mrima coast south of Tanga by Whiteley (1956) does not provide much material: his description of the phonology shows very little difference with the Zanzibar dialect (one feature it shares with Pemba is the

absence of palatalization of ky to ch in terms like kyumba versus
[Unguja] chumba). The main characteristic of Mtang'ata is a special
set of singular subject prefixes for the perfect and past affirmative
tenses (22, 28-32), i.e. si for the 1st person, ku for the 2nd person,
and ka for the 3rd person, which also occur in Vumba (Lambert 1957:
40, 43-46). Pemba and Hadimu also show the forms ka- and ku- in
the 2nd and 3rd person, respectively, but the 1st person form is
n(i)- (Whiteley 1958: 12). As in these dialects the negative verbal
pre-prefix k'(a)- is currently used where standard Swahili has h(a)-.
As for Mrima, in general it is now 'almost identical with Kiunguja'
according to a leading Swahili writer (Whiteley 1956: 3).

[13] Whiteley's study (1958) does not provide any data on the
phonological peculiarities of the dialects, except for the absence of
palatalization of k before i; the analysis of the morphology is limited
to pointing out the main discrepancies versus standard Swahili, i.e.
Unguja. A full listing of noun classes is provided, as well as a table
of the tense markers with dialectal variation within Pemba; the latter
is accompanied by a rather extensive illustrative sampling (14-17).
The lexical material collected is limited, but reflects the vocabulary
of daily usage; the place where the terms were recorded is indicated,
but no attempt is made to determine the geographical area over which
they are used, though it is pointed out that, while absent in standard
Swahili, they 'occur in other dialects of this cluster, notably Hadimu,
Vumba and Mtang'ata' (55).

[14] Forms like fyoma for soma 'read' (Bantu *pióm- [C.S. 1543])
were considered as 'archaic' in Mrima and Mvita at the time Sacleux
(1939: 241) collected the data for his dictionary (from the end of the
nineteenth century until the early twenties); fyoma is still used in Pemba (Guthrie 1970: iv. 64). Occasionally fy- has been maintained in
Unguja, e.g. in fyonza 'suck.'

[15] Reflexes of Bantu *di- are also found in Pemba z(i)-, e.g.
zicho 'eye,' ziko 'kitchen' (: standard Swahili jicho, jiko), parallel
with Comoran (Ngazija) dz(i)-, in dzitzo, dziho (Ingrams 1924: 540,
542).

[16] This confirms the findings of Sacleux (1941: 538), who also
mentions mwomo for Tumbatu and Pemba, with the alternate form
muyomo in Hadimu and Pemba.

[17] According to Sacleux (1941: 544), mfaume also occurred in
the coastal dialects, namely in Mgao (in the Kilwa area), in Mrima,
and in Amu (cf. also fn. 3).

[18]The compilers of the Swahili Dictionary (in <u>Swahili</u> 36.2 [1966]: 181) point to the use of <u>karua</u> with the meaning 'boat' in the area of the Kavirondo Gulf. Patel (1967: 63) considers the term as a borrowing from Gujrati <u>kharvo</u> 'sailor' with a restricted meaning in Swahili. Etymologically, the Gujrati term appears to have meant 'carrier of salt' (< Skt. <u>ksār(a)</u>- 'alkali' +√<u>vah</u>- 'transport').

[19] In Zaïre, the phrase <u>mashini ya baridi</u> seems to prevail according to Kajiga (1975: 192).

[20]On the processes of consonant strengthening and weakening, cf. in particular, Hyman 1975: 164–69.

[21] Here again, comparing the local Swahili forms with the area Bantu languages provides the clue to the phonological changes. Thus, <u>nzaa</u> 'hunger,' <u>nzia</u> 'path' corresponds to Sukuma <u>nzala</u>, <u>nzila</u>, respectively. (For a parallel development in Lubumbashi Swahili, cf. Polomé 1968b: 18.) Similarly, where the local vernacular fails to show a voiced counterpart to the sibilant /s/,* voiceless realizations of Swahili /z/ are likely to occur. Some changes cut widely across the country, especially those affecting Swahili phonemes appearing characteristically in Arabic loans, e.g. the fricatives /θ/, /ð/, and /ɣ/, spelled respectively < th >, < dh >, and < gh >: the interdental fricatives are shifted to the corresponding alveolar /s/ and /z/ by changing the feature [-strident] to [+ strident], e.g. in <u>thamani</u> 'value, <u>kithiri</u> 'increase,' <u>theluthi</u> 'one-third,' etc.; <u>dhambi</u> 'sin,' <u>kadhalika</u> 'likewise,' <u>idhini</u> 'sanction, permission,' etc.

(1) the voiced velar fricative /ɣ/ is strengthened to the corresponding stop /g/ by changing the feature [+ continuant] to [-continuant], e.g. in <u>ghali</u> 'expensive, scarce,' <u>bughudha</u> 'ill feeling, slander,' <u>ghasia</u> 'confusion, disturbance,' etc.

Also widespread is the weakening of /h/ to Ø, e.g. <u>(h)asara</u> 'damage,' <u>(h)uruma</u> 'compassion,' <u>kwa (h)eri</u> 'goodbye,' <u>(h)ajui</u> 'he doesn't know,' etc.—entailing the use of hypercorrect forms with <u>h</u>-, e.g. <u>hasali</u> 'honey,' <u>maharufu</u> 'well-known,' etc.

---

* This is currently the case in the Chaga dialects, where Machame <u>fyaa</u> corresponds to Swahili -<u>zaa</u> (dialectal -<u>vyaa</u>) 'give birth to,' both reflecting Proto-Bantu *<u>bíád</u>- 'bear(child)' (Guthrie 1970: 3: 48), and Machame <u>nrye</u> to Swahili <u>nzige</u> 'locust,' both reflecting Proto-Bantu *-<u>gìgè</u> (Guthrie 1970: 3: 219), while the loanword -<u>suri</u> from Swahili appears with initial <u>s</u>-.

A typical regional feature on the morphological level is the occurrence of such prefixes as the diminutive ka-, e.g. katu (instead of kijitu 'little man'), kameza 'small table,' kapaka 'kitten,' in the Ngoni-speaking area, where the augmentative gu- is also found, e.g. gumtu (instead of jitu 'very big man'), gumeza 'large table,' gusimba 'big lion.'

It may be worth noticing that some of these features also occur in Kenya Swahili pidgin, characterized by (a) devoicing of v to f (e.g. ngufu 'force, strength,' kufaa 'put on (clothes),' etc.); (b) weakening of h to Ø (e.g. apana 'no,' roo 'heart,' etc.); (c) diminutives in ka- (e.g. kamtu 'dwarf,' kamto 'brook,' kalevi 'little drunkard,' etc.) (Heine 1973: 75, 84-85).

[22] For a comprehensive survey of the Swahili derivational patterns, see Polomé 1967: 77-94. The 'virtually unlimited' productivity of a pattern of derivation—the nouns of action in -o—is described by Knappert (1962-63); the extent to which extensions can be added to verbal roots and the complex structure of the derivations is surveyed by Whiteley (1968: 56-68 and tables II-IV), with a sample based on fung- 'fasten' (107-10).

[23] On compounds with mwana-, cf. Temu 1971: 4, 12. The connotations of mwananchi are discussed by Scotton 1965: 528-34; Philippson 1970: 531; Besha 1972: 30-31.

[24] The list submitted by the Tanzania Episcopal Conference and based on the Catholic Swahili catechism (Swahili 35.1 [1965]: 77-91) was revised and republished with Swahili explanations a few years later (Kiswahili 42.2/43.1 [1973]: 86-96; 43.2 [1973]: 98-112). In the meantime, Omari (1969) had pointed out some of the problems connected with the creation of a Christian theological terminology (Knappert's papers on 'The Divine Names' [Swahili 31 (1960): 180-98] and 'Swahili Theological Terms' [African Language Studies 8 (1967): 82-92] deal exclusively with Islamic concepts).

[25] On the rules governing the phonological adaptation of loans, cf. Polomé 1967: 175-76. It should, however, be observed that 'irregularities' occur, e.g. jemi 'jam,' midila 'medal,' likurutu 'recruit' (the last case, with final -u presumably due to vowel harmony).

REFERENCES

1. Origin of Swahili

Berg, F. J. 1968. The coast from the Portuguese invasion to the
    rise of the Zanzibar Sultanate. In B. A. Ogot and J. A.
    Kieran, eds., Zamani. A survey of East African history.
    Nairobi: East African Publishing House, pp. 119–41.
Broomfield, G. W. 1931. The re-Bantuization of the Swahili language.
    Africa 4: 77–85.
Chittick, Neville. 1965. The 'Shirazi' colonization of East Africa.
    Journal of African History 7, 3: 275–94.
_____. 1968. The coast before the arrival of the Portuguese. In
    B. A. Ogot and J. A. Kieran, eds., Zamani. A survey of
    East African history. Nairobi: East African Publishing
    House, pp. 100–118.
Freeman-Grenville, G. S. P. 1962a. The medieval history of the
    coast of Tanganyika, with special reference to recent archaeo-
    logical discoveries. London: Oxford University Press.
_____. 1962b. The East African coast. Selected documents from
    the first to the earlier nineteenth century. Oxford: Clarendon
    Press.
Gray, Sir John. 1950. Portuguese records relating to the Wasegeju.
    Tanganyika Notes and Records 29: 95–96. (See Whiteley,
    1968: 37: 113.)
Guthrie, Malcolm. 1967-71. Comparative Bantu. An introduction to
    the comparative linguistics and prehistory of the Bantu lan-
    guages. 1. The comparative linguistics of the Bantu languages.
    2. Bantu prehistory, inventory and indexes. 3-4. A catalogue
    of common Bantu with commentary. Farnborough: Gregg Press.
Harries, Lyndon. 1962. Swahili poetry. Oxford: Clarendon Press.
Heine, Bernd. 1970. Status and use of African lingua francas. (IFO-
    Institut für Wirtschaftsforschung München—Afrika Studien,
    vol. 49.) München: Weltforum Verlag.
Hinnebusch, Thomas J. 1976. Swahili: Genetic affiliations and evi-
    dence. Studies in African Linguistics. Supplement 6, pp. 96-
    108. (Papers in African Linguistics in Honor of Wm. E.
    Welmers.)
Ingham, Kenneth, 1962. A history of East Africa. London: Longmans,
    Green.

Johnson, F. 1930. Zamani mpaka siku hizi. London (quoted in
    Reusch 1953: 22).
Kimambo, Izaria N. 1969. The interior before 1800. In I. N. Ki-
    mambo and A. J. Temu, eds., History of Tanzania. Nairo-
    bi: East African Publishing House, pp. 14-33.
Knappert, Jan. 1968. The Hamziya deciphered. African Language
    Studies 9: 52-81.
_____. 1969. The discovery of a lost Swahili manuscript from the
    eighteenth century. African Language Studies 10: 1-30.
_____. 1971. Swahili Islamic poetry. 1. Introduction. The celebra-
    tion of Mohammed's birthday. Swahili Islamic Cosmology.
    2. The two Burdas. 3. Mi'rāj and Maulid. Leiden: E. J.
    Brill.
Krumm, B. 1932. Wörter und Wortformen orientalischen Ursprungs
    im Swaheli. Hamburg: Friederichsen, de Gruyter.
Mathew, Gervase. 1963. The East African coast until the coming of
    the Portuguese. In Roland Oliver and Gervase Mathew, eds.,
    History of East Africa, vol. 1, pp. 94-127. Oxford: The
    Clarendon Press.
Ohly, Rajmund. 1973. The dating of Swahili language. Kiswahili 42.2/
    43.1, 15-23.
Reusch, R. 1953. How the Swahili people and language came into
    existence. Tanganyika Notes and Records 34: 20-27.
Sacleux, C. 1939-49. Dictionnaire Swahili-Français. Part I, A-L
    (1939); Part II, M-Z (1941). (Travaux et mémoires de
    l'Institut d'Ethnologie. Université de Paris, vols. 36-37.)
_____. Dictionnaire Français-Swahili. (2d ed., same series, vol.
    44, 1949.) Paris: Musée de l'Homme.
Struck, B. 1921. Die Einheitssprache Deutsch-Ost-Afrikas. Kolon-
    iale Rundschau, 1921, pp. 164-96.
Sutton, J. E. G. 1966. The East African coast. An historical and
    archaeological review. (Historical Association of Tanzania,
    Paper no. 1.) Nairobi: East African Publishing House.
Tolmacheva, Marina. 1975. The Zanj language. Kiswahili 45.1:
    16-24.
Turner, R. L. 1966. A comparative dictionary of the Indo-Aryan
    languages. London: Oxford University Press.
Whiteley, Wilfred. 1969. Swahili. The rise of a national language.
    (Studies in African history, vol. 3.) London: Methuen.

Wrigley, Christopher. 1970. Speculations on the economic prehistory
     of Africa. In J. D. Fage and R. A. Oliver, eds., Papers
     in African prehistory. Cambridge (U. K.): University Press,
     pp. 59-73.

2. The Present Situation

This bibliography makes no claim to exhaustiveness, but covers the
materials used for the discussion of the development of Swahili.

Akida, Hamisi M. 1971-75. Msamiati wa Muda wa Sayansi (Elimuvi-
     umbe). Kiswahili 41.1 (1971): 8-45; 42.2 (1971): 95-102;
     42.2/43.1 (1973): 97-101; 43.2 (1973): 116-20; 45.1 (1975):
     57-63.
Alidina, M. M. R. 1975. The switch-over to Swahili. Kiswahili
     45.1: 51-54.
Baldi, Sergio. 1976. A contribution to the Swahili maritime termin-
     ology. (Collana di Studi Africani, vol. 2.) Rome: Istituto
     Italo-Africano.
Besha, R. 1972. Lugha ya Kiswahili hivi leo: hasa katika siasa.
     Kiswahili 42.1: 22-38.
Eastman, Carol M. 1969. Some lexical differences among verbs in
     Kenya coastal Swahili dialects. African Language Review 8:
     126-47.
Frankl, P. J. L., et al. 1970. Maneno ya Utaalamu wa Sayansi ya
     Lugha. Kiswahili 40.2: 1-5.
Goldklang, Harold A. 1967/68. Current Swahili newspaper terminol-
     ogy. Swahili 37.2: 194-208; 38.1: 42-53.
Gurnah, Abdulla M. 1974. Agricultural terms in kiSwahili. In
     Kiswahili 44.2: 32-44.
Guthrie, Malcolm. 1967-71. Comparative Bantu. 4 vols. Farnbor-
     ough: Gregg Press.
Heine, Bernd. 1973. Pidgin-Sprachen im Bantu-Bereich. (Kölner
     Beiträge zur Afrikanistik, vol. 3.) Berlin: Dietrich Reimer.
Hyman, Larry M. 1975. Phonology. Theory and analysis. New
     York: Holt, Rinehart & Winston.
Ingrams, W. H. 1924. The dialects of the Zanzibar Sultanate. Bull-
     etin of the School of Oriental Studies 3: 533-50.
Kajiga, Balihuta. 1975. Dictionnaire de la langue Swahili. Goma:
     Librairie Les Volcans.

Knappert, Jan. 1962/63. Derivation of nouns of action in -o̱ in
    Swahili. Swahili 33.1: 74–106.

Lambert, H. E. 1957. Ki-Vumba. A dialect of southern Kenya
    coast. (Studies in Swahili dialect—II.) Kampala: East
    African Swahili Committee.

_____. 1962/63. (ed. H. E. Lambert) Haji Chum: A vocabulary
    of the Kikae dialect. Swahili 33,1: 51–68.

Madalla, Amos. 1972. Mechanical engineering terminology. Kiswahi-
    li 42.1: 75–86.

Madoshi, F. F. 1971. KiSwahili words peculiar to Mwanza. Kiswa-
    hili 41.1: 85–88.

Mkelle, M. B. 1971. Change in content and meaning of words. Kis-
    wahili 41.1: 100–105.

Ohly, Rajmund. 1973. Word and civilization. Kiswahili 43.2: 52–57.

_____. 1975. The conception of State through Swahili. Kiswahili
    45.1: 25–33.

_____. 1976. Lexicography and national language. Tanzania Notes
    and Records 79/80: 23–30.

Omari, C. K. 1969. Towards the development of Swahili theological
    terms. Swahili 39.1/2: 119–24.

Ostrovsky, V., and J. Tejani. 1967–68. Second tentative word list.
    Swahili 37.2: 209–24 (A-I); 38.1: 54–99 (J-T); 38.2: 164–68
    (T-Z).

Patel, R. B. 1967. Etymological and phonetic changes among for-
    eign words in Kiswahili. Swahili 37.1: 57–64.

Philippson, Gérard. 1970. Etude de quelques concepts politiques
    swahili dans les oeuvres de J. K. Nyerere. Cahiers d'Etudes
    Africaines 10: 530–45.

Polomé, Edgar C. 1967. Swahili language handbook. Washington,
    D. C.: Center for Applied Linguistics.

_____. 1968a. Geographical differences in lexical usage in Swahili.
    Verhandlungen des zweiten internationalen Dialektologen-
    kongresses II (= Zeitschrift für Mundartforschung. Beihefte.
    N. F., vol. 4), pp. 664–72.

_____. 1968b. Lubumbashi Swahili. Journal of African Languages
    7: 14–25.

_____. 1978. The earliest attestation of Swahili. Indian Linguistics
    39: 165–73.

Prins, A. H. J. 1970. A Swahili nautical dictionary. Dar es Salaam:
    Chuo cha Uchunguzi wa Lugha ya Kiswahili.

Rupper, G. 1965. Suggested list of terms for stars and constellations. Swahili 35.1: 75-76.

Sacleux, C. 1909. Grammaire des dialectes swahilis. Paris: Procure des PP. du St. Esprit.

_____. 1939-41. Dictionnaire Swahili-Français. 2 vols. Paris: Institut d'Ethnologie. Musée de l'Homme.

Scotton, Carol M. M. 1965. Some Swahili political words. The Journal of Modern African Studies 3: 525-42.

Stigand, C. H. 1915. A grammar of dialectic changes in the kiSwahili language. Cambridge: University Press.

Tejani, J., V. Ostrovsky, and Ali Kondo. 1966-67. Tentative list of new words. Swahili 36.2: 169-85 (A-K); 37.1: 103-23 (L-Z).

Temu, Canute W. 1971. The development of political vocabulary in Swahili. Kiswahili 41.2: 3-17.

Trager, Lillian. 1973. The formation of nouns from verbs in Swahili. Kiswahili 42.2/43.1: 29-50.

Weinreich, Uriel. 1953. Languages in contact. Findings and problems. New York: Linguistic Circle of New York.

Weston, A. B. 1965. Law in Swahili—problems in developing the national language. Swahili 35.2: 2-13.

Weston, A. B., and Sheikh Mohamed Ali. 1968. Swahili legal terms. Dar es Salaam: The Legal Research Centre Faculty of Law, University College.

Whiteley, W. H. 1956. Ki-Mtang'ata. A dialect of the Mrima coast—Tanganyika. (Studies in Swahili dialect—I.) Kampala: East African Swahili Committee.

_____. 1958. The dialects and verse of Pemba. An introduction. (Studies in Swahili Dialect—IV.) Kampala: East African Swahili Committee.

_____. 1959. An introduction to local dialects of Zanzibar. Part I. Swahili 30: 41-69.

_____. 1961. Political concepts and connotations. Observations on the use of some political terms in Swahili. St. Antony's Papers 10. African Affairs I (edited by K. Kirkwood), pp. 7-21.

_____. 1964. Problems of a lingua franca: Swahili and the trade-unions. Journal of African Languages 3: 215-25.

_____. 1968. Some problems of transitivity in Swahili. London: School of Oriental and African Studies, University of London.

Anon.   1972.   Msamiati wa muda wa Masomo ya Maendeleo.   (Development Studies.)   Kiswahili 42.1: 70-74.

Anon.   1974.   Msamiati wa Muda wa Chuo cha T. A. N. U.   Kivukoni. Kiswahili 44.1: 67-70.

Anon.   1974.   Msamiati wa Muda wa Saikolojia.   Kiswahili 44.2: 75-81.

10 | Lubumbashi Swahili

The development of an important urban concentration by
rapid industrialization of the Katangese mining district has entailed
remarkable linguistic consequences.[1] While multilingualism was
already common in Katanga before the penetration of Europeans, the
tremendous development of the Union Minière du Haut-Katanga has
produced a considerable influx of migrant labor from all neighboring
areas, but mainly from the Kasayi, the northern and western districts
of Katanga, Rwanda-Burundi, as well as Rhodesia. Swahili, which had
already been introduced before the Belgian occupation by the baYeke
from uNyamwezi, had been adopted as a lingua franca by the colonial
administration in the area. Many of the immigrants from the eastern
areas of the Congo as well as from Rwanda-Burundi also used it as a
language of intertribal communication, so that it soon emerged as the
common language of social intercourse in the mushrooming urban communities of the Katangese mining district. It was, however, strongly
influenced by the Luba speakers from the Kasayi and northwest Katanga, as well as by the local Bantu languages, mainly Bemba. Intertribal marriage led to detribalization and Swahili emerged as the
mother tongue of part of the younger generation of the Katangese city
dwellers. The teaching of Swahili in schools, however, was discontinued and soon the only East Coast Swahili to which the speakers of
Katanga Swahili were exposed was that used in the local press, on the
radio, and in religious instruction. Consequently folk plays and current conversation show a local creolized variety, diverging considerably from east coast Swahili, but showing many of the features of the
Congo Swahili known as kiNgwana. As a matter of fact, the Swahili
spoken in a town like Lubumbashi (formerly Elisabethville) could be
described as a linguistic continuum ranging from the rather sophisti-

cated speech of those taught in the East Coast standard version (Swahili safi, literally 'clean Swahili') to the potopoto-Swahili (literally
'muddy Swahili') of the uneducated speakers, acquired through daily
contact in intertribal social intercourse.[2] This paper focuses on the
characteristics of the creolized variety of Swahili spoken by people
without formal education in East Coast Swahili.[3]

In order to indicate more clearly the background against
which this Katangese Swahili creole developed, it is worthwhile to
direct attention to the lexical interchange to which the long coexistence
of Africans and Europeans gave rise. This extended linguistic contact
not only led to the borrowing of technical as well as everyday words
from French into Swahili, but also involved the taking over of various
Swahili words and phrases into the local French. Typical of the French
spoken in Lubumbashi are some loan words from Swahili, which are
perfectly integrated into the colloquial language, e.g. pimer 'to size
up,' from (ku)pima 'test, try out,' e.g. 'ce gars-là, je l'ai pimé: il
n'a pas de mayele' ('I sized up this guy: he has no brains')—mayele
being the local substitute for coastal Swahili akili 'intelligence, clever-
ness'; pinduler 'to turn over,' e.g. 'sa voiture a pindulé à la Munama'
('his car turned over at the Munama'), from kupindu(l)a 'turn over,
capsize'; Lubumbashi expatriates call a 'letter' a mukande, French
pronunciation of local Swahili mukanda, borrowed from Lingala mo-
kandá to replace the Arabic loan barua; a 'tip' is a matabishi, actually
a borrowing from African Portuguese matabicho; any insect will be
called bilulu; the shorts commonly worn by Africans and expatriates
are known under the name of kaputula, a word that may ultimately
derive from Nyanja.[4] An interesting case is also the hybrid fungula-
teur for a 'can opener,' derived with the French suffix for instruments
from the Swahili verb stem -fungu(l)a 'open,' just as the Kinshasa
hybrid zibulateur 'can opener' is derived from the liNgala verb stem
-zibola 'open.' A rich set of exclamations from Swahili will also make
the expatriate's speech more picturesque, e.g. wapi, to express his
disbelief; mama yangu 'oh mother!' to express astonishment or admiration; mungu moya, literally 'one god,' accompanied by the gesture
of cutting one's throat, to confirm that he speaks the truth; kazi yako
'(that's) your business.' Particularly striking is il l'aura à son book
'he'll have to pay the piper,' where the English word applies to the
labor record booklet of African servants, in which fines for unjustified
absence, gross errors, breakage, etc. were noted in colonial days.

Conversely, the French loanwords cover a wide scope of subjects in Swahili: obviously they are mostly related with the effects of the colonial administration and the partial Westernization of urban life. Such are words like lopitalo (or less Swahilized opital), contrat (especially in kazi ya contrat, i.e. non-permanent job for menial tasks like gardening), facture ('bill'), buloko 'jail'—a Swahilization of French slang 'bloc' in 'mettre au bloc' (= 'to put in the cooler'), etc. Typical Western products are evidently borrowed with their name, e.g. articles of clothing: chapeau 'hat,'[5] chemise 'shirt,' chaussettes 'socks,' pantalon 'pants,' cravate 'tie,' etc., when they represent items which originally were typically used only by the expatriates and which were eventually taken over by the more sophisticated members of the African community. On the contrary, those commonly used by the average African worker show an adaption to his way of speech which has practically Bantuized them, e.g. salubeti 'overalls,' from French salopette. This vocabulary also contains older English loans like kochi from koti with palatalization—presumably already brought in from the east coast. The same is true of pieces of furniture: fauteuil 'armchair' is strictly French and of recent date, but bafwa 'bath' and kabati '(small) cupboard' have been known since the early days. The lack of understanding of French by lower-level Africans of the working class leads to curious misunderstandings: a small chest of drawers is, indeed, described as kabati kiloko kwa macomptoirs, i.e. the collective prefix ma- + the French word for 'counter' instead of tiroirs 'drawers.' The desire to impress, or perhaps a rather subtle distinction between indigenous and imported varieties of flowers or fruits leads to the apparently unnecessary substitution of mafleurs for maua and mafruits for matunda. In many cases, the French word also gradually replaces the less common east coast word, e.g. prafond, with r for l, from Fr. plafond 'ceiling' instead of the Arabic loan dari; allumetti 'matches' instead of the Arabic loan kiberiti; this is especially the case when the French word designates a special variety of the species under consideration, e.g. sitéron from Fr. citron 'lemon,' instead of ndimu, which rather designates 'lime.' The French words belonging to the current speech of the lower-class inhabitants of Lubumbashi have been phonetically reshaped to conform with the phonotactics of their language: this entails the breaking up of unusual clusters by the insertion of svarabhakti vowels, whose quality is determined by the coarticulation features of the preceding consonant as in apusan with the high back rounded vowel u after p from French absent 'absent' [apsã] or with

the front high unrounded vowel i after s in sitopo from the French use
of English stop for a 'stop sign,' also applied in Lubumbashi Swahili
to the 'brakes.' In certain cases, the quality of the epenthetic vowel
is determined by vowel harmony especially with clusters followed by
[ã], e.g. palanton 'orderly,' tarante 'thirty,' but also with [i], as
shown by the local designation of the Methodist Church as sipiling,
from the name of the minister in charge for so many years, Rev.
Springer. More complex phonetic adaptation is likely to take place
when the cluster involved is totally alien to the system of Bantu, e.g.
[ks] in French accident, which is reshaped into akistan with meta-
thesis of the [i], since the cluster st is more common in Swahili,
though hatari, actually 'danger,' is used by metonymy for 'accident,'
e.g. in official documents instead of East Coast msiba. In French
klaxonner 'to hoot,' the whole first syllable has been dropped by hap-
lology so that only sonner, homonymous with Fr. sonner 'to ring,'
has been preserved in the hybrid phrase kupika sone.

    Meanings are also changed in the process of borrowing: thus,
Fr. guidon which designated the handle bar of a bike, now applies to
the fork in Sw. kido; Fr. contact is used as such for the contact key
of a car, etc.

    The impact of the Rhodesians on some industries has led to
the preference of English words above French in certain fields; thus,
the current substitute for E. Coast dirisha is windo; Lubumbashi workers use hama side by side with Congo Swahili sando for 'hammer'
instead of E. Coast nyundo. The English loans tauni 'town,' komponi
'compound,' kona 'corner' attest to the participation of migrant labor
from the south in the development of the city; contributing to the popu-
larity of the futubol, they have also added (ku)luza 'to lose' to the English terminology current in Lubumbashi Swahili. Their impact on
economic life is also shown by the current word chipi 'cheap' in the
phrase bei chipi translating French 'bon marché.' Even the name of
the cat—E. Coast paka—is an English loan pushi, with Western Katangese palatalization of s to [ʃ] from pussy-cat.

    This palatalization is, indeed, one of the typical features of
Lubumbashi Swahili phonology: most common is the change of [s] to
[ʃ] before [i], e.g. bushiku 'night,' -epeshi 'quick' versus East
Coast Swahili usiku, -epesi; usually, however, the shibilant is optional,

e.g. pashipo 'there is not,' used prepositionally in the meaning of
'without,' mweushi 'black' (adjective with 1st class concord), alternating with pasipo, mweusi. Parallel, [z] is palatalized to [ʒ] before
[i], e.g. in mbuzi 'goat' pronounced ['mbuʒi]. The phenomenon is
obviously ascribable to the influence of native speakers of Luba languages on Katanga Swahili, since the palatalization of [s] and [z] to
[ʃ] and [ʒ], respectively, before [i] is a characteristic feature of
their language. This is further confirmed by the Luba loan mukaji
'wife' [mu'kaʒi] corresponding to kiKongo ŋŋkazi; in the Bemba rural
dialect of Kafubu, about ten miles from Lubumbashi, this term appears,
indeed, as mukashi. Maybe Bemba influence is accordingly responsible
for the sporadic devoicing of the resulting shibilant, e.g. in bushingi-
shi 'sleep,' muloshi 'sorcerer' versus East Coast Swahili usingizi,
mlozi. Hypercorrect forms have also developed as a result of these
palatalization processes, e.g. kuziba 'to have enough to eat,' instead
of East Coast kushiba. More difficult to explain is, however, the
change of [s] to [ʃ] without palatalizing factor in -pashwa for -paswa,
e.g. in inapashwa 'it is necessary': maybe the shibilant is ascribable
to the influence of -pasha 'cause to get'?[6]

   Another palatalization process due to Luba influence is the
sporadic change of [ti] to [tʃi], e.g. kiti, plural viti 'chair(s),' alternating with kichi, plural bichi. Even English loans like koti, pronounced ['kotʃi] can be affected by it. That the phenomenon is typically
Luba is shown by the form muchi for 'tree,' usually muti, since the
neighboring Bemba dialect of Kafubu has muti. Similarly, [di] becomes [dʒi] in mukindi 'corn,' pronounced [mu'hindʒi].

   Shared with the kiNgwana is the devoicing of [g] to [k], except after nasal, e.g. in kifakio versus (East Coast) ufagio 'broom';
kani versus (East Coast) gani 'which' (e.g. in the common phrase
habari kani? 'what's the news?,' used for 'how are you?'); mukongo
versus (East Coast) mgongo 'back'; mboka versus (East Coast) mboga
'vegetable.' In most cases, [g] is also heard, except in certain words
in which [k] is constant, e.g. makalashi 'eye-glasses; window-panes,'
actually a borrowing from English glass, with the 'collective' prefix
ma- (kalashi shows k- from g-, the following -a- being due to vowel
harmony [in contrast with -i- in the East Coast form gilasi] and -sh-
results from s before i, the normal paragogic vowel after final dental
in foreign loans). Sometimes, this leads to homophony between

originally contrasting pairs, e.g. pika (from [East Coast] piga 'strike'):
pika (=[East Coast] pika 'cook'). The maintenance of [g] after -n-
seems to motivate the insertion of an epenthetic [ŋ], e.g. in mangar-
ibi versus (East Coast) magharibi;[7] perhaps it occurs for the purpose
of differentiation from possible homonyms in mungazi (: [East Coast]
mgazi) 'ladder,' versus mukazi 'work-day' (also with palatalization of
[z] to [ʒ], and, then, homonymous with the Luba loan mukaji 'wife')?

Occasionally [v] is also devoiced to [f], but, in such cases,
[v] also occurs apparently in free variation, e.g. mafi ~ mavi 'excre-
ment,' ndefu ~ ndevu 'beard,' mbafu ~ mbavu 'rib.' In a few cases,
however, the contrast is phonemically pertinent, e.g. kitovu 'navel':
kitofu 'range'; there are also cases where v never appears, e.g. kufuta
'smoke (tobacco)' (: [East Coast] kuvuta).

Typically Central Bantu is the shift of [r] to [l], e.g. Katanga
Swahili kilaka 'patch,' kuluka 'to fly,' lafiki 'friend,' felo 'iron,' versus (East Coast) kiraka, kuruka, rafiki, Portuguese ferro. Conversely,
[l] in the (East Coast) adjective -kali 'sharp, cutting' always appears
as [r] in the stereotyped form makari. There are also numerous cases
of weakening of [d] to [l], e.g. (East Coast) udongo 'ground, earth,'
damu 'blood': (Katanga) bulongo, lamu. Stem initial r- is seldom preserved in low-level colloquial Lubumbashi speech and such words as
radio or kurudia 'come back' will then be heard as lario and kuluria,
but there is, of course, considerable individual variation, though [l]
is constant in certain words like bule (: [East Coast] bure) 'of no
value.'

Apparently, in comparison with East Coast Swahili, -l- is
automatically inserted between two heterosyllabic vowels, e.g. (East
Coast) kiatu 'shoe,' kukaa 'to sit down,' kufua 'wash (linen),' kaanga
'peanut': (Katanga) kilatu, kuikala, kufula, kalanga. This epenthetic
-l- is optional in the 'applicatives' in -ea, e.g. tembe(l)a 'stroll,'
pote(l)a 'forget,' but obligatory in the 'reversives' in -ua, e.g. pindula
'turn over,' pasula 'tear.' However, a comparison with the local languages, e.g. Bemba, shows that Lubumbashi Swahili has actually reshaped its forms on their model, as shown, e.g., by the stem initial
i- of ikala (= Bemba -ikala 'sit down'). Sometimes, we have actually
a direct substitution of the 'local' form as in nzila, alternating with
nji(l)a 'road,' or nzala, alternating with njala 'hunger,' which are out-

right Luba forms (the corresponding Bemba forms are nshila and nsala). By analogy this epenthetic -l- is also introduced into Arabic loans as well, e.g. in jamala 'family': (East Coast) jamaa.[8]

Characteristic of Congo Swahili as well as of some of the northern coastal dialects like kiGunya and kiAmu is the merger of the Swahili voiced palatal j[ʝ] or [dʒ]) with y[j], except after nasal, e.g. in mayi 'water,' yulu 'above,' yambo 'hello': (East Coast) maji, juu, jambo.

The influence of the local languages is especially obvious in the shape of the class prefixes, as shown by:

(1) the i-prothesis before N- with monosyllabic stems, e.g. imbwa 'dog,' inchi 'country, nation,' inje 'outside' (versus [East Coast] mbwa, nchi, nje with syllabic nasal);
(2) the replacement of syllabic [m̩] in class 1 and 3 by mu-, e.g.

	Lubumbashi	East Coast
(cl. 1)	muzungu 'white man'	mzungu
	muzee 'old man'	mzee
	mugeni 'foreigner'	mgeni
	mutoto 'child'	mtoto
(cl. 3)	mukate 'bread'	mkate
	mulango 'door'	mlango
	mufuko 'bag'	mfuko
	musumari 'nail'	msumari

Similarly, [mu] is found instead of [m̩] in the pronominal prefix of the 2nd person plural, e.g. in mutaona 'you (all) will see,' and in the pro-nominal 'infix' of the 3rd person singular, e.g. in anamuita 'he calls him,' as well as in clusters of m plus obstruent or resonant, e.g.:

Lubumbashi	East Coast
pumuzika 'rest, go on leave'	pumzika 'breathe'
teremuka 'slip, slide'	telemka
amuri 'rule, law'	amri
namuna 'kind, sort'	namna

Accordingly, we are dealing with a typically dialectal phonetic devel-opment of syllabic nasals;

(3) the mostly optional substitution of <u>ba</u>- for <u>wa</u>- in the second class,
e.g. <u>wazungu</u> ~ <u>bazungu</u> 'white men'; <u>ba</u>- is always used in <u>bantu</u>
'men' (: [East Coast] <u>watu</u>) and <u>basendji</u>[9] 'uncouth savages'
(: [East Coast] <u>washenzi</u>), when used derogatorily for persons
without any culture at all (then also with <u>ba</u>- for a single person,
in Lubumbashi French as well, e.g. <u>c'est un basendji</u> 'he is a
boor');

(4) the substitution of <u>bi</u>- for <u>vi</u>- in the eighth class, only for a limited
number of words of very current use, e.g.:

<u>bilashi</u> (: <u>viazi</u>) 'potatoes'
<u>bilatu</u> (: <u>viatu</u>) 'shoes'
<u>bilulu</u> 'insects'

—but always <u>visu</u> 'knives,' <u>vipande</u> 'pieces.' The local origin of
<u>bi</u>- is implied by the co-occurrence of <u>kichi</u>, plural <u>bichi</u> 'chairs'
besides <u>kiti</u>, plural <u>viti</u>. The latter East Coast form prevails among
the more educated speakers, whereas the former is used in socially
lower levels of speech;

(5) the substitution of <u>li</u>- for <u>ji</u>- in the fifth class, only for a limited
number of words of very current use, e.g. <u>licho</u> 'eye,' <u>lino</u> 'tooth'
—but always <u>jina</u> 'name';[10]

(6) the substitution of <u>bu</u>- for <u>u</u>- in the fourteenth class, e.g. in <u>bu-</u>
<u>longo</u> 'ground,' <u>bunga</u> 'flour,' <u>bushanga</u> 'pearl,' versus (East Coast)
<u>udongo</u>, <u>unga</u>, <u>ushanga</u>. Note also <u>busubui</u> 'morning' for <u>asubui</u>
(with <u>a</u> > <u>u</u> by vowel harmony?) and <u>bongo</u> 'lie'[11] for <u>uwongo</u>.

A strictly morphological feature ascribable to the local languages is
the use of the prefix <u>ka</u>- to form diminutives, e.g. <u>kachupa</u> 'small
bottle,' <u>kanyumba</u> 'small house,' <u>kanyama</u> 'small animal' (cf. Luba
<u>muchi</u> 'tree': <u>kachi</u> 'small tree'; Bemba [Kafubu] <u>libwe</u> 'stone': <u>kabwe</u>
'small stone'). Other typical morphological characteristics of Lubum-
bashi Swahili are:

(a) the loss of the locatives in -<u>ni</u> of which only a few are preserved
in lexicalized forms, e.g. <u>mgini</u> ~ <u>mukini</u> 'town, village' (: [East
Coast] <u>mjini</u> 'into town'[12]: <u>mutoni</u> (instead of <u>mto</u>) 'river.' They
are replaced by prepositional phrases like <u>ndani ya nyumba</u> 'inside
the house' or the (East Coast) pattern with <u>katika</u>, e.g. <u>katika</u>
<u>mahospitali</u> 'in the hospitals.'[13] To indicate a direction, <u>ku</u> is
used with names of objects and <u>kwa</u> with names of persons, e.g.

anakwenda ku magasini 'she is going to the shop': kwenda kwa
Bwana Lebrun 'go to Mr. Lebrun'; this corresponds essentially
to Bemba (Kafubu) usage, where kwa is used in the singular for
persons and ku elsewhere, e.g. kwa Mulungu 'to God': ku mushi
ku mwetu 'to the village to our home';
(b) the complete disruption of the concord system, e.g. (Lubumbashi)
imbwa yangu mukubwa tatu, versus (East Coast) mbwa zangu wakubwa watatu 'my three big dogs.'

Where East Coast Swahili shows complex rules of class
agreement for the possessives in noun phrases with animate nouns,
Katanga Swahili shows only one stereotyped form with initial y-
(yangu 'my,' yako 'your,' yake 'his,' yetu 'our,' yenu 'your (pl.),'
ya(b)o 'their'), e.g. kambo yako (instead of wako) 'your grandfather,'
nguo yake (instead of zake) 'his clothes,' etc.

The adjectives are invariable, usually showing a stereotyped
prefix, mostly mu-, e.g. kipande mukubwa 'a big piece' (instead of
kikubwa), ng'ombe mukubwa mbili 'two big cows' (instead of wakubwa
wawili), wanawake muzuri 'beautiful women' (instead of wazuri).
Occasionally, vi- is, however, used in the plural for objects, e.g.
vipande vikubwa 'big pieces.' Some adjectives show special prefixes;
thus, -kali 'sharp, fierce' always appear as makari, e.g. kisu makari
'sharp knife,' imbwa makari 'vicious dog,'[14] and -dogo 'small' as
kiloko (which actually reflects [East Coast] kidogo 'a little'), e.g.
bilauri kiloko tatu 'three small glasses.' Some are actual nouns used
as adjectives, e.g. mafuta, actually meaning 'grease, oil,' but currently used for 'fat' besides munene; similarly, nguvu—literally
'force, strength'—in the phrase iko nguvu kabisa 'it is very difficult.'

The adjectives with the stereotyped prefix mu- are also used
as adverbials instead of the forms with the prefixes vi- or u- of East
Coast Swahili, e.g. mubaya 'bad,' in minasema mubaya kabisa 'I
speak very badly' (applying to kiSwahili and indicating the adjectival
origin of the adverbial); muzuri 'well, fine' in minasikia muzuri 'I
understand well'; mwepeshi (also mupeshi) 'fast,' in mitafanya mwepeshi sana 'I'll do it very quickly.'

The numerals are also invariable: moya 'one,' mbili 'two,'
tatu 'three,' ine 'four,' etc.

The demonstratives have also developed stereotyped forms: to indicate proximity in space, hiyi is used for things and huyu for persons, e.g. kitenge hiyi 'this piece of cloth': mutoto huyu 'this child'; to indicate distance in space, ile is used for things and persons if placed before the noun, e.g. ile kintu 'that thing,' ile muntu 'that man,' but, in postposition, ule is used for persons, e.g. mutoto ule 'that child.'

The verbal system has also been deeply affected by the disruption of the concord system: for things, a stereotyped pronominal prefix and 'infix' i prevails, e.g. kama bintu yote inaisha kukauka, uitoshe na kamba 'when everything is dry take it off the wire': with the antecedent bintu ([East Coast] vitu), the concord of the eighth class vi would be expected in vyote vinaisha and uvitoshe, but instead, only i and its morphophonemic alternant y occur; similarly, in kufula yote inaisha 'the washing is all done,' y- and i- replace the concords of class 15 with the infinitive kufula. For persons, however, the same personal prefixes as in East Coast Swahili appear, except for the 1st person singular where the prefix mi- is regularly substituted for ni- in the -na- tense and occasionally in the -ta- tense, e.g. minajua kazi yote 'I know all the work' (i.e. 'I can do everything'), mitafanya ile muzuri 'I'll do that well,'[15] and for the 3rd person plural where the prefix appears optionally as ba- instead of wa-. As a substitute for the verb 'to be,' the quasi-verbal complex iko 'there is' is used in the present with the personal subject prefixes as well as with the locative ku-, e.g. kuiko pombe tena 'there is still beer (available)'; the 3rd person singular, however, shows a zero prefix, e.g. muzungu iko wapi? 'where is the white man?,' versus (3rd person plural) bote beko muzuri 'they are all fine' (in which beko represents ba- plus -iko). This -iko complex combines with the connective na to mark possession and to translate 'to have,' e.g. niko (~ miko) na kazi mingi 'I have a lot of work.' In the other tenses, the verb kuwa appears regularly, e.g. 'we will have,' is translated by tutakuwa na as in East Coast Swahili. The negative forms of the present of 'to be' and subsequently, 'to have,' are, however, also aberrant: actually, Katanga Swahili uses the East Coast form expressing 'not to have' for 'not to be' and optionally adds a redundant na to the form when 'not to have' is meant. Thus, the 1st person singular 'I am not' appears as shina ~ sina (= [East Coast] sina 'I have not'); similarly, the 2nd person singular is huna or hauna and the 3rd hana; for things haina is used, e.g. haina

bei nguvu 'it is not expensive.' 'I have no buttons' appears as shina
na boutons. The whole system of the conjugation of the indicative is
practically reduced to the three main tenses: present, characterized
by the marker -na-; past, characterized by the marker -li-; future,
characterized by the marker -ta-. The -me- tense, expressing 'completion,' is replaced by a periphrastic form with kuisha 'to finish,'
e.g. minaisha kupika bilashi 'I have finished cooking the potatoes.'[18]
The negative tenses corresponding to the main tenses seldom occur
in colloquial speech, except for a few, almost lexicalized forms like
sijui 'I don't know,' sitaki 'I don't want,' sisikii 'I don't hear' (i.e.
'understand'). However, instead of sikusahau 'I did not forget,' a
less educated Katangese is more likely to say mi hapana sahabu or
mi hapana potela. Hapana plus infinitive or verbal stem is, indeed,
the standard negative in Katangese Swahili, e.g. kesho mi hapana
kuenda ku mukini 'tomorrow I'll not go to the village.' Even where
the original negative form still occurs, as in the negative 'adhortative,'
e.g. usifunge mulango 'don't close the door,' the hapana form is always more current in colloquial speech, e.g. hapana kufunga mulango.

Similarly, in the affirmative form, though an 'adhortative'
such as umuite 'call him' can be used, the imperative ita ye is more
likely to be heard. Nevertheless, even poorly educated people are
familiar with the form and occasionally resort to it in definite contexts, e.g. when a brewery hand whose overalls have been stolen
writes to the police and requests that whoever stole it should give it
back, he uses uludishe (= [East Coast] urudishe) 'that you return (it).'
On the other hand, the -ki- tense, which occasionally occurs in print,
is always replaced by the conjunction kama and one of the three main
tenses, e.g. kama utatumika machine utageusha ile moteur mpaka
minutes ine 'when you work with the machine, you will make the motor
run for only 4 minutes.' A stereotyped form of the -ki- tense marking a simultaneous process may be contained in the adverbial kiisha
(= [East Coast] kisha) 'then, afterwards' (literally 'finishing').

The whole complex of aspectual connotations presenting the
realization of the process as depending on a certain condition, marked
in East Coast Swahili by the -japo-, -nga-, -nge-, and -ngali- tenses,
has totally disappeared from Katanga Swahili. Only the so-called -sipo-
tense, expressing a restrictive supposition introduced by 'unless,'
appears occasionally in official writings, e.g. at the Post Office on

boards indicating exceptions to parking restrictions, e.g. isipokuwa
tu magari ya kazi ya pahali, literally 'except only for vehicles of work
of the place,' isipokuwa kadiri dakika 60 'only for 60 minutes.' These
inscriptions were, however, presumably concocted by some educated
local police clerk, who wanted to produce a text in Swahili safi. This
would also account for the occurrence of an isolated -me- tense form
in the same location, translating literally the French 'Il est défendu
d'uriner' by an impersonal passive perfect imekatazwa kukoyola 'it
has been forbidden to urinate.'[17] Otherwise, as already pointed out,
-me- is always replaced by the periphrastic form with -isha, which
is occasionally also used with the same additional connotations as in
East Coast Swahili, e.g. anaisha kutoka 'he has already gone.' The
unmarked present appears sporadically in direct style in the rather
stereotyped asema 'says he' when reporting somebody else's statement.

Of the compound forms with 'to be,' only the progressive
present seems to be used, e.g. tuiko tunakufa 'we are dying' (literally
'we are we die').' Very frequent, however, is the use of taka 'want'
as an auxiliary, e.g. minataka kuuza nguo 'I am going to buy clothes';[18]
anataka kuisha 'he has almost finished'; minataka kulala 'I'd like to
sleep.' The relative forms do not occur at all in the spoken language,
though they may occasionally be found in written texts, e.g. in the
local press, in advertisements, etc. In an advertisement for a radio
set, the firm promises to repair any set, stating, PH atakutengen-
ezeayo 'PH will repair it for you';[19] at the zoo, a poster announces
that kila ticket munayonunua ni ticket ya tombola 'each ticket you buy
is a sweepstake ticket.' However, the driver's manual contains statements like kinga ni chombo chenye kutumia kwa kuchukua 'the bicycle
is the implement that is used to transport,' in which a phrase with
-enye, which is currently employed in East Coast Swahili with a noun
or infinitive to express a state or condition, e.g. watoto wenye kusin-
zia 'drowsy children,' appears as a substitute for a relative form;
similarly, drivers are referred to as 'Congolese who drive vehicles,'
which reads in Katanga Swahili wakongomani wenye kuongoza magari
(instead of wanaoongoza), and an advertisement describes sabuni yenye
kuitwa ZURI for 'the soap that is called ZURI.' Like every marginal
language, Congo Swahili shows remarkable archaisms, e.g. lexicalized
phrases with the -nga- tense of -li- 'to be' (with the meaning Bishop
Steere illustrates for archaic kiUnguja with examples like ningali hai
'while I am still alive'), e.g. kingali pombe (more colloquially: kuiko

pombe tena) 'there is still beer'; akingali muzima 'he is still alive.'
Another example is the occurrence of the 'continuous' suffix -aka, e.g.
anaikalaka kwa shangazi 'she stays permanently with an aunt' (the stem
-ikal- 'stay' [East Coast -ka(a)] showing a derivation in -ak-, parallel
to -ag- occurring elsewhere in kiNgwana). As a matter of fact, it
should be stressed that, while the conjugation system was by and
large reduced to its three main tenses, the derivational system of
applicatives, causatives, passives, statives, etc. remained remarkably operative, presumably also on account of its striking correspondences with the system of the local languages.

        Though the syntax of Katanga Swahili has not diverged consid-
erably from the East Coast Swahili patterns which are basically similar to those of central Bantu, the practice of literal translation has led
to the transference of some French patterns into this variety of Swahili, especially in its written form, e.g. unakuwa katika hatari on the
model of 'tu es en danger' ('you are in danger'), fanya ile plaisir na
miye, word for word 'fais-moi ce plaisir' ('do me this favor'). It
went even as far as taking over idiosyncracies of Belgian French, like
the postpositional use of 'avec' with certain verbs, e.g. 'du fil pour
coudre avec' ('thread to sew with'), rendered faithfully as uzi ya
kushona nayo.

        In the process of rebantuization which went on under the in-
fluence of the local languages, a considerable number of new words,
unknown in coastal Swahili, were introduced into the language. They
belong to various areas of the lexicon: the diversity that already characterized Swahili in East Africa as regards animal names[20] is even
more obvious here, where a considerable number of local terms are
used instead of the East Coast Swahili words, e.g. mpevu instead of
mende for 'cockroach,' fwifwi instead of bundi for 'owl.' For 'gazelle'
the kiNgwana term pongo has replaced paa; the hare is called kalulu,
as in Bemba, and its East Coast Swahili name sungura is only known
through storybooks; the French nickname jacko has replaced kasuku
for the parrot; instead of ngiri or mbango the wild hog is called lupenge
—a term that corresponds to kiLuba mpenge; similarly, the local name
of the hippotragus niger variety of antelope—fumbo—corresponds to
kiLuba mfumbo. Local names of plants are also quite common, e.g.
lusonga for 'spurge' instead of mchongoma, but by far more numerous
are the Katanga names of instruments or other technical terms, e.g.
kitofu 'range,' mbabula 'fire basket,' posholo 'shovel,'[21] ngolofano

'wheelbarrow,' dilata 'sheet, iron,' swakala 'lime,' chapu 'workshop,'
dikuta 'pierced coin,' etc. Many have developed in the daily conversation of workers in the copper industry, and in some cases the redupli-
cative forms indicate their popular 'expressive' origin, e.g. kingo-
longolo 'token,' changachanga 'head of personnel' (obviously from the
verbal stem changa 'muster, levy'). This type of formation is especially common in colloquial names, of vehicles, like the onomatopoetic
tukutuku for the 'Vespa' type of motorbike or the Swahili version of
French pousse-pousse 'rickshaw' in pushipushi ya wagonjwa 'invalid
chair' (literally 'rickshaw of the sick'). Typical is the Lubumbashi
colloquial name of the big city buses—chachacha—based on the noise
made by their hydraulic brakes, whereas the smaller-sized public
vehicles are called fulafula—possibly because their noise is associated
with that of washing linen (Katanga Swahili kufula)? Expressive redup-
lication is also very widespread in verbal forms, e.g. kutafutafuta 'to
look for (thoroughly),' kusemasema 'to drivel' (: kusema 'to speak'),
etc.

A further characteristic of Katanga Swahili is semantic change
found in Swahili words, due to the loss of terms with more specific
meanings. Thus shingo 'neck' also means 'nape,' for which East Coast
Swahili has the special term ukosi; similarly, matako 'buttocks' also
indicates thighs, for which East Coast Swahili uses mapaja; mupila,
corresponding to East Coast Swahili mpira 'rubber,' has acquired the
new meanings 'spring' and 'T-shirt'; kuchacha 'to ferment' also means
'to hurry'; hamu 'desire, anxiety,' has replaced kiu in the meaning of
'thirst,' e.g. in the phrase kusikia hamu 'to be thirsty' (literally: 'to
hear a longing'). All kinds of phrases, unknown to the East Coast, are
commonly used in Lubumbashi, e.g. kulala zamu 'to keep watch during
the night' (literally: 'to sleep a turn of guard duty'), kutuma singa 'to
telephone' (literally: 'to use the wires,' Swahili singa 'hairs,' having
taken over the meaning 'wires' from kiLuba nshinga 'wire'). To designate the local railway (mostly known as B. C. K., abbreviation for 'Bas-
Congo-Katanga'), the phrase mashua ya ntoto (literally: 'boat of the
rail') is used, instead of the East African gari la moshi (literally:
'wagon of smoke').

These few examples illustrate the fact that on the strictly
colloquial level the speech of uneducated speakers of Katanga Swahili
will hardly be understandable to East Coast Swahili speakers. At a
higher level of sophistication, the educated speakers who have been

widely exposed to Swahili safi or Swahili ya kitabu, i. e. the Swahili which used to be taught in the schools and which conforms by and large to the patterns of East Coast Swahili, will use a form of the language which will be mutually intelligible to East Coast and Katanga Swahili speakers. The songs of the popular Katangese composer, Jean Bosco, are written in this language, as are the weekly paper Uhaki and the fortnightly Mwana Shaba formerly published by the Union Minière du Haut-Katanga. This has created the illusion in East Africa and elsewhere that Katanga Swahili is but slightly different from East Coast Swahili. However, in its colloquial form, with its phonology reshaped, mainly under the influence of Luba and the local languages, and its widely simplified morphology, it is undoubtedly a Creole, which is further developing quite independently from the East Coast standard.

NOTES

[1] This paper was read at the Conference on Pidginization and Creolization of Languages (Mona, Jamaica, April 1968) and at the First European Summer Institute of Linguistics (Kiel, Germany, July 1968). I am deeply indebted to my colleagues Earl Stevick (Foreign Service Institute, Washington), Irvine Richardson (Michigan State University), Carol Eastman (University of Washington, Seattle), and especially Marcel Van Spaandonck (University of Texas, Austin) for valuable comments and remarks.

[2] For further details, see my articles: 'Cultural Languages and Contact Vernaculars in the Republic of the Congo,' in The University of Texas Studies in Literature and Language 4, no. 4 (Winter 1963): 499-511 (esp. 502-4); 'The Position of Swahili and Other Bantu Languages in Katanga,' in the same journal 11, no. 2 (1969): 905-13; 'The Choice of Official Languages in the Democratic Republic of the Congo,' in J. A. Fishman, C. A. Ferguson, and J. Das Gupta, eds., Language Problems of Developing Nations (New York: Wiley, 1968), pp. 295-311 (esp. 298, 306-8). On kiNgwana, cf., e.g., B. Lecoste, 'Le Ngwana. Variété congolaise du Swahili,' in Kongo-Overzee 20, no. 4-5 (1954): 391-408; 'Vocabulaire Ngwana,' in Kongo-Overzee 21, no. 304 (1955): 289-97; 'A Grammatical Study of Two Recordings of Belgian Congo Swahili,' in Swahili 31 (1961): 219-26. A comprehensive bibliography on Congo Swahili can be found in M. van Spaandonck,

Practical and Systematical Swahili Bibliography. Linguistics, 1850–
1963 (Leiden: E. J. Brill, 1965), pp. 50–54.

[3] The material used in this sketch of the characteristics of
Lubumbashi Swahili is based on personal notes and on the excellent
collection of samples contained in Le Swahili Véhiculaire by Camille
Annicq (Lubumbashi: Imbelco, 1967). Some useful data are also to
be found in A. Verbeken, Petit cours de kiSwahili pratique (Elisabeth-
ville: Imbelco, 1953; 6th ed.). The data on the Bemba of the area of
Lubumbashi are taken from the Eléments de Grammaire kiBemba by
Father E. Noël (Kafubu: Préfecture du Luapula Supérieur, 1953).

[4] Elaborating on F. Johnson's suggestion (A Standard Swahili
English Dictionary [London: Oxford University Press, 1939], p. 173,
s.v. kaputula) that the word derives from the Nyanja verb kubudula
'cut off' and was introduced into Swahili during World War I, when
shorts became in fashion in East Africa, Earl Stevick (personal letter
of May 2, 1968) indicates that some Nyanja dialects have a distinction
between implosive ɓ, ɗ and aspirated bh, dh. The aspirates are rare,
except in ideophones, and unmarked in D. C. Scott and A. Hetherwick,
Dictionary of the Nyanja Language (London: Lutterworth Press, 1929),
which lists kabudula (p. 168). The verb -budula 'cut off' is related to
an ideophone budu; if, then, the Nyanja forms actually have bh dh,
they are presumably the source of Shona kabhudhura, and ultimately
Bemba and Swahili kaputula can be referred to the same origin.

[5] Kofila (= East Coast kofia) is used only for a soldier's cap.

[6] Apparently, the East Coast Swahili contrast between -pasa
'befit' and -pasha 'cause to get' has been partly leveled in Lubumbashi
Swahili, since -pasha occurs beside -pasa in the meaning 'oblige,
compel.'

[7] Reflexes of East Coast gh [γ] seldom occur in Katanga Swahili; when the relevant Arabic loans have been preserved, they constantly show [g], e.g. luga ~ ruga 'language' (East Coast lugha).

[8] The insertion of -l- is actually a widespread Congo Swahili
phenomenon, which reflects the tendency to reshape successive syl-
lables with vowels in hiatus according to the prevailing Bantu pattern
/CV/.

[9] -ndj- represents the nasal cluster [ɲd³], the Lubumbashi
reflex of (East Coast) Swahili -nz- —articulated [nd^Z]—under the influence of the palatalization by final -i.

[10] Whereas the use of mu-, ba-, bi-, bu-, ka-, as well as
the occurrence of i- before the N- prefix of monosyllabic stems, is

also current in kiNgwana, the appearance of li- is restricted to this
area. Since the form of the prefix is undoubtedly not Luba, its source
may be Bemba, though the relevant noun stems are definitely Swahili
(cf. Kafubu Bemba linso 'eye': Lubumbashi Swahili licho: East Coast
Swahili jicho).

[11] Also used in Lubumbashi French as an interjection to express disbelief.

[12] Note the [g] for (East Coast) [ʝ], with subsequent devoicing
of [g] to [k]; cf. parallel, (Lubumbashi) semeki 'brother- or sister-
in-law': (East Coast) shemeji.

[13] The form (ma)hospitali is apparently influenced by the Dutch
form of the word: hospitaal (versus French hôpital [opital], whence
Lubumbashi Swahili (l)opital(o)).

[14] This use of ma- may be due to the influence of liNgala,
where the prefix ma is widely used in colloquial speech instead of the
regular adjectival concord, e.g. bato malámu 'good men' instead of
bato balámu; monɔ makási 'strong medicine' instead of monɔ mokási.

[15] The use of mi- instead of ni- may well be from the emphatic
pronoun mimi (cf. former British Army Swahili miminajua 'I know');
this is also confirmed by the use of the unreduplicated form of the
emphatic pronoun enclitically after the verbal form instead of the object 'infix,' e.g. mitapika we 'I'll hit you' (East Coast nitakupiga).

[16] This construction, which also occurs in East Coast Swahili
to emphasize completion, more than the -me- tense, has become here
the only way to express it.

[17] In the buses, where a less sophisticated public has to get
the message, the interdiction to smoke and to spit is bluntly stated
with the local negative hapana plus the relevant infinitives, nl. hapana
kufuta tumbaka 'no smoking,' hapana kutema mate 'no spitting (saliva).'

[18] In colloquial Katanga Swahili uza, which means 'sell' in
East Coast Swahili, has replaced nunua 'buy'; 'to sell' is expressed by
means of its causative uzisha.

[19] Notice the occurrence of the relative referential -yo (applying to the direct object 'radio') in final position instead of being inserted between the tense marker -ta- and the object 'infix' -ku-.

[20] Cf. E. Polomé, 'Geographical Differences in Lexical Usage
in Swahili,' in Verhandlungen des zweiten internationalen Dialektolo-
genkongresses, vol. 2 (Wiesbaden, 1968), p. 664.

[21] Ultimately from Kitchen Kafir and Zulu (cf. Bemba fosholo).

Part III. Creolization

11 | Creolization Theory and Linguistic Prehistory

In a paper presented at the workshop on Pidgins and Creoles at the 12th International Congress of Linguists in Vienna (Austria), G. Manessy (1977: 14) defended the view that pidginization and creolization processes are in direct correlation with the presence or absence, or the strength and weakness, of a sociocultural tradition shared by the users of the variety of speech in which they are observed. Having ascribed the structural changes characterizing pidgins essentially to the breakdown of the normative constraints of the target language, he emphasizes that creolization entails a restructuring of the linguistic system along totally different channels and for totally different reasons: the development of a new group solidarity, with the creole as its code. Progressively stricter constraints are imposed on the modes of expression of the grammatical categories and of the semantic relations, while the morphophonemic rules increase in complexity. This would define 'creolization' as an 'evolutive process liable to operate on any type of speech'—vernacular, pidgin, or other variety—as soon as its sociolinguistic conditioning has been established with the formation of the relevant group.

This approach has far-reaching consequences for diachronic linguistics. If we limit ourselves to the history and prehistory of the Indo-European languages, a number of relevant cases immediately comes to mind. G. Manessy himself (1977: 4) refers to the Romance languages: the study of the language situation in the Roman Empire (Polomé 1977: 20-24) shows that the penetration of Latin was a very slow process, and in Gaul there is abundant evidence of the continued use of Celtic until the fourth century A.D. and even later: there are inscriptions in Gaulish; the father of the poet Ausonius, a distinguished Gaul who practiced medicine in Bordeaux, is said to speak Celtic at

home and to have a rather poor knowledge of Latin; the rural areas
remain essentially pagan and speaking Gaulish at the beginning of the
fourth century. It is actually the vigorous apostolic fervor of (Saint)
Martin to Christianize Gaul, using Latin as the vehicle of evangelization that ensured the late romanization of the whole territory. At the
end of the fourth century, there must already have been some distinct
form of Gallo-Latin in Central Gaul, designated by contemporary
Latin writers like Sulpicius Severus as 'Celtic' or 'Gallic,' and characterized by the fronting of [u] to [y] and by 'lenition' (voicing intervocalic voiceless obstruents and fricativizing intervocalic voiced
stops). But much earlier a pidginized form of Latin must have been
common around the army camps, and in the third century, Dio Cassius
echoed current complaints about the gruffness of the Latin spoken by
soldiers in Gaul. When the Roman Empire collapsed and new patterns
of political, social, and economic organization emerged, following
various, often transitory, periods of alien domination, Gallo-Romance,
when compared with Latin, had become a 'new' language through a
process showing a set of features of creolization: repatterning of
phonology, 'deflection,' reshaping of the conjugation system, restructuring of syntax, renewal of lexicon. However, the phonological
changes which are usually expected to produce a simplification of the
phonemic contrasts are in the direction of greater complexity, e.g.
with diphthongization and palatalization rules.

    That the application of the creolization theory to diachronic
linguistics creates problems is further illustrated by the study of N.
Domingue on Middle English (1977). This language looks like a creole
because of its innovative characteristics (absence of grammatical gender; only remnants of noun categories, case endings and verbal inflec-
tions; no rounded vowels), but the amount of mixing is insufficient:
the French borrowings were only introduced 'when French as a language failed to be available to many,' but the concepts had to be expressed in English—the popular language which had now spread to 'all
areas of the society and of the culture it lived by (Domingue 1977: 96).'
Such a situation, N. Domingue concludes, might be better characterized as hybrid than creole. In passing (1977: 97), however, she mentions that 'Proto-Germanic could be considered as a creole language.'
This view was already expressed five decades ago by S. Feist (1928):
on the basis of the prevailing view that the Illyro-Venetes, also associated with the Lusatian civilization, were responsible for the prehis-

toric trade in amber and other precious articles between northern
Europe and the Mediterranean, the German scholar assumed that they
'indo-europeanized' the pre-Germanic population in the southern Baltic
area. This argument was, however, based on erroneous interpretations of the Venetic materials in which he saw evidence to account for
the Germanic consonant shift. The fact that Germanic shows this important phonological change in the consonantal system, added to the
very restricted paradigmatical structure of its conjugation (only a
past and a preterit; only limited evidence of the medio-passive; etc.),
has led a number of scholars to assume that Germanic had lost a considerable part of the inherited Indo-European verb morphology and
thoroughly changed its phonology as a result of the population merger
that must have taken place when the Indo-European invaders of northwestern Europe settled together with the agriculturists established
there since the fourth millennium B. C. This remains, however, as
conjectural as the claim that the Eddic myth of the war of the AEsir
and the Vanir reflects what happened in those early days of the Indo-
European conquest and restructuration of Germanic society.

A better case can be made for Hittite: it represents the language of the Indo-European conquerors of the land of Hatti in Asia
Minor; they were preceded by the Luwians who may have arrived as
early as the middle of the third millennium B. C. and who occupied the
south coast of Anatolia. Hittite and Luwians share a series of alleged
'losses' of Proto-Indo-European grammatical categories: (1) the mas-
culine/feminine genders; (2) the dual number; (3) the comparative and
superlative of adjectives; (4) a number of moods and tenses. Moreover, the distinction between the different stems in the nominal declen-
sion is widely leveled out; almost all of them have the same case endings, and only traces of the Ablaut remain in Old Hittite. On the other
hand, the Anatolian languages partly preserved the Proto-Indo-European
laryngeal(s) which disappeared elsewhere (except—to some extent—in
Armenian). Otherwise, the direction of phonological change seems to
be toward simplification, though the cuneiform writing system makes
it rather difficult to assess the outcome with certainty. Thus, Hittite
seems to share with Hurrian—a non-Indo-European language of Anatolia—the 'neutralization' of voice as a relevant feature in the stops. The
loss of the dual cannot be ascribed to any external factor, but as the
need to mark out objects coming in pairs, like the body parts, seems
to disappear, the dual also disappears as grammatical category, e.g.

in Germanic. The problem of the gender is a different issue: is the
primary system of Indo-European a distinction between masculine,
feminine, and neuter, or does the contrast animate : inanimate constitute the oldest form of gender distinction, as Meillet suggested?
A recent careful investigation of the Hittite material relating to the
gender of cognates of PIE feminines concluded 'that the theory of a
lost feminine should be eliminated from the Hittite handbooks' (Brosman 1976: 157). The use of syntactic devices instead of adjectival
suffixes to express the degrees of comparison is frequent in non-Indo-
European languages and in more recent developments of Indo-European
languages like Hindi, e.g. chatrii-see barsaatii acchii hai 'a raincoat
is better than an umbrella.' As this construction also occurs in Armenian, it has been ascribed to Caucasian influence in the case of
Hittite, but how much difference is there between Hittite DINGIR^MEŠ_
naš humandaš ^DZašhapunaš šalliš 'of all the gods Z. great' (= 'Z. is
the greatest of all gods')—and—Hindi iee šaher-mẽẽ sab-see ũũcii
imaarat hai 'of all in town this is the high building' (= 'this is the
highest building in town')?

        As for what occurred to the nominal flection, A. Kammen-
huber rightly pointed out (1969: 254) 'no non-Indo-European influences
in Anatolia should be made responsible for changes already recognized
in proto-Hittite-Luwian.' The process started, according to her, even
before their migration and continued independently in both dialects for
several centuries. To judge from what happened in such languages as
Middle High German, it is indeed easily acceptable to ascribe this
leveling of the inflectional system to strictly internal factors.

        More complex is the problem of the verb system: here we
are confronted with the problem that Vedic shows an elaborate conjugation with an active, a middle, and a passive voice; four moods: the
indicative, the imperative, the subjunctive, and the optative, to which
remnants of a fifth, the injunctive, may be added; seven tenses: present, imperfect, aorist, perfect, pluperfect, future, conditional. It
is paralleled by Greek, which has an active and a middle, the passive
being restricted to the aorist and future; four moods and seven tenses.
In contrast to this wealth of forms, Hittite merely shows a 'minimal'
system with an active and a medio-passive, two moods (indicative
and imperative), and two tenses (present and preterit)—a situation
rather similar to that of Gothic, with an active and a passive, three

moods (indicative, imperative, optative), and two tenses (present and preterit).

Have the Hittite and Germanic conjugation system undergone a radical transformation due to a contact situation, which entailed far-reaching simplification of the morphology of both languages ? Other elements might suggest interference of non-related linguistic entities, in particular the lexicon: in both cases, the percentage of terms without a readily available Indo-European etymology is especially high, and very basic words like the correspondents of pater, mater, dexter, *dō- 'give,' *bher- 'carry,' *bhū- 'be(come),' etc. are missing in Hittite, while Germanic lost the Indo-European terms for 'give' (*dō-), 'drink' (*pō-), etc.

Confining ourselves to Hittite, we should, however, point out that the conquest of Anatolia by the Indo-Europeans was not the result of a massive invasion, but rather the action of enterprising chieftains with a small retinue, who progressively strengthened their grip of the land and were reinforced by a continued influx of immigrants (Bittel 1950: 52, 60-61). Though they assimilated to the local culture, taking over its religion, they steadfastly maintained and imposed their language as the administrative medium of their kingdom as well as the official language of all legal and diplomatic documents. A tightly knit feudal aristocracy, they asserted their power in a strongly hierarchized society and their conservatism also involved their language, which shows much less change until the fall of the Old Kingdom than Indo-Aryan from Vedic to Classical Sanskrit. Moreover, that language does not show the restructuration that 'creolization' would entail: whether it be the French-based creole of Mauritius or the Swahili-based creole of Nairobi, Kenya, the process is essentially the same—the original morphological markers of 'aspect' have been lost and a new system has been elaborated, e.g. as shown in the tabulation at the top of the following page.

Whereas French marked the tense difference within the morphology and gave special weight to the perfective aspect expressed by compound forms with the auxiliary have, the progressive aspect was usually unmarked, and the distinction between indefinite and definite future was not part of the conjugation system, e.g. Mauritius French /mo a get li pli tar/ 'I may see her later on' = French 'Il se peut que

Mauritius French (Baker 1972: 107-10):

Tense: Aspect →	unmarked	progressive	perfective	indefinite future	definite future
Aorist/Present (unmarked)	—	/pe/	/fin/	/a/	/pu/
Past	/ti/	/ti pe/	/ti fin/	/ti a/	/ti pu/

Nairobi Swahili (Heine 1973: 90-94):

	unmarked	progressive	perfective	negative
Aorist	/na+/		/kwiʃa/	/hapana/
Past		/li+kuwa/ + Aorist		/bado/
Future	/ta+/	/ta+kuwa/ + Aorist		{ /hapana weza/ /hawezi/

je la voie plus tard' or 'Je la verrai peut-être plus tard' (/pu/ would
indicate that I would definitely see her later!). In Coastal Swahili,
there is a separate negative conjugation of which hawezi 'he cannot'
preserves a form, whereas, e.g., Coastal Swahili mtu huyu hajafanya
kazi = Nairobi Swahili mtu hii bado fanya kazi 'this man has not yet
done any work.' Furthermore, -na- and -ta-, as well as -li- are
tense markers, but they have to be preceded by a pronominal prefix
indicating the person and/or class of the grammatical subject: the
perfective form is usually marked by the morpheme -me-, e.g. Coastal Swahili kisu changu kimeanguka 'my knife has fallen down' = Nairobi
Swahili kisu yangu kwisha anguka.

Nothing of the kind happens in Anatolian: the forms of Hittite
show features of striking archaism. As Kuryłowicz (1964: 148) and
others have shown, in a descriptive pattern of speech, the marked,
positive member of the opposition between the persons involved is the
first person, the person of the 'speaker,' whereas as the negative member is the second person, the person of the 'hearer,' the third person
being neutral—a kind of ∅ person, which accounts for the third person
being representative of all nouns. This would also explain why, as
Watkins (1969: 49-54) has convincingly argued, the third person singular has originally a ∅-ending in Proto-Indo-European, a fact that is
still reflected by archaic middle forms in Old Hittite, where the third

person singular merely shows the reflex of a middle ending -o̧, e.g.
O. Hitt. kiya̧, corresponding to Vedic (a̧)saya̧(t); in a younger stage of
the language, however, the characteristic -t- marker is inserted in
the same form, which, then, appears as Hitt. kitta̧, corresponding to
Gk. keîto. This archaism of Hittite can even be better appreciated
when one considers the formal correspondence between the second
person imperative and the third person indicative in the thematic conjugation, e.g.

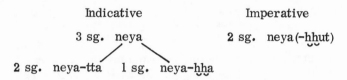

In the imperative, the second person is the neutral or ∅-person (Watkins 1969: 120-21), and the Hittite situation is strikingly paralleled by
Greek where imperative 2nd sg. lége 'read!' corresponds to indicative
3 sg. légei, i.e. lege + the deictic particle -i marking the present
(HIC and NUNC).

        It is also fairly well established that the Hittite hi- conjuga-
tion and the Indo-European perfect derive from a common source
(Kammenhuber 1969a: 330-32), and Hittite shares the -r- middle
forms with Latin, Celtic, and Tocharian, as well as Armenian and
Phrygian. It has been assumed (Kammenhuber 1969a: 345) that this
-r- medio-passive was a recent innovation of Proto-Indo-European in
which Greek and Indo-Iranian would no longer have participated. Such
a hypothesis is contradicted by the dialect-geographical evidence,
which indicates a discontinuous area, with the occurrence of the -r-
forms in the marginal territory at the outskirts of the Indo-European
area of expansion—in Old Irish and in the Tocharian dialects—which
would point to greater antiquity. Moreover, the relative chronology
of the movements of the ancestors of the Greek and the Indo-Iranians
versus the conquerors of central Europe in the fourth and third millennia B. C. needs to be tightened up. Anyhow, to revert to Anatolia,
every component in the Hittite conjugation system is Indo-European,
and the whole system shows remarkable archaic features. Proto-
Hatti, the language of the conquered people, hardly could affect it and
obviously did not: the Hatti verb does not mark tense, or person; it

does not have a medio-passive, or infinitive, or participle, but operates with enclitic particles, essentially prefixes like the negative taš-
or the optative te- (Kammenhuber 1969b: 499-507), none of which appears to have influenced Hittite in any traceable way. On the other
hand, Hurrian, with a verbal system with a present, preterite, and
future, and moods functioning like Indo-European optatives and sub-
junctives (Friedrich 1969: 17-18), would hardly have been responsible
for the 'loss' of the Indo-European optative and subjunctive in Anatolian and for the absence of a 'future' tense in Hittite and Luwian. To
be sure, Anatolian shares some features with the language of the non-
Indo-European people of the area, e.g. the weak articulation of nasal
before stops (Sommer 1947: 71-72, 75, 99). From an Ægean language,
it has the suffix -umna-/-um(m)a-, used in masculine names of persons and also found in Etruscan and Prehellenic Greek names (Kammenhuber 1969a: 268). But there is no cogent evidence of strong interference entailing structural changes in Anatolian.

If then Anatolian has been a 'conservative' Indo-European
dialect, how are we to account for the 'simplification' of its verb
morphology as compared with Vedic and Homeric Greek?

A first question is: Has there ever been a 'simplification'?
In other words, can we not conceptualize a type of Proto-Indo-European
which is not based on the triad: durative (or linear) present: punctual
aorist: stative perfect? The development of Proto-Indo-European
must have been a long process, and assuming that M. Gimbutas is
right in linking it with the so-called 'Kurgan' culture, we are talking
about a cultural tradition that encompasses three millennia with socioeconomic and religious changes reflected by the archeological material
(Gimbutas 1974: 290-94). Apparently, the linguistic community con-
solidated itself through trade and incessantly growing mobility in the
fifth millennium B.C., when the horse had been domesticated. No
later than the middle of the fourth millennium B.C., the two-wheeled
cart appeared, and in the second half of that millennium, the Balkans
become the staging area for the vast movement of the corded ware-
battle axe complexes, which will indo-europeanize central and northern
Europe in the third millennium B.C. It is in the light of this diachronic
perspective that Indo-European data have to be evaluated: as W. Meid
(1975: 209-13) pointed out, at least three periods might be distinguished
in the development of Indo-European:

(a) <u>early Indo-European</u>, reflected by <u>archaisms</u>, evidenced in cor-
     respondences between east and west, or cases where the eastern
     forms appear to be older than the western or vice versa;
(b) <u>middle Indo-European</u>, reflecting the recent structures shared by
     east and west;
(c) <u>late Indo-European</u>, reflecting innovations versus the two previous
     types: here, Greek and Indo-Iranian constitute one subgroup
     (Birwé 1955), and the Old European subgroup (Meillet's 'North-
     West-Indo-European') another.

If one accepts with Neu (1976: 252-53) that Proto-Indo-European has
built its verbal system around a contrast <u>active : perfect</u>, and that
the middle is a secondary development, Anatolian appears like a
dialect which separated from the Indo-European community at an
early date, before the preterit and mood had developed from the non-
present active in the structural pattern proposed by Neu:

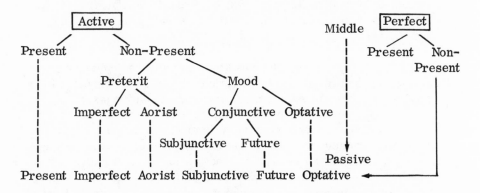

Indo-Iranian, on the contrary, would reflect the completely elaborated
system. Though the detail of the reconstruction of the above model
remains open for discussion, most scholars would agree nowadays
that Anatolian provides a valuable record of a relatively early stage
of development of Indo-European.

       But then, Germanic, with a rather similar system, no trace
of the assumed 'preterit' development (imperfect: aorist, cf. Polomé
1964), no subjunctive, no future, may also reflect an archaic form of
Indo-European. The archaism of Germanic has already been pointed

out for a number of reasons, e.g. its dialect-geographical position,
but the consonant shift added to the 'innovations' in the lexicon and
the 'simplification' of the morphology has given rise to various theories
of hybridization, as if it reflected an Indo-European dialect altered by
being acquired by an alien population. The changes involved in the
consonant shift could indeed—partly at least—be explained by the type
of interference that occurs when bilinguals reinterpret distinctions
that occur in the target language by means of features in their primary
system, e.g.

$$\begin{matrix} & C \\ \begin{bmatrix} +\text{voice} \\ -\text{tense} \end{bmatrix} & \rightarrow & [-\text{voice}] \end{matrix}$$

as in the case of Romansh spoken by a native speaker of Schwyzer-
tütsch (Weinreich 1953: 17). However, recent studies on the phonology of Proto-Indo-European would rather indicate that Germanic,
here again, has been more conservative than the other western Indo-
European languages (Hopper 1973; Bomhard 1975; Normier 1977).
Under those conditions, is it justified to speak of 'creolization' of
Indo-European in the case of Germanic?

       The rather negative results of this discussion do not at all
imply that the process of 'creolization' should not be resorted to as a
method to explain prehistoric developments in languages undergoing
apparently profound structural changes. What is important is to
assess the sociocultural situation with sufficient precision and detail
to make it possible to assume that from a contact situation between a
ruling minority and a subjugated mass, a language of intergroup communication developed which was based on the language of the upper
levels of society, but was considerably altered by features of 'creolization.' Much to my regret I cannot find any older Indo-European language that fits that pattern at this time!

BIBLIOGRAPHY

Baker, Philip. 1972. Kreol. A description of Mauritian Creole.
        London: C. Hurst & Co.
Birwé, Robert. 1955. Griechich-arische Sprachbeziehungen im

Verbalsystem. Walldorf-Hessen: Verlag für Orientkunde,
    Dr. H. Vorndran.
Bittel, Kurt. 1950. Grundzüge der Vor- und Frühgeschichte Klein-
    asiens. 2nd ed. Tübingen: Ernst Wasmuth.
Bomhard, Allan R. 1975. An outline of the historical phonology of
    Indo-European. Orbis 24: 354-90.
Brosman, Paul W., Jr. 1976. The Hittite gender of cognates of
    PIE feminines. Journal of Indo-European Studies 4:2: 141-59.
Domingue, Nicole Z. 1977. Middle English: Another creole?
    Journal of Creole Studies 1:1: 89-108.
Feist, Sigmund. 1928. Die Ausbreitung des indogermanischen
    Sprachstammes über Nordeuropa in vorgeschichtlicher Zeit.
    Wörter und Sachen 11: 29-53. Shortened English version:
    1932. The origin of the Germanic language and the Indo-
    Europeanizing of North-Europe. Language 8: 245-54.
Friedrich, Johannes. 1969. Churritisch. In Altkleinasiatische
    Sprachen (Handbuch der Orientalistik I.2. Part 1/2, Section
    2), pp. 1-30. Leiden/Köln: E. J. Brill.
Gimbutas, Marija. 1974. An archaeologist's view of PIE in 1975.
    Journal of Indo-European Studies 2, 3: 289-307.
Heine, Bernd. 1973. Pidgin-Sprachen im Bantu-Bereich (Kölner
    Beiträge zur Afrikanistik, Bd. 3). Berlin: Dietrich Reimer.
Hopper, Paul J. 1973. Glottalized and murmured occlusives in Indo-
    European. Glossa 7: 141-66.
Kammenhuber, Annelies. 1969a. Hethitisch, Palaisch, Luwisch und
    Hieroglyphenluwisch. In Altkleinasiatische Sprachen (Hand-
    buch der Orientalistik I.2. Part 1/2, Section 2), pp. 119-357.
    ———. 1969b. Hattisch. In Altkleinasiatische Sprachen (Handbuch
    der Orientalistik I.2. Part 1/2, Section 2), pp. 428-546.
Kuryłowicz, Jerzy. 1964. The inflectional categories of Indo-
    European. Heidelberg: Carl Winter.
Manessy, G. 1977. Pidginisation, créolisation, évolution des
    langues. Workshop on Pidgins and Creoles, 12th International
    Congress of Linguists, Vienna (Austria), August 30, 1977.
Meid, Wolfgang. 1975. Probleme der räumlichen und zeitlichen
    Gliederung des Indogermanischen. In Helmut Rix, ed.,
    Flexion und Wortbildung. (Akten der 5. Fachtagung der
    Indogermanischen Gesellschaft), pp. 204-19. Wiesbaden:
    Dr. Ludwig Reichert Verlag.

Neu, Erich. 1976. Zur Rekonstruktion des indogermanischen Verbal-
	systems. In A. Morpurgo Davies and W. Meid, eds., Studies
	in Greek, Italic, and Indo-European linguistics offered to
	Leonard R. Palmer, pp. 239-54. Innsbruck: Institut für
	Sprachwissenschaft.
Normier, Rudolf. 1977. Idg. Konsonantismus, germ. "Lautverschie-
	bung" und Vernersches Gesetz. Zeitschrift für vergleichende
	Sprachforschung 91: 171-218.
Polomé, Edgar C. 1964. Diachronic development of structural pat-
	terns in the Germanic conjugation system. In Proceedings
	of the Ninth International Congress of Linguists. Cambridge,
	Mass., 1962, pp. 870-80. The Hague: Mouton.
_____. 1977. The linguistic situation in the western provinces of
	the Roman Empire. In W. Haase and H. Temporini, eds.,
	Aufstieg und Niedergang der römischen Welt. Berlin-New
	York: W. de Gruyter, forthcoming.
Sommer, Ferdinand. 1947. Hethiter und Hethitisch. Stuttgart: W.
	Kohlhammer.
Watkins, Calvert. 1969. Indogermanische Grammatik. Bd. III.
	Formenlehre. I. Geschichte der indogermanischen Verbal-
	flexion. Heidelberg: Carl Winter.
Weinreich, Uriel. 1953. Languages in contact. Findings and prob-
	lems. (Publications of the Linguistic Circle of New York —
	N. 1). New York.

12 | Creolization Processes and Diachronic Linguistics

After giving support to Valkhoff's theory that South African Dutch was creolized in the seventeenth century, Loreto Todd makes a number of rather challenging statements in the last chapter of her short but substantial survey of Pidgins and Creoles (1976: 89-90): noticing that modern English compared with the language used before the Norman Conquest or French compared with the Latin of the classical authors shows "features consistent with pidginization," she assumes that "many languages which have not been classified as creoles and whose histories are not known may also have undergone processes of simplification." If so, the creole universals derived from the close analysis of the world's pidgins and creoles might throw a new light on those historically poorly documented languages, and if, furthermore, "the processes of simplification and accommodation are similar wherever people, not rigidly bound by conventions of 'standard languages,' come into contact, then the linguistic features which are common to pidgins and creoles may prove as valuable a parameter in the study of the history of languages as the study of sound changes was in the past."

Such a view would tend to assume pidginization or language simplification and adjustment for a large number of cases where languages come into contact. This is precisely where the crux of the problem lies: at all times, when a group of speakers of a definite language of higher prestige managed to impose its language upon a larger mass of speakers of another language (mostly unrelated to theirs), either by administrative and political coercion or by social and economical pressure, or by any other means, the speakers of language B would take over language A with some changes that reflect features of the phonology and the grammar of their own language. This is the basic assumption that underlies the substratum theory, which was used to explain

why Latin ū and Germanic ū appear as front rounded vowels [y :]
without the action of any umlaut factor in French and in Dutch. Actually, the whole process of Indo-Europeanization of Europe and parts
of Asia would provide ample evidence of such phenomena: if, as K.
Bittel (1950: 52, 60-61) describes it, the Hittite penetration in Asia
Minor was due to the action of invading groups of warriors under
chieftains who got hold of some limited territories and had the local
people work for their benefit and that of their retinue, it would be
understandable that Hittite would appear as a strongly simplified Indo-
European language, when compared with Vedic Sanskrit or Homeric
Greek. F. Sommer (1957: 81-100) and a number of other linguists
ascribed this to the influence of the non-Indo-European component of
the Hittite population in the Old Kingdom, but recent research tends
to show that the 'simplification' did not go along the lines of the grammatical structure of the Anatolian non-Indo-European languages and
that Hittite may represent an older stage of Indo-European in which
grammatical categories which it is assumed to have lost had not as
yet been developed by the time the proto-Hittites left the Indo-European homeland (Polomé 1979: 6-11).

Similarly, the major phonological change that differentiates
Germanic from the other Indo-European languages—the Germanic consonant shift, known as Grimm's Law—has often been considered as
due to the articulatory characteristics of the obstruent system of the
pre-Indo-European population of Northern Europe, and Sigmund Feist
(1928, 1932) developed a hypothesis ascribing to Illyro-Venetic traders in amber and furs the Indo-Europeanization of the local natives.
It was, however, based on an incorrect interpretation of the Venetic
script[1] and on presently quite inacceptable chronological assumptions.[2]
Moreover, in recent years, the research of Paul Hopper (1973) in
this country and of T. Gamkrelidze and V. Ivanov (1973) in Russia
tends to show that, actually, Germanic has preserved the status of
the Indo-European consonantal system better than many other Indo-
European languages (Normier 1977: 172-91; Polomé 1979: 11).

These examples should caution us against hasty conclusions
and generalizations of the principle implied by Loreto Todd's approach.
In a paper read at the 1978 annual meeting of the Association for Asian
Studies, Michael Shapiro warned in the same way against considering
that pidginization and creolization may account for some of the structural features of modern Hindi.

The main thrust of his paper was to show that the views developed by Frank Southworth over recent years (especially 1971 and 1974), in order to determine the social contexts in which linguistic convergence took place in South Asia and the role of pidginization and/or creolization in feature transmission, could not apply to Hindi. There are indeed essential differences between Hindi and Marathi: first of all, the term Hindi is applied to a variety of linguistic contexts—it refers to India's national language, based on Delhi speech as well as on dialects historically close to Braj, enriched with Sanskritized forms, written in devanāgarī; it designates a number of literary dialects like the mixture of Braj and Avadhi used to Tulsīdās or the early type of eastern Hindi appearing in Kabīr's poetry; it covers a set of regional vernaculars reflecting the continuation of four distinct Middle Indo-Aryan Apabhraṃśas[3] (Chatterji 1960: 164-68; 188-91). Urdu—originally the 'language of the imperial camp'—is based on the same Delhi dialect as Hindi and has practically the same grammar; their main difference consists in their source of borrowing, Urdu using Persian and Arabic loans where Hindi relies on Sanskrit, but the most obvious contrast is the script, Urdu being written in the nasta'līq Persian script. Both contrast with the bāzār-Hindustani, which is essentially a trade language, based on the North Indian vernaculars without either Sanskrit or strong Perso-Arabic component. There were, however, various levels in Hindustani: one designated a language used in daily life with a fair amount of Perso-Arabic elements, but also limited Sanskritization—this is the Hindustani Gandhi advocated strongly as the common language for India (Das Gupta 1970: 37, 111-12).[4] Therefore, Michael Shapiro recognized that the Indian situation lends itself fairly nicely to a comparison with the creole continua described for Hawaii or Jamaica. The vernacular varieties of Hindustani would constitute the low-prestige basilects, presumably with literary Hindi or Urdu, as the case might be, at the other end of the range—a situation that would be particularly plausible in the peripheral areas where Hindustani was used as lingua franca by non-native speakers in multilingual urban communities (Shapiro-Schiffman 1975: 261-64). The lack of sufficiently detailed studies on variation in the Hindu-Urdu speech community makes it impossible to examine this problem further. While it is possible to determine a few features shared by all identifiable varieties of Hindi-Urdu, we lack time depth in the description of the complex diasystem that they represent. All the documentation available for earlier developments consists, indeed, of literary

texts, mostly poetry. Therefore, Michael Shapiro feels that there
is no satisfactory corpus of data to illustrate the history of a speech
continuum of the complexity of the Hindi-Urdu one, nor to assume
that Hindi is the result of a process of creolization, i.e. the "systematic integration of material of at least two distinct linguistic stocks."
Hindi definitely shows strongly innovative features in comparison with
the regional vernaculars, but the dialects on which it is based are
completely surrounded by closely related Indo-Aryan speech forms,
whereas Marathi, for example, occupies a marginal position in the
geographical area where Dravidian and Indo-Aryan languages meet.
Relexification has hardly affected the grammatical structure of Hindi,
although the phonology and the word formation show distinct features
of Persian and Arabic influence in Urdu. On the whole, however, a
major part of the innovations of Hindi-Urdu consists in the analogical
extension of preexisting processes to new contexts in the language.
Therefore, Michael Shapiro is presumably right in assuming that
creolization is not involved in the development of the complex multi-
dimensional system of Hindi-Urdu.

        Where Michael Shapiro deplores the lack of adequate linguis-
tic evidence to prove into the past of the North Indian speech continuum, Frank Southworth (1971: 256-59) deliberately reconstructs the
sociolinguistic situation obtaining in the subcontinent after the Aryans
had achieved their dominant status: the language of high prestige was
presumably colloquial Aryan speech ("the upper class, while fiercely
maintaining the purity of their ritual language, can ... afford to take
a much more relaxed attitude about their language of worldly intercourse"); non-native speakers would vary in their ability to approximate the Aryan speakers from near-native control to a true pidgin—
the latter most likely to occur with lower-class individuals ("The non-
appearance of ... pidginized forms of Indo-Aryan in early texts is
accounted for by the fact that all writing and scholarship has traditionally been in the hands of Brahmins, the guardians of the purist
tradition."). As for the development of the pidgin into a creole, it
was often a matter of sheer survival in the early period of Aryan-
Dravidian contact, e.g. for groups of slaves having no other language
in common.

        To back up this hypothesis, Frank Southworth examines the
evidence of reduction and unexpected restructuring of the features of

the Indo-Aryan languages, with focus on the Marathi-speaking area.
Undoubtedly, these languages have undergone a set of sweeping changes by the time the inscriptions of Ashoka were written in the third
century B. C., and between that time and the earliest Marathi texts
(tenth century A. D.), additional changes have drastically altered the
phonological structure of the language. However, as Southworth himself recognizes (1971: 260-61), the changes occurring in Indo-Aryan
and Marathi are in no way more extreme than those undergone by
Germanic in Scandinavian languages like Swedish, where they do obviously not "correlate with specific kinds of social upheaval." He therefore puts more weight on restructuring which involves modifications
in the direction of Dravidian, e. g. shift of the word stress to the initial syllable, development of dental and palatal affricates, development of glides before initial e̱ and o̱ (→ ye̱-, wo̱-)—changes which,
again, do not per se provide evidence for pidginization, but whatever
limited material is available on social variation in Marathi indicates
that the speech of uneducated non-Brahmins carries through the changes in the direction of Dravidian more thoroughly and fails to restore
lost Indo-Aryan contrasts reintroduced in educated speech in Sanskrit
loans, e. g. the palatal and retroflex sibilants ś and s̱. Actually,
Southworth's strongest arguments in favor of creolization are phonological irregularity, grammatical changes, semantic similarities with
Dravidian and vocabulary replacement. On the basis of these, he assumes a process parallel to the development David De Camp (1971)
described for the Jamaican post-creole continuum: whereas the upper
classes would use the Maharashtrian Prakrit, a large segment of the
population would develop a Maharashtrian Pidgin Prakrit from the
Prakrit and the local languages; out of the Maharashtrian Prakrit and
the corresponding pidgin a creolized form would ultimately emerge,
which is continued by present-day Marathi (Southworth 1971: 268-70).[6]
In his argumentation, Frank Southworth is putting much weight on the
regularity of sound change, showing 21 percent of the Marathi tatsamas
(i. e. words derived by diachronic development from Sanskrit or Prakrit) in a list of 200 lexical items reflect "non-systematic sound change,"
whereas only 13 percent do in Hindi. These figures look more impressive, indeed, when one notices that, in the 200-word list, tatsamas
reflecting regular sound change constitute only 32 percent of the total
corpus in Marathi and 44 percent in Hindi. Nevertheless, in view of
the respective geographical location of the languages under reference
in the Indo-Aryan linguistic area (marginal for Marathi; central for

Hindi), this situation is rather to be expected, as outlying areas may
be more exposed to outside influences without implying pidginization/
creolization. Moreover, Southworth appears to neglect the impact
of internal interdialectal borrowing, evidenced, e.g., by Bengali
pāhārolā from Hindi parahāwālā/versus 'native' Bengali pāhār-
ālā 'watchman, constable'; bārīolā < Hindi bārīwālā beside genuine
Bengali bārīcīlā 'house owner, landlord,' etc. (Chatterji 1960: 121).
Similarly, the difference in rate of replacement of the vocabulary (45
percent of retention of Sanskrit terms in Marathi and 65 percent in
Hindi) gives only a weak support to a pidginization hypothesis: though
his methodology in counting cognates is open to improvement (Polomé
1977: 182-83), Malcolm Guthrie's statistical studies on Bantu languages
(1967: 96-103) show similar rates of replacement over a similar span
of time without any traceable pidginization. Moreover, the preservation of Common Bantu items appears to be higher in the east where
there is apparently strong cultural and even linguistic evidence of
Sudanic influence (Ehret 1967, 1968). Without a clear picture of the
sequence of the Bantu migrations (Polomé 1977: 195-201; Philippson
1978), it is nearly impossible to assess the true significance of such
statistical data, and mutatis mutandis, one could say the same about
the situation in the Indian subcontinent, since so much remains uncertain about the process of Indo-Aryanization and its linguistic consequences. Where Southworth assumes that Indo-Aryan was thoroughly
restructured under Dravidian influence and correlates this process
with the social and linguistic stratification within the complex society
that resulted from the Aryan expansion,[8] much of the restructuring
may be typologically motivated by the shift to a rigid SOV pattern, due
mainly to deflexion as a result of the fixation of the stress on the initial syllable. The archaic system of Vedic based on timbre and quan-
tity, and defined by morphological rules, had completely disappeared
after Pāṇini, but the information derivable from Middle Indic sources
makes it difficult to explain the evolution of Indo-Aryan accentuation
to the present day: an intensity accent or stress is documented for
the modern languages, but its position may be determined by divergent
rules in the different languages, and Middle Indic does not offer any
decisive clue as to the presence of "a regular stress accent in the
vulgar language" (Bloch 1965: 50-51). Obviously, much more work
needs to be done in this area, but as matters stand now, little evidence
appears to substantiate Southworth's claim that pidginization has been
operating in the contacts between Dravidians and Indo-Aryans and that
this accounts largely for the structural borrowing and conversion in

South Asia. Unless it can be established that Dravidian influence is
responsible for the shift of Indo-Aryan to an OV-pattern, India will
just appear as part of a larger complex with a dominant 'left-branching'
syntactic pattern, as described by Colin Masica (1976: 19-39). Besides,
as Shapiro and Schiffman (1975: 185) pointed out: "it is very likely that
cross-language contact areas in ancient India had individuals or communities displaying some form of bi- or multilingualism—not of a sort
in which the speakers contain full control of fully autonomous codes,
but instead have expanded linguistic repertoires enabling them to communicate at least minimally across cultural and linguistic boundaries."
This is the type of convergence Gumperz and Wilson (1971) described
for the rural areas along the Mysore-Maharashtrian border, where a
single syntactic (surface) structure is used with three different lexical
codes: local (Kupwar) Urdu, Marathi, and Kannaḍa. The question is,
as Shapiro and Schiffman (1975: 255) correctly put it: shall we call
'pidginization' in Marathi what we call 'borrowing' in Hindi, "because
Marathi represents an extreme tendency of which Hindi is also a lower-
degree example," whereas, usually, the two processes are considered as separate?

     Some of Southworth's statements to back up the pidginization
hypothesis also give us pause, e.g. the fact that "the English verb <u>have</u>
(in the meaning 'possess' or 'own') translates into a number of Indian
languages with expressions containing the postposition which also has
the meaning 'near' (Southworth 1971: 265-66), e.g. Marathi <u>mājhā kaḍe</u>
<u>pustak āhe</u>; Hindi <u>mere pās pustak</u> (or <u>kitāb</u>) <u>hai</u> 'I have a book' (liter-
ally: 'me near book is'). It is well known that the oldest method to
indicate possession in Indo-European was by means of the verb 'be'
with an oblique case for the person; this is the normal type in Indo-
Iranian, both in Avestan and Sanskrit where the genitive is used, as
well as in the Celtic languages down to the present day. With deflection a substitute for the genitive was used, just as a substitute was
used for the instrumental in constructions like the original neutral impersonal passive already described by Pāṇini (e.g. <u>ihāhinā srptam</u>
'the serpent has crawled here'; Gonda 1951: 103-4; Renou 1961: 198),
which expanded considerably in later Sanskrit to become ultimately the
source of the Hindi 'ergative' construction (e.g. <u>maĩ ne citthī likhī</u>;
Gaeffke 1967: 82-85).

     Similarly, the impact of Dravidian on Indo-Aryan phonology
can hardly be described in terms of 'simplification' if we consider the

addition of a new series of consonantal phonemes—the retroflex consonants—to their phonemic system as a result of prehistoric contacts
between the two linguistic communities, presumably due to the influence of "bilingual speakers who recognized a phonemic contrast between dentals and retroflects in the foreign (i. e. indigenous Dravidian)
language, came to interpret the allophones of proto-Indo-Aryan in
terms of the foreign system"[7] (Kuiper 1967: 144). It is indeed remarkable that, originally, retroflexes were rather low in frequency of
occurrence in the Vedic texts, but that this frequency increased from
the Ṛgveda to the Atharvaveda and later. Apparently, lexical borrowing from Dravidian introduced the new phonemes which then expanded
their area of occurrence.

It seems, therefore, that the views of Southworth, challenging as they are, fail to convince: more evidence is needed to substantiate his claim that "pidginization took place throughout the Indo-Aryan
area, but that its long-range linguistic effects were tempered or reinforced by other social factors (caste structure, diglossia, and sanskritization)" (1971: 270-71).

The case of Swahili provides additional evidence of the difference between the acquisition of a new language and its spread with
trade and migration and the development of pidgins and creoles:
coastal Swahili is definitely a Bantu language—its alleged Arabization
has not entailed drastic changes in the morphology or the syntax. The
Arabic loans have been integrated into the language system, with
some minor adjustments; thus, the adjectives of Arabic origin do not
take the class concord of the noun that governs them, e.g. mtu hodari
'a clever man,' mti hodari 'strong wood' versus mtu mwororo 'a mild
person,' mti mwororo 'soft wood'; chumba safi 'clean room' versus
chumba kirefu 'a long room' (-ororo and -refu are adjectives of Bantu
origin). As for the nouns, they are either included into the Bantu
class that best fits their semantic content, or they remain unchanged
and require the concords of the n-class or, for animate beings, of
the personal classes unless their initial syllable is homophonous with
a class prefix, in which case they may be considered as members of
that class in the concord system. Thus, maasi 'disobedience, riot,
revolt,' maarusi 'bride and bridegroom (on wedding day),' maki
'thickness' all belong to the 6th class, characterized by the prefix
ma-; this also fits semantically as the class contains terms desig-

nating sets of two, conveying an abstract idea of totality (a non-item-
izable whole, as in mass nouns), indicating processes, etc. However,
some Arabic terms which would fit neatly into these categories belong
to class 9/10 (the n-class) with a zero prefix, e.g. maarifa 'knowledge, erudition,' maradufu 'doubling' (older 'twill'), mali 'property,'
etc. The integration is total in the case of forms like kitabu 'book,'
from Arabic kitāb, whose plural appears as vitabu according to the
Swahili pattern ki-ti, plural vi-ti 'chairs,' or wakati 'time' from
Arabic waqt, with a plural nyakati after the model of uta 'bow,' plural
nyuta (Polomé 1967: 171-72).

As regards the phonology, here again additional phonemes
have been integrated into the system of the language, namely the dental fricatives /θ/ and /ð/, and the velar fricative /γ/, for which the
graphemic representation < th>, <dh>, and <gh>, respectively, has
been introduced. The phonemic status of Arabic [χ] has not been recognized, and it has mostly merged with [h] except in a few cases
where it is written kh, e.g. subalkheri 'good morning'; it then alternates with h, e.g. khasara ~ hasara 'loss'; in other cases, an alternation hs ~ ks is found, e.g. maksai ~ mahsai 'castrate.' This last
example provides evidence of the way Arabic has partly affected the
syllable structure of Bantu in Swahili by introducing clusters hitherto
unknown, e.g. sequences of two obstruents as in labda 'maybe, probably,' which, accordingly, is often resyllabified according to the
current CV-pattern labuda. Another disturbing factor resulting from
this resyllabification was the maintenance of the stress in its original
position, e.g. in Swahili nusura 'almost' (from Arabic nusra 'help')
with stress on the first syllable, where the word stress regularly
falls on the penult in Swahili. Elsewhere, a different stress pattern
simply prevails in the Arabic loans, e.g. in Swahili lázima 'necessity'
(Arabic lâzima 'necessity, duty'). This gives rise to stress doublets
like barábara 'exactly' versus barabára 'highway' (Polomé 1967: 50-51).

An often mentioned typical result of Arabic influence on
Swahili is supposed to be the loss of tone as a distinctive feature in
the morphology and the lexicon—a function it used to have in Proto-
Bantu and maintains in the majority of the Bantu languages. There
are indeed no identifiable minimal pairs based on tonal contrasts in
Swahili or its dialects as far as the records go, though Hadimu on
Zanzibar Island is reported to still have tone. It should, however,
be kept in mind that the loss of tone does not depend on outside influ-

ence; thus Tumbuka, the major language of northern Malawi, has lost
tone though no dialect mixture or impact of another language can be
adduced to account for the phenomenon.

When Swahili penetrated upcountry with the slave trade and
with European colonization in the nineteenth century, its use as lingua
franca spread further, and a number of pidginized forms developed with
urbanization—some of which developed into creoles, e.g. Shaba Swahili in Zaïre.

The situation, here, is different: coastal Swahili was presumably originally a language closely quite connected with Pokomo
and the Sabaki subgroup of Northeast Coastal Bantu, known as Mijikenda (Polomé 1978: 165-66), which spread over a long strip of coast-
land over the centuries, developing dialectal differentiation, especially
in the north. The Swahili pidgins are contact vernaculars originally
used for limited communication purposes in trade and/or industrial
enterprises, e.g. copper mining in Katanga, railway building in Kenya,
leading to the foundation of major cities like Elisabethville (now Lubumbashi) and Nairobi, where people of most divergent ethnic and linguistic background are brought together in new socioeconomic contexts.
In these contexts, simplification and restructuration of the phonemic
system, the morphology and the syntax, and renewal of the lexicon
took place to a large extent (Polomé 1968; Heine 1973: 70-118). Here
we deal undoubtedly with pidgins, whereas in the case of coastal Swahili, the Bantu system is maintained as well as in any other language
which has not been exposed to a centuries-long and particularly strong
outside influence: the contribution of Arabic to coastal Swahili is practically exclusively lexical, since all other features (adding phonemes;
morphological peculiarities of the loans) are only corollaries of massive borrowing.

If we look at the problem of language substitution in a contact
situation from a historical point of view, two situations can obtain:
(a) a new language is acquired, with the impact of the other language(s)
limited essentially to phonology and the lexicon; (b) pidginization and
creolization with thorough restructurization by the native population
of the language introduced by the invaders. The difference may be
more a matter of documentation than of factualness: the former presumably reflects the language of the 'elite' in which the impact of the

'alien' elements is consciously minimized; the latter, the language of the bulk of the population, as it appears to be continued in present-day languages—a typical example would be 'classical' Latin versus 'popular' Latin, from which the Romance languages developed.

This situation has been depicted by Pulgram (1958: 311-23), when he emphasizes the growing distance between spoken and written Latin and the early dialectalization of Latin, pointing to the basic class division of Roman society as the source of the linguistic dichotomy and to further social stratification as the main reason for further breakdown, with some overlapping, of either of the two basic groups— the patricians and the plebeians, the 'haves' and the 'have-nots.' 'Classical' Latin remained the norm of the upper class until the end of the Empire, but continued with increasing deviations from the norm and outright 'mistakes' in the Merovingian and Langobardic documents, while the new sociocultural structures created by the Germanic invasions led to the creation of new literary languages out of the spoken languages current in the Romania in late Carolingian times.[8] This scheme does not, however, take into account the process of Romanization and its impact on the provincial spoken language: recent research has shown how vigorously some Italic dialects maintained themselves, e.g. Oscan, which was still currently used in Pompeii graffiti in 79 A.D., and it took the settling of sizable numbers of veterans in Samnium under Augustus to ensure its latinization after Sulla had ruthlessly subdued the territory in 82 B.C. (Polomé 1977: 14). Outside of Italy, Romanization was even slower, and Gaulish is used in inscriptions until the fourth century A.D., though Latino-Celtic Mischsprache already occurs in graffiti in the third century and is still found in the fifth century. There is even indirect evidence that Gaulish was still spoken in Switzerland at the time of the Alamannic invasion (Polomé 1977: 22-23). Under those circumstances, it becomes rather appealing to assume that in the contacts between the Gaulish lower class and the Romanized upper class, as well as the Romans, a pidginized form of Latin developed for practical purposes of communication, and such a hypothesis does not appear totally unfounded in the light of some statements by Roman authors about the gruffy Latin of soldiers from Gaul or about the deviant form of spoken Latin used there (Polomé 1977: 21). It is, however, unwarranted to use the scanty evidence available to build far-reaching theories of pidginization and creolization to account for the Romance languages. The Roman authors were not interested in linguistic issues; the amount of information we have about the complex language situation in the Empire is appallingly poor. In centuries of contact with the Germanic peoples, for example, there is no document outside the Germania of Tacitus that attempts to provide a picture of their culture, and even this ethnographic sketch, published in 98 A.D., though it contains genuine Germanic words and names, fails to identify the Aestii (i.e. Balts) and the Venedi (i.e. Slavs) as non-Germanic.

Any hypothesis about the existence of a lingua franca along the long boundaries of the Empire and 'free' Germania and/or along the coasts of the North Sea has therefore to be treated most cautiously: that bi- or even multilingualism must have prevailed in the trading centers and among the Germanic tribes resettled on Roman territory, like the Ubii, is obvious from their votive inscriptions which contain a number of transparent Germanic names—mostly epithets of the deity identified under its interpretatio romana or simply designated as mater/matrona ('mother [goddess]'), to say nothing of their onomastics. Piracy and trade often went hand in hand, and long before Carausius (285-86 A.D.) (Hancock 1977: 284), the Germanic seafaring tradition had started in 47 A.D. with Gannascus, a Canninefate chieftain, who led a fleet of light vessels manned by Chauci and plundered the coast of Gaul, also establishing 'colonies' in Ireland long before the Vikings (Much-Jankuhn-Lange 1967: 147, 409). One wonders what the language of communication may have been there?

But from a less speculative point of view, the contact between Germanic and Celtic which took place on British soil is interesting to examine in its linguistic reflexes. In conclusion of a careful analysis of the available evidence, Kenneth Jackson (1953: 245) states:

> The Britons learned the language of their conquerors, and they acquired its sound system and vocabulary very completely, their own phonetics having no discernible effect on the new language and their own vocabulary very little. There must have been at least some degree of close relationship and intermarriage through which British personal names were taken into Anglo-Saxon. All this suggests a bilingual stage, when the Britons knew both Anglo-Saxon and British, though it is not likely to have been a long one, especially in the

East; and it is not probable that the conquerors learned
much of the language of the conquered.

British place-names were anglicized; a few popular terms were taken
over by Old English, e.g. binn 'basket,' bratt 'overcoat, mantle,'
brocc 'badger,' etc. Morphology and syntax remained practically un-
affected, and whatever other Celtic elements are found in later Old
English were introduced by the Irish missionaries, especially such
vocabulary items as cursian 'curse' or drȳ 'sorcerer' (O. Ir. drūi,
plur. drūid 'druid, soothsayer, sage').

If we survey the process of Indo-Europeanization or of
Romanization, or, for that matter, the expansion of the western languages through the imperialistic policies of the colonial period, it is
obvious that the way the new language is taken over and the form in
which it ultimately prevails depend on a multiplicity of factors. Mostly a smaller number of strongly organized invaders impose their rule
on larger communities: one only needs to think of Cortes or Pizarro,
but after the power of Aztec and Inca crumbled, the missionary, the
trader, and the estate development entrepreneur moved in, and all of
them used the same language as the King's autocratic administration—
did any Spanish pidgins develop under the native population of Mexico
and Peru in this context? The type of political system resulting from
the conquest may be relevant and the situation that obtains in a large
empire ruled with an iron hand by a centralized authority may differ
from the one in small feudal states or necessarily less cohesively
united strings of islands. Attitudes are also of major importance:
the language loyalty of the conquered may be strengthened by potent
correlates like religion, whereas the language consciousness of the
conqueror may react strongly against 'adulteration' of its 'sacred
tongue' by alien elements and provide all kinds of pressures to impose its language in its accepted norm. Numbers may also be affected by the ruthlessness with which the conquest was effected: if the
local population is decimated or ousted, its impact is likely to be
minimal, but in spite of often exaggerated statements of contemporary chronicles, conquerors seldom destroy the indigenous masses
whom they need to serve their purposes. Thus,the argument that
Celtic has practically had no influence on Anglo-Saxon in Britain,
because after the conquest, the country was depleted by immigration
to Brittany and by ousting or extermination of the Celts who remained

behind, is unacceptable, as shown by Kenneth Jackson (1953: 194-
246). To be sure, movements of population, wars, invasions, trade
are likely to promote the development of contact languages—pidgins.
Within human memory one could mention the birth, growth, and also
death of a number of such pidgins: in Europe during World War II, a
pidginized German with an essentially Slavic lexicon (Czech, Polish,
Russian terms; cf. Unbegaun 1947: 177-93) developed in the German
concentration camps, like Buchenwald, while the European population
under German occupation also created limited-scope linguae francae,
which partly survived with a shift of lexical code from German to
English after the Liberation in 1944-45 and disappeared when things
went back to normal. The flood of foreign workers—the so-called
Gastarbeiter—in Germany gave rise to new patterns of linguistic simplification in German in recent years, with a number of varieties depending on the national or linguistic background of the aliens (Yugo-
slav, Turkish, etc.).

This leads up to a certain level of bilingualism if it gets
sufficiently stabilized (one could mention the Swahili-based pidgins
in Eastern Africa and Zaïre as a typical example of the complement-
ary function of the pidgin as intertribal/interracial means of communication, especially for uneducated lower-class people). Such a situation, in turn, promotes adaptation processes over language boundaries within the area where the contact languages prevail: this is the
way Sture Ureland approaches the problem of the Sprachbund, when
he tries to establish (1977) that such a linguistic area may have existed in the Baltic in the Viking age: according to him (p. 18), "a mixed
language of North Germanic, East Slavic and some other languages
(Finno-Ugric or Turkic) ... [would] have existed as a kind of pidgin
language in the trading centers and settlements along the main thor-
oughfares of the Dvina, the Neva, the Dnepr, the Dnestr, and the
Volga." This language would be responsible for the prehistoric
Baltic language area in which speakers of Finno-Ugric or Turkic languages apparently acted as morphosyntactic and syntactic innovators
through the interference of their grammatical structures when they
spoke Indo-European languages (North Germanic, Baltic, or East
Slavic).

As in South Asia, historical evidence is sufficient to show
that multilingual contact accounts for the features shared across

linguistic boundaries. Whether it proves the existence of pidgin is a
more disputable issue. The challenging paper of Nicole Z. Domingue
(1977) commands our attention in this context: noticing that there is
no evidence anywhere that a pidgin or "mixed language" was spoken
in Britain prior to the development of Middle English, she carefully
analyzes the sociocultural background on which this process took
place, as well as the characteristics of Middle English for which it
would qualify as a creole. If Middle English is rated by the amount
of mixing, it appears to be rather 'incomplete' in its relexification;
if the kind of mixing is considered, it fails to show the features of a
creole syntax. This is the reason why Nicole Domingue prefers to
call Middle English a hybrid (1977: 98).

On the whole, this paper may seem to betray a rather negative and hypercritical attitude. Actually, it is more a matter of defining with more precision which factors allow us to assume pidginization and/or creolization in the historical development of a language.
In my opinion, to do so, one should focus on two types of motivations
to interpret the processes involved as reflecting a pidginization (entailing creolization at a further stage):

(a) linguistic motivations: (1) the target language undergoes a dras-
    tic reduction of its phonological and morphological inventory; (2)
    the syntax shows a major shift in the structural pattern, e. g.
    from a synthetic (i. e. inflexional) to an analytic type (with com-
    pound forms);
(b) non-linguistic motivation: a strong dominance of an originally
    external language of a prestige group over the (local) language
    of the majority would be expected.

Neither of the linguistic changes should, of course, be readily ex-
plainable by strictly internal factors, like the fixation of the stress
on the initial syllable entailing the loss of case and verbal endings—
a phonologically conditioned 'deflection' which, in turn, makes rigid
word order imperative and brings about the use of auxiliaries and
pre- or postpositions, as has been historically the case in Hindi or
in English (the process described as 'drift,' e.g. by Vennemann 1975).

As has already been illustrated by Brigitte Schlieben-Lange
in her discussion of the origin of the Romance languages (1976), a

number of conditions need to be met if we want to assume creolization
processes as the source of language change in the past: (1) there must
be clear evidence of a break in continuity in language development; (2)
there must be linguistic features characteristic of creolization (successive phases of simplification [by reduction and fossilization of the preserved material] and restructuration); (3) there must be adequate evidence of the socioeconomic or politico-cultural conditions by which
deculturation/acculturation processes of outsiders acquiring the language can be documented.

      Ideally, an intermediate stage at which pidginized forms of
the language are found would also be desirable, but such type of material is seldom available. Otherwise what looks like creolization is presumably nothing but a parallel case of linguistic development giving
evidence of some of the typological features usually characteristic of
creoles.

NOTES

      [1] In 1924, F. Sommer had proposed to interpret the Venetic
graphemes < ɸ >, < z >, and < χ > as fricatives, and S. Feist saw
in cases like Venetic zoto: Greek ἔδοτο or Venetic vhuχiia = Latin
Fugia a parallel to the Germanic consonant shift. It was, however,
soon recognized that the Venetic graphemes < ɸ >, < z>, and < χ >
represented the voiced stops b, d, g (cf. e.g. Lejeune 1974: 31-32).
      [2] At the time Sigmund Feist was writing, it was believed that
the Venetic people of pre-Roman northeastern Italy were part of a
vast Illyrian complex, assumed to have played a major part in the Indo-
Europeanization of Western Europe and the Mediterranean area and
connected with the Lusatian civilization in North East Saxony and Lower
Silesia ca. 1200 B. C. A number of leading scholars promoted these
views in the late thirties and the forties, such as Hans Krahe and Julius
Pokorny, but recent research has shown the 'Illyrian' hypothesis to
be ill-founded (cf. Kronasser 1962; Polomé 1978a) and it is now generally abandoned.
      It is now generally recognized that the homeland of the Ger-
manic tribe in Northern Europe has not undergone any major cultural
or ethnic change since the arrival of the 'single-grave'group of invaders

(Einzelgrabvolk) in Neolithic times (Much-Jankuhn-Lange 1967:45-47),
but the Jastorf culture ca. 600 B. C. appears to be the first distinctly
Germanic culture in northern Germany and the Jutland Peninsula
(Keiling 1976).

[3] Apabhraṁśa designates an aberrant form of a prākrit, which
mixes forms from the popular (spoken) language with the (literary)
prākrit (Renou-Filliozat 1947: 83).

[4] The ambiguity of the term Hindustani is particularly well
illustrated by its fate in the Census: when the term Hindustani was
used alone, without giving their respondents the alternate choice between Urdu and Hindi, it scored very high in Uttar Pradesh and Bihar,
e.g. 1921, 99.75 percent; 1931, 99.68 percent; when Urdu and Hindi
could also be marked, it dropped dramatically, e.g. 1951, 10.67 percent; 1961, 0.1 percent, whereas Hindi scored high percentages (1951,
79.82 [Urdu, 6.8]; 1961, 85.39 [Urdu, 10.7]; Brass 1974: 188-97).

[5] A situation that Southworth (1971: 270) illustrates by the
following diagram:

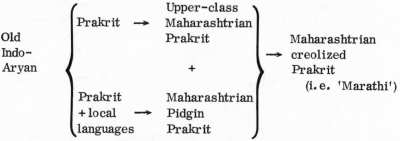

[6] In his view (Southworth 1971: 268), 'pidginized forms of Indo-
Aryan were created and stabilized in the context of trade and joint
agricultural activities within multicaste settlements.' In the Aryan
settlements in the originally Dravidian (and/or Munda) speech community, the language situation was presumably as follows, according to
Southworth: (a) Sanskrit (confined mainly to ritual activities); (b) Prakrit (colloquial Indo-Aryan spoken by the upper class); (c) local lan-
guage(s) (spoken by the indigenous population); (d) pidgin (principal
medium of communication between lower-class cultivators and their
Aryan superiors). At a later stage of development, two processes are
assumed to take place: (a) the local language is given up in favor either
of the pidgin or of the Prakrit (in the latter case, with drastic changes
in the structure of the Prakrit); (b) the pidgin and Prakrit become gradually convergent as they now constitute both ends of a continuum.

[7] E.g. in the case of dentals preceded by voiced sibilants
(either the dental [z] or the palatal [ž], as in the participles līḍha-
'licked,' gūḍha 'hidden,' etc., where late IE ('satem') *ĝdh- (from
*ĝh-t- by Bartholomä's Law) had become Indo-Aryan *ždh, in which
the sibilant was lost with compensatory lengthening of the preceding
vowel, while the dental became a retroflex.

Indo-Aryan *s was affected by the so-called ruki-rule, i.e.
s became ṣ after the 'vowels' ī, ū, e, o, and ṛ, and after r(l) and k,
if followed either by a vowel or a dental consonant, or m, y, or v,
e.g. Loc. Pl. pitṛṣu 'at the fathers'; deveṣu 'at the gods,' etc. versus bālāsu.

Indo-Aryan *s combines with a preceding palatal or guttural
to yield kṣ, e.g. 2nd sg. vakṣi 'you speak': vacmi 'I speak,' vakti
'he speaks'; vakṣi 'you want': vaśmi 'I want'; etc.

[8] This was schematized by Pulgram as follows:

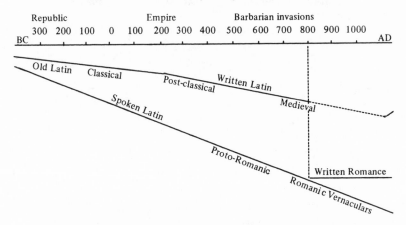

| Republic | | | | | Empire | | | Barbarian invasions | | | | |
| 300 | 200 | 100 | 0 | 100 | 200 | 300 | 400 | 500 | 600 | 700 | 800 | 900 | 1000 |

BC ⎿_____⏌ AD

Old Latin   Classical   Post-classical   Written Latin
Spoken Latin   Medieval
Proto-Romanic
Written Romance
Romanic Vernaculars

REFERENCES

Bittel, Kurt. 1950. Grundzüge der Vor- und Frühgeschichte Klein-
        asiens. 2nd ed. Tübingen: Ernst Wasmuth.
Bloch, Jules. 1965. Indo-Aryan from the Vedas to modern times.
        English edition by Alfred Master. Paris: Librairie d'Amé-
        rique et d'Orient. Adrien-Maisonneuve.

Brass, Paul R. 1974. Language, religion and politics in North India. Cambridge: University Press.

Chatterji, S. K. 1960. Indo-Aryan and Hindi. Calcutta: K. L. Mukhopadhyay.

Das Gupta, Jyotirindra. 1970. Language conflict and national development. Group politics and national language policy in India. Berkeley/Los Angeles: University of California Press.

DeCamp, David. 1971. Toward a generative analysis of a post-creole speech continuum. In D. Hymes, ed., Pidginization and creolization of languages. Cambridge: University Press, pp. 349-70.

Domingue, Nicole Z. 1977. Middle English: Another creole? Journal of Creole Studies 1, 1: 89.

Ehret, Christopher. 1967. Cattle-keeping and milking in Eastern and Southern African history: the linguistic evidence. Journal of African History 8: 1-17.

_____. 1968. Sheep and Central Sudanic peoples in Southern Africa. Journal of African History 9: 213-21.

Feist, Sigmund. 1928. Die Ausbreitung des indogermanischen Sprachstammes über Nordeuropa in vorgeschichtlicher Zeit. Wörter und Sachen 11: 29-53.

_____. 1932. The origin of the Germanic languages and the Indo-Europeanising of north Europe. Language 8: 245-54.

Gaeffke, Peter. 1967. Untersuchungen zur Syntax des Hindi (Dissertationes Rheno-Trajectinae, vol. 11). The Hague: Mouton.

Gamkrelidze, T., and V. V. Ivanov. 1973. Sprachtypologie und die Rekonstruktion der gemeinindogermanischen Verschlüsse. Vorläufiger Bericht. Phonetica 27: 150-56.

Gonda, J. 1951. Remarks on the Sanskrit passive. Leiden: E. J. Brill.

Gumperz, John J., and Robert Wilson. 1971. Convergence and creolization: A case from the Indo-Aryan/Dravidian border. In D. Hymes, ed., Pidginization and creolization of languages. Cambridge: University Press, pp. 141-50.

Guthrie, Malcolm. 1967. Comparative Bantu: An introduction to the comparative linguistics and prehistory of the Bantu languages. Farnborough (England): Gregg Press.

Hancock, Ian F. 1977. Recovering pidgin genesis: Approaches and problems. In A. Valdman, ed., Pidgin and creole linguistics. Bloomington: Indiana University Press, pp. 277-94.

Heine, Bernd. 1973. Pidgin-Sprachen im Bantu-Bereich. (Kölner
    Beiträge zur Afrikanistik, vol. 3.) Berlin: Dietrich Reimer
    Verlag.
Hopper, Paul J. 1973. Glottalized and murmured occlusives in Indo-
    European. Glossa 7: 1-166.
Jackson, Kenneth. 1953. Language and history in early Britain: A
    chronological survey of Brittonic languages first to twelfth
    century A. D. Edinburgh: University Press.
Keiling, Horst. 1976. Die Herausbildung der germanischen Stämme
    (ab etwa 6. Jahrhundert vor unserer Zeitrechnung). 1. Die
    Entstehung der Jastorfkultur und zeitgleicher Kulturen im
    Rhein-Weser-Gebiet und deren geographische Verbreitung.
    In Die Germanen: Ein Handbuch. Vol. 1, pp. 83-102.
    Berlin: Akademie-Verlag.
Kronasser, Heinz. 1962. Zum Stand der Illyristik. Balkansko
    ezikoznanie—Linguistique Balkanique 4: 5-23.
Kuiper, F. B. J. 1967. The genesis of a linguistic area. Indo-
    Iranian Journal 10: 81-102.
Lejeune, Michel. 1974. Manuel de la langue vénète. Heidelberg:
    Carl Winter.
Masica, Colin P. 1976. Defining a linguistic area: South Asia.
    Chicago/London: University of Chicago Press.
Much, Rudolf, Herbert Jankuhn, and Wolfgang Lange. 1967. Die
    Germania des Tacitus erläutert. Heidelberg: Carl Winter.
Normier, Rudolf. 1977. Idg. Konsonantismus, germ, "Lautver-
    schiebung" und Vernersches Gesetz. Zeitschrift für ver-
    gleichende Sprachforschung 91: 171-218.
Phillipson, D. W. 1977. The spread of the Bantu language. Scien-
    tific American 236(4) (April 1977): 106-14.
Polomé, Edgar C. 1967. Swahili language handbook. Washington,
    D. C.: Center for Applied Linguistics.
_____. 1968. Lubumbashi Swahili. Journal of African Languages
    7(1): 14-25.
———. 1977a. Le vocabulaire proto-bantou et ses implications
    culturelles. Paleontologia Linguistica. Atti del VI. Convegno
    Internazionale di Linguisti, Milano, settembre 1976. Brescia:
    Paideia Editrice, pp. 181-201.
_____. 1977b. The linguistic situation in western provinces of the
    Roman Empire. To be published in H. Temporini and W.

Haase, eds., Aufstieg und Niedergang des Römischen Reichs. Berlin/New York: Walter de Gruyter, forthcoming.

Polomé, Edgar C. 1978a. Illyrian-Thracian-Daco-Mysian. To be published in Cambridge Ancient History 3: 2. Cambridge: University Press, 1982.

_____. 1978b. The earliest attestations of Swahili. Indian Linguistics 39: 165-73.

_____. 1979. Creolization theory and linguistic prehistory. In Festschrift for Oswald Szemerényi, ed. by Bela Brogyanyi. Amsterdam: John Benjamins, pp. 679-90.

Pulgram, Ernst. 1958. The tongues of Italy. Prehistory and history. Cambridge, Mass.: Harvard University Press.

Renou, Louis. 1961. Grammaire sanscrite. Deuxième édition. Paris: Librairie d'Amérique et d'Orient Adrien-Maison-neuve.

Renou, Louis, and Jean Filliozat. 1947. L'Inde Classique. Manuel des Etudes Indiennes, vol. 1. Paris: Payot.

Schlieben-Lange, Brigitte. 1976. L'origine des langues romanes—un cas de créolisation. In J. M. Meisel, ed., Langues en contact—pidgins-créoles. Tübingen: Gunter Narr, pp. 81-101.

Shapiro, Michael C., and Harold F. Schiffman. 1975. Language and society in South Asia. U.S. Department of Health, Education, and Welfare, International Studies Branch, Office of Education.

Sommer, Ferdinand. 1947. Hethiter und Hethitisch. Stuttgart: W. Kohlhammer.

Southworth, Franklin C. 1971. Detecting prior creolization. An analysis of the historical origins of Marathi. In D. Hymes, ed., Pidginization and creolization of languages. Cambridge: University Press, pp. 255-73.

_____. 1974. Linguistic stratigraphy of North India. In F. Southworth and M. Apte, eds., Contacts and convergence in South Asian languages (International Journal of Dravidian Linguistics 3,1), pp. 201-23.

Todd, Loreto. 1974. Pidgins and creoles. London/Boston: Routledge & Kegan Paul.

Unbegaun, B.-O. 1947. Les argots slaves des camps de concentration. Mélanges 1945: V. Etudes Linguistiques. (Publications de la Faculté des Lettres de l'Université de Strasbourg, vol. 108.) Paris: Société d'Editions 'Les Belles Lettres.'

Ureland, P. Sture. 1977. Aspects of prehistorical bilingualism in
    the Baltic language area and Russia. (Paper presented at
    the XIIth International Congress of Linguists, Vienna, Aus-
    tria, August 30, 1977.)
Vennemann, Th. 1975. An explanation of drift. In Charles N. Li,
    ed., Word order and word change. Austin: University of
    Texas Press, pp. 271-305.

13 | Creolization and Language Change

The problem of creolization and language change has received increased attention in recent years. It has been examined by prominent creolists, such as Gabriel Manessy (1979), and historical linguists, such as Elizabeth Closs-Traugott (1977), and it has found a place in textbooks on historical linguistics (e.g. Bynon 1977: 256-61).

The importance of creoles for diachronic studies was apparently highlighted by the assumed derivation of the European-based creoles and pidgins from a Portuguese proto-pidgin (Whinnom 1965). This monogenetic approach lent itself to a family-tree representation of the relationship between those pidgins and creoles, grouping them into two major subfamilies—the Atlantic Portuguese Pidgin and the Indo-Pacific Pidgin (Todd 1974: 40)—corresponding to the two major trading routes. This sweeping monogenesis theory which ultimately derives those pidgins from the Mediterranean Lingua Franca (Whinnom 1977) is, however, fraught with difficulties: the tree pattern fails to describe the wave after wave that led to the expansion of the proto-pidgin;[1] the similarities between the Portuguese-based pidgins and creoles and those based on Bantu remain unaccounted for. In the latter case, typological features, cutting across genetic groupings are involved, such as the limitation of the tense-aspect markers to basically three covering the semantic categories of (1) anteriority; (2) 'irrealis' (i.e. 'not actualized'); (3) non-punctual (Markey 1979: 7).[2] Therefore, Elizabeth Closs-Traugott (1977) prefers to look for the relation between pidginization, creolization, and language change in the direction of the investigations of the generativists of the sixties in language acquisition. Innovativeness in creoles may indeed be due to the fact that 'first generation creole speakers are presumably subject to relatively little suppressive judgment by older speakers' (p.

87), because, as Le Page (1977: 238) shows, different generations of
speakers have different goals. Closs-Traugott (p. 88) combines this
acquisition model of change with Bailey's 'dynamic wave theory' (1973),
which describes changes as 'unidirectional wavelike patterns of generalization'—especially of comparative simplification resulting from
children's failure to learn all the constraints of the innovated form.
In this procedure, Closs-Traugott (p. 91) sees a fruitful new approach
to the study of language as a social instrument. It is indeed on the
simplification process that creolists tend to focus: the 'ideal pidgin'
grammar is a reduced model of grammar, presumably governed by
some universal criteria of simplicity, but it is nevertheless quite characteristically structured (Ferguson-De Bose 1977: 114-15).

   The case of the African pidgins of Bantu origin provides a
neat example of such a situation: Fanagalo, the Zulu-based language
of communication in the South African mining industry (Heine 1970:
47-54), underwent a considerable process of simplification in the nominal classification system characteristic of Bantu. Whereas Zulu still
has thirteen classes of nouns, regrouped two by two to mark number
contrasts, Fanagalo divides the nouns into two groups: count-nouns
and mass-nouns. The mass-nouns are not marked for number; the
count-nouns fall into two categories:

(a) those with the prefix <u>um-</u>, e.g. <u>umfazi</u> 'woman, wife,' <u>umlilo</u> 'fire';
(b) those 'without prefix' (+ a few relic forms of the old class system),
 e.g. <u>nwele</u> 'hair,' <u>khanda</u> 'head,' <u>litshe</u> 'stone' (formerly a Zulu
 class 5 noun, with the prefix <u>li-</u>).

Their pluralization follows a rule, in which the environmental constraints are either semantic or phonological, i.e.

$$
\text{Pl.}
\begin{bmatrix}
\text{category (a)} \\[2ex]
\text{category (b)}
\end{bmatrix}
\rightarrow
\begin{bmatrix}
\begin{cases}
\underline{\text{ba}}\text{- in the environment—}N \;\text{category (a)[+ Human]} \\
\underline{\text{mi}}\text{- elsewhere}
\end{cases} \\
\begin{cases}
\underline{\text{zi}}\text{- in the environment—[+ nasal]} \\
\underline{\text{ma}}\text{-}
\end{cases}
\end{bmatrix}
$$

e.g. <u>um</u>fazi — <u>ba</u>fazi;
  <u>um</u>lilo — <u>mi</u>lilo;

nwele — zinwele;
khanda — makhanda;
litshe — matshe (Heine 1973: 124-26).

Thus, Fanagalo has reorganized whatever it preserved from the Zulu class system into a new structure.

Describing the linguistic features of a pidgin or creole and contrasting them with those of the base language does not, however, provide sufficient clues to understand the processes involved. Brigitte Schlieben-Lange (1976: 94) has proposed a typology of the conditions that determine the course of historically documented processes of creolization. The facts that require prior analysis are:

(1) the type of historical situations and events;
(2) the types of contact between two or more languages;
(3) the type of development of a language;
(4) the type of linguistic structure per se.

To respond to the fourth criterion it would be necessary to define which kind of linguistic phenomena occur typically in creole languages, while they are not found as a rule in 'non-creole' languages: would the substitution of aspect for tense qualify, as has often been suggested? Presumably not, since the history of definite Indo-European languages such as Gothic illustrates the same trend (cf. also Hall 1966: 59, fn. 4). As for the third point, creoles are contrasted with non-creoles by assuming that their development implies a break in continuity: what is mainly involved is a drastic reduction of the communicative functions of the language as well as its takeover by non-native speakers under a fossilized form, i.e. without any more feedback from the base language. The result of such a 'break' is extensive change in the phonology, morphology, and syntax, characterized by a reduction of the linguistic inventory of phonemes, grammatical categories, word classes, paradigms, phrase structures, as well as a fossilization of the preserved material, i.e. the forms of the base language are preserved in a stereotype form on which the original rules of inflection and derivation do no longer operate. Lubumbashi Swahili in the Shaba province of Zaire provides clear evidence of such a state of affairs. After Swahili had been introduced by immigrants from central Tanzania in the precolonial period and reinforced by an influx of East Coast personnel in the early days of King Leopold's administration, the contact with the native speakers along the Indian Ocean was practically broken, and a pidginized form of the language served as means of intertribal and interracial communication. Its early development is unfortunately undocumented, but when it is recorded in the fifties, it shows all the expected features of a pidgin: its phonemic inventory has been reduced, not only by the elimination of the Arabic fricatives /θ/, /ð/, and /γ/ as elsewhere in upcountry Swahili dialects, but also by the merger of / ɟ/ and /j/, blurring the contrast between <j> and <y> (for which minimal pairs like jua 'know': yua 'wobble' were anyhow only exceptional); the whole morphological system has been utterly simplified by the complete disruption of the concord system: adjectives appear with stereotyped prefixes (usually mu-); numerals and demonstratives have fixed forms; the conjugation is reduced to three tenses: present (non-punctual), past and future (the na-, li-, and ta- tenses); the copula is replaced by the 'locative' iko 'there (is)'; the negative conjugation has been lost, except for a few lexicalized relic forms; the relative forms have disappeared from the spoken language, though they occur occasionally in writing (Polomé 1968). Moreover, the impact of the prevailing alien population which adopted the local Swahili as lingua franca on the phonology is noticeable in the occurrence of a number of variants such as byforms with nz- for nj- (e.g. nzala 'hunger' versus East Coast Swahili njaa), occasional devoicing of v to f and palatalization of s to š and z to ž, etc.—features which are characteristic of the influential Luba component of the immigrant population (Polomé 1969, 1971a; Heine 1970: 88).

This raises the question of the type of contact between the languages coexisting in the Lubumbashi area, as suggested by Schlieben-Lange's second point. We do not deal here with a diglossic situation as exists, e.g., in Jamaica or in Haiti, but rather with what M. H. Abdulaziz (1972) calls triglossia, i.e. the coexistence of three languages, each with different functions, depending on prestige, social status, political, cultural, economic, or other important roles of their speakers—one, at least, being confined to very specific roles (e.g. at home). There is indeed still a strong prevalence of French as the prestige language, used in education and in the upper levels of economic and sociocultural life; Swahili (in its local form) is the market language, the current means of intertribal communication, the urban dialect in which everyday business is conducted at work, in the

shops, in public offices; it is used in broadcasting and by popular pop
musicians; it is the language of the youth among their peer groups;
the vernacular is restricted to the family, if both parents speak it,
and to relations with the home village. Important is the fact that detribalization in the urban context leads to mixed marriages, where
the home language tends to become Swahili; children growing up in
such an environment adopt Swahili as their first language (Polomé
1972: 70-71; Heine 1979: 85-86). By this process Shaba Swahili shifts
from lingua franca to creole[3] in the urbanized centers of the Katangese
copper industry with the present generation. This entails an extensive
relexicalization which is marked by borrowings from local sources,
either French or Bantu languages, also English from neighboring
Zambia, loan translations, new word formations, etc. Typical Lubumbashi terms are kinga for 'bicycle' (East Coast Swahili baiskeli),
mashua ya ndege for 'plane' (East Coast Swahili eropleni), mashua ya
ntoto for 'train' (East Coast Swahili gari la moshi), kalulu 'rabbit'
(East Coast Swahili sungura). Obviously, many neologisms are due
to semantic shift, as shown by the use of mashua literally 'boat,' for
other vehicles (a boat is mashua ya mayi in Lubumbashi, i.e. 'of
water'), or of kambo, literally 'step-parent' for 'grandfather.' Others
are lexicalized Bantuized French forms, e.g. loro 'gold,' musiketele
'mosquito net,' falanga 'money,' or belong to the common vocabulary
of the Zaire contact vernaculars, e.g. mukanda 'letter' (East Coast
Swahili barua), matabishi 'tip' (Polomé 1968; 1972: 71).

   If we consider the first point of Schlieben-Lange, the socioeconomic perspective of creolization which is its major non-linguistic
conditioning appears to be the most neglected factor when creolization
processes are assumed to account for linguistic change in the past.
Robert Chaudenson (1977) has sketched an eloquent picture of the
socioeconomic structure of the plantation system in the French islands
of the Indian Ocean and in the Caribbean, showing how it favored the
rapid process of deculturation of African slaves and their acculturation to their new creole-speaking environment. Similarly, the new
creoles that have developed in recent years in Africa are a result of
socioeconomic phenomena. Again, the case of Shaba (or Lubumbashi)
Swahili is particularly instructive: 80 years ago there was nothing
but wooded savannah where the sprawling city of Lubumbashi has now
got a population of about half a million people. Up to the Depression
the mining industry took only manpower on contract, a large number

of them from the south (Rhodesia—present-day Zambia), but Swahili
was already used as lingua franca in the workshops and plants of the
big copper-processing company, though the missions in the neighboring rural area used Bemba as the language of primary education. In
the thirties the policy changed and a settlement for factory workers
was built near the plants. As production increased and more manpower
was required, recruiters brought in workers from various parts of the
Congo and Ruanda-Burundi. Some of them already knew Swahili and
reinforced the use of the language as lingua franca. Soon schooling
and preaching in Swahili was initiated by the Protestant missions, and
until the shift to French as the language of the curriculum after World
War II, Swahili was effectively the medium of education at the primary
level. Meanwhile, as was already indicated, a growing number of
workers stopped returning to their village to get married and found
their spouses locally. These new families used Swahili as their first
language, so that it became their children's mother tongue, and by the
middle fifties, most of the school-going children would play and con-
verse with their peers almost exclusively in Swahili (as demonstrated
by statistics; cf. Heine 1970: 88-89).[4] This generation has now grown
up and is founding new families of Swahili speakers, spreading the language even further as first language, but this Swahili is not East Coast
Swahili: it is a creolized form resulting from the relexicalization of
the pidginized Swahili used as lingua franca by earlier generations
(Polomé 1971a,b).[5]

The way it spread illustrates the pattern of language acquisition as described by the generativists, and it has not taken more than
two generations to solidly establish the pidginized Swahili lingua franca
of the copper industry as the prevailing urban creole of Shaba province
in Zaire—but the motivation was strictly socioeconomic.

If, then, we want to assume creolization processes as the
source of language change in the past, a number of conditions need to
be met:

(a) there must be clear evidence of a break in continuity in language
    development;
(b) there must be linguistic features characteristic of creolization
    (successive phases of simplification [by reduction and fossilization
    of the preserved material] and restructuration);

(c) there must be adequate evidence of the socioeconomic or politico-
cultural conditions by which the deculturation/acculturation processes of outsiders acquiring the language can be documented.
(See the concluding section of Chapter 12.)

Ideally, an intermediate stage at which pidginized forms of
the language are found would also be desirable, but such type of material is seldom available.[8] Otherwise, what looks like creolization is
presumably nothing but a parallel case of linguistic development giving
evidence of some of the typological features characteristic of creoles.
As Brigitte Schlieben-Lange (1976: 101) points out, there is a constant
relation between historical situations and the types of linguistic development that obtain, but then there are different types of historical situations, and the political situation (in the broadest sense) certainly has
a considerable impact on language development. Her remarks applied
in particular to the situations that must have existed in the Roman
Empire, since a number of scholars have considered the origin of the
Romance languages as a possible case of creolization. Usually the
matter is very fervently debated: the arguments pro and con are
fiercely defended ('the system of the language has been radically simplified'—'the structure of Latin has not been deeply altered'—'the process of acquisition of Latin in contact with the Romans was never
really completed'—'the inhabitants of the provinces were totally assimilated and learnt Latin thoroughly'—etc.). But the main argument,
that apparently clinches it all, is that, actually, there has never been
a break in the diachronic development of Latin.[7] To this, the 'creolists'
retort that there are two distinct periods to consider:

(a) the Roman period during which spoken Latin develops into so-called
'Vulgar Latin';
(b) the German invasions which disrupt the evolution process and lead
to a 'creolization' of Latin, as it is more and more spoken by the
'barbarian' invaders.

This is allegedly evidenced linguistically by a phase of <u>simplification</u>,
followed by a phase of <u>restructuration</u>. A diglossic situation ultimately
prevails in which one form of the language enjoys a higher prestige so
that the community identifies itself with it.

For all the possible parallelism with historical creoles, it is
obvious that the conditions that characterize the development of the

latter will be expected to have their counterpart in the alleged creolization processes of the past. As far as the Romance languages are concerned, it goes without saying that the policy of Rome in the conquered
territories was quite different from the plantation economy that prevailed in the Caribbean, for example, and that therefore the basic conditions for language development were quite different. Romanization
was essentially promoted by the introduction of a uniform system of
administration, by the establishment of an efficient network of roads
and by the creation of colonies of Roman citizens. The main purpose
of Rome was, however, to establish its political power on solid foundations, and it was not directly concerned with its sociocultural impact
on the linguistic situation of the area: schooling was only fully accessible to the upper classes, and even a higher education in Greek and
Latin did not entail giving up one's mother tongue, as is shown by the
case of the father of the fourth-century poet Ausonius, who spoke Gaulish at home and Greek with his friends, and had only a poor knowledge
of Latin though he practiced medicine in Bordeaux. The persistence
of Celtic in Gaul is confirmed by numerous other testimonies as well
as by linguistic evidence (Polomé 1977: 22): thus, the statement of
Dio Cassius that a Roman senator was very upset by the gruff Latin
spoken by soldiers from Gaul is confirmed by the contemporaneous
graffitti on spindle whorls in a mixture of Latin and Celtic (Meid 1980).
This and other material make it plausible that there may already have
been a distinct form of Gallo-Latin in Central Gaul at the end of the
fourth century, which was different enough from classical Latin for its
use to be labeled as Celtice or Gallice loquere. The pattern of Christ-
ianization shows that the rural areas in Gaul had remained essentially
pagan and speaking their Celtic dialects at the beginning of the fourth
century. It took the vigorous apostolic fervor of Saint Martin to
Christianize them, using Latin for that purpose. The triumph of
Christianism, therefore, also achieved total romanization at that late
date (Whatmough 1970: 75). That the Germanic invasions led to extensive disorganization need not be emphasized (Musset 1965), and a
break in the continuity of the development of Latin is clearly documented by Merovingian Latin.

These facts would, accordingly, tend to confirm the view of
the propounders of the 'creolization' theory, but, again, what applies
to Gaul is not necessarily valid for other parts of the Roman Empire.
The situation in the Iberian Peninsula, for example, is quite different:

intense Roman colonization essentially in the second half of the first century B. C. made the cities prosperous, except in the Celtiberian area where the population remained predominantly rural and stuck to its old traditions with limited Roman impact. Baetica seems to have been more thoroughly romanized at an earlier date, but the pre-Roman languages appear to regress rapidly in Lusitania and Tarraconensis toward the end of the Republic, except in the northwest, including the present-day Basque territory, which, however, does not provide any clue as to its linguistic situation. By the time of the Visigothic invasion, only Latin seems to have been found by them in the upper classes and the administration—a Latin characterized by its high level of 'correction,' which would hint at the depth of the romanization. Nevertheless, the Latin of Spain revealed by the inscriptions already displays a number of the typical lexical features which distinguish Ibero-Romance from the rest of the Romanitas (Polomé 1977: 16-18).

Putting such regional differentiations into perspective, Devoto (1968: 251-61) has shown how the decentralization of the Roman administration by the Diocletian reform has favored the strengthening of the preexisting dialectal trends in Latin and led to greater regional variation. Some of the differences may reflect the lingering influence of the pre-Roman languages, but nevertheless the regional features constitute incipient varieties, which a significant political and social change could develop into full-fledged Proto-Romance dialects. The turmoil of the fifth century and the ensuing breakdown of the Empire will provide the external element to trigger this evolution.

Does this favor the creolization hypothesis? It remains undoubtedly disputable; each area of the Empire has problems sui generis, and what applies to Spain or Gaul is not necessarily valid for Italy or Rumania. Moreover, how much do we really know about the process that should have preceded 'creolization'? Undoubtedly, there must have been many instances of 'pidginization,' but how transient were they and how much impact did they make? If we take Britain as an example, it is obvious that it was never deeply romanized (Polomé 1977: 25-26). As many soldiers recruited in the Germanic border areas served there in the third century and married locally, one cannot but start wondering how much Latin they actually knew and what language they spoke at home, when their votive inscriptions reveal that they maintained their Germanic gods under Roman garb. Unfortunately, the Romans were not interested in sociolinguistic problems: what interesting reading the reports of their proconsuls would have provided otherwise for modern 'creolists' concerned with the origin of the Romance languages!

For lack of such evidence, the problem of creolization as the source of the split between Latin and its 'daughter languages' must needs remain unsolved, and similarly many hasty recent assumptions of creolization to account for language of the past will have to be carefully reassessed in the light of the principles advanced by B. Schlieben-Lange and briefly discussed in this study.[8]

NOTES

[1] It has been assumed that the New World creoles developed mainly through extensive relexification from a Portuguese-base proto-pidgin located in West Africa (Voorhoeve 1973): there are, however, arguments to assign the Portuguese component in the creole languages of Surinam to another source (Le Page 1977: 250-51) and to date back some lexical correspondences between Sranan and Krio to a late sixteenth/early seventeenth century West African variety of English (Hancock 1977: 282-83).

[2] Kenya Pidgin Swahili (as spoken in Nairobi) illustrates this situation: it has:
(a) an 'aorist,' marked by na, e.g. yeye naleta pombe 'he brings beer';
(b) a past, marked by the auxiliary kwisha—a 'perfective' marker—
    e.g. yeye kwisha funga mlango 'he has (already) shut the door';
(c) a future, marked by ta, e.g. sisi tapata kazi? 'are we going to get work?' (Heine 1973: 90-92).

[3] Creole is taken here in the same meaning as when it applies to the vernacular language of Haiti (De Camp 1977: 5): evolved from a pidginized variety of its base language, Lubumbashi (or Shaba) Swahili has begun to 'be acquired as a native language.' It performs 'a wide range of communicative and expressive functions' and has an extensive lexicon and an adequate grammatical structure to meet all the needs of a so-called 'normal language.' It is, however, often unintelligible to East Coast Swahili speakers and cannot simply be considered as a dialect of the same.

[4] After being exposed to French in school for a number of
years, more advanced students will alternately use this more prestigious language with their peers and with strangers, switching being a
common feature in the conversation (for statistics of language use by
high school students, cf. Polomé 1971b: 372-73).

[5] Besides expanding its vocabulary, it has acquired new syntactic patterns which differentiate it considerably from East Coast
Swahili, e.g. the use of -enye as a substitute for the relative form
with the infinitive in sentences like this statement from the Highway
Code defining a cycle track: ni kipindi cha njia chenye kufunguliwa
kwa watu wenye makinga na tukutuku-kinga 'it is a part of the road that
is open to people with bicycles and motorbikes' (in East Coast Swahili
-enye is only used with nouns to indicate 'possession' as in the second
case in this example). It has also reorganized its morphology, rein-
troducing, e.g., the 'diminutive' ka-class, which has been lost in
East Coast Swahili, e.g. kasafisha ya meno 'toothbrush' (from the
verb -safisha 'clean'), or the 'continuative' suffix -aka, unknown in
standard Swahili but common in eastern Bantu language (as -aga), e.g.
ule anafanyaka mayele 'that one tries to be smart all the time.' It has
developed its own morphophonemic rules, e.g. about the treatment of
the original syllabic nasals: i + nasal in class 9 versus nasal + u in
class 1/3, e.g. imbwa 'dog': mukate 'bread' (East Coast Swahili
mbwa: mkate, both with [m̩]).

[6] Hancock (1977) has collected evidence on a number of cases,
but the material is scant so that the conclusions often remain inevitably
speculative, as in the case of the linguistic situation in Britain under
the Roman Empire (see, e.g., Jackson 1953: 97-106).

[7] It is not possible to survey within the scope of this paper the
considerable literature on the subject from Schuchhardt to the present
day. Meillet (1928: 236) compared explicitly the restructuration of
the Latin pronominal system in the Romance languages with what happened in the European-based creoles. B. Schlieben-Lange (1976: 82-
93) had provided an excellent analysis of the most important views expressed on the subject by Otto Jespersen, Marius Valkhoff, José de
Carvalho, Helmut Lüdtke, Klaus Heger, Marcel Cohen, and others.
The main argument against the creolization hypothesis is summarized
by Hall (1974: 76): 'there probably existed various pidginised versions
of Latin, spoken wherever Romans came into contact with non-Romans,
especially along the borders in military camp and in markets ... However, we have no direct record of any such, nor can any of the later

developments of Latin into Romance be ascribed with any certainty to
any kind of Pidgin Latin which later became creolised. All the Romance developments ... could have taken place in the course of normal
slow linguistic change over the centuries, without the sharp break and
drastic restructuring which is by definition involved in pidginisation.'
This is also the view of Coseriù (1978: 265), who explains the origin
of the Romance languages as the direct continuation of 'das sich in
ununterbrochener Differenzierung befindende, <u>sich entwickelnde Latein</u>,'
which he contrasts with classical Latin, whose development was practically stopped in the first century B. C. :

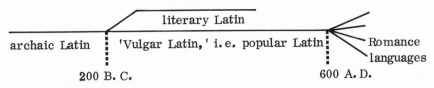

archaic Latin ⋮ 'Vulgar Latin,' i.e. popular Latin ⋮ Romance
                                                          languages

       200 B. C.   600 A. D.

[8] A preliminary version of this paper was read at the annual
meeting of the Modern Language Association of America in the section
'Language Change' on December 29, 1979, in San Francisco, California.

BIBLIOGRAPHY

Abdulaziz-Mkilifi, M. H. 1972. Triglossia and Swahili-English bi-
        lingualism in Tanzania. Language in Society 1: 197-213.
Bailey, Charles-James N. 1973. Variation and linguistic theory.
        Arlington, Va.: Center for Applied Linguistics.
Bynon, Theodora. 1977. Historical linguistics. Cambridge/London:
        Cambridge University Press.
Closs-Traugott, Elizabeth. 1977. Pidginization, creolization, and
        language change. In Albert Valdman, ed., Pidgin and creole
        linguistics. Bloomington: Indiana University Press, pp.
        70-98.
Coseriù, Eugenio. 1978. Das sogenannte 'Vulgärlatein' und die ersten
        Differenzierungen in der Romania. In Zur Entstehung der
        romanischen Sprachen. Darmstadt: Wissenschaftliche Buch-
        gesellschaft, pp. 257-91.
De Camp, David. 1977. The development of pidgin and creole studies.

In Albert Valdman, ed., Pidgin and creole linguistics.
Bloomington: Indiana University Press, pp. 3-20.

Devoto, Giacomo. 1968. Geschichte der Sprache Roms. Heidelberg:
Carl Winter.

Ferguson, Charles A., and Charles E. De Bose. 1977. Simplified
registers, broken language, and pidginization. In Albert
Valdman, ed., Pidgin and creole linguistics. Bloomington:
Indiana University Press, pp. 99-125.

Hall, Robert A., Jr. 1966. Pidgin and creole languages. Ithaca,
N. Y.: Cornell University Press.

_____. 1974. External history of the Romance languages. (Com-
parative Romance Grammar, vol. 1.) New York/London/
Amsterdam: American Elsevier Publishing Co.

Hancock, Ian. 1977. Recovering pidgin genesis: approaches and
problems. In Albert Valdman, ed., Pidgin and creole linguistics. Bloomington: Indiana University Press, pp. 277-94.

Heine, Bernd. 1970. Status and use of African lingua francas.
(IFO—Institut für Wirtschaftsforschung München—Afrika-
Studien, vol. 49.) Munich: Weltforum Verlag.

_____. 1973. Pidgin-Sprachen im Bantu-Bereich. (Kölner Beiträge
zur Afrikanistik, vol. 3.) Berlin: Dietrich Reimer.

_____. 1979. Sprache, Gesellschaft und Kommunikation in Afrika.
(IFO—Institut für Wirtschaftsforschung München—Afrika-
Studien, vol. 103.) Munich/London: Weltforum Verlag.

Jackson, Kenneth. 1953. Language and history in early Britain.
Edinburgh: University Press.

Le Page, Robert. 1977. Processes of pidginization and creolization.
In Albert Valdman, ed., Pidgin and creole linguistics.
Bloomington: Indiana University Press, pp. 222-55.

Manessy, Gabriel. 1979. Pidginisation, Créolisation, Evolution des
Langues. Sprache und Geschichte in Afrika 1: 55-74.

Markey, Thomas L. 1979. Deixis and diathesis: The case of the
Greek k-perfect. Manuscript.

Meid, Wolfgang. 1980. Gallisch oder Lateinisch? Soziolinguistische
und andere Bemerkungen zu populären gallo-lateinischen
Inschriften. (Innsbrucker Beiträge zur Sprachwissenschaft—
Kleine Schriften, vol. 24.) Innsbruck.

Meillet, Antoine. 1928. Esquisse d'une histoire de la langue latine.
Paris: Hachette.

284   Language, Society, and Paleoculture

Musset, Lucien. 1965. Les Invasions: Les Vagues Germaniques.
     (Nouvelle Clio, vol. 12.) Paris: Presses Universitaires de
     France.
Polomé, Edgar C. 1968. Lubumbashi Swahili. Journal of African
     Languages 7: 14-25.
_____. 1969. The position of Swahili and other Bantu languages in
     Katanga. Texas Studies in Language and Literature 11: 905-13.
_____. 1971a. The Katanga (Lubumbashi) Swahili-creole. In Dell
     Hymes, ed., Pidginization and creolization of languages.
     Cambridge: University Press, pp. 57-59.
_____. 1971b. Multilingualism in an African urban center: The
     Lubumbashi case. In W. H. Whiteley, ed., Language use
     and social change. Problems of multilingualism with special
     reference to Eastern Africa. London: International African
     Institute/Oxford University Press, pp. 364-75.
_____. 1972. Sociolinguistic problems in Tanzania and Zaire. In
     Sunday O. Anozie, ed., Language systems in Africa (= The
     Conch 4, 2). New Paltz, N. Y.: Conch Magazine, pp. 64-83.
_____. 1977. The linguistic situation in western provinces of the
     Roman Empire. Manuscript. (To appear in H. Temporini
     and W. Haase, eds., Aufstieg und Niedergang des Römischen
     Reichs. Berlin/New York: Walter de Gruyter.)
Schlieben-Lange, Brigitte. 1976. L'origine des langues romanes—
     un cas de créolisation? In Jürgen M. Meisel, ed., Langues
     en contact—pidgins—creoles—languages in contact. Tübingen:
     Gunter Narr., pp. 81-101, 267-85.
Todd, Loreto. 1974. Pidgins and creoles. London/Boston: Routledge
     & Kegan Paul.
Whatmough, Joshua. 1970. The dialects of ancient Gaul. (The quota-
     tion is from Κελτινα, reprinted as Prolegomena to the vol-
     ume, from Harvard Studies in Classical Philology 45 [1944]:
     1-85.) Cambridge: Harvard University Press.
Whinnom, Keith. 1965. The origin of the European-based creoles
     and pidgins. Orbis 14: 509-27.
_____. 1977. Lingua franca: historical problems. In Albert Vald-
     man, ed., Pidgin and creole linguistics. Bloomington:
     Indiana University Press, pp. 295-310.

Part IV. Language, Paleoculture, and Religion

14 | Old Norse Religious Terminology in Indo-European Perspective

If we were to apply the principles of comparative linguistics to the reconstruction of Indo-European religion, we would not get very far, as A. Meillet (1948) recognized many years ago: there is no common term to designate religion itself, or the cult, or the priest, or even personal gods. The only term the Indo-European peoples share is the word for 'god'—*deywos—conceived as 'luminous' and 'celestial' and thus contrasted with 'human' and 'terrestrial,' as illustrated by the connection homo: humus in Latin. Therefore, recent work on Indo-European religion has been focused on the structural analysis of myths and beliefs, as well as cult practices and rites, and a close association between the social structure of the Indo-European community and the organization of its pantheon has been emphasized, in particular, by G. Dumézil (e.g. 1958).[1] But as the recent work of E. Benveniste (1969) on Indo-European institutions has demonstrated, the careful study of the vocabulary also provides interesting clues: thus, whereas there is no specific term in common Indo-European to designate the 'sacred,' Latin, Greek, Iranian, and Germanic show a characteristic double designation which reflects the fundamental dichotomy of the 'sacred' into a positive and a negative aspect: 'fraught with divine presence' versus 'forbidden to human contact.' After a careful analysis of the Germanic terminology of the 'sacred,' W. Baetke (1942) has referred the duality of concepts of the 'sacred' reflected by Gmc. *wīhaz versus *hailagaz to the contrastive aspects of the numinosum defined by R. Otto (1936):

> Ich sehe es als das Ergebnis unserer Untersuchung an, dass *wīhaz im Germanischen die Seite des Numinosen bezeichnete, von der es dem Menschen als das 'Andere,' von der profanen Welt wesentlich Unterschiedene erscheint—dasjenige,

was zu ihm in Distanz steht, was in ihm die Gefühle der Ehr-
furcht und der Scheu erweckt (i.e. Otto's mysterium tremendum, the awe-inspiring aspect of the deity); ... durch unsere
Untersuchung dürfen wir auch dies als erwiesen ansehen,
dass *hailagaz auf die dem Menschen und der Welt zugekehrte
Seite des Numinosen, das Fascinosum, geht, also das be-
zeichnet, worauf die kultische Handlung letzlich gerichtet
ist: das Heil das von der Gottheit ausgeht, die in die Welt
hineinwirkende Segenskraft, aus der alles Wachsen, Gedeihen
und Gelingen kommt (Baetke 1942: 213, 215).

I consider as the result of our investigation the fact that, in
Germanic, *wīhaz designates the aspect of the numinous in
which it appears to man as the 'Other,' essentially different
from the profane world—that which stands aloof from him,
which awakens feelings of reverence and shyness in him (i.e.
Otto's mysterium tremendum, the awe-inspiring aspect of
the deity); ... we may also consider as demonstrated by our
research that *hailagaz applies to the side of the numinous
turned toward man and the world, the fascinosum, and that,
accordingly, it designates the ultimate target of the cultural
process: the blessing bestowed by the deity, its beneficent
power operating in the world, from which all growth, thriv-
ing, and success derive. (Translation by E. C. Polomé.)

In spite of the etymological relationship between sacer and
sanctus, the recognition of this conceptual duality must have been
Indo-European, but each language has reinterpreted it along its own
lines (Benveniste 1969: 1.179-207): in Greek, hierós and hagiós show
clearly the positive and negative aspects of the concept: hierós (cognate with Vedic isirah 'lively, vigorous,' applying to deities) focuses
on what is 'animated with power and sacred vitality'; hagiós indicates,
originally, 'what is forbidden, what men should have no contact with'
—hence hágnos, applying to the 'forbidden' territory of a god, but
also meaning 'ritually pure,' i.e. in the required state for a ceremony,
which explains the relationship with Skt. yájati 'shows reverence to
the gods with sacrifices and prayers.' In Latin, sacer specifically
stresses the state of being cut off from the world of men: that is why
a cursed man is called homo sacer, because he is severed from all
human connection, just as a sacrificed animal is made 'sacred' by

being cut off from the world of the living. The contrast with sanctus
is more difficult to define: sacer is what is implicitly sacred and
worthy of veneration; sanctus is explicitly sacred, as the result of an
interdiction promulgated by men or a prescription sanctioned by law.
Avestan also contrasts spǝnta- as a natural quality with the state of
yaoždāta- 'pure': 'to make yaoš' is to cause to conform with the prescriptions, to put in the state required by the cult. In Avestan spǝnta-,
as in Gk. hierós, the basic notion is that of a power bubbling over with
vitality, full of fertility. To this corresponds Gothic hails, whose
basic notion is that of 'wholeness'—a power protecting the object or
the living being against any 'diminishing.' This original meaning is
confirmed by the Balto-Slavic cognates: OCS čelŭ 'whole, healthy,
salvus,' OPruss. kailūstiskun (acc. fem. sg.) 'good health,' i.e. en-
joying physical wholeness. This quality has definite religious connotations; it is a divine grace: the deity is inherently endowed with
'wholeness, salvation, and luck' and can impart these to man in the
form of physical health (Gothic hails translating Gk. hugiēs) and pre-
dicted good fortune (ON heil, OE hǣl 'good omen'). The choice of
*hailag- by the Anglo-Saxon church to translate Latin sanctus is there-
fore linked with the primacy, for its missionaries, of the concept of
'salvation.' As for Gmc. *wīhaz, it reflects the notion of 'sacred' as
'separated from the profane, dedicated to the gods for their exclusive
possession': this is especially evident in the ON noun vē 'temple, holy
place'—'ein der Gottheit geweihter und für einen sakralen Zweck abge-
sonderter Platz,' as Baetke (1942: 196) defines it. Hence, the verb
(Gothic weihan, OHG wīhen) which indicates the magico-sacral process by which the object is separated from the profane (Markey 1972:
373-75)—a meaning which is also perfectly in keeping with the etymology of the Germanic term: its only close cognate is indeed Latin victima 'the sacrificial animal,' which was carefully picked out and dedicated to the relevant god. There were very specific rules as to which
animals had to be chosen for particular gods: Jupiter and Juno were
to get white animals, male for the god and female for the goddess, but,
whereas Jupiter wanted castrated males, Mars received them whole;
when the earth was teeming with growing crops, fordae 'pregnant cows'
were delivered to Earth (Dumézil 1966: 534-35; 1970: 559). The Umbrian ritual of Iguvium has given us elaborate details on the selection
of the animals, insisting, e.g., on the necessity of checking them
and solemnly pronouncing them free from blemish: only then may
they be consecrated to the god (Poultney 1959: 190ff)! Strikingly

enough, the verb designating this process is Umbrian eveietu, attested
in the imperative and reflecting an Italic prototype *ē-weig-ē-tōd—
a verb of the second conjugation derived from the theme *wey-g-,
whose final voiced velar alternates with the voiceless velar in Latin
and Germanic. Though the derivation of Latin victima is rather unusual—it is based on a participial form *vict(o)- plus a complex suffix -ima which occurs elsewhere only in the adjective sacrima, preserved in a Festus gloss, designating the sweet wine offered as first-
lings to Bacchus—the correspondence in the root constitutes a major
cultural isogloss between Germanic and Italic, which can be added to
the important set of correspondences between these two languages in
the field of religion and social organization (cf. Polomé 1972: 59-63).
Thus, projecting the results of Baetke's analysis of the terminology
of the 'sacred' in Germanic onto the Indo-European institutional framework defined by Benveniste proves quite instructive and provides more
depth and substance to the argument on the original dichotomy of the
concept of the 'sacred' based on Otto's research.

It appears, therefore, legitimate to look further into a few
other fundamental terms of the Old Norse religious vocabulary, in
order to see what can be learned from their IE background and how
they can be integrated into the larger framework of the IE heritage:

One of the most commonly quoted correspondences in the
Indo-European religious vocabulary is the assumed Latin-Indic isogloss flāmen : brahmán 'sacrificer, priest.' Their identity of function
in both ancient societies, their social status in ancient Rome and
ancient India, the parallel correspondence of an impressive number
of religious terms in Indo-Iranian and Italo-Celtic, are a number of
arguments pleading in favor of the correspondence, but there exist
some major phonological and semantic difficulties: first of all, it
would imply a rather complex prototype *bhlaĝh(s)mĕn, designating
the priest reciting the ritual chants at the sacrifice. However, Latin
flāmen is apparently an old neuter indicating the performance of the
sacrifice, whereas a thorough analysis of Vedic bráhma and its Iranian
cognates points to the oldest retrievable meaning of 'Formung, Gestaltung, Formulierung,' as P. Thieme (1952: 102-4) has demonstrated.
The oldest form is the Vedic neuter bráhman-, also personified in the
later god Brahman-; the oldest meaning of the masculine brahmán-
is 'poet, singer,' i.e. 'creator of forms.' Middle Persian/Parthian

brahm also means 'form, appearance, style' and points to an Iranian
*brazman-, which actually occurs in a controversial Old Persian in-
scription: this limits the prototype of the Indo-Iranian terms to a
form *b(h)^{r}/$_{1}$Vgh-, to which the closest cognate would be ON bragr
'poetry' (NIcel. bragur 'Weise, Art, Sitte, Ton, Gedicht, Melodie')
as H. Osthoff (1892: 118-21) suggested long ago, indicating, furthermore: 'Vielleicht war so etwas wie "Formung, Gestaltung" der
gemeinsame Grundbegriff.' This puts the lesser Germanic god of
poetry Bragi into a new light: instead of connecting his name with ON
bragr 'first, most important' and OE brego 'lord, prince' on account
of the Old Norse and Old Swedish anthroponym Bragi (cf. e.g. Kuhn
1951: 43), he might be considered as the god of the cultual song (cf.
e.g. De Vries 1956: 458; 1957: 272-74): his having Iðunn for a wife
suggests his command over life-dispensing formulas; the short passage in the Lokasenna (stanzas 11-18) is also very instructive. Bragi
is obviously not good at fighting with weapons, but appears as the
'pride of the bench,' the manipulator of 'taunting words,' which suggests for him a role as praiser and censor similar to that of the poet
in ancient Vedic, Roman, and Celtic society, as described by G.
Dumézil (1943) in connection with the Latin-Indic isogloss censeō:
śámsati.

As for Latin flāmen, the basic meaning *'Opferhandlung'
makes a connection with ON blōt 'sacrifice' obvious, since it can easily
be derived from a verbal stem *bhlād- 'sacrifice' with the suffix -men;
this stem is well represented in Gmc. by Gothic blōtan, ON blóta, OE
blōtan, OHG blōzan, to which the following derivations and compounds
can be added: OHG bluostar 'sacrifice': plōzhus 'temple'; ON
blótgoðe 'priest'; Goth. guþblostreis 'worshiper.'

This striking correspondence in the field of the sacrifice is
paralleled by a few others, e.g. ON tafn 'sacrifice; food': Lat. daps
'meal'; Arm. tawn 'feast,' to which Latin damnum 'damage' < *dapnom
and Gk. dapánē 'expense' are also related. This set of divergent meanings obviously requires a careful semantic analysis with due consideration of the cultural features involed (cf. Benveniste 1969: 1. 74-77;
2. 226-29). Latin daps originally designated the ritual meal of offering
following the sacrifice to the gods. There is ample evidence that it
involved rather lavish spending and an ostentatious display of generos-
ity, as reflected by the adverb dapatice 'sumptuously,' applying to the

manner in which people have been entertained. Such lavishness was a
kind of 'sacrifice' insofar as, in a usually parsimonious society, such
prodigality was a sheer loss for the sponsor (hence, the term damnum
'damage'), but he presumably felt compelled to go through these extrav-
agant expenses (cf. Gk. dapáne) to assert his status and humiliate his
rivals, as in the well-known potlatch festivals. One of the aspects of
such a solemn feast (cf. Arm. tawn) is the large consumption of food
(cf. ON tafn). This places the ON term in its proper context, but the
underlying IE theme *dap- forbids connecting it further, as is usually
done, with OE tīfer, tīber 'sacrificial animal, sacrifice' and OHG
zĕbar 'sacrificial animal,' which reflect an IE prototype *dīp-, also
occurring in the late MHG ungezībere, G. Ungeziefer 'vermin,' actually 'impure animal, not fit for sacrifice,' in Gothic *tibr 'offering'
(if the correction from aibr is justified) and perhaps also in ON tívurr
(Vǫluspá 31)—if it means 'victim,' and not 'god.' It is attractive to
connect these with Gk. deîpnon 'meal,' which would point to the collective consumption of the sacrificial animal as part of the ceremony.[2]
The animal involved was always of an edible species, also as hinted at
by the Romance loans: Engadin. zepra 'bait'; O. French atoivre 'draft
animal.'

Besides valuable hints on the original nature of the sacrifice,
the study of the ON vocabulary provides indications as to the procedures involved in the ceremony.

As Benveniste (1969: 2.233-54) has shown, the oral performance in formulaic speech is an important component of the ritual:
one condition of the sacrifice is for the offerer to make the object of
the oblation ritually fit for this purpose; it must be free of any blemish,
and the Avestan verb yaoždā- 'make pure' is the technical term for
effecting this in compliance with the ritual prescriptions; the cognate
Latin iūs, which is the foundation of the concept of 'law' in Ancient
Rome, also expresses this compliance with the rules. The IE theme
*prek- in Latin precor 'pray' expresses the strictly verbal request
addressed to the gods to obtain what one expects from them. A third
term, IE *weg^wh-, reflected by Latin uoueō 'vow,' indicates the solemn pledge of the offerer in response for the benefit to be granted by
the deity; the vow is pronounced in faithfully repeated fixed formulas
and binds the devotee in the strictest way.

In the Germanic world, the notion of formulaic speech appears to be expressed by ON þula—the technical term for alliterative strings of words and, probably, the ultimate outcome of a poetic form in which specific knowledge was communicated in concise form. As the Edda indicates, this could often be done in questions and answers, and, presumably, the person entrusted with this knowledge, the guardian of the traditional heritage, would function as 'cultual orator' (G. Kultredner). Though the evidence is scanty, þulr most have fulfilled this essential role of oral performer of the cult, mediating between men and gods (cf. Vogt 1927). Described as sitting on a hill, pronouncing mysterious words, he must have communicated with the deity by means of special prayer formulas.

Unfortunately, the etymological explanations supplied hitherto to account for these hardly account for this function of the þulr. Some connections are purely arbitrary, such as Loewenthal's (1919) comparison with the obscure Latin term tullii, found in Ennius and glossed by Festus as vehementes proiectiones sanguinis arcuatim fluentes or Trier's (1944: 119) reference to Russian toloka 'day-long work in common of all peasants of a village in the fields,' Lithuanian talkà 'group of workers called up and treated to a banquet upon completion of their assigned task.' In view of the OE gloss þyle 'orator,' van Blankenstein's (1909) connection with OCS tlŭkŭ, Russian tolkŭ 'meaning, concept, teaching; interpreter' makes better sense, but the Slavic words are further related to Ir. ad-tluch, to-tluch 'pray' and, possibly, Latin loquor 'speak,' which do not show the religious connotations implied by ON þulr (cf. Vasmer 1958: 115). No better is the rather unconvincing link with ON þaul, found only in the phrase mæla sik í þaul(ar) 'sich festreden' and surviving in Icel. þaul in compounds like þaularvágr 'Bucht in der man festsitzen bleiben kann,' þaulsætinn 'unbeweglich sitzend,' for which the closest cognates appear to be Norw. tula 'toil,' tyla 'hesitate,' to which Lett. tūl'uôt 'tarry' is compared (cf. Jóhannesson 1956: 450). Obviously, þulr has not been satisfactorily explained because it has not been placed in the proper context. In a set of Hittite texts the verb talliia- occurs, which applies to humans propitiating the gods. E. Laroche, in a recent study on the vocabulary of the Hittite prayer (1964), indicates that it presumably means 'solemnly call upon the god (to do something), which is what one expects the mediator between man and deity to do in formulaic speech. Accordingly, this would provide a quite attractive etymological connection for ON Þulr: the IE root would be *tel-, of which the reduced grade would be reflected by Gmc. *Þul-, as in Gothic Þulan from IE *tel(ə)- 'lift up, carry, bear.' This new etymology would be a valuable addition to the list of Germanic-Hittite isoglosses (cf. Polomé 1953, 1954), which include such common terms as:

(1) Hitt. dankwis 'dark': ON døkkr, O. Swed. diunker, O. Fris diunk < Gmc. *diŋkwa- < IE *dheng^w- 'dark';

(2) Hitt. sak(u)wa- 'eyes': Goth. saiƕvan 'see,' ON sjā, OE sēon, OHG sehan—a special semantic development of the root *sek^w- 'follow';

(3) Hitt. gank- 'hang': Goth., OHG hāhan, Du. hangen < IE *kenk- 'hang';

(4) Hitt. lis(s)āi- 'gather': OHG lesan 'gather, pick, glean,' ON lesa, Goth. galisan (with a divergent meaning, also Lith. lesù, lèsti, 'forage');

(5) Hitt. hassus 'king': Gmc. *ansuz 'sovereign god' (ON ǫss, plural æsir; OE ōs 'god,' Goth. ansis (acc. plur.) 'ancestors, semi-gods'), to which Indo-Iranian *asura- 'lord' is presumably to be added;

(6) Hitt. mald- 'recite invocations, promise solemnly': OHG meldōn 'announce, reveal,' OE meldian 'proclaim, announce, declare'—originally a term with strong religious connotations, as shown, e.g., by Lithuanian meldžiù, melsti 'pray,' but whose content has been secularized in Gmc.;

(7) Hitt. *alwanza- 'struck by a spell': Run. alu '(magic) charm': ON ǫl, OE ealu, aloþ 'ale,' as the beverage of libation.

An interesting case is also that of biðja, the ON reflex of the common Germanic word for 'pray' (= Goth. bidjan, OE biddan, OS biddian, OHG bittan, etc.). Two etymologies have been proposed: the first, based on the parallel between Vedic jñubādh- 'kneeling for prayer' and ON knébeðr 'hassock,' OS kneobeda 'prayer (while kneeling),' refers the terms to IE *bhedh- 'bow, bend down,' to which Toch. A poto, B peti 'veneration' may also belong; the second connects them with Gk. peíthō 'persuade' and Lat. fidēs 'faith, confidence' (cf. Benveniste 1969: 1.119-20; 2.247). Both are perfectly in keeping with the IE prayer, which emphasizes two attitudes: (a) entreating, beseeching—also expressed by Goth. aihtron, Gk. líssomai, etc.; (b) calling upon the security the gods provide (this is a result of the

reciprocal confidence between man and the deity: the faith that man
has in god assures of a divine protective guarantee).

The vocabulary of the oath could be analyzed in a similar way
(cf. Benveniste 1969: 1.164-65): one of the main features in oath-
taking was the ceremonial march to the place where the rite was performed; this is illustrated by the Germanic and Celtic words: Goth.
aiþs, ON eiðr, OHG eid, OE āþ 'oath' and OIr. ōeth 'oath, ' which
reflect an IE prototype *oyto- 'going' from the root *ey- 'go. ' On the
other hand, the exchange of pledges reflected by Latin spondeō 'pledge,
commit myself to': respondeō 'promise in return' is also illustrated
by Goth. swaran 'swear' versus ON svara, OE andswarian 'answer';
the underlying verbal *swer- means 'vouch for, ' as shown by its only
cognate, Oscan sverrunei 'to the guarantor, ' and *andswaran is originally to Latin respondēre as Gothic swaran is to spondēre.

Thus, the studies of Benveniste have opened a stimulating
area of investigation for gaining depth into the study of Germanic institutions by projecting them onto their common IE heritage.

NOTES

[1] On the views of G. Dumézil, see, in particular, Scott-
Littleton 1966.
    [2] Cf. De Vries 1956: 362. Frisk 1960: 358, and Chantraine
1968: 258, however, indicate the Greek has no satisfactory IE etymology and may be of Mediterranean origin.

BIBLIOGRAPHY

Baetke, Walter. 1942. Das Heilige im Germanischen. Tübingen.
Benveniste, Emile. 1969. Le vocabulaire des institutions indoeuro-
        péennes. Paris.
Chantraine, Pierre. 1968. Dictionnaire étymologique de la langue
        grecque. Histoire des mots. A - Δ. Paris.

De Vries, Jan. 1956. Altgermanische Religionsgeschichte. I. Einleitung. Vorgeschichtliche Perioden. Religiöse Grundlagen des Lebens. Seelen- und Geisterglaube. Macht und Kraft. Das Heilige und die Kultformen. 2nd ed. Berlin.

_____. 1957. Altgermanische Religionsgeschichte. 2. Die Götter. Vorstellungen über den Kosmos. Der Untergang des Heidentums. 2nd ed. Berlin.

Dumézil, Georges. 1943. Servius et la Fortune. Essai sur la fonction sociale de Louange et de Blâme et sur les éléments indo-européens du cens romain. Paris.

_____. 1958. L'idéologie tripartite des Indo-Européens. Collection Latomus 31. Brussels.

_____. 1966. La Religion Romaine Archaïque. Paris.

_____. 1970. Archaic Roman Religion. Chicago.

Frisk, Hjalmar. 1960. Griechisches etymologisches Wörterbuch. Heidelberg.

Jóhannesson, Alexander. 1956. Isländisches etymologisches Wörterbuch. Bern.

Kuhn, Hans. 1951. Es gibt kein balder "Herr." Erbe der Vergangenheit. Germanistische Beiträge. Festgabe für Karl Helm, pp. 37-45. Tübingen.

Laroche, Emmanuel. 1964-65. La prière hittite: Vocabulaire et typologie. Ecole pratique des Hautes Etudes, Ve Section, Sciences Religieuses; Annuaire 72. 3-29.

Loewenthal, John. 1919. Zur germanischen Wortkunde. 115. an. þulr. Arkiv för nordisk filologi 35. 236.

Markey, Thomas L. 1972. Germanic terms for temple and cult. Studies for Einar Haugen presented by friends and colleagues, ed. by E. S. Firchow, K. Grimstad, et al., pp. 365-78. The Hague.

Meillet, Antoine. 1948. La religion indo-européenne. Linguistique historique et linguistique générale 1. 323-34. 2nd ed. Paris.

Osthoff, Hermann. 1896. Griechische und lateinische Wortdeutungen. 14. victima, umbr. eveietu; got. weihan, aind. vinakti. Indogermanische Forschungen 6. 39-47.

_____. 1899. Allerhand Zauber etymologisch beleuchtet. 2. Aind. bráhma, air. bricht: aisl. bragr; lat. forma. Beiträge zur Kunde der indogermanischen Sprachen 24. 113-44.

Otto, Rudolf. 1936. Das Heilige. 23rd ed. Munich.

Polomé, Edgar. 1953. L'étymologie du terme germanique *ansuz
"dieu souverain." Etudes Germaniques 8.36-44.
_____. 1954. Notes sur le vocabulaire religieux du germanique.
1. Runique alu. La Nouvelle Clio 6.40-55.
_____. 1972. Germanic and the other Indo-European languages.
Toward a grammar of Proto-Germanic, ed. by Frans van
Coetsem and Herbert L. Kufner, pp. 43-69. Tübingen.
Poultney, James. 1959. The bronze tables of Iguvium. Baltimore.
Scott-Littleton, C. 1966. The new comparative mythology. An anthro-
pological assessment of the theories of Georges Dumézil.
Berkeley-Los Angeles.
Thieme, Paul. 1952. Bráhman. Zeitschrift der deutschen morgen-
ländischen Gesellschaft 102.91-129.
Trier, Jost. 1944. Pflug. Beiträge zur Geschichte der deutschen
Sprache und Literatur 67.110-50.
van Blankenstein, M. 1909. Etymologien. 5. Aisl. þulr. Indoger-
manische Forschungen 23.134.
Vasmer, Max. 1958. Russisches etymologisches Wörterbuch. 3.
Sta-Y. Heidelberg.
Vogt, Walther Heinrich. 1927. Stilgeschichte der eddischen Wissens-
dichtung. I. Der Kultredner (þulr). Schriften der Baltischen
Kommission zu Kiel 4.1. Breslau.

15 | A Few Thoughts About Reconstructing Indo-European Culture and Religion

In recent years, considerable work has been done in the field of Indo-European culture and religion. This activity is mainly due to three new approaches to old problems:

(a) in the field of archeology, extensive excavations in Russia and the Balkans has led to a better understanding of the prehistoric cultures and population movements of the fifth to the third millennium B. C.;
(b) in the field of lexical and semantic analysis, the traditional compilation of lengthy lists of correspondences has been supplemented by studies in depth of the diachronic development of the specific connotations of technical terms to discover their original functional meaning;
(c) in the field of comparative mythology, a search for the basic organization of the pantheon has led to the recognition of the correlation between social structure and internal hierarchization of the world of the gods.

These new trends can best be illustrated by the works of Marija Gimbutas, Emile Benveniste, and Georges Dumézil.

In a number of studies since 1956, Marija Gimbutas has connected the Proto-Indo-Europeans with the Kurgan people, infiltrating Europe and the Near East from the Dnieper-Volga steppe.[1] The only major change in her views was a revised dating of the process, presented at the Indo-European conference in Philadelphia in 1966. Briefly, the Kurgan culture starts in the fifth millennium B. C., beginning its move to central Europe via the Danube in the fourth millennium B. C. In the second half of that millennium, a new culture appears in the northern part of the Balkans, east-central Europe, central Europe,

and Trans-Caucasia, marked by complex changes due to 'kurganiza-
tion': the horse and vehicle are evidenced; in the eastern Balkan hills,
strategic positions are converted to strongholds. But the tribal groups
dominated by Kurgan elements really prevail in the third millennium
B. C.: this, for Marija Gimbutas, is the time when most of Europe
gets 'kurganized.' The groups have increased their mobility, and
their expansion lays the foundation for the IE-speaking peoples of the
Bronze and Iron Age: the Germanic tribes deriving from the Corded
Ware/Battle-Axe complex in the northwest, the Baltic tribes from the
East Baltic-Central Russian Battle-Axe complex; the Slavic tribes
from the north Carpathian Corded Ware/Battle-Axe complex; the Celtic-
Italic-Illyrian-Phrygian tribes to the Central European Corded Ware/
Battle-Axe complex; etc.

     For Marija Gimbutas, this Kurgan culture was not limited to
the common feature of the barrow, important as it may have been. She
also listed such features as a patriarchal society, a class system, the
existence of small tribal units ruled by powerful chieftains, a predominantly pastoral economy including horse breeding and plant cultivation,
small subterranean or above-ground rectangular huts of timber up-
rights, small villages, and massive hill forts, crude unpainted pottery
decorated with impressions or stabbing, religious elements indicating
a sky/sun god and thunder god, horse sacrifices, and fire cults.

     Benveniste's searching probes into the vocabulary of Indo-
European institutions[2] appear to confirm these views: he depicts a
society with closely knit kinship links, reinforced by cross-cousin
marriage; the individual is involved in a complex network of allegiances,
based on mutual trust, support, and confidence in the concentric system of the community: (nuclear family →) expanded family → clan →
tribe → people, as well as in the social hierarchy which put the ruling
caste of priest-magician-lawmaker on top and the majority of the
cattle raisers/horse breeders/producers at the bottom, with the warrior caste, the defenders of the group, in the middle. This society is
essentially ethnocentric and xenophobic: it is very hospitable to in-
siders but excludes aliens; within the group, services are rendered as
pure favors, without expecting anything in return besides the normal
cycle of exchange, where something is offered to obtain something else
by way of reciprocation. In the Indo-European society described by
Benveniste, the 'king's' basic function is to set the rules, to determine

what is 'right,' which accounts for his functions being more religious than political. As the IE tribes move on the warpath, the need grows for a more dynamic leadership: the people in arms march under the direction of powerful chiefs.

Benveniste does not examine the Indo-European pantheon: his concern about religion remains restricted to the examination of a few basic concepts, e.g. the 'sacred' whose dual aspect: (a) filled with divine power, (b) forbidden to human contact, is described strictly on the basis of internal evidence (by studying the connotations of the relevant terms in the IE languages, without recourse to the concepts of mana and tabu like Wagenvoort or Gonda,[3] but, unfortunately, without discussions of the views of Baetke[4] on Germanic, based on Otto's dichotomy of the 'sacred').

Georges Dumézil has relentlessly labored since the thirties in a sustained and continued series of efforts to reconstruct the Indo-European functional system of divine powers and some of the great myths in which they are involved.[5] This basic postulate which he derives from Durkheim and Meillet, is that the IE gods are essentially features of the social system: having recognized, with Benveniste,[6] that a number of early IE societies show a hierarchized tripartite social organization, he uses this as the framework underlying the pantheon of the IE peoples. Each level has its specific concerns, namely:

(a) the first function (the priestly stratum)—the maintenance of magico-religious and juridical sovereignty and order;
(b) the second function (the warrior stratum)—physical prowess;
(c) the third function (the herder-cultivator stratum)—the provision of sustenance, the maintenance of physical well-being, plant and animal fertility, and related activities.

It is Dumézil's assumption that this tripartite 'ideology,' reflecting three fundamental components of human social behavior and their correlated supernatural counterparts, existed as such in the Proto-Indo-European homeland, that the tradition was carried with them by the migrating groups all over the vast expanse of the territory later dominated by Indo-Europeans, and that elements of it can still be identified in their myths and epics, from the Veda to the Mahābhārata in India, and from the Edda to the Heimskringla in the Germanic North.

The identification of archeological data with linguistic data
is always a rather risky enterprise, and the recent fate of 'Illyrian'
which, in the late thirties, was considered as one of the major components of the IE world should give us pause. Indeed, after some of
the most prominent European archeologists linked the Lusatian civilization and the spread of the urnfields with the migrations of the
alleged Proto-Illyrians,[7] these became the agents of the early Indo-
Europeanization of large territories in Europe and even in the Middle
East, since Krahe identified them with some of the 'people of the sea'
mentioned in Egyptian documents and with the Philistines.[8] Nowadays,
the term 'Illyrian' has been reduced to size and applies strictly speaking only to a small territory in the southeastern part of Dalmatia.[9]
The problem has recently led Rüdiger Schmitt[10] to question Marija
Gimbutas' Kurgan hypothesis; his main argument is against her assumption that the Proto-Indo-European culture is the only candidate
to fit the Kurgan material. Rüdiger Schmitt claims that whatever we
assume for Indo-European, e.g. inferring social structure from habi-
tation patterns and burial rites, may have existed in other language
(and ethnic) groups. The presence of roots like *wegh- 'drive' or
terms for the vehicle, its wheels, its axle, nave, pole, yoke, etc.
is not compelling evidence either, since we can reconstruct Proto-
Semitic roots for 'drive,' 'yoke,' and the like. Vehicles were known
to the Proto-Finno-Ugrians as well. Along this line of argument, he
concludes, with Kronasser (in a 1961 position paper),[11] that linguistic
paleontology should remain an autonomous method: only when a particular cultural group has been proved to be IE, i.e. when the linguistic data are sufficiently specific should coordination with archeological finds or other extralinguistic data be attempted.

The critique of Rüdiger Schmitt in the case of Marija Gimbutas is, however, in many respects rather unfair, since a large
number of her assumptions are based on well-established, carefully
researched Indo-European data. If we examine the domestication of
animals, it is undoubtedly obvious from the lexicon with terms for
'kine,' 'bull,' 'steer,' and related activities ('milking') that cattle
raising was the major economic activity of the Indo-Europeans. As
Benveniste[12] has demonstrated, the possession of livestock was the
symbol of wealth and status, as in the cow-keeping kingdoms of the
African Great Lakes region. If one looks at the relative chronology
of animal husbandry in prehistoric Europe, the introduction of cattle

breeding antedates the penetration of the Kurgan culture in a rather
striking way:[13] the early European agriculturists of the Neolithic who
established themselves in Greece before 5000 B. C. and reached the
Low Countries before 4000 B. C. mainly reared sheep and goats, although they had some cattle, pigs, and dogs. The Linear Pottery
culture, responsible for the transmission of agriculture across Europe
from Hungary to Holland between 4500 and 3700 B. C. , consisted essentially of cattle breeders, who castrated a large portion of their animals,
and the cultures that developed later in France, Britain, Scandinavia,
as well as in central Europe continued to practice cattle breeding
(besides wheat cultivation) as the basis of their subsistence economy
until the end of the Neolithic Period. With the Copper Age, two main
animal breeding traditions appear in Europe: one centered on cattle
rearing in the early copper-mining cultures deriving their ore from
the Carpathians; the other based on the breeding of goats and sheep
spreading over Europe from 3900 to 2000 from Greece to France, with
its point of origin somewhere in the Near East in the fifth millennium.
This second group appears in east-central Europe ca. 3000 B. C. at
the time when the Carpathian copper center is declining and when the
copper starts being imported from the south, especially from Anatolia
and the Near East. It is also at this stage that the horse, in the form
of the tarpan, appears to have been first domesticated. The earliest
evidence comes from the Tripolye culture in southern Russia, and its
spread over the rest of Europe is linked with the increase in sheep
farming and the mounting trade in copper from the south. Important
for the problem of the Indo-Europeans is the fact that the penetration
of the horse in northern Europe may be connected with the Single Grave
Complex. It should also be noted that cattle prevail over goats, sheep,
pigs only in the Bronze Age in European settlements, as bone counts
in archeological sites have shown. Recent work on the history of domestic animals[14] tends, accordingly, to weaken arguments based on
the cattle economy to identify certain prehistoric cultures as Indo-
European,[15] but the connection with the horse is particularly significant. The horse has, indeed, acquired a privileged position among
the IE domestic animals: it had not only the indispensable auxiliary
of the warrior, whether it pulled the chariot or he rode it, but it had
also become closely associated with him in life and death: his horse's
neighing and whinnying would tell the warrior what fate had in store
for him—the Greek heroes of Homer believed in the oracular powers
of their horses, and so did the Persians according to Herodotus and

the Germanic 'nobility' according to Tacitus, and medieval chronicles tell us about the 'clues' the Slavs were getting from their horses;[16] the typical sacrifice of the warrior caste, performed by the highest among them—the victorious king [rājan-], is the aśvamedha in India, and parallel horse sacrifices are to be found in Ireland at the coronation of the kings of Ulster, in ancient Gaul, in Thracia, and especially in Rome, where the Equus October is offered to Mars according to a ritual that shows some similarity with the Indian;[17]—and when the warrior dies, the symbiosis of man and horse is illustrated by the cremation of the animal on his funeral pyre. Theriomorphic gods appear as horses, e.g. the Celtic goddess Epona, but most characteristic is the equine nature of the divine twins and Dioscures, the sons of the Sky God who appear as 'owners of horses' (Aśvinau) in the Veda, having 'white horses' in the Greek tradition, bearing equine names in the Germanic euhemeristic tale of Hengist and Horsa about the Saxon conquest of Britain.[18]

In view of the importance of the horse, it is rather significant that Hittite, which has the first complete treatise on horse training ever written—the Kikkuli text dating back to the fourteenth century B.C.—does not show the word for 'horse': throughout the text it is represented by the Sumerian ANŠE.KUR.RA, which means literally 'donkey of the foreign country' (occasionally, Accadian SISU 'horse' is also used). However, there is a hieroglyphic Hittite ašuua- 'horse,' which could reflect IE *ek'wos, without having to be borrowed from the Mitanni-Aryan *aśva- 'horse' (= Skt. aśva-). Directly derived from this source, however, is the title by which Kikkuli designates himself: Hittite ᴸᵁaššuššanni- 'master of the stables.'[19] In this case, the ending -ni indicates Hurrian suffixation, so that the term must have reached Hittite via Hurrian.[20] The Mitanni-Aryans lived, indeed, in close contact with the Hurrians, and from the middle of the fifteenth century B.C., on the whole, Near Eastern culture seems to have been influenced by new Mitanni-Hurrian techniques of hunting and fighting from a chariot, as these motives appear in the art of Egypt, Syria, Mesopotamia at that time. The innovators are obviously the Mitanni-Aryans, who must have become known as the best horse trainers in the Middle East. If, however, the chariot is an innovation introduced by them, the only common IE heritage is the heavy four-wheeled cart;[21] the terminology is old with terms for 'wheel' like Latin rota OHG rat (secondarily, Skt. ratha 'chariot'), or Gk. kuklos, Skt.

cakra- (secondarily, 'cart' in Tocharian A kukäl, B kokale); the words for 'axle' and 'hub' are originally names of parts of the body ('shoulder' [G. Achsel] and 'navel'); 'shaft' and 'harness' provide good Old Indic: Hittite parallels, namely -īsā = hiṡṡa- and dhur- = tuziia-; etc.

All of this tends to show that a time perspective must be carefully preserved in the discussion of the cultural material. When we are examining Indo-European society, we have to keep in mind that, like any other human community, it is not static. In spite of all the impressive material assembled by Georges Dumézil, and the enlightening solution his approach has brought to some problems, his tripartition of Indo-European society postulates an early specialization of a military caste, which may more tend to reflect the situation of an expanding society conquering new territories or threatened in its homeland. The case of the Germanic peoples may illustrate this state of things: their unsophisticated techniques necessitated the yearly rotation of the fields, and in some areas, the reallocation of arable land was done on the basis of individual needs by the representatives of the community. This 'agrarian communism' is, however, only on record for the regions close to the Roman border,[22] where a substantial part of the male population had to be more or less permanently mobilized, whereas the less apt to fight and the women carried the burden of providing for the needs of the community. This accounts for the situation described by Tacitus in his Germania: chieftains would gather a retinue of young warriors who would be 'their pride in time of peace, their support on the battlefield,' and the comitatus, as it was called, developed a code of honor in keeping with the ethics of a warrior caste.[23] But there is no evidence that the same system prevailed elsewhere in 'free Germany': there, people owned their land and house, and were free to sow wheat, rye, oats, barley in their fields and to rear horses, kine, pigs, sheep, goats, and poultry as they wanted. With the movements of population that prevailed after the third century A.D., the military element became undoubtedly a major group in the social complex, and a leader chosen from among them presided over the destiny of the people. Actually, the original IE pastoralist may very well have been both a producer and a warrior: in peacetime, his energies are focused on his animal husbandry, also partly on hunting, but if his group is threatened or goes on the move, his function becomes essentially military—though he may return home to his cattle and fowl like Cincinnatus when the battle is done. The fact that gods like Mars have agrarian connotations can be better understood in this context;[34] similarly, the connection of Thor with the peasants may reflect more than his role as atmospheric god on account of his hammer Mjǫlnir, the thunderbolt. But Mars has also another function: he is the god associated with the old Italic practice of the uer sacrum, which was a religious decision to 'swarm,' i.e. to send the young generation away to find a new habitat. Mars would then appear to them in animal shape and lead them to their new site, and they would be henceforth named after this animal, e.g. the Picentes, after the woodpecker (picus) which shows them the way.[25] This practice of gradual occupation of the soil must have been inherited from IE, and may be the motivation of their migrations, far away, presumably in small groups of young warriors with a chieftain, submitting or expelling the former occupant of the area they conquered. This is the way the earlier Hittites present themselves: their invasion of Anatolia is not a massive migration, but rather a slow infiltration, a progressive build-up.[26] The Indo-European penetration had started already in the third millennium B. C. with the arrival of the Luwians;[27] by and by they unified the country, but their institutions still reveal in the oldest documents the survival of an assembly of the Hittite nobility—the pankuš—which not only advised the king but also exercised some important juridical prerogatives[28]—just like the Germanic þing. This is in keeping with the growing complexity in social organization and the stages of social evolution, with the staggered appearance of definite institutions.[29] In the comparative scheme emerging from a worldwide study of cultures both contemporary and archeologically investigated in the Old and New World, at the tribal stage unranked descent groups, pantribal associations—'fraternal orders' of all those of the same descent—prevail, but as the community grows and diversifies, the extended family 'swarms' for economic reasons: moving to establish new settlements leads to profound social changes: ranked descent groups, full-time craft specialization, and even the central accumulation and redistributive economy evidenced by the Germanic 'agrarian communism' or by the 'feudalism' developed by the Hittites.[30] A further important change was produced by the shift from a rural to an urban habitat: when the Achaean warriors made the πόλις the center of their social, political, and economic activity, the old social ranking based on descent groups was progressively replaced by the groupings defined by their common habitat[31]—true law and social stratification were now established. By the time the Vedic Indians entered the subcontinent the tripartite division may have been further elaborated, since the hymn to the Aśvins in the Eighth Book of the Rigveda (35: 16-18) explicitly mentions the priestly order, the nobility, and the commoners as the social levels worthy of their blessings. The later Puruṣa hymn (RV X, 90: 11), however, already mentions the four classes resulting from the partial integration of the conquered people in the Aryan society: in the cosmogonic myth, the primeval 'man's' mouth becomes the bhramans, his arms (symbols of strength) the rājanyas ('ruling nobility'), his thighs (supports of the body) the vaiśyas (the 'producers'), and his feet, the śudras (the original 'outsiders'). Though only the three upper classes are allowed to participate in the cultural and ritual activities of the Aryans, and the śudras were considered as 'unclean,' the three other classes showed a lot of flexibility: there was no restriction on intermarriage; the class membership was not hereditary; the warriors, in particular, were drawn from the Aryan community at large. Interesting in this context is also a hymn to Indra in the older part of the Rigveda (III. 43), where the poet asks the god to make him a 'herder of men'—like the Homeric ποιμὴν λαῶν —and gives his choices in the following order: 'make me king'—and if not, 'make me a priest'—if not, 'give me unperishable riches.'

It is important to keep these facts in mind when evaluating Dumézil's sociological interpretation of the pantheon. Another point is the impact of the dynamic character of Indo-European society on the same pantheon: to be sure, the Indo-Europeans had a god of the bright luminous sky. His name, *dyeus, is connected with the Latin word for 'day' (diēs) as well as 'god' (deus—adjectival dīvus 'divine'), which survives ON tívar 'gods,' OPruss. deiwas 'god,' etc. As a god Dyaus had receded to the background by the time the Vedic hymns were composed, though references to his former role in the hierogamy with Mother Earth—in the compound Dyāvaprthivī, his omniscience and his creativity—as Father Sky—Dyaus pitā parallel to Jupiter, still occur in the text. The changeover made Varuna—together with Mitra —the 'powerful and sublime master of the sky'—he 'separated the two worlds,' he established order in the universe, he became the universal sovereign, sahasrākṣa—'with a thousand eyes'—informed of everything, wielding an ominous magical power—the māyā—[32] which makes him fit in Dumézil's classification as the Vedic embodiment of magic sovereignty at the first function level. But his position as ruling god is threatened, and the Rigveda gives evidence of the conflict between Varuṇa-centered religion and Indra-centered religion.[33] The result of the alteration of the original sky god can be very complex, and when Dumézil reclassifies Týr, the Germanic descendant of *dyeus, as the representative of the Mitra aspect of sovereignty, i.e. the judicial component of the first function (Odin being the Germanic 'magic sovereign'), one cannot escape the impression that this focuses only on one aspect of his functional role, namely his breaking a solemn promise and sacrificing his arm to ensure the safety of his kin in a heroic gesture paralleling that of Mucius Scaevola in ancient Rome.[34] Actually, the Germanic god *Tīwaz (> ON Týr) has been associated in the interpretatio romana with Mars as appears from the translation Tuesday for dies Martis, but on account of the votive inscription to Mars Thincsus by Roman auxiliary troops from the Germanic Low Countries found along Hadrian's Wall in Great Britain, and of the German and Dutch words for Tuesday: Dienstag/dinsdag, both containing the genitive of the old designation of Germanic tribal assembly of free men, the þing, this has been seen as a confirmation of the juridical functions of *Tīwaz.[35] There may, however, be another way to approach the problem: there seems to be some evidence that *Tīwaz was venerated as tribal god by the Suebians along the Roman limes; on the other hand, the Saxon chronicle of Widukind mentions that they celebrated their victory over the Thuringians by erecting huge columns to Mars, whom they called (H)irmin—a term which reappears in Irminsul, the idol Charlemagne is supposed to have destroyed after his victory over the Saxons in 772, and which is described as a cosmic pillar —by Rudolf of Fulda—universalis columna quasi sustinens omnia.[36] On the other hand, in the abjuration formula the vanquished Saxons had to swear upon conversion to Christianity, the main gods mentioned were Donar, Wodan, and their tribal god Saxnôte. The question, then, arises: if *Tīwaz is identified with Mars, if the Saxons venerate a cosmic god under the name of (H)irmin and the symbol of a cosmic pillar and identify him with Mars, if the major god of the Saxons, besides Donar and Wodan, is their tribal god Saxnôte, is it not plausible that (H)irmin and Saxnôte are merely two names of the old sky god *Tīwaz under his specific functions of cosmic sovereign and protector of the tribe?[37] His close association with the tribal assembly— the þing—would obviously follow from the second aspect of his personality.

But perhaps the most troubling problem about Dumézil's
sociological approach is what it leaves out; to limit ourselves to a
few issues: (a) what is the position of the sun worship in his system?
To be sure, the sun deity, Sūrya, occupied a secondary position in the
Rigveda, and the sun cult was not important in ancient Rome and
Greece, but in northern Europe its rich symbolism appears on the
rock drawings and the sun chariot of Trundholm attests to the importance of the cult.[38] There are also myths about the sun's chariot and
its horses closely associated with the divine twins. It is therefore
the more puzzling that the validity of Caesar's statement about the
Germanic people, that the sun, the fire, and the moon—Sol, Vulcanus,
Luna—are their main deities, cannot be properly established, but then
also Agni, the Vedic fire god, does not fit in Dumézil's system,[39]
whereas the antiquity of two Indo-European terms for 'fire,' one 'profane'—Hittite pahhur, Gk. πῦρ, G. Feuer, E. fire—the other 'sacred'
—Skt. agnih, Lat. ignis—also a god name in the Hittite nomenclature
Agniš.

(b) Why does the system not work for Greece? Palmer has
tried to establish some traces of the tripartite division in the reparti-
tion of the land in the Mycenaean world,[40] but apart from a few samples
like the judgment of Paris or the social organization of Plato's Republic, Dumézil and his disciples have not been able to come up with
much that fits their pattern in the Greek mythological world.[41]

(c) Why is the Anatolian world completely left out, except
for the Mitanni documents? To be sure, like most of the Near Eastern people at that time, the Indo-European invaders of Anatolia have
taken over most of the Sumero-Babylonian mythological tradition and
reinterpreted it to suit their own specific needs, and the surprising
appearance in the treatises of the fourteenth century B. C. of the Vedic
god names Mitra, Varuna, Indra, and Nāsatyā as the deities of the
Mitanni-Hurrian princes in Upper Mesopotamia contrasts with the ap-
parent total loss of Indo-European religious traditions by the earlier
Anatolian immigrants. Should one assume that the Anatolians have
'lost' the Indo-European social structure in their new homeland to
take over the Oriental type of divine kingship? That is definitely not
true until the middle of the second millennium B. C., in the period of
the 'Old Kingdom.' Actually, the Indo-Europeans that came into the

Middle East in the third millennium B. C. may have represented a
less elaborated stage in their societal development so that what appears as a 'loss' is actually an archaic feature. What is suggested
here is similar to what is slowly being recognized in the linguistic
field: up to quite recently, Hittite was considered as a strongly adulterated type of Indo-European—a kind of creolized Indo-European developed in the Middle Eastern territories conquered by the Hittites
under the influence of the submitted and surrounding Semitic and other
non-Indo-European populations. Upon closer examination, one fails
to recognize such a repatterning of Hittite on the basis of the languages
with which it has come into contact: the Hittite system has not become
closer to the Semitic or the Hurrian or any other non-Indo-European
Anatolian linguistic pattern.[42] Whatever can be recognized as strictly
Indo-European in Hittite appears to be more archaic, though losses
are possible as well, e.g. the dual which has totally disappeared,
whereas it should have been preserved under Semitic influence. If
we look at the verb system, we find a model consisting of:

(1) an indicative and an imperative, but only the indicative has a paradigmatic structure, contrasting present and non-present; active
and medio-passive; active ('infectum') and perfectum ;
(2) paradigmatic endings characterizing the 'active' versus the perfectum and appended vocalic suffixes marking the present versus the
non-present as well as the medio-passive.

This system, as Meid has shown,[43] can form the basis from which the
later IE system evidenced by Sanskrit and the classical languages has
developed (see table). Thus, on the linguistic level as well as on the
social and religious level, a difference in time perspective would account for the Sonderstellung, for the alleged particular position of
Anatolian: it would merely reflect an earlier stage of the Indo-European complex—and maybe in the light of all this we should give Sturte-
vant's Indo-Hittite hypothesis a new look!

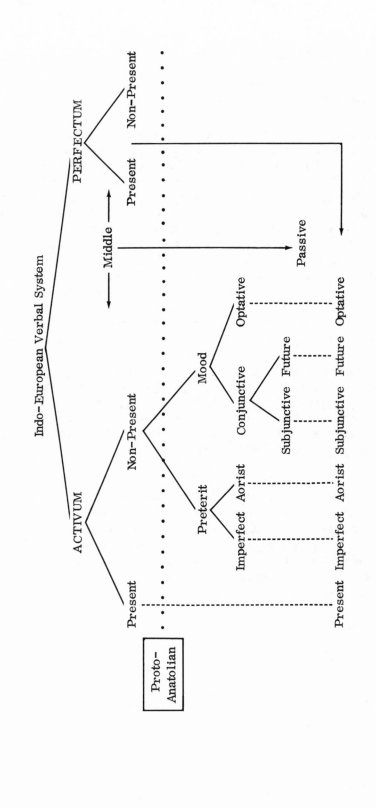

REFERENCES

[1] The Kurgan people represent a civilization characterized by burial rites with a central grave in a barrow (= Russian kurgan). The most significant writings of M. Gimbutas on this subject are:

1956. Prehistory of Eastern Europe. I. Mesolithic, Neolithic and Copper Age cultures in Russia and the Baltic area. American School of Prehistoric Research, Peabody Museum, Harvard University, Bull. 20, Cambridge, Mass.

1963. The Indo-Europeans. Archaeological problems. American Anthropologist 65: 815-37.

1965. Bronze Age cultures of Central and Eastern Europe. The Hague: Mouton.

1970. Proto-Indo-European culture: The Kurgan culture during the fifth, fourth and third millennia B. C. In G. Cardona, H. Hoenigswald, and A. Senn, eds., Indo-European and Indo-Europeans. Philadelphia: University of Pennsylvania Press, pp. 155-97.

1973. Old Europe c. 7000-3500 B. C.: The earliest European civilization before the infiltration of the Indo-European peoples. Journal of Indo-European Studies 1: 1-20.

1974a. The gods and goddesses of Old Europe 7000-3500 B. C. London: Thames and Hudson.

1974b. An archeologist's view of PIE in 1975. Journal of Indo-European Studies 2: 289-307.

1978. La fin de l'Europe ancienne. La Recherche 9 (nr. 87): 228-35.

[2] Le vocabulaire des institutions indo-européennes. 1. Economie, parenté, société. 2. Pouvoir, droit, religion. Paris: Les Editions de Minuit, 1969. (English translation by Elizabeth Palmer; Coral Gables, Fla.: University of Miami Press, 1973.)

[3] Cf., e.g., H. Wagenvoort, Imperium. Studien over het "mana"—begrip in zede en taal der Romeinen (Amsterdam: H. J. Paris, 1941). Jan Gonda, Some Observations on the Relations between "Gods" and "Powers" in the Veda, a propos of the phrase sūnuh sahasah (The Hague: Mouton, 1957). Jan Gonda, Die Religionen Indiens. I. Veda und älterer Hinduismus (Stuttgart: W. Kohlhammer, 1960; esp. 'Die Mächte,' pp. 26-47).

[4] Das Heilige im Germanischen (Tübingen: C. B. Mohr, 1942).

[5] An excellent survey of Dumézil's views in a historical per-

spective is given by C. Scott Littleton in The New Comparative Mythology. An Anthropological Assessment of the Theories of Georges
Dumézil (Berkeley–Los Angeles: University of California Press,
1966, rev. ed. 1973). This volume contains an extensive bibliography
of Dumézil's writings up to 1971. G. Dumézil himself has given a
synthesis of his views in his study L'idéologie tripartie des Indo-
Européens (Collection Latomus, vol. 31; Brussels, 1958). In recent
years, a number of his works have become available in English:

1970a. Archaic Roman religion. 2 vols. Translation by Phillipp
  Krapp of La religion romaine archaique (Paris: Payot,
  1966). Chicago: University of Chicago Press.
1970b. The destiny of the warrior. Translation by Alf Hiltebeitel of
  Heur et malheur du guerrier (Paris: Presses Universitaires
  de France, 1968). Chicago: University of Chicago Press.
1973a. Gods of the ancient Northmen. Translation edited by Einar
  Haugen of Les Dieux des Germains (Paris: Presses Universitaires de France) and four articles on Germanic religion.
  Berkeley–Los Angeles: University of California Press.
1973b. The destiny of a king. Translation by Alf Hiltebeitel of lectures given in Chicago, Philadelphia, and Los Angeles, 1969–
  70. Chicago: University of Chicago Press.

Besides, G. Dumézil has been steadily revising and reorganizing his
earlier work in a corpus published in the Bibliothèque des Sciences
Humaines (Gallimard, Paris). It includes:

1968. Mythe et épopée. I. L'idéologie des trois fonctions dans les
  épopées des peuples indo-européens. (Rev. ed., 1974.)
1969. Idées romaines.
1971. Mythe et épopée. II. Types épiques indo-européens: un héros,
  un sorcier, un roi.
1973c. Mythe et épopée. III. Histories romaines.
1975. Fêtes romaines d'été et d'automne, suivi de Dix questions romaines.
1977. Les dieux souverains des Indo-Européens.

  [6] Cf. Scott Littleton 1973: 50–52; see also Benveniste 1969:
1. 279–92; 1973: 227–38.
  [7] Cf., e.g., Julius Pokorny, Zur Urgeschichte der Kelten
und Illyrier (Halle: M. Niemeyer, 1938).

[8] Cf., e.g., Hans Krahe, 'Das Problem der "ägäischen" Wanderung in sprachwissenschaftlicher Beleuchtung.' Geistige Arbeit 5: 18 (1938). 1-2; 'Der Anteil der Illyrier an der Indogermanisierung Europas,' Die Welt als Geschichte 6 (1940): 54-73; Die Indogermanisierung Griechenlands und Italiens (Heidelberg: C. Winter, 1949).

[9] In the fifties, H. Krahe himself toned down his claims on the expansion of the "Illyrians" and substituted "Alteuropäisch" for (Proto-)Illyrian to denote the common elements identifiable in the hydronymy of large areas in Europe. Cf. Sprachverwandtschaft im alten Europa (Heidelberg: C. Winter, 1951); Vorgeschichtliche Sprachbeziehungen von den baltischen Ostseeländern bis zu den Gebieten um den Nordteil der Adria (Wiesbaden: F. Steiner, 1957); 'Vom Illyrischen zum Alteuropäischen. Methodologische Betrachtungen zur Wandlung des Begriffs "Illyrisch," ' Indogermanische Forschungen 59 (1964): 201-13.

The problem was thoroughly reviewed by H. Kronasser in his study 'Zum Stand der Illyristik, ' in Balkanska ezikoznanie/Linguistique Balkanique 4 (1962): 5-23. The Illyrian onomastic territory was carefully redefined by R. Katičić in 'Die illyrischen Personennamen in ihrem südöstlichen Verbreitungsgebiet,' Živa Antika 12 (1962): 95-120; and 'Das mitteldalmatische Namengebiet,' Živa Antika 12 (1963): 255-92. See also his Ancient Languages of the Balkans (The Hague: Mouton, 1976), vol. 1, pp. 154-88.

[10] 'Proto-Indo-European Culture and Archaeology: Some Critical Remarks,' Journal of Indo-European Studies 2 (1974): 279-87.

[11] 'Vorgeschichte und Indogermanistik,' in Theorie und Praxis der Zusammenarbeit zwischen den anthropologischen Disziplinen (Horn: F. Berger, 1961), pp. 117-36; reprinted in A. Scherer, ed., Die Urheimat der Indogermanen (Darmstadt: Wissenschaftliche Buchgesellschaft, 1968), pp. 478-509.

[12] 'Les valeurs économiques dans le vocabulaire indo-européen, in G. Cardona, H. Hoenigswald, and A. Senn, eds., Indo-European and Indo-Europeans (Philadelphia: University of Pennsylvania Press, 1970), pp. 307-20; see also Le vocabulaire des institutions indo-européennes (Paris: Editions de Minuit, 1969), vol. 1, pp. 47-61 (English translation, 1973, pp. 40-51).

[13] Jacqueline Murray, The First European Agriculture. A Study of the Osteological and Botanical Evidence until 2000 B.C. (Edinburgh: University Press, 1970), esp. pp. 110-11; 'Einige Gesichtspunkte über die Beziehung zwischen Viehzucht und archäologischen Kulturen im Spätneolithikum in Europa,' in J. Matolcsi, ed.,

Domestikationsforschung und Geschichte der Haustiere. Internationales Symposium in Budapest 1971 (Budapest: Akadémiai Kiadó, 1973), pp. 177-86.

[14] E.g. S. Bökönyí, History of Domestic Mammals in Central and Eastern Europe (Budapest: Akadémiai Kiadó, 1974).

[15] Benveniste, in Le vocabulaire des institutions indo-européennes, vol. 1 (Paris: Editions de Minuit, 1969, pp. 21-45; English version 1973, pp. 19-39), illustrated the importance of sheep, goats, and pigs in Indo-European animal husbandry. As Marija Gimbutas has shown (e.g. 'La fin de l'Europe ancienne,' La Recherche 9 [no. 87, March 1978]: 230), what took place is a confrontation of two cultures: the matriarchal agricultural society of ancient Europe, established in sizable farming communities and the patriarchal pastoral—more mobile, dynamic, and expansionistic Kurgan civilization. The role of cattle in the Indo-European world is illustrated by its myths, especially those described by Bruce Lincoln in 'The Indo-European Cattle-Raiding Myth,' History of Religions 16,1 (1976): 42-65.

[16] Rudolf Much, Die Germania des Tacitus erläutert (3rd ed., revised by W. Lange and H. Jankuhn; Heidelberg: Carl Winter, 1967), p. 198.

[17] Cf. especially G. Dumézil, Archaic Roman Religion (Chicago: University of Chicago Press, 1970), pp. 224-27; Fêtes romaines d'été et d'automne (Paris: Gallimard, 1975), pp. 145-56.

[18] Donald Ward, The Divine Twins. An Indo-European Myth in Germanic Tradition (Folklore Studies, vol. 19; Berkeley-Los Angeles: University of California Press, 1968), pp. 11-12; 54-56.

[19] Cf. Annelies Kammenhuber, Hippologia Hethitica (Wiesbaden: O. Harrassowitz, 1961), pp. 13-14, 23-34, 354, 362, 364; M. S. Drower, 'The Domestication of the Horse,' in P. Ucko and G. Dimbleby, eds., The Domestication and Exploitation of Plants and Animals (Chicago-New York: Aldine-Atherton, 1969), pp. 471-78, esp. p. 472.

[20] Manfred Mayrhofer, Die Indo-Arier im alten Vorderasien (Wiesbaden: O. Harrassowitz, 1966), p. 10, fn. 4; Annelies Kammenhuber, Die Arier im Vorderen Orient (Heidelberg: Carl Winter, 1968), pp. 208-11, 223-24. Mayrhofer (Die Arier im vorderen Orient—ein Mythos? [Vienna: Österreichische Akademie der Wissenschaften, Philosophisch-historische Klasse. Sitzungsberichte, vol. 294, Nr. 3, 1974], p. 15) considers the form simply as 'Aryan' and does not list

it among the derivations with the Hurrian morpheme -ne (> Hittite -nni) in the Kikkuli horse-training treatise.

[21] Cf. Kammenhuber, Hippologia Hethitica (Wiesbaden: O. Harrassowitz, 1961), pp. 24-25 (with fn. 101); R. A. Crossland, 'Immigrants from the North,' in Cambridge Ancient History, vol. 1, part 2, 3rd ed., chap. 27 (Cambridge University Press, 1971), pp. 844, 873-74. The four-wheeled cart was introduced in Europe by the Kurgan culture as early as 3000 B. C. A clay model dating back to 2000 B. C. was found at Budakalász, north of Budapest.

[22] Caesar, De Bello Gallico VI, 22 (cf. G. Dumézil, Mitra-Varuna [Paris: Gallimard, 1948; 2nd ed.], pp. 154-59; Les dieux souvérains des Indo-Européens [Paris: Gallimard, 1977], p. 202.

[23] Tacitus, Germania, chaps. 13-15. (Cf. R. Much, Die Germania des Tacitus erläutert, 3rd ed. by W. Lange and H. Jankuhn [Heidelberg: Carl Winter, 1967], pp. 221-44.) On the significance of the institution in the Germanic world, cf. especially D. H. Green, The Carolingian Lord (Cambridge: University Press, 1965). On its Indo-European context, see E. Benveniste, 1969, pp. 103-21; 1973, pp. 84-100.

[24] As. K. Latte points out (Römische Religionsgeschichte [Munich: C. B. Beck, 1960], p. 114), he is functionally connected with the 'hostile, unfamiliar outside world' (cf. Benveniste, 1969, p. 314; 1973, pp. 256-57); but G. Dumézil (Archaic Roman Religion [Chicago: University of Chicago Press, 1970], pp. 213-40) is definitely right in rejecting the view that he was essentially an 'agrarian' god. (Cf. also Latte's argument [pp. 114-21] on the 'military' [kriegerisch] character of the ritual activities connected with Mars.)

[25] Latte, 1960, p. 124; Dumézil, 1970, p. 208.

[26] Kurt Bittel, Grundzüge der Vor- und Frühgeschichte Klein-asiens (Tübingen: F. Wasmuth, 1950, 2nd ed.), p. 52.

[27] Bittel, 1950, pp. 54-55; R. A. Crossland, 'Immigrants from the North,' in Cambridge Ancient History, vol. 1, Part 2, 3rd ed., chap. 27 (Cambridge: University Press, 1971), p. 842. Friedrich Cornelius, Geschichte der Hethiter (Darmstadt: Wissenschaftliche Buchgesellschaft, 1976), pp. 43-45, 292-93.

[28] Cf. Albrecht Götze, Kleinasien (Munich: C. H. Beck, 1957), pp. 86-88. On the IE context of the Hittite pankuš, cf. F. Cornelius, 1976, pp. 54-56 (based on his Geistesgeschichte der Frühzeit 2,2 [Leyden: E. J. Brill, 1967], pp. 13-16, 241-42).

[29] John E. Pfeiffer, The Emergence of Society (New York: McGraw-Hill, 1977), p. 103.

[30] Bittel, 1956, p. 43; Götze, 1957, pp. 102-7; Cornelius, 1976, pp. 68-70.

[31] Benveniste, 1969, pp. 309-10; 1973, pp. 252-53.

[32] Mircea Eliade, Patterns in Comparative Religion (New York: Meridian Books 1963), pp. 66-72.

[33] Edgar Polomé, 'Approaches to the Study of Vedic Religion,' in Paul Hopper, ed., Studies in Descriptive and Historical Linguistics. Festschrift for Winfred P. Lehmann (Amsterdam: J. Benjamins, 1977), pp. 405-15.

[34] Cf., e.g., Mitra-Varuna (Paris: Gallimard, 1948; 2nd ed.), pp. 165-69, 174-77; Mythe et épopée, vol. 1 (Paris: Gallimard, 1968), pp. 424-28; vol. 3 (Paris: Gallimard, 1973), pp. 268-74.

[35] Cf., e.g., G. Dumézil, Gods of the Ancient Northmen (translation edited by E. Haugen; Berkeley-Los Angeles: University of California, 1973), pp. 42-48. On Tuesday as translation of dies Martis, cf. especially Udo Strutynski, 'Germanic Divinities in Weekday Names,' Journal of Indo-European Studies 3 (1975): 363-84.

[36] See, in particular, Jan de Vries, 'La valeur religieuse du mot germanique irmin,' Cahiers du Sud, 1952, pp. 18-27.

[37] Jan de Vries, Altgermanische Religionsgeschichte, vol. 2 (Berlin: W. de Gruyter, 1957, 2nd ed.), pp. 16, 18.

[38] Cf., e.g., Peter Gjelling and Hilda Ellis Davidson, The Chariot of the Sun (London: J. M. Dent, 1969), pp. 9-26, 136-37, 140-45, 180-83. See further J. de Vries, Altgermanische Religionsgeschichte, vol. 1 (Berlin: W. de Gruyter, 1956; 2nd ed.), pp. 110-15, 355-58.

[39] He is described as a kind of marginal god on account of his appearance at the beginning or/and the end of the list of the Vedic divinities to whom sacrifices are offered. (Cf. G. Dumézil, Ancient Roman Religion [Chicago: University of Chicago Press, 1970], pp. 322-23; see also C. Scott Littleton, The New Comparative Mythology [Berkeley-Los Angeles: University of California Press, 1973; 2nd ed.], pp. 15-16, 106.)

[40] L. R. Palmer, Mycenaeans and Minoans (London: Faber & Faber, 1961), pp. 93-99.

[41] Cf. G. Dumézil, 'Les trois fonctions dans quelques traditions grecques,' in Hommage à Lucien Febvre, vol. 2 (Paris: Armand

Colin, 1953), pp. 25-32; C. Scott Littleton, 'Some Possible Indo-European Themes in the "Iliad,"' in Jaan Puhvel, ed., Myth and Law among the Indo-Europeans (Berkeley-Los Angeles: University of California Press, 1970), pp. 229-46.

[42] See, e.g., Annalies Kammenhuber, Hethitisch, Palaisch, Luwisch und Hieroglyphenluwisch, pp. 266-69. (Handbuch der Orientalistik 1.2:1-2. Altkleinasiatische Sprachen [Leiden: E. J. Brill, 1969], pp. 119-357.)

[43] Wolfgang Meid, 'Probleme der räumlichen und zeitlichen Gliederung des Indogermanischen,' in Helmut Rix, ed., Flexion und Wortbildung. Akten der V. Fachtagung der Indogermanischen Gesellschaft (Wiesbaden: L. Reichert, 1975), pp. 204-19. The model presented here is taken from Erich Neu, 'Zur Rekonstruktion des indogermanischen Verbalsystems,' in A. Morpurgo Davies and W. Meid, eds., Studies in Greek, Italic and Indo-European Linguistics offered to Leonard R. Palmer (Innsbruck, 1976), pp. 239-54, esp. p. 252. Basic arguments for this analysis of Indo-European verbal morphology are to be found in J. Kuryłowicz, The Inflectional Categories of Indo-European (Heidelberg: Carl Winter, 1964), pp. 56-147; and C. Watkins, Geschichte der indogermanischen Verbalflexion (= Indogermanische Grammatik. III. Formenlehre, vol. 1 (Heidelberg: Carl Winter, 1969).

16 | The Reconstruction of Proto-Bantu Culture from the Lexicon

Though the close kinship of the Bantu languages has long been recognized since the work of W. H. J. Bleek (1862-69), the systematic reconstruction of the Proto-Bantu lexicon[1] was only started several decades later when Carl Meinhof (1899, 1910, 1932), applying the methods of Schleicher and the Neogrammarians, tried to reconstruct the phonological system of Proto-Bantu. His reconstructions, based on a limited number of languages, did not serve as a basis for a hypothesis on Proto-Bantu culture, because Meinhof was at that time the main promoter of the hypothesis of the Hamitic pastoral expansion as a major civilizing element in Africa south of the equator (Meinhof 1912, 1936). Other German linguists added progressively numerous new comparisons to those of Meinhof, on the basis of the steadily increasing available linguistic information, mainly as a result of the study of the languages of the interior, first by missionaries, later by linguists. Especially important were the collections of O. Dempwolff (1916-17) and W. Bourquin (1923), to which the contributions of Belgian linguists like A. Coupez (1954) and A. de Rop (1958) may be added. In 1969, the accumulated material was sufficient for A. E. Meeussen to compile an extensive repertory of Proto-Bantu roots under the title Bantu lexical reconstructions. The following year, the first volume of Malcolm Guthrie's comparative Bantu vocabulary appeared, soon followed by the second volume, both constituting parts 3 and 4 of his monumental Comparative Bantu (1967-71). This contained a systematic synthesis of twenty years of research, compilation, and checking of materials in about two hundred languages, presented under the form of some 2,300 lexical correspondences based on a shared semantic content and phonologically closely related forms. The total number of Proto-Bantu roots was much smaller, however, since the lemmas of the dictionary include a considerable number of derivations, e.g. verbs, nouns of agent, nouns of action, reversives and causatives, based on the same root. Moreover, every significant semantic difference leads to positing homonymous but separate "roots." Thus, the term *cîmbà is listed under three lemmas: (a) "wild-cat (leopard)"; (b) "genet"; (c) "lion," whose reflexes cover extensive areas of the Bantu territory, whereas the meaning occurring in the various regions seems to depend on the ecology of the habitat of the relevant animal. On the other hand, when reconstructing Proto-Bantu, Guthrie establishes at a very early date a dialectal contrast between a western area (Proto-Bantu A̲) and an eastern area (Proto-Bantu B̲). When a "root" has valid reflexes in both areas, it is assigned to original Proto-Bantu (Proto-Bantu X̲), but this does not necessarily imply that terms which do not appear all over the Bantu territory have to be excluded from the Proto-Bantu vocabulary: the absence of reflexes in a given region may be due to lack of information (in particular as regards the zones A, B, and C of Guthrie in the northwest). The occurrence of different terms in the two areas (P.B. A̲ and P.B. B̲) does not necessarily exclude the existence of a common concept at an early date: thus, the fact that the term for "door" is *bédò in the west and *yìbì (*yìgì) in the east may simply reflect a difference in construction technique. And should one doubt the existence of terms for "scorpion" or "chameleon" at an early date because only very localized terms are found for the former, whereas no set of comparable terms is attested for the latter? When one thinks of the magical power ascribed to the chameleon, it is not surprising that its original name may have been made tabu: hence, the absence of a common term! Nevertheless, the abundance of terms occurring mostly in the southern and eastern part of the Bantu territory and the frequent absence of correspondences in Guthrie's zones A, B, C have led a number of scholars to wonder about the possibility of an early split of the languages of these zones from the rest of Proto-Bantu. Though this question must, for the time being, remain open, it is obvious that Guthrie's work, in spite of some of its methodological weaknesses, provides us with a rich and valuable picture of the culture of the early Bantu world. Detailed in certain respects, it remains, however, fragmentary in others. As regards the environment, the vocabulary rather points to a landscape of wooded savanna than to tropical forest: wide stretches of bush, with various kinds of palm trees, baobabs, thorn trees, etc. The fauna is essentially that of the savanna: lion, genet, jackal, hyena, elephant, numerous varieties of antelopes, from the

kudu to the impala, wart hog, leopard, and so many others. Some
terms indicate different varieties of ecological environment, e.g.
dense thickets in which the rhinoceros wanders or rivers in which
crocodiles swarm and hippopotamuses bathe leisurely. There is a
very extensive and precise nomenclature of animal names, including,
among others, the monkey, the rat, the bat, the monitor lizard, the
ant, the termite, the spider, the millipede, the cricket, the locust,
the grasshopper, the fly, the mosquito, the cockroach, the turtle, the
frog, the porcupine, etc. Living in close contact with nature, the
Bantu has an adequate and specific set of terms at his disposal to
describe it. This applies, however, to a lesser degree to the birds
and the fish: merely a few species of birds are specifically designated
in the common vocabulary, except for the birds of prey. There is no
linguistic evidence of direct contact with the sea: terms like "crab"
apply to the terrestrial varieties that abound among the palm trees;
the only specific fish name is that of the "eel" which could be caught
in fresh water. A more precise terminology applies to cultivated
plants and domestic animals.

There is no doubt that the Proto-Bantus were agriculturists
and grew cereals, especially millet. They also seem to have become
familiar, at a very early date, with the sugar cane and the banana.
For vegetables, they appear to have grown mainly pumpkins and beans.
Important were also the oil-yielding plants, especially the palm nut.
As for the agricultural techniques, the vocabulary points out that the
Bantus cleared the land with axes and cultivated it with hoes. The
cereals were threshed and winnowed; they were stored in safe places.
When they wanted to obtain flour, they used two techniques: (a) grind-
ing between two stones; (b) stamping in a mortar.

The Proto-Bantus must also have been picking fruit, but the
only known name of fruit tree in their lexicon (except for the palm
trees) is the fig tree. Among the techniques connected with agriculture,
it should also be mentioned that they had developed a method for brew-
ing beer. On the other hand, they also practiced cattle breeding on a
large scale: besides cows and bulls, which were penned up in kraals
for their protection, they also kept goats, sheep, pigs, chickens, and
of course dogs. As regards their livestock, they may already have had
castrated steers. As for preparing food, cooking seems to have been
the common practice: a set of verbs indicates the various techniques—

"frying, " "roasting, " "boiling, " "baking in hot ashes"; there is a
term to indicate that the food is getting cooked enough, and one of the
words for vegetables applies specifically to "cooked vegetables. "
They prepared broth and, with millet, a rather thick mush. Fish was
also part of their usual diet. The Proto-Bantus fished with hook and
line or caught the fish in basket traps, as the waGenia still do nowadays in the rapids of Zaire.

Pottery and basketry were very popular crafts: there are
terms for "molding the clay"; a distinction is made between pots to
cook food in and jars to preserve drinking water in. There were bas-
kets of all sizes and shapes, from the hamper to the small box. Nothing, however, indicates any knowledge of spinning and weaving,
though, besides the sheep, a kind of wild cotton was abundantly available as a source for spinning thread. Clothing was presumably limited
to a strict minimum to cover the genitals, but animal skins must have
been used in particular circumstances. Several terms also indicate
the use of feathers, especially as headdress. For the ladies, beauty
care must already have included intricate methods of plaiting the hair.
It is more difficult to ascertain if the practice of shaving had been generalized for men. Many other activities contributed to the well-being
of the community: hunting had been practiced for centuries and was
still very much in favor; the techniques used were trapping, throwing
the javeline and shooting with bow and arrow. The lexicon also indicates that the Proto-Bantus caught birds with lime and that, in the
east zone at least, they built traps that fell down on their prey. There
are several words for "arrow, " and the homonymy of some of them
with the term for the midrib of the palm frond indicates that the latter
was used at an early date to make arrows. We do not have any indication as to the wood used for bows (the only specific name of wood mentioned in Proto-Bantu is "ebony"). Sinews may have been used as bow-
strings, but the occurrence of specific words for "string rope" points
to the existence of a technique for turning fibers into strings and ropes.
Another activity practiced by the Proto-Bantus was the gathering of
honey. They also used the beeswax, though we do not know specifically
for what purpose.

As for housing, they built huts—presumably of rather different shapes—thatched with palm of banana leaves and divided inside by
screens. A special roomier hut was reserved for the chief. The huts

were provided with a door, which could be barred during the night.
The furniture was rather minimal: wooden stools and headrests; bed-
stead with bedding consisting presumably of animal skins. The building techniques were still very unsophisticated, e.g. to put a bridge
over a small river, a tree trunk was simply laid across it.

The main cultural feature of the Proto-Bantus was presumably
their knowledge of the metallurgy of iron. This is amply evidenced by
the lexicon: common terms for "iron," "hammer," "bellows," "char-
coal," "iron ore," etc. There is even a technical term for "beat with
a hammer," "sharpen the edge," etc.

In the field of social life, activities were regulated by the
rhythm of the seasons: dry season following upon rainy season; the
day of the last rain seemed to be particularly important, as well as
the day on which the first fruit of the new crop were eaten. There
must have been feasts with music, songs, and dances. They already
knew the drum and the <u>marimba</u>. Religious life also played an important part in social activities: witchcraft was practiced on a large scale;
the witch doctor protected the crops with spells. He presumably controlled the tabus and acted as a go-between with the spirits. Several
terms point to an extensive use of fetishes and charms. There was even
a regional term for a special type of skin eruption ascribed to the breaking of a tabu. There is a Proto-Bantu word indicating the "deity": it
is found essentially in the west, but its etymology remains obscure
and it is not possible to derive any clue concerning its cult.

Society was apparently organized according to the clanic system: there is a special term for "clan brother" distinct from natural
"brother," but unfortunately the lexicon does not throw any light on the
kinship system. Parents, grandparents, brothers and sisters, mater-
nal uncles, in-laws are all indicated by specific terms, but without any
clue as to patrilinear or matrilinear features of kinship.

Interesting facts are the following: (a) marriage appears to
imply the payment of a sizable bride-price to the parents of the bride;
(b) mothers carry their child on the back with a kind of sling: the terms
designating this baby sling and this way to carry a child are homonymous
with the words for "skin" and "bear a child (in pregnancy)," so that
apparently this behavior was considered as the normal continuation of
the development of the fetus outside the mother's womb.

Polygamy was common practice, and there is a specific term for "taking a second wife."

As for economic activity, there must have been a certain amount of bartering between neighboring groups. The system of numerals is well attested in Proto-Bantu from "one" to "five," but there are no common terms for numerals "six" to "nine"; for "ten," there is again a common Proto-Bantu term, whereas "hundred" is expressed by different words in the west and in the east. The concept of "measure and "measuring" seems quite widespread, but one does not know what particular entities it applies to (time was measured in lunar months, and the same term is used regularly for "moon" and "month").

The Bantus were in contact with the former populations of their territory, especially the pygmies (*túá), whose name was also derogatory. The contacts between tribes were sometimes violent, as is shown by the various words for "war." There were different types of arms: bows and arrows, javelins, spears, shields, etc. Prisoners captured in combat were presumably the source of the "slaves" existing in the Proto-Bantu community.

Internal strife was settled according to customary law; an indication of it is given by the terms designating a "fault," a "punishment," or meaning to "settle a dispute." Swearing an oath also seems to play an important part in the practice of tribal law.

Such is the society which the Proto-Bantu lexicon describes to us. To what extent can these lexical data be correlated with the archeological data?

The studies of paleobotanists, like Raymond Postères (1970: 47, 51, 53), have indicated that several varieties of millet, sorghum, and even rice were known in subsaharan Africa prior to the development of the Bantu world. It appears, accordingly, that upon their arrival in central, southern, and eastern Africa, the Bantus found populations practicing agriculture and that their contribution consisted of an expansion of that activity owing to the technical progress made possible by the use of iron, which also determined their superiority at war as well as in hunting. This, at least, is the conclusion reached by Christopher Wrigley (1970: 66-69, 71) in his analysis of the pre-

historic economy of Africa. It agrees rather well with the views of
J. H. Greenberg (1963: 38), who considers the central valley of the
Benue as the original homeland of the Bantus. There, the Nok culture
was one of the earliest to use iron in subsaharan Africa. Though M.
Guthrie rejects this area as the Proto-Bantu homeland for rather unconvincing reasons and tries to make them come from the Chad region,
the matter is of secondary importance for the subject under discussion.
The main thesis is that a population nucleus coming from the northern savanna area has, at a definite moment of prehistory, crossed
the tropical forest to come and settle in the southern savanna area.
On the basis of radiocarbon datings, this migration must presumably
have taken place during the first centuries of our era. Settling down
in Katanga, in the present-day Luba territory, the newcomers would
have progressively expanded and strengthened their grip over wider
territories. This is confirmed by a number of linguistic and archeological facts:

(a) As the extensive study of linguistic geography undertaken by M.
    Guthrie has shown, the Luba-Bemba area of Katanga shows the
    highest percentage of retention (Guthrie 1970a: 135).
(b) The technique of iron making, improving agricultural tools, was
    accompanied by the introduction of better varieties of sorghum
    and millet. At a very early date, contact was established with the
    Indian Ocean, entailing the introduction of the banana and the coco-
    nut, originally imported to Madagascar from Southeast Asia by the
    Indonesian conquerors. It is even possible to date this contact:
    the Periplus of the Erythrean Sea (first century A. D.), describing the
    coast of the Indian Ocean as far south as the Rufiji, does not show
    any knowledge of Bantu-type poeple living in this region. However,
    a fourth-century compilation of Ptolemy's Geography mentions
    them as "man-eating Ethiopians" (Oliver 1970: 148). At that time,
    the Bantu nucleus had expanded from Katanga along the savanna
    belt from the mouth of the Congo to the south of Tanzania, facing
    Madagascar, where Indonesian colonization had taken place in the
    first five centuries of our era.

        The banana will supply an opportunity for further expansion:
the region of the great lakes and the coast of the Indian Ocean offer
an ideal climate for its cultivation, and during the second half of the
first millennium A. D. , Bantu will spread over these territories. The

expansion toward the northwest and the south of the presently Bantu
territory will, however, occur only in the second millennium A. D. ,
but during this last stage Bantu appears to be already deeply differentiated dialectally.

The Proto-Bantu vocabulary on which Guthrie's study is
based is essentially that of the first and second stages in this diachronic development of the Bantu linguistic territory, i. e. (1) the settling
of the central nucleus by the Proto-Bantus; (2) the expansion along the
savanna belt from the Atlantic to the Indian Ocean. At the second
stage, already a western group and an eastern group are getting progressively more sharply differentiated. At the third stage, at the
time of the expansion from the central area to the great lakes, several
dialectal changes like Dahl's Law start occurring. However, Swahili,
developing from the groups settling at that time along the east coast
of Africa, still appears to be very conservative in its vocabulary. At
the fourth stage, the degree of retention of the Proto-Bantu lexicon
becomes weaker, especially as one moves farther off to the northwest.
Besides, Bantuization has never been complete during stages 3 and 4
and many remnants of former populations survive until nowadays in
the territories newly occupied by the Bantus, whose oral traditional
history often confirms with remarkable accuracy the migrations and
their chronology (Oliver 1970: 150).

The views of Malcolm Guthrie and their confirmation by historians like Roland Oliver (1970) have, however, been considerably
challenged in recent years. The archeologist J. Desmond Clark (1970:
9), indicating that the introduction of the metallurgy of iron in the
Congo basin took place about 0 A. D. , wonders whether or not the
Proto-Bantus had a knowledge of iron working when they migrated:
their movement to Katanga could have been earlier, but by a people
with knowledge of cultivation and water transport. "The archaeological evidence, slight as it is, lends some support to the belief that
iron-working may have been diffused to an already sedentary and
cultivating Proto-Bantu in a somewhat more extended region than
Professor Guthrie's 'nuclear area.'" He also notices that cultivation
of the sorghums and millets was presumably confined to the drier and
more drained areas on the periphery of the Congo Basin, so that it is
unlikely that these plants were carried from the north across the basin
by the ancestors of the Proto-Bantus. "It seems more probable that

these cereals, together with iron, reached the Proto-Bantus at a later date than the initial migration, by the way of the northwestern route, on the one hand, and down the high country east of the forest, on the other" (Clark 1970: 13). This latter route, probably through country free of tsetse, must have favored cattle raising: pastoral stone-using people were occupying the high grassland of the eastern Rift and the Victoria basin in the first millennium B. C. and continuing at least in the first few centuries A. D. Further complexity is added to the archeological problem by the connections between Guthrie's eastern zone of Proto-Bantu and the Dimple Based and Channel Ware (Clark 1970: 15; cf. also Posnansky 1968; Sutton 1971: 159-61): these would imply that the ancestors of the Proto-Bantus settled in Katanga even earlier still.

This hypothesis remains quite disputable. If the ancestors of the Proto-Bantus crossed the equatorial forest, this movement may have stretched over a longer period than M. Guthrie and R. Oliver surmise (Posnansky 1968: 11). If such is the case, the linguistic arguments of J. Greenberg (1972: 193-95), against the archaism of the central area and in favor of the northwest region of the Bantu territory as the original area of differentiation, deserve special attention. As we already pointed out, the solution may be found in a different dichotomy of Proto-Bantu: this is the conclusion reached by Bernd Heine (1973) after a detailed lexicostatistical study of the Bantu languages. According to Heine, there must have been three waves of expansion: the first started from the region between the Benue and the Sanaga, moving partly to the east, across the watershed of the Ubangi-Mbomu-Uele up to the foothills of the East African plateau and Lake Albert (this group included essentially the peoples of the Benge-Baali, Bira and Nyali branches in zones C and D of Guthrie); the bulk of the migrants, however, occupied the territory between central Cameroon and the Ogove (zones A and partly B of Guthrie), but a splinter group seemed to have moved further south to the shores of the Congo River. There they constituted the nucleus of a coherent group from which the second wave will later originate: this migration covered the whole Congo Basin and the highlands of Southwest Africa, including zones H, K, R, and the Lunda branch of zone L of Guthrie, besides the remainder of his zones B and C. Their point of departure would have been the Lower Congo, and one group branching off to the southeast of the equatorial forest would later have become the nucleus from which the third and last migration originated, which took the Bantus from Mount Kenya to the deep south of Africa.

These views contrast, in turn, with those of J. C. Sharman
(1974: 119-20), who believes in a migration from the Cameroon highlands to the east as far as Lake Albert, then southward along the
watersheds, from Semliki to the Rukwa, always essentially in savanna
regions, down to Guthrie's "central nuclear area." This would imply
a relatively early occupation of the northeast, which the percentage
of reflexes of Proto-Bantu terms identified there by Sharman (1974:
125) seems to confirm. The problem of the eastern zone is further
complicated by the possibilities of Sudanic and Cushitic influences
studied by the historian Christian Ehret (1967, 1968, 1972, 1973,
1974) on the basis of lexical comparisons. If his views according to
which the practice of agriculture and of cattle raising was, to a large
extent, borrowed by the Proto-Bantus from the Central Sudanese of
the interlacustrine zone, the whole linguistic prehistory of East Africa
would have to be revised.[2]

By way of conclusion, we may say that Guthrie's work has
undoubtedly opened new fields of research in Proto-Bantu, but by
offering an abundance of lexical data illustrating the culture of the
speakers of Proto-Bantu, he has faced us with new, more complex
problems as to the origin of the Bantus, their oldest migrations and
routes of penetration to their present territories, their level of culture
in prehistory in correlation with the too scanty and incomplete data
available in African archeology.

NOTES

[1] This paper was presented in two preliminary versions at
linguistic meetings: (a) the Proto-Bantu cultural vocabulary was discussed at the 6th International Meeting of Linguists sponsored by the
Istituto Lombardo (Accademia di Scienze e Lettere) and the Sodalizio
Glottologico Milanese, in Milan (Italy), on September 6, 1974; (b) the
recent discussion of Guthrie's views was summarized in a paper read
at the Symposium on Patterns in Language, Culture, and Society: Subsaharan Africa, at the 6th Conference on African Linguistics, in
Columbus, Ohio, on April 11, 1975.
      An extensive French version, with critical apparatus, has
appeared in the Proceedings of the Milan convention (Paleontologia

<u>Linguistica</u>. Atti del VI. Convegno Internazionale di Linguisti.
Brescia: Paideia, 1977, pp. 181-201).
[2] With all due regard for the stimulating pioneering work
done by C. Ehret, one cannot help noticing that the linguistic argumentation is often rather weak: too many semantic changes remain undocumented (e.g. why does P. B. *gànà mean "100," while its assumed
Mangbetu cognate (ka)na means "1"?); too much use is made of
"mobile" prefixes *t- or *k- with "characteristic" vowels; some phonological rules appear to be rather ad hoc; etc.

REFERENCES

Bleek, W. H. I. 1862. A comparative grammar of South African
    languages. Part I. Phonology. London.
_____. 1869. A comparative grammar of South African languages.
    Part II. The concord. Section I. The noun. London.
Bourquin, Walther. 1923. Neue Ur-Bantu-Wortstämme. Berlin:
    Dietrich Reimer (Ernst Vohsen). (Beiheft 5 zur Zeitschrift
    für Eingeborenen-Sprachen.)
Clark, J. Desmond. 1970. African prehistory—opportunities for
    collaboration between archaeologists, ethnographers and
    linguists. In Dalby 1970: 1-19.
Coupez, A. 1954. Etudes sur la langue Luba. Annales du Musée
    Royal du Congo Belge. Sciences de l'Homme. Linguistique,
    vol. 9.
Dalby, David, ed. 1970. Language and history in Africa. New York:
    African Publishing Corp.
Dempwolff, O. 1916-17. Beiträge zur Kenntnis der Sprachen in
    Deutsch-Ostafrika. 9. Ostbantu-Wortstämme. Zeitschrift
    für Kolonial-Sprachen 7: 134-60, 167-92.
de Rop, Albert. 1958. Eléments de phonétique historique du Lomongo.
    Léopoldville: Editions de l'Université (Studia Universitatis
    "Lovanium." Faculté de Philosophie et Lettres, vol. 5.)
Ehret, Christopher. 1967. Cattle-keeping and milking in eastern
    and southern African history: The linguistic evidence. Jour-
    nal of African History 8.1: 1-17.
_____. 1968. Sheep and Central Sudanic peoples in southern Africa.
    Journal of African History 9.2: 213-21.

Ehret, Christopher. 1972. Bantu origins and history: Critique and interpretation. Transafrican Journal of History 2.1: 1-9.

———. 1973. Patterns of Bantu and Central Sudanic settlement in central and southern Africa (ca. 1000 BC-500 AD). Transafrican Journal of History 3.1-2: 1-71.

———. 1974. Agricultural history in central and southern Africa, ca. 1000 BC to ca. 500 AD (mss. to appear in Transafrican Journal of History 4).

Fage, J. D., and R. A. Oliver, eds. 1970. Papers in African History. Cambridge: University Press.

Greenberg, Joseph H. 1963. The languages of Africa. Bloomington: Indiana University, Publication 25 of the Research Center for Anthropology, Folklore and Linguistics.

———. 1972. Linguistic evidence regarding Bantu origins. Journal of African History 13.2: 189-216.

Guthrie, Malcolm. 1967-71. Comparative Bantu. An introduction to the comparative linguistics and prehistory of the Bantu languages. 4 vols. I (1967). The comparative linguistics of the Bantu languages. II (1971). Bantu prehistory, inventory and indexes. III-IV (1970). A catalogue of common Bantu with commentary. Farnborough: Gregg International Publishers.

———. 1970a. Some developments in the prehistory of the Bantu languages. In Fage and Oliver 1970: 131-40. Originally published in Journal of African History 3.2 (1962): 273-82.

Heine, Bernd. 1973. Zur genetischen Gliederung der Bantu-Sprachen. Afrika und Übersee 56.3: 164-85.

Meeussen, A. E. 1969. Bantu lexical reconstructions. Tervuren (xeroxed mss.).

Meinhof, Carl. 1899. Grundriss einer Lautlehre der Bantusprachen. Leipzig.

———. 1910. Grundriss einer Lautlehre der Bantusprachen. Berlin, 2nd ed.

———. 1912. Die Sprachen der Hamiten. Hamburg.

———. 1932. Introduction to the phonology of the Bantu languages. Translated by N. J. v. Warmelo. Berlin: Dietrich Reimer/ Ernst Vohsen.

———. 1936. Die Entstehung der flektierenden Sprachen. Berlin: Dietrich Reimer.

Oliver, Roland. 1970. The problem of Bantu expansion. In Fage
    and Oliver 1970: 141-56. Originally published in Journal of
    African History 7.3 (1966): 361-76.
Portères, Raymond. 1970. Primary cradles of agriculture in the
    African continent. In Fage and Oliver 1970: 43-58. Origin-
    ally published in French as "Berceaux agricoles primaires
    sur le continent africain, " in Journal of African History 3.2
    (1962): 195-210.
Posnansky, Merrick. 1968. Bantu genesis—archaeological reflec-
    tions. Journal of African History 9.1: 1-11.
Sharman, J. C. 1974. Some uses of common Bantu. In Whiteley
    1974: 115-27.
Shinnie, P. L., ed. 1971. The African Iron Age. Oxford: Claren-
    don Press.
Sutton, J. E. G. 1971. The interior of East Africa. In Shinnie 1971:
    142-82.
Whiteley, W. H., ed. 1974. Language in Kenya. Nairobi: Oxford
    University Press.
Wrigley, Christopher. 1970. Speculations on the economic prehis-
    tory of Africa. In Fage and Oliver 1970: 59-73. Originally
    published in Journal of African History 1.2 (1960): 189-204.

17 | Indo-European Culture, with Special Attention to Religion

Pastoralism was the basis of the economy of the Indo-European invaders of Europe. Their first wave and its aftermath, from the middle of the fifth millennium B. C. until about 3700 B. C., appears to have played a decisive role in the way of life of the territories extending from Rumania to the Low Countries (Gimbutas 1977). They were essentially cattle breeders, but they also domesticated sheep, goats, pigs, and dogs. Their technique must have been sufficiently sophisticated to practice castration and, presumably, to use the oxen as draft animals. Though cattle breeding continued to prevail through the centuries, e.g. in the Linear Pottery cultures, there was some fluctuation in the relative importance of the various species involved in animal husbandry, e.g. the flocks of smaller ruminants decreased, while the herds of swine increased in number (Murray 1973: 178–79).

While the cultures of Indo-European origin favored cattle over any other domestic animal, other cultures of the fourth and third millennia B. C. concentrated on the swine (for example, the coastal culture of southern Sweden about 2400–2200 B. C.), or on ovicaprid breeding (for example, the Dimini culture in Greece)—but prevalence of the smaller ruminants also occurs in some Indo-European cultures like the Baden culture in Hungary (end of the fourth millennium B. C.), though the bovine continues to play a prominent part in their ritual practices, as is shown by some carefully buried skeletons. It is interesting to note that such changes are unparalleled by the change in the size of cattle; as Bökönyi (1974: 117–18) pointed out, at the end of the Copper Age and the beginning of the Bronze Age, the size of cattle had diminished so markedly that "perhaps with the Baden culture, a great number of dwarf cattle had reached Central Europe."

By the end of the Neolithic period, cattle no longer served exclusively to provide meat—very little was obtained by hunting game, as appears from the scanty remains of bones of wild animals. Now, the cows were milked (from the rear, like goats).

These facts shed a particular light on the Indo-European lexicon covering animal names: the 'bovine' shows a common term *g^wou-, attested in Indo-Iranian, Greek, Latin, Germanic, and Celtic, and represented in Slavic *govedo 'head of cattle'; similarly, there is a generic word for 'sheep,' *owi-, represented by cognates in Old Indic, Greek, Latin, Old Irish, Baltic, and Slavic, and meaning 'ewe' in Germanic, and a number of languages show old correspondences for 'lamb.' In both cases, technical terms associated with animal husbandry are also found: 'to milk' represented by a verbal theme, *(H)melĝ-, shared by Greek, Latin, Germanic, Celtic, and Slavic, and 'wool,' found already in the Hittite (hulana-) and preserved in Indo-Iranian, Greek, Latin, Celtic, Germanic, Balto-Slavic. Furthermore, there is a generic term for the porcine, *sū-, but it must originally have designated the wild pig, as it still does in Indo-Iranian. Another term has equal claim to IE origin, *porko-, which must have meant 'young pig,' and denoted the domestic variety. It is also found in the oriental part of the Indo-European area, proving that domestication was originally practiced everywhere, but abandoned at an early date in India and Iran (Benveniste 1973: 23-31). It is, therefore, all the more astonishing that no generic word for 'goat' is to be found. The goat is the earliest ruminant to have been domesticated. It spread in Europe before the coming of the Indo-Europeans. Two types prevail: the scimitar-horned goats and the twisted-horn goats, but none of the limited lexical correspondences point to any of their features: Gk. aíks, Arm. aic, Av. izaēna (adj.) 'of [goat's] skin' is derived from a root indicating its movement, just as Goth. gaits 'goat': Latin haedus 'kid,' usually compared with Lith. žáidžiu, žáisti 'play' < originally 'jump, gambol,' and Skt. aja-: Lith. ažys, possibly from the root *aĝ- 'drive'; OHG ziga (Ger. Ziege): Gk. díza [: aíks, Lákōnes] (Hesychius), Arm. tik 'leather bag' is isolated. Obviously, the Indo-Europeans did not have a common term for the 'goat,' or perhaps they eliminated it as a consequence of some ecological change: at an early stage of colonization, the goat as destroyer of woods may have been useful, but once open wastelands had been created by impoverishment

of the soil through primitive agricultural practice, the sheep, as a
grass feeder, definitely proved more valuable (Zeuner 1963: 145-46).

Unfortunately, the counts of bones provided by archeologists
do not distinguish between sheep and goats and simply contrast the
ovicaprid with the bovine elements in the herds; from these data, it
appears that in the third millennium there were two coexisting and
partly overlapping animal husbandry activities prevailing in Europe—
cultures keeping flocks of sheep, which traded copper implements and
ornaments with the Near East and Caucasus areas, and cultures concentrating on cattle breeding, with characteristic pottery styles and
metal objects produced locally from their own ores (Murray 1970: 111).
Nevertheless, however valuable these data may be, and in spite of the
problems they raise regarding definite cultures, e.g. in Switzerland,
in the Middle and Lower Danube areas, and in the Ukraine, they do not
throw any light on the linguistic question.

The instrument of Indo-European mobility and a major asset
to their conquering power is undoubtedly the horse. Apparently the
oldest appearance of the domesticated horse is to be located in the
southern Ukraine—originally dated around 3000 B.C. (Bökönyi 1973:
238), it is now assigned to an earlier period, between 4400 and 3400
B.C., which coincides with the first invasion wave of Indo-European
steppe pastoralists toward Europe (Gimbutas 1977: 284). That the
horse was, with the dog, man's closest companion on these moves
appears both from the archeological finds and from the lexicon: both
*eḱwo- 'horse' and *ḱwōn-/ḱun- 'dog' are represented in all the major
IE dialects, though their reflexes, such as Gk. híppos or Lat. canis,
may sometimes present us with rather puzzling phonological problems.
It is striking that, though the major implement used for horse riding
—namely, antler-cheek pieces with the attached bridle—is found in
the earliest Indo-European settlements (Gimbutas 1977: 281-82), no
corresponding common lexical item has come down to us.[1] Neither
is there a common Indo-European term for 'riding a horse,' though
'riding a vehicle' is expressed by *weǵh-, documented in all the major
Indo-European languages, also as the root for the common term for
a wheeled vehicle. Cartwrights are presumably among the oldest
craftsmen among Indo-Europeans, and their technical terminology
goes back to the older periods of the speech community: words for
'wheel,' *kʷelo-s/*kʷolo-s, reduplicated *kʷekʷlos and *retH-, both

Table 1. Indo-European Words for 'Wheel'

		Baltic			Toch. B. *kokale* A. *kukäl*
Gmc.	OE *hwēol*	OPruss. *kelan*	OCS *kolo*		
	OHG *rad*	Lith. *ratas*			
Celtic	OIr. *roth*		Greek *kúklos*	Avest. *čaxra-*	: *raθa-* ('chariot')
Latin	*rota*			Skt. *cakra-*	: *ratha-* ('chariot')

from verbal roots indicating motion, and both very old, as evidenced
by their areal distribution (see Table 1); 'axle' (*aks-), 'yoke' (*yugom),
etc. (Devoto 1962: 236-37, 269-70). The problem, however, is what
kind of vehicles are we talking about during the earliest Indo-European
migratory movements? No doubt the first carts were drawn by cattle,
but these were soon replaced by horses (Bökönyi 1974:249). The four-
wheeled cart seems to have been the earliest vehicle: did it appear
with the first Indo-Europeans or only at the turn of the third and second
millennia B. C., followed by its variant with spoked wheels a few centuries later?[2] The latter dating is usually correlated with the first
occurrence of the four-wheeled vehicle in the Uruk culture of Mesopotamia around the middle of the fourth millennium B. C. Military use
is only documented since the twenty-eighth century B. C., and it will
take until the fifteenth century B. C. before the Mitanni charioteers on
fast chariots with two spoked wheels revolutionized the tactics of combat in the Middle East (Kammenhuber 1961: 9-14). That this new instrument of victory was introduced by the Aryan aristocracy of Mitanni
in Mesopotamia is most significant, for the improvement of the chariot appears to be an Indo-European achievement in the early Bronze
Age, as is confirmed by Mycenaean data. This late date explains the
absence of a common term for 'felly' or 'spoke,' for example, though
the correspondence between Gk. [w]ītus and Latin vitus points to the
use of the wood of the willow for the rim of the spoked wheel. All
these facts would tend to show that the horse was first used for riding
and only later for drawing carts, but one question remains to be clarified: how to account for the common Indo-European terminology if
the cartwright's trade postdates the first migrations by more than a
millennium?

        In order to appreciate the way of life of early Indo-European
cultures in Europe, it is also interesting to assess the relative importance of hunting in their daily diet; bone finds provide valuable data
which show considerable variation as to the percentage of game versus
meat of domesticated animals consumed by these populations. Thus,
in the fourth millennium B. C., the Baden culture in Hungary shows
93. 2 percent of bones of domestic animals versus 6. 8 percent of bones
of game, mainly deer, but also aurochs and wild boar (Murray 1970:
363), whereas the older Altheim culture in Germany shows a considerable fluctuation depending on the sites:

Bones of animals	Domestic	Wild
Altheim	92.9	7.1
Altenerdingen	81.5	18.5
Pasternacker	51.7	48.3
Pölling	approx. 27.5	approx. 72.5

It stands to reason that in cases like this the ecology of the environment must be greatly responsible for the discrepancies. The main wild animals involved are the red deer, to a lesser degree the wild pig and the bear—which is in keeping with the lexical data where the dialects of IE show two terms for 'deer,' one (Gk. élaphos, Lith. élnis, OCS jelenĭ, W elain 'doe,' Eng. elk, Arm. ełn 'doe') presumably from a root denoting the reddish color, and the other (Lat. cervus, W carw, OE heorot, OPruss. sirwis) connected with the term for 'horn.' The bear must also have a common IE name, but it was tabuized at an early date—hence, the Germanic and Slavic substitutes for the correspondents of Skt. ŕksa-, Arm. arj, Gk. árktos, Lat. ursus, OIr. art, and presumably Hitt. hartagga-. Striking is the practical absence of bird remains, as the goose and the duck—for which the major Indo-European languages show a common term—were apparently hunted from time immemorial. On the other hand, one site contains the bones of at least ten beavers, representing 6.8 percent of the total number of animals consumed there—the familiarity of early IE with the animal being confirmed by the correspondence: Avest. bawri- : Lat. fīber : Corn. befer : OHG bibar : Lith. bēbrus : OCS bebrŭ. Unfortunately, such data are not available for another important activity in the economy of the early IE cultures, namely beekeeping. Although the PIE term for 'bee' is not known (the root *bhī- shared by Germanic, Celtic, and Balto-Slavic is presumably onomatopoeic), the occurrence of *melit- for 'honey' in Greek, Latin, Celtic, Germanic, Armenian, Albanian, besides the use of *medhu- 'mead'—the name of the intoxicating drink made from it—for 'honey' in Balto-Slavic, guarantees that apiculture was part of the IE heritage. Acquaintance with the habits of the bees is documented since the end of the Neolithic—"it was not domestication, but simple exploitation of the guests by the host species," as Zeuner (1963: 496) points out. Finding the bees was not a problem; their natural habitat stretched over most of the South Russian steppe to the greater part of Europe.

But if such were the main sources of food for these originally nomadic peoples of the steppe, what was their social organization? What were their beliefs?

Indo-European society, as far as we can judge, was agnatic and ethnocentric, its basic unit being the patriarchal, patrilinear, and essentially patrilocal extended family. Kindred was the foundation of its concentric structure, grouping the families in clans, claiming descent from a common ancestor, and the clans in tribes, presumably deriving their origin from some eponymous founder. Ethnic solidarity became especially manifest in contrast with outsiders—whether the Vedic term arí, which has been the object of such vehement polemic regarding its basic meaning,[3] expresses this awareness of an ethnic community, recognizing the same ancestry and practicing the same cults, is a moot question. The main point is the emphasis on the contrast inside versus outside which prevails at each level of the social structure and conditions human relations. Inside his group, with his kith and kin, the Indo-European is safe; outside lurk the dangers. Inside his family, his clan, his tribe, he enjoys all the rights and privileges that pertain to free members of the community: 'to be free' is indeed to be one of the group, as the first element of Slavic svoboda 'freedom' and Skt. svādhīna 'free' indicates. These terms and other derivations from the reflexive pronoun stem *swe- point to the status of the individual in the society: born in his proper social context, he will grow up into a free adult, receiving the love and affection people give to their own, as is evidenced by the Germanic term for 'free,' related with Skt. priyá- 'loved,' and the Greek eleútheros and Latin līber 'free,' from the IE verbal stem *(H$_1$)lewdh- 'to grow,' which also yielded Lat. līberī 'children' and OCS ljudŭ, OHG liut 'people,' as well as the name of the god of growth and fertility, Latin Līber and (maybe) ON Lóðurr (Polomé 1969: 287-90; 1972: 66-67; Benveniste 1973: 262-72). The symbolism of the door, the persistence of the ritual separation of inside and outside in the sacralization of places, like sanctuaries, or later, cities, tend to show how this contrast pervades the conceptual world of the Indo-European and gives some validity to the view of Jost Trier (1942): "Am Anfang steht der Zaun. Tief und begriffsbestimmend durchwirken Zaune, Hegung, Grenze die von Menschen geformte Welt." Nowhere is this more obvious than in the field of the sacred, where the dichotomy involved placing out of bounds to human beings whatever was consecrated to the deity. In another context, the <u>ambiguous attitude toward outsiders</u> led the Indo-Europeans to treat them either as <u>enemies</u>, reduced to a state of servitude or, mostly in individual cases, to grant them most generously their <u>hospitality</u>—often a lasting pledge passed on to the following generation.

But if we consider the vertical structure of society, a question arises: was there a <u>hierarchy of social levels</u> in the original Indo-European society? Or did those families of pastoralists live more or less independently from each other, each clan respecting the grazing land of the other and the heads of the clan meeting only in case of emergency? Was there a clan of priests in charge of their religious activities, or were there only shaman-medicinemen, seers, or the like, to respond to their daily needs, in case of illness or death of people or cattle, to provide guidance in important decisions, to ward off ill-fortune, etc.? Undoubtedly, there is strong evidence that historical Indo-European peoples had a tripartite social organization, described by Emile Benveniste and Georges Dumézil as consisting essentially of three functional classes: (1) the priests, in charge of the religious traditions of the community and entrusted with the performance of its rituals; (2) the warriors from among whom the "king" would usually emerge; (3) the clansmen—the pastoralists concerned with their living.[4]

One can, however, wonder whether such a neat discrimination between social levels already existed among the early Indo-Europeans of the fourth and third millennia B. C. It is, to say the least, astonishing that the Germanic tribes, for example, as they are described by the earliest sources, appear to have a rather egalitarian society, in which the leading men seem to be the clan elders whose council practically runs the show with the backing of the assembly of all the free adult males able to carry arms. As for religious activities, no mention is made of priests, but several of the sacred and magical functions are discharged by "holy women." Thus, in the tripartite system, the first function would be represented by these <u>seeresses</u>, whereas the <u>warrior</u> class would contain practically the <u>whole adult male population</u>; and the <u>aged</u>, the <u>women</u> and <u>children</u> would constitute the <u>third</u> group, working in the communal fields and tending the herds. It stands to reason that this cannot represent a genuine social hierarchy—but it could be objected that this reflects a special

development of Germanic society owing to the danger of living close
to aggressive neighbors and the need to be constantly ready for combat.
True—but, then, why does the type of society claimed for the Indo-
European society develop in the same area after the same Germanic
tribes have convinced the Romans of the futility of conquering their
land and both have lived peacefully as neighbors for about a century?[5]

At any rate, even in the societies where the tripartite organization was well established from the earliest times on, the class status
was not hereditary and there was no restriction on intermarriage, as
several examples from Vedic times indicate (Altekar 1958: 226). Moreover, even later, there was room for upward mobility within the framework of the three-generational unity of the lineage evidenced by the Germanic and Celtic kindred systems (Pearson 1973: 159-60). Obviously,
any societal framework is open for adaptation to changed conditions:
with the urbanization of society and the development of new trades, some
IE cultures added a fourth class to their social hierarchy to include all
the artisans—hence, Avestan hūiti 'occupation, craft' and Gk. dēmiour-
goí 'artisans.' Elsewhere, the fourth estate applied to people of the
lowest category, originally non-Aryans, excluded from participation
in the rituals, like the ancient Indian śūdrás. On the other hand, if the
third functional class covers essentially the producers who ensure the
survival of the society, the craftsmen can easily be included as a subgroup, just as the agriculturists have their place beside the original
pastoralists in the same estate.

The beliefs of early Indo-European society are difficult to
assess, let alone retrieve. Undoubtedly, the ecology of their steppe
environment must have influenced them. Their pastoral economy, and
the problems and conflicts linked with it, were certainly reflected in
their earliest myths, as recent research by Bruce Lincoln (1975, 1976,
1981) has confirmed. The dichotomy of the "holy" along the lines indicated by Rudolf Otto (1917) is definitely inherent to the terminology of
the "sacred" analyzed by Baetke (1942), Benveniste (1973: 445-69),
and others; "divination," the interpretation of signs and omens, must
have been common practice since time immemorial, as may have been
some ritual procedures of sympathetic magic like invultuation or hoo-
doo. But more important is the problem of the Indo-European concept
of the "supernatural." How did they visualize their gods? Were they
really merely personified social processes, as Meillet (1907) would

have when he brilliantly analyzed the Vedic god Mitra as the divine
symbol of the contractual agreements that are basic to all human relations—friendship, hospitality, marriage, etc.?[6] Are the gods the
embodiment of the essential social functions? Does the internal struc-
turation of the pantheon reflect the ideal human society in grandiose
Durkheimian terms? Or is the idea of "god" connected with celestial
sacrality—with light and "transcendence," as the etymological link
*dyeus 'god (as celestial sovereign and spouse of Mother Earth)':
*deywos 'god'/'divine': Latin diēs '(light of) day' would suggest? Un-
doubtedly, celestial and atmospheric gods abound in the pantheon of
the Indo-European peoples whether they be connected with the thunder
or the wind or designate the sun, for example. Or is the universe
full of magical forces, perhaps more powerful than the gods—impersonal powers that can adhere to any being or object, can be trans-
ferred and may prove either useful or dangerous, like the Melanesian
mana?

It is doubtful that the nomadic Indo-European pastoralists
developed much of a structured agricultural activity in which the regular rhythm of the seasons would have given rise to the development of
the calendrical rites characteristic of organized religions with a specialized priestly caste (Titiev 1972). In a society like theirs, critical
rites would be essential to counteract the personal emergencies,
though, occasionally, the community as a whole might be affected,
e.g. when a prolonged drought threatened the survival of their herds.
The rituals performed under such circumstances would rather be the
special function of seers, medicine men, diviners, and such, than of
a priestly hierarchy, though they may have included some "specialists"
like rainmakers. But on the whole, their performance would be closer
to what is traditionally labeled magic. Does that mean that we should
follow those who see "magical potency" at work in the cosmos?

To be sure, it is attractive to project into Indo-European
such Vedic concepts as asu, rta, and māyā. The "numinous" is in-
trinsically nameless and formless, residing in an invisible sphere;
only its influence is felt to exist. By its own will, it projects itself
into a sphere visible to Vedic man, where deities will perform their
creative act. These deities (Asuras) are "charged with vital energy"
(asu) and endowed with creative power (māyā) (Srinivasan 1975: 141).
Because of māyā, one of them wields sovereign power over the uni-

verse (Varuna), where he "enforces and upholds a self-operating cosmic power (ṛta), which establishes, governs, and directs physical norms in worldly, human and ritual activities, causing these to appear as right and true." Dandekar, one of the main propounders of this view, shared to a large extent by Jan Gonda (1960: 75-81), even goes so far as to claim that asu is the "primary and most basic religious concept of the early Vedic period," and he describes it as "a somatic magic potence [that] permeated through nature and the human world and thereby constituted the essential basis of their existence and functioning." Obviously, he identifies it with mana, when he adds: "The concept of an all-pervading somatic magic potence such as this is ... common to the religious ideologies of many primitive peoples" (1971: 287). But Vedic asu as 'vital energy,' just as Sumerian me (the impersonal, immanent 'divine power' of the earliest Mesopotamian religion), never occurs quite independently from personalized deities, so that if there is at all a power involved in Indo-European religion that is axiomatic to all that is supernatural, it should not be conceived as impersonal, but as depersonalized. It is, however, quite possible that "creative power" is no more than one of the attributes shared by a number of gods with a number of functional restrictions specifying their respective role in the creative act. Thus, after the searching analyses of Gonda (1972: 27-28; 1974: 197), Minard (1956: par. 809b), and Renou (1956: 58; 1961: 4), it seems fairly well established that dakṣa reflects Varuṇa's 'creative energy' and kratu, Mitra's 'power of deliberation'—Mitra conceptualizes, Varuṇa gives shape.

If, then, we are to consider that the Indo-Europeans had personalized gods, it is important to determine, as Mircea Eliade (1978: 188-89) pointed out, to what extent "pastoral nomadism, vigorously reorganized for war and conquest, encouraged and facilitated the emergence of specific religious values." This task is made difficult by the fact that in their migrations and expansion, the Indo-Europeans constantly came in contact with sedentary agricultural populations, which they subjugated and "absorbed" into their social structure, but this symbiosis must have created from the very earliest days the kind of tensions between heterogeneous and often antithetical orientations that Georges Dumézil (1970a: 65-76; 1973: 7-16, 20-25) has illustrated in his comments on the Sabine War and the parallel conflict opposing the Æsir and the Vanir in Scandinavian mythology: on the one hand, a powerful leader and heroic fighters, who prevail through potent

magic when sheer physical strength fails; on the other hand, wealthy
agriculturists, who do not hesitate to use the lure of gold to corrupt
their adversary, but are ultimately willing to compromise, so that
from the merger of the two originally disparate elements a complete,
viable, unified society results.

What was the situation prior to that "merger"? It has long
been assumed that their oldest religious concepts were associated
with nature and the cosmos—the supreme god being Father Sky (Vedic
Dyaus pitā, Gk. Zeús patēr, Lat. Juppiter, etc.), whose main functions were sovereignty and creativity, the latter being manifested both
in the cosmogony and his paternity in divine and human genealogies.
As Eliade (1963: 82-86) has shown, sky gods seldom maintain their
cardinal role beyond the initial creative act, and often they yield their
place to storm gods. It stands to reason that in the ecological milieu
of the steppe where a long spell of dry weather can be disastrous for
the grazing lands and endanger the cattle and horses, a deity controlling the thunder and unleashing the rains can be of prime importance,
as it was for the Semites who invaded the fertile Sumerian alluvial
irrigation lands of the south from semi-arid steppes in the northwest.
Symbolically, the widespread mythological theme of the battle of the
storm or thunder god with the monster that "imprisoned" the waters
undoubtedly alludes to this ecological reality, but it would be simplis-
tic to confine it to this naturalistic interpretation. As Norman Brown,
in particular, has indicated (1978: 31-32, 40-42), the myth has cosmogonic significance, marking the triumph of life over sterility and
death—in particular, in the case of Indra and Vrtra. Indra puts an end
to inertia and transforms the "virtuality" of the world fashioned by
Tvastr into the actuality of the cosmos. In other words, to quote Eliade
(1978: 207): "The world and life could not come to birth except by the
slaying of an amorphous Being. "

But, reverting to the original Indo-European religion, a number of important elements need to be considered, such as the prominent role held by the sun in prehistoric and protohistoric belief among
the Indo-Europeans, though the Sun god seems to recede to a secondary
position later on. Here again, an archaic society like the Germanic
world could be mentioned with Caesar's reference to the sun cult and
archeological finds such as the sun chariot of Trundholm and the numerous Scandinavian rock engravings of the sun disk in the Bronze Age

(Gelling and Ellis Davidson 1972: 9-26, 140-45), contrasted with the total absence of reference to its cult in later Roman writers like Tacitus and the very episodic role played by Sunna in the Germanic tradition. Another cosmic hierophany would be the wind of the steppes, represented by the Indo-Iranian deity Vāyu, in which some want to see an incarnation of brutal violence, acting readily on its own, whereas its appearance in certain contexts rather suggests an "initial" god, like Janus or, to some degree, Heimdall (Dumézil 1970b: 59, 90, 139; 1973: 126-30). With supernatural beings whose mythology is limited to one Indo-European subgroup and partly of ambiguous interpretation, it is hardly possible to extrapolate anything valid into Indo-European. As for the fire, it seems that its domestic cult was already quite significant in early Indo-European times; it was believed to have been kindled by lightning and regarded, therefore, as of celestial origin. In Vedic, the god Agni is the embodiment of the sacrality of the fire, but that does not restrict his cosmic affinities and ritual activities. Just as his Iranian counterpart, Atar, is the son of Ahura Mazdā, Agni has Dyaus for a father; "born" in the sky, he descends in the form of lightning, but he is also in the waters—he is called āpam garbhah 'embryo of the Waters' and invoked as springing from the womb of the Waters (Eliade 1978: 208-9). On the other hand, he is also involved in an archaic cosmological idea, conceptualizing creation as the union of an igneous element (fire, heat, and human sperm) with the aquatic principle (the "waters," seat of all "virtualities")—an idea which will ultimately be elaborated in the speculations about the Golden Embryo (Hiranyagarbha). Nevertheless, he has no important mythology, but he is omnipresent in religious life; Agni is indeed the "messenger" through whom the offerings reach the gods. Therefore, he is the archetypal priest, but he is also grhaspatih 'the master of the home,' which indicates the prominent role he must have played from the very beginning. He keeps out the evil spirits, drives away sickness, protects against witchcraft—in a word, people are closer to him than to any other god, and they invoke him with full confidence. Again, of course, it remains rather speculative to assume that such a situation already obtained in early Indo-European times, but the striking correspondences between the implicit Roman theory of fires clarified by Dunézil (1970a: 311-22) and the explicit Indian theory demonstrate the survival of Indo-European traditions. Again, a far echo comes from the Germanic world. Besides the two great celestial luminaries, the Germanic people, according to Caesar, worship Volcanus, i.e. the fire, and for centuries, they continued to kindle the New Fire at the winter solstice (de Vries 1956: 360-61, 462); just as in Rome, the perpetual fire was put out and solemnly rekindled once a year, on March 1.

The Indo-Europeans must have elaborated an extensive mythology; their tradition was transmitted orally, and after some of them acquired the skill of writing, a taboo was maintained against putting down in writing their religious lore. Their gods were close to them, though their attitude toward them was ambivalent, characterized by (1) awe, and (2) trust, tinged with a certain familiarity. The religious fear was inspired by their holiness, and the reserved attitude of the Indo-Europeans was translated in their piety by a set of interdictions. As the gods were, however, accessible and interested in human affairs, the Indo-Europeans respected them for it, while giving them their full confidence, showing their feelings of trust and admiration for their deities in their prayers, their offerings, and their entire cult. The cult was celebrated in consecrated enclosures, in the open—a technique developed at an early date by the Indo-Europeans seems to be the sacralization of space, for which they may have had special rituals. They did not build sanctuaries and made their offerings in the fire, a fact illustrated by the lexical correspondence: Hitt. hašša- 'hearth, fireplace': Lat. āra (Olat. āsa) 'altar': Skt. ā́sa 'ash(es)'; etc.

The Indo-European lexicon contains a number of archaic correspondences which reflect the old religious vocabulary. They include such terms as Hitt. mald- 'recite invocations': Lith. meldžiu, melsti 'pray' (: OHG meldōn 'announce, reveal'); Hitt. šaklaiš 'rite, custom': Lat. sacer; Hitt. talliia- 'solemnly call upon the gods': ON þulr 'Kultredner'; etc. (Polomé 1975: 660-62)—or designations for the "libation" (Skt. juhoti 'offers sacrifice': Gmc. term for 'god' < *ǵhu-tó-m 'to whom libations are poured'; Hitt. šipant-, Gk. spondḗ 'libation': Lat. spondeō), the "ritual feast," the "sacrifice," the "prayer," etc. Particularly important is the act of speech, not only because of solemn verbal engagements (= 'vow,' linked with the root *wegʷh-, found in Lat. uoueo, Gk. eúkhesthai, etc.), but also as creative act, which may account for the glorification of the entity Vā́c 'speech' in RV 10.125 as "the common foundation of all reality" (Dumézil 1970a: 392). The root *ḱens- illustrates the ambivalence of speech and its power as an efficient but also scathing weapon, e.g. for the priest in a society where authority is still insufficiently established and people are more restless:

praise, extolling their heroic deeds, enhances the prestige of the chiefs
and the power of the gods; criticism can lash out at undeserved fame
and bring down to size tyrannical usurpers or crush despicable arro-
gants. Such a society was disappearing in India (which accounts for the
limited derogatory use of the Skt. śams-), but it was undoubtedly still
a prevailing type in the Celtic world where kings feared satirists (Dumézil 1969: 103-8; Benveniste 1973: 416-20).

The most important problem in connection with Indo-European
religion is, however, the validity of the Dumézilian hypothesis of the
trifunctional religious ideology for the earliest period, as a reflex in
the world of the divine of the fundamental structure of the nomadic pastoral society. The problem is complex and fraught with controversial
issues, but if we consider the fragmented and heterogeneous heritage
of the Vedic Indians, of ancient Rome, and of medieval Scandinavia and
Ireland, and the scattered elements provided by archeology, votive
inscriptions, runic formulae, onomastics, reports of ancient authors
and early Christian missionaries, capitularia of Charlemagne, epic
poetry and medieval historiography, and what not, it is undeniable that
a set of striking correspondences emerges in which myths preserved
in the Rigveda will find parallels in the legendary history of the kings
of Rome as reported by Livy and in Scandinavian mythography in the
collection compiled by Snorri Sturluson, as well as in some passages
of the Irish epics. And, more important still, these traditions will be
organized around a tripartite structure of the pantheon and of the corresponding society, the three social divisions—priests, warriors, and
cattle breeders and agriculturists—corresponding to the three functional
levels of the religious ideology—magical and juridical sovereignty; physical and martial force; fertility, health, and economic prosperity. With
all its consistency, the system shows a definite flexibility, allowing
for shifts and expansions according to local contingencies. Thus, the
couple of sovereign gods Mitra-Varuṇa will be completed by associated
deities like Aryaman and personified concepts such as Bhaga 'allotted
fate,' Aṃśa 'share,' Dakṣa 'creative energy,' which will specialize in
certain aspects of the first function such as preserving the cohesive
unity of the Aryan community and ensuring its continuity, parceling out
the goods, etc. (Dumézil 1977: 86-114). On the other hand, in Scandinavia, the magical sovereign Óðinn will become essentially involved with
war and the nobility—the jarls—on the second function level, while the
fighting champion of the Æsir, Þórr, will, as thunder god, control the

fertility of the lands and become very close to the lower class—the
karls. However, the preservation of the tripartite scheme—illustrated,
for example, by the theme of the "three sins of the warrior" in the
Indian, Iranian, Greek, and Scandinavian traditions (Dumézil 1970b:
65-104)—indicated that the general structure of the trifunctional ideology must have been elaborated prior to the dispersal of the Indo-Europeans. This does not imply that it covers all the religious thought
and speculation peculiar to the Indo-Europeans, nor that the complexity of religious practices and conceptions linked with the tripartite
ideology had developed beyond the incipient stage. It stands to reason
that when we compare Latin iūs with Avestan yaoz̆-dā and Vedic śám
yóh we can immediately measure the particular contribution of each
society to the elaboration of the concept. Rome is a city of laws, and
iūs defines the maximal area of action or claim resulting from the
nature or conventional status of an individual or group; it is mutatis
mutandis for the organization of society what Vedic r̥ta is for the cosmos: the observance of rules contrasted with chaos. Rome establishes juridical ethics contrasting with the "frenzy" of the Barbarians,
but they do not acquire a religious value. On the contrary, the Indo-
Iranian world, stressing the religious consciousness of man, uses
*yaus̆- with a double polarity: (1) it maximizes a state (to be reached
from a given state—whether mystico-ritual or physico-material)—
hence, Avest. yaoz̆-dā in the meaning 'sanctify'; (2) it brings back to
normal, "restores" what is in an impure or diseased state—hence,
Avest. yaoz̆-dā 'restore ritually, purity,' Ved. śám yóh associated
with healing (Benveniste 1973: 389-96; Dumézil 1969: 31-45). The
study of key words like Latin fās, fetialis versus Vedic dhā́tu, Latin
augur, augustus versus Vedic ójas, etc. provides additional illustration of this further elaboration of the basic ethico-religious concepts
of the Indo-Europeans within the sociocultural framework of the new
societies they had shaped (Dumézil 1969: 61-102; Benveniste 1973:
407-15, 420-23).

    Actually, it seems to me that the absorption of the sedentary
agricultural populations of the conquered territories was a major factor in triggering the transformation of Indo-European societies. Obviously, their pastoral society could not coexist in complete independence side by side with the cultivators, and their economy and religion
were bound to affect their mode of living and thinking in the new symbiosis. In the stabilized society, the tripartite system jelled into a

hierarchized community in which a priesthood became the guardian of
the ethnic heritage and a ruler emerged from the warrior group, while
farming combined cattle and horse breeding with cultivation of grains
and vegetables. Celtic society provides a good example of such an
organization up to historical times. All through the Indo-European
tradition, there are reminders of the major difficulty encountered in
establishing an integrated society. Besides the Sabine War and the
struggle between the Æsir and Vanir, one could mention the fact that
the Nāsatyas were at first challenged by the other gods, because they
had "mingled with men." They were even momentarily denied participation in the sacrifice ritual which was exclusively reserved for the
Aryans—a fact that gains particular significance in the light of their
occasional mention in later literature as belonging to the śūdras, the
very lowest level in the hierarchy, practically outside the organized
Aryan society.

As attractive as this hypothesis may be, it is, however, fraught
with problems: if the tripartite system became fully operative when
symbiosis with agriculturists acted as a catalyst on the incipient ideology of the Indo-European pastoralists, why is it that the Mitanni Aryans show a completely developed trifunctional pantheon in the fourteenth
century B.C. in Asia Minor, with gods like Mitra, Varuṇa, Indra, and
the twin Nāsatyas? It must then be assumed that the development had
already taken place in the staging area of the Indo-Iranian invasions,
which only complicates the problem since we do not agree on the location of this area, or on the kind of socioeconomic situation that prevailed there! On the other hand, how do we account for the Germanic
situation, unless we admit that Caesar was "misinformed" and that
Tacitus' Mercurius = Wōðanaz, Mars = Tiwaz, Hercules = *Þunraz,
were already valid in the days of Ariovistus—disregarding the profound
transformation of Germanic sociocultural and politico-economic life
brought about by the Germanic wars of the reign of Augustus and intense
trading and other contacts for more than a century along the Rhine-
Danube limes.

Also, the fate of the Indo-European ideology in Anatolia remains puzzling if it predated the Indo-European moves toward this
area, since nothing reminds us of the trifunctional pattern in the traditions of the Luwians, Hittites, and other Indo-Europeans of the Old
Kingdom, which, otherwise, preserved quite a few archaic Indo-European features in its organization and in its language.

Anyhow, whatever the chronology of its elaboration, the tripartite ideology is definitely subjacent to a considerable number of myths and rituals in the Indo-Iranian, ancient Roman, Germanic, and Celtic world, and its prevalence is clearly evidenced by the ouster or radical transformation of such archaic Indo-European religious concepts as the sky god as creator, sovereign, and father: in India, Dyaus pitā has been driven out by Varuṇa, who appears to be threatened by the rising glory of Indra in the Veda. In Rome, Juppiter has considerably widened his dominion, becoming the symbol of the power and the mission of conquest of Rome. In the Germanic world, *Tīwaz appears as (a) the equivalent of the Roman god Mars (hence, the survival of his name in Tuesday); and (b) the protector of the assembly of the people in arms, the þing (hence, Ger. Dienstag); and (c) a tribal god of the Saxons, also represented by a huge column, symbolizing the axis mundi, propping up the sky (de Vries 1957: 10-26). Nevertheless, it is important to keep the whole matter in perspective. The trifunctional hierarchization of society and the corresponding tripartite ideology are only part of the total picture. They have to be viewed diachronically as part of a dynamic process of development: the staggered establishment of specific institutions keeps pace with the growing complexity in social organization and the stages of social evolution. In the older pastoral society, we rather expect unranked descent groups. As the community grows and diversifies, the extended family "swarms" for economic reasons; moving to establish new settlements leads to profound social changes with ranked descent groups and full-time craft specialization (Pfeiffer 1977: 103). Therefore, in my opinion, the tripartite ideology is more recent than some of the purely pastoralist traditions that comparative mythology has been retrieving. It originated as the Indo-European community started breaking up—maybe after the departure of the Proto-Anatolians?

Postscript

After completing this study, O. Szemerényi pointed out to me regarding my paper "The Gods of the Indo-Europeans," The Mankind Quarterly 21.1 (Winter 1980): 151-64, that he had suggested new interpretations for a series of terms discussed here in his monograph Studies in the Kinship Terminology of the Indo-European Languages,

with special references to Indian, Iranian, Greek and Latin, in Acta
Iranica, vol. 16, Varia (Leyden: E. J. Brill, 1977), pp. 1-240.

    Particularly important with regard to our discussion are the
new etymologies proposed for the terms for 'free': IE *priyo- (reflected by Goth. freis, OHG frī, etc.) originally designated 'people
belonging to the same household' (as Ernst Risch suggested [Museum
Helveticum 22 (1965):194, fn. 4], the term was a derivative from
*per- 'house'; Szemerényi 1977: 122-24). The IE reflexive *swe/o-,
contained in Slavic svoboda 'freedom,' is considered by Szemerényi
(1977: 43-46) as a thematic adjective derived from *su-, possibly the
earliest expression for 'joint family, clan,' so that it would originally
designate 'people of the same ilk.' As for Gk. eleútheros: Lat. līber,
Szemerényi (1977: 109-11) believes they should be separated as Venetic
(Cadore) Loudera proves that Lat. līber has to be traced back to *loud-
heros, denoting a member of the 'people, nation,' and as such free-born,
whereas Gk. eleútheros (Mycenaean ereutero) is to be compared with
Hitt. arawa- 'free of impost.' However, Szemerényi becomes more
difficult to follow when he assumes that (a) Mycenaean ereutera was
borrowed from the more advanced Anatolian area via the Hittite abstract arawatar 'freedom of impost' (1977: 116); and (b) Hitt. arawa-
'free' has nothing to do with ara- 'companion, mate' and reflects
*n-rə -wo- 'not giving' (not obliged to render any financial or physical
service), versus IE *rē- 'give, bestow' (1977: 115). These views tie
in with his reinterpretation of the current connection of Indo-Iranian
*arya- with the Anatolian terms: for Szemerényi (1977: 144-48), Hitt.
ara-, denoting a close relationship between equals, corresponds to
Ugaritic ảry 'kinsman' (: Egyptian ỉry 'companion') and must be a
borrowing from a neighboring non-Indo-European language. This, in
turn, implies that "part of the future Indo-Iranians which had via the
Caucasus entered the peripheral area of the Near East acquainted itself with the important local term for 'kinsman, companion' and adopted it in the form arya-, which, transmitted to the kindred tribes further east, later became the overall term for their nationality" (Szemerényi 1977: 148). What makes such a hypothesis rather disputable is
that it postulates a rather uncommon pattern of name-giving for such
a widespread ethnicon as *arya-, apart from the fact that there is still
considerable disagreement as to the routes followed by the Indo-Iranians
in their migrations. They may as likely have moved east of the Cas-

pian Sea as via the Caucasus, and there is no evidence that the group branching off toward a dead end in Mitanni served as a transmitter of Middle Eastern cultural features to the other tribes at any time.

NOTES

[1] The often alleged correspondence Gk. hēníai 'reins': MIr. ḗ(i)si (plural) 'bridle,' reflecting, respectively, *ansi(y)ā and *ansi(y)o-, would point to an original meaning 'halter' (Pokorny 1959: 48; 'dem Zugvieh umgelegter Zügel'), as the further connection with Lat. ānsa 'handle,' Lith. asà 'handle, slip knot,' ON ōes 'hole for the thong in a sandal' would also suggest. The derivation remains uncertain, however (Chantraine 1970: 413).

[2] The early date of the arrival of the Indo-Europeans on the basis of their identification with the so-called Kurgan culture has also been challenged in recent work on the European Bronze Age (e.g. Milisauskas 1978: 183–84; Coles and Harding 1979: 6–8).

[3] On the controversy between Dumézil, Thieme, and Gershevitch over the interpretation of ari-, see Scott-Littleton 1973: 186–92; cf. further Benveniste 1973: 301–4. An extensive survey of the problem and the relevant literature is presented by Cohen in his forthcoming article on "Arya" in the Journal of Indo-European Studies (1981).

[4] On the elaboration of this idea, see Scott-Littleton 1973: 7–19, 49–53, 58–79; Rivière 1979: 35–66. Cf. further Dumézil 1958; Benveniste 1973: 227–38.

[5] On the changes affecting the material civilization and social organization of the Germanic territories described by Roman authors from the time of Julius Caesar (51 B. C.) to the time of Tacitus (A. D. 98), cf. especially Thompson 1965: 1–71. See also Much 1967: 154–60, 167–70, 201–11, 221–27, 236–37, 331–42.

[6] Recently, the view of Meillet has come under criticism, especially by J. Gonda (1975: 48–52). A review of the discussion is given by H. P. Schmidt (1978), who proposes a more general meaning 'alliance, allegiance.' B. Lincoln (1981: 54–55) derives *mitra- from IE *mey- 'join together, bind,' and ascribes the meaning 'that which joins together' to the original form.

BIBLIOGRAPHY

Altekar, A. S. 1958. Vedic society. In S. K. Chatterji, N. Dutt, A. D. Pusalker, and N. K. Bose, eds., The cultural heritage of India. Vol. 1, The early phases. 2nd ed. Calcutta: The Ramakrishna Mission Institute of Culture, pp. 221-32.

Baetke, Walter. 1942. Das Heilige im Germanischen. Tübingen: J. C. B. Mohr (Paul Siebeck).

Benveniste, Emile. 1973. Indo-European language and society. Translated by Elizabeth Palmer. Coral Gables, Fla.: University of Miami Press.

Bökönyi, Sándor. 1974. History of domestic mammals in Central and Eastern Europe. Budapest: Akadémiai Kiadó.

Chantraine, Pierre. 1968-80. Dictionnaire étymologique de la langue grecque. Histoire des mots. Paris: C. Klincksieck.

Coles, J. M., and A. F. Harding. 1979. The Bronze Age in Europe. New York: St. Martin's Press.

Dandekar, R. N. 1971. Hinduism. In C. Jonco Bleeker and George Widengren, eds., Historia religionum. Handbook for the history of religions. Vol. 2, Religions of the present. Leyden: E. J. Brill, pp. 236-345.

Devoto, Giacomo. 1962. Origini Indeuropee. Firenze: Sansoni.

de Vries, Jan. 1956. Altgermanische Religionsgeschichte. I, Einleitung-Vorgeschichtliche Perioden-Religiöse Grundlagen des Lebens-Seelen- und Geisterglaube-Macht und Kraft-Das Heilige und die Kultformen. 2nd ed. Berlin: Walter de Gruyter.

_____. 1957. Altgermanische Religionsgeschichte. II, Die Götter-Vorstellungen über den Kosmos-Der Untergang des Heidentums. Berlin: Walter de Gruyter.

Dumézil, Georges. 1958. L'idéologie tripartie des Indo-Européens. (Collection Latomus, vol. 31.) Brussels: Latomus. Revue d'Etudes Latines.

_____. 1969. Idées romaines. Paris: NRF-Gallimard.

_____. 1970a. Archaic Roman religion. Translated by Philip Krapp. Chicago: University of Chicago Press.

_____. 1970b. The destiny of the warrior. Translated by Alf Hiltebeitel. Chicago: University of Chicago Press.

_____. 1973. Gods of the Northmen. Edited by Einar Haugen. Berkeley/Los Angeles: University of California Press.

Dumézil, Georges. 1977. Les dieux souverains des Indo-Européens. Paris: NRF-Gallimard.

Eliade, Mircea. 1963. Patterns in comparative religion. Translated by Rosemary Sheed. Cleveland: Meridian Books (The World Publishing Company).

———. 1978. A history of religious ideas. Vol. 1, From the Stone Age to the Eleusinian Mysteries. Translated by Willard R. Trask. Chicago: University of Chicago Press.

Gelling, Peter, and Hilda Ellis Davidson. 1972. The chariot of the sun and other rites and symbols of the Northern Bronze Age. London: J. M. Dent.

Gimbutas, Marija. 1977. The first wave of Eurasian steppe pastoralists into Copper Age Europe. Journal of Indo-European Studies 5.4: 277-338.

Gonda, Jan. 1960. Die Religionen Indiens. I, Veda und älterer Hinduismus (Die Religionen der Menschheit, vol. II). Stuttgart: W. Kohlhammer.

———. 1972. The Vedic god Mitra. Leyden: E. J. Brill.

———. 1974. The dual deities in the religion of the Veda. (Verhandelingen der Koninklijke Nederlandse Akademie van Wetenschappen. Afd. Letterkunde. N. R. 81.) Amsterdam: North-Holland Publishing Company.

———. 1975. Mitra in India. In John R. Hinnells, ed., Mithraic studies. Manchester: University of Manchester Press, pp. 40-52.

Hamp, Eric P. 1973. Religion and law from Iguvium. Journal of Indo-European Studies 1: 320-22.

Kammenhuber, Annelies. 1961. Hippologia Hethitica. Wiesbaden: Otto Harrassowitz.

Lincoln, Bruce. 1975. The Indo-European myth of creation. History of Religion 15: 121-45.

———. 1976. The Indo-European cattle-raiding myth. History of Religion 16: 42-65.

———. 1981. Priests, warriors and cattle. A study in the ecology of religions. Berkeley/Los Angeles: University of California Press.

Meillet, Antoine. 1907. Le dieu indo-iranien Mitra. Journal Asiatique 10: 143-59.

Milisauskas, Sarunas. 1978. European prehistory. New York-London: Academic Press.

Minard, A. 1956. Trois énigmes sur les cent chemins, vol. II.
(Publications de l'Institut de Civilization Indienne, Nr. 3.)
Paris: E. de Boccard.

Much, Rudolf. 1967. Die Germania des Tacitus erläutert. 3rd ed.,
by Wolfgang Lange and Herbert Jankuhn. Heidelberg: Carl
Winter.

Murray, Jacqueline. 1970. The first European agriculture. A
study of the osteological and botanical evidence until 2000
B. C. Edinburgh: University Press.

_____. 1973. Einige Gesichtspunkte über die Beziehung zwischen
Viehzucht und archäologischen Kulturen im Spätneolithikum
in Europa. In János Matolcsi, ed., Domestikationsforschung
und Geschichte der Haustiere. Internationales Symposion in
Budapest, 1971. Budapest: Akadémiai Kiadó, pp. 177-86.

Norman Brown, W. 1978. India and Indology. Selected articles, edited by Rosane Rocher. Delhi: Motilal Banarsidass.

Otto, Rudolf. 1917. Das Heilige. Munich.

Pearson, Roger. 1973. Some aspects of social mobility in the early
history of Indo-European societies. Journal of Indo-European
Studies 1: 155-62.

Pfeiffer, John E. 1977. The emergency of society. A prehistory of
the establishment. New York: McGraw Hill.

Pokorny, Julius. 1959. Indogermanisches etymologisches Wörterbuch. Bern: A. Francke.

Polomé, Edgar C. 1969. Some comments on Vǫluspá, Stanzas 17-18.
In Edgar C. Polomé, ed., Old Norse literature and mythol-
ogy. A symposium. Austin/London: University of Texas
Press, pp. 265-90.

_____. 1972. Germanic and the other Indo-European languages.
In Frans van Coetsem and Herbert L. Kufner, eds., Toward
a grammar of Proto-Germanic. Tübingen: Max Niemeyer
Verlag, pp. 43-69.

_____. 1975. Old Norse religious terminology in Indo-European
perspective. In Karl-Hampus Dahlstedt, ed., The Nordic
languages and modern linguistics, vol. 2. Stockholm:
Almquist and Wiksell International, pp. 654-65.

Renou, Louis. 1956. Etudes védiques et pāṇinéennes, vol. II.
(Publications de l'Institut de Civilisation Indienne, Nr. 2.)
Paris: E. de Boccard.

_____. 1961. Etudes védiques et pāṇinéennes, vol. VIII. (Publica-

tions de l'Institut de Civilisation Indienne, Nr. 14.) Paris:
E. de Boccard.

Rivière, Jean-Claude. 1979. Georges Dumézil. A la découverte
des Indo-Européens. Paris: Copernic.

Schmidt, Hans-Peter. 1978. Indo-Iranian Mitra: The state of the
central problem. In Etudes Mithriaques. Actes du 2nd
Congrès International, Téhéran, 1975. (Acta Iranica, vol.
17.) Leyden: E. J. Brill, pp. 346-93.

Scott Littleton, C. 1973. The new comparative mythology. An anthro-
pological assessment of the theories of Georges Dumézil.
Rev. ed. Berkeley/Los Angeles: University of California
Press.

Srinivasan, Doris. 1975. The religious significance of multiple
bodily parts to denote the divine: Findings from the Rig-
Veda. Asiatische Studien/Etudes Asiatiques 29: 137-79.

Thompson, E. A. 1965. The early Germans. Oxford: Clarendon
Press.

Titiev, Mischa. 1972. A fresh approach to the problems of magic
and religion. In William A. Lessa and Evon Z. Vogt, eds.,
Reader in comparative religion. An anthropological approach,
3rd ed. (Reprinted from the Southwestern Journal of Anthropology 16 [1960]: 292-98.) New York/Evanston: Harper & Row.

Trier, Jost. 1942. Zaun und Mannring. Beiträge zur Geschichte
der deutschen Sprache und Literatur 66: 232-64.

Zeuner, Frederick E. 1963. A history of domesticated animals.
New York/Evanston: Harper & Row.

18 | Lexical Data and Cultural Contacts: A Critique of the Study of Prehistoric Isoglosses and Borrowings

Language contact affects the languages involved at all levels: phonological, grammatical, lexical, but to various degrees depending on the kind and length of cultural interchange between the speech communities involved. Syntactic patterns are taken over, but a thorough change in the syntactic structure will require a prolonged period of influence during which the social prestige of one language is likely to play a prominent role—the impact of Latin models on Hungarian syntax since the oldest texts is a typical example—but this principle does not always hold true. Swahili, in spite of centuries of strong cultural exposure to Arabic, has preserved a typically Bantu syntactical system. In bilingual cities like Brussels, it works both ways: the local dialect of Dutch abounds in French syntactic patterns, and Brussels French regularly uses 'prepositional verbs' of the Germanic type, e.g. 'tu peux venir avec' (Dutch mee-komen 'accompany' with separable prefix); 'il a couru après' (Dutch [er] achter lopen 'run after'). Similar remarks could be made for the morphology: when Swahili borrowed Arabic terms, it simply integrated them into its class system, e.g. mismār 'nail' was swahilized as misumari, but interpreted as a plural form in mi-, so that a new singular msumari was made on it; on the other hand, kitāb 'book' became Swahili kitabu, which was interpreted as a noun of the ki- class, hence the plural vitabu. The same process operated with English loans: a singular digadi was formed on the plural madigadi, a Swahili reinterpretation of E. mudguard (Polomé 1967: 171-72, 176). These examples, however, point to the main source of innovation due to language contact: borrowing, and the phonological impact of a strong influx of words whose sound pattern, syllabification, stress, and tone features may differ thoroughly from the receiving language. To continue briefly with Swahili, long consonants and complex consonant clusters constituted a major

problem in borrowing from Arabic: the participial form mu?allimun
from ?allama 'to cause to know,' becomes mwalimu 'teacher' in Swahili; on the other hand, waqt 'time' becomes wakati; šuyl → shughuli
'job, concern'; barf → barafu 'ice'—all of them with epenthetic vowels
whose quality is determined partly by vowel harmony, partly the coarticulation features of the Arabic final consonant, in order to restore
the Bantu syllable pattern /CV/ (Polomé 1967: 169-70, 179).[1]

It is plausible that, under similar circumstances, the same
phenomena would have occurred in prehistoric times. It may be significant for the location of the original homeland of the Venetes that
they share with Germanic the pronoun of 'identity' sselboisselboi:
Gothic silba, OHG (with 'expressive gemination') der selbo selbo;
that isolated feature is not sufficient to postulate closer relationship
with Germanic, however (Polomé 1957).[2] Besides such grammatical
correspondences, one would expect a sizable set of lexical items
pointing to shared cultural features; this vocabulary would consist
essentially of two types of terms:

(a) common innovations;
(b) borrowing, either from each other or from a third, possibly un-
    identifiable source.

In the case of Venetic, such evidence is hardly available:
all the data consist of disputable etymologies, e.g. of the divine
name (dat. sg.) Vebelei 'weaver' or 'bather' (Lejeune 1974: 87,
145, 340) or warrior goddess (Prosdocimi 1967: 2.195-97)—or of
the proper name Goltanos 'with golden hair' (Polomé 1957: 90-91),
whose initial g- as a reflex of IE *gh- contrasts with the h- in the
proper name Hostihavos.[3] This kind of problem is largely due to
the type of information available on Venetic, which is only known
through about 250 votive and funeral inscriptions consisting of short,
mostly similar formulas with numerous anthroponyms. If we examine the Latin and Italic material as compared to the early Germanic
texts, we have a large corpus of data including various areas of
sociocultural and religious life. Common innovations appear in the
semantic development of certain inherited terms like IE *moyno-, a
nominal form derived from the root *mey- 'exchange,' which appears
only in Latin and Germanic with the specific sociolegal connotation,
expressed by Lat. communis 'common'—literally 'who shares the
duties' (cf. mūnia 'official function, duties of a magistrate')—and

OHG gimeine 'common,' gimeinida 'community.' The presence of a
hierarchized society, with a sense of duty under the law is further
confirmed by the specialization of the root *deyk- 'to show, point at'
in Latin (ius dīcere, causam dīcere, multam dīcere, etc.) and in
Germanic (OHG zīhan 'to indict, accuse') or by the correspondences
between Oscan sverrunei (Cippus Abellanus). iurato ('sworn in')
and Gothic swarjan 'swear,' or Oscan tanginom (Tabula Bantina).
sententiam ('opinion'), O. Lat. tongēre (Ennius) and Gothic þagkjan
'to think' (Benveniste 1969: 1.96-97; 2.108-9, 114; 2.165; Polomé
1972: 60-61).

These contacts predate by far the varying neighborhood relationships between Germanic tribes and the Roman Empire: they took
place in prehistoric times in northern Europe in the original homeland
of the ancestors of the Latino-Faliscans and Osco-Umbrians prior to
their migrations to the south. From a linguistic point of view, the
prehistoric correspondences can be identified as such in Germanic,
because the relevant terms show the first consonant shift and all the
recent phonological changes occurring in Germanic prior to its major
dialectal splits. On the other hand, the arrival of the waves of Indo-
European invaders in Italy can be dated archeologically so that an
approximate time for the Germanic-Latin-Italic common development
can be assumed (presumably before 1500 B. C. ?). The major dangers
involved in this kind of procedure is the misinterpretation of alleged
correspondences; a number of things can indeed have happened which
the sources do not reveal:

(a) the common 'innovation' was developed independently at different
    times in the linguistic communities under consideration: thus,
    OCS cělŭ: Goth. hails 'whole, healthy' seem to provide a perfect
    isogloss, both in their phonological and semantic correspondence,
    but closer examination of the use and meaning of the Germanic
    adjective shows that it belongs originally to the Indo-European
    religious vocabulary and applies to the benefic vitality emanating
    from the gods. The meaning 'whole, healthy' derives secondarily
    from that of 'god-given well-being'; the semantic correspondence
    with OCS is merely due to a parallel, but most probably indepen-
    dent development (Polomé 1970: 62-63).
(b) the isogloss was shared by a larger group of languages, but pre-
    served only in the two languages examined, as a consequence of
    the limited amount of data available and/or of their specialization

to definite subjects, e.g. religious texts, laws, etc. One thinks
of the morphological isogloss of the -r- passive used as a major
argument for positing an Italo-Celtic phase in the development of
western Indo-European prior to the discovery of Tocharian and
Hittite.

(c) the isogloss reflects recent developments, not properly accounted
for in the relevant literature, e.g. a number of acceptable Balto-
Germanic isoglosses are actually recent borrowings, as, for instance, Lith. snãkè 'snail,' which has been compared with OHG
snecko, but is merely a loan from East Prussian snâk 'snail,
poisonous snail' (Polomé 1974: 111).

Borrowings made at a very early date may no longer be identified as such, in view of their total integration into the system of the
recipient language. Perhaps the greatest danger in using lexical
material is the often indiscriminate use by historical and comparative
linguists of two types of data:

(a) vocabulary that is not actually attested in context or glosses, dat-
able, clearly interpretable and assignable to a definite language
or dialect. This applies in particular to glosses in classical sources, especially lexica like Hesychius' compilation. A great number of glosses have, for instance, been labeled Macedonian,
which have little to do with this language.[4]

(b) Lexical elements derived from the etymological interpretation of
onomastic data or less clearly identified linguistic sources and
assigned to a definite language or dialect on the basis of nonlinguis-
tic arguments (local cultural history and prehistory, geographical
features and their impact on name-giving, etc.).

The whole concept of an Illyrian language as part of the Indo-
European family was based on such evidence. For four decades,
Krahe and others accumulated an impressive set of etymologies and
built up a network of hypotheses which sent the Proto-Illyrians emerged
from the Lusatian urnfield culture of the middle of the second millennium B.C. all over the Western World and as far east as Palestine.
The hydronomy of practically all of Europe was basically 'Illyrian';[5]
isoglosses between Baltic and Celtic, as well as Slavic and Celtic, of
which Pokorny (1938) provided substantial lists were assumed to be
either borrowings from Illyrian or vocabulary shared in common with

Illyrian—all of this while there was not one text in Illyrian extant (the only alleged short inscription on a ring found near Scutari proved to be an early medieval Christian formula in Greek),[8] if one treats Messapian as a separate entity, as most scholars now tend to do.[7] 'Illyrian' is represented by onomastic data only, recorded in Latin inscriptions. The studies of Katičić (1963, 1964, 1965, 1968) parallel to the work of Untermann on Venetic anthroponyms (1961) have defined three major onomastic areas (Namengebiete) in the 'Illyricum': (a) Southeastern Dalmatia (containing the Illyrii proprie dicti); (b) Central Dalmatia, with the closely related Pannonian area; (c) Liburnia, with the region of Ig, belonging, with Istria, to the larger Venetic territory.

This approach is essentially based on distributional criteria applying to roots and derivational morphemes, and while making use of limited comparative material, it relies only minimally on etymologies (Katičić 1976: 171-84).

Another example of similar inferences about the prehistoric presence of an ethnic group on the basis of etymologies of onomastic data and obscure terms is the case of Pelasgian. Here we have to distinguish the effort at interpretation of the 'Aegean' words which have resisted IE etymologizing for years, from the 'new' Pelasgian elements collected by Georgiev (1966: 112-13), to serve as a basis for his assumption of a consonant shift similar to Grimm's Law:

> p → ph, e.g. aleíphō (Pelasgian) 'anoint': lípos (Greek) 'fat';
> bh → b, e.g. ámbōn (Pelasgian) 'crest of a hill': Lat. umbō
>   'navel of a shield'—cf. Gk. omphalós 'navel';
> b → p, e.g. therápnē (Pelasgian) 'dwelling' > IE *terəb-na;
>   cf. Gk. téramnon 'dwelling.'

Most of these connections have been proposed before with various degrees of assertiveness: without the Pelasgian hypothesis, aleíphō is explained as *(ə)lei-bh- versus *lei-p- (in the Ø- grade in lípos); IE *(ə)lei- is also found in Lat. linō, Gk. alinō (Chantraine 1968: 1.57). As for ámbōn, the semantic link is uncertain; others consider the concept of 'height' as primary (cf. Gk. anabainō 'walk up'). Finally, taking the meaning 'dwelling' as the basis for therápnē is contrary to the facts: the oldest meaning appears to be 'servant' (therápōn) and for all we know, the Greek terms may have been borrowed from Hittite

(Gk. théraps 'servant ← Hitt. tarpassa- [Van Brock 1959]). As
Hester (1965), who reviewed the materials most thoroughly, pointed
out, only a handful of 'Pelasgian' etymologies resist criticism, and
one Aegean term—purgos 'tower'—receives a satisfactory explanation
—hardly enough to postulate the existence of a separate Pelasgian
language as an IE dialect of pre-Hellenic Greece, in spite of Katičić's
noncommittal attitude (1976: 86-87).

Projecting unsolvable problems into IE is not a satisfactory
way of coping with them, even when this type of material is connected
with a prehistoric culture as seemed to be the case with the pre-Celtic
'Belgian' assumed by Gysseling (1952): besides the characteristic
names in -apa- which stretch into Hessen, the Rhineland, and the Ruhr,
this language has the following features:

(a) an ablaut between a ~ i ~ u, as in the place-names of Hus-id-inniu
    (Heusden; Houdaing): His-id-inniu- (Hesdin);
(b) initial p- weakened to h-, e.g. in Han-aciu- (*pan-; cf. Gmc.
    *fanja > Du. veen, Fr. fagne; Celt. annā 'mud');
(c) suffixes like -are (e.g. Tamare > Demer), -one (e.g. Bibr-one,
    'beaver brook').

The idea was developed by Kuhn in a series of articles (especially
1959 and 1961), concentrating on the forms with suffix -st-, the words
with initial p- and the names in -apa.[8] The outcome was a book written in collaboration with two prehistorians, defending the thesis that
the major part of the territory between the Main and the coast between
the Rhine and the Weser had only been germanized at a late date, presumably around the time of the Roman conquest of Gaul (Hachmann/
Kossack/Kuhn 1962). Earlier a population which was neither Celtic
nor Germanic was claimed to have occupied this northwestern area,
stretching down to the Aisne. These views have triggered very strong
criticism for the following methodological reasons: (1) they failed to
examine the rise and origin of the non-IE component of the Germanic
vocabulary; (2) they fail to exhaust the possibilities of Gmc. explanations for the allegedly aberrant forms.

It has been claimed that about one-third of the Germanic lexicon was not IE: though such statistics are per se always disputable,
it is obvious that the IE conquerors of northern Europe did not move

into a vacuum, and it can be assumed that the local languages contributed to the constitution of the Gmc. lexicon as well as neighboring people like the Lapps. Moreover, the usual factors renewing the vocabulary of any language have been active in Gmc. as elsewhere. Presumably, increasing involvement with seafaring was one motivation for lexical expansion; new products brought early loans like Go. alew, presumably borrowed from second-century B. C. spoken Latin *olēuom by the Cimbri and Teutones in northern Italy (Polomé 1953). As for the etymologies, while Kuhn (1961) lines up an impressive series of terms with initial p-, which can be of different origins, he completely misses the point with the suffix -ei/-ey—allegedly pre-Gmc.—since OS saharai: OHG saharahi 'marsh grass' shows that Low German -ei/-ey reflects Gmc. *-ahja (Oberdt. -ahi > -ach; Dittmaier 1963). Meid (1964),[9] Neumann (1971), and others have further demonstrated the shakiness of the validity of Kuhn's assumptions.

However, prudent investigation of all the non-linguistic evidence can be used to support the assumption of prehistoric ethnic contact. Thus, it can be established that the word for lead was borrowed from Celtic by Germanic (OE lēad, MLG lôd: O. Fr. luaide 'lead,' from IE *pleu-d- 'running [i. e. melting] easily'), because they got the technique of soldering from them not earlier than the middle of the first century A. D. This timing also accounts for its phonological form *lauda- (the borrowing took place before Celtic *ou was monophthongized to ū) (Birkhan 1970: 147-52).

Parallel work in other linguistic areas, e.g. Bantu, indicates that the same restrictions are valid there as for the reconstruction of cultural artifacts in the IE territory (Polomé 1977).

NOTES

[1] On the problem of Arabic loan words in Swahili, cf. especially B. Krumm, Wörter und Wortformen orientalischen Ursprungs im Suaheli (Hamburg: Friedricksen, De Gruyter & Co., 1932—English version, Words of Oriental Origin in Swahili [London, 1940]); Sharifa M. Zawawi, Loanwords and Their Effect on the Classification of Swahili Nominals (Leiden: E. J. Brill, 1979).

[2] Since the lost bronze situla on which the inscription occurred must have dated back to the second or first century B. C. (Pellegrini and Prosdocimi 1967: 1.451), sselboisselboi has sometimes been considered as a borrowing from Germanic, but even with the transitory presence of the Germanic Cimbri and Teutones in northern Italy, this remains extremely improbable. Presumably, as Prosdocimi suggests (Pellegrini and Prosdocimi 1967: 2.168), the Venetic form merely represents an āmredita formation (with double inflexion) parallel to the Germanic karmadhāraya (with inflexion only of the second component) OHG (der) selb selbo, similar to Latin ipsipse and Greek aútautos.

[3] Though Lejeune (1974: 148-51) decides in favor of the etymologies that derive initial h- from IE *gh-, he does not provide any explanation for the initial g- in the anthroponyms Galknos (gen. sg.) and Goltanos. It should be noted, however, that Goltanos occurs in an inscription from the Valle di Cadore where Venetic h- corresponds graphically to Latin f- in huttos: FVTVS; houvonikos: FOVONICVS (Pellegrini and Prosdocimi 1967: 2.99-103). The alternation h ~ ∅ in the names with Osti-, e.g. Hostihavos (Padua): ostiiarei (Trieste), OSTIALAE (Padua), makes the connection of this onomastic theme with IE *ghosty- 'stranger' less convincing (cf. on these personal names Polomé 1957: 93-94; 1966: 78; Untermann 1961: 117-29, 134-35, 160-61; Pellegrini and Prosdocimi 1967: 2.103-4, especially fn. 1, p. 103, 148-50).

[4] Cf. e.g. the comments of Otto Hoffmann, Die Makedonen, ihre Sprache und ihr Volkstum (Göttingen: Vandenhoeck and Ruprecht 1906), pp. 2-17, on the glosses ascribed to Amerias, the Macedonian, a third-century B. C. grammarian.

[5] In spite of strong criticism of such scholars as Vittore Pisani (1938) and Paul Kretschmer (1943), H. Krahe maintained the view that the 'Illyrians' played a major role in the Indo-Europeanization of Europe (1940), especially Greece and Italy (1949). However, as he analyzed the structure of the oldest European hydronymy, he came to the conclusion that the toponymic correspondences spanning territories stretching from the Adriatic to the Baltic (1957) could no longer be labeled 'Illyrian,' and he coined the term 'Alteuropäisch' (1964), which essentially serves the purpose of tagging the Indo-European features shared by the earliest onomastic material of the area.

[6] On the 'Illyrian' interpretation of the text, cf. Krahe 1955: 12. The correct translation of the inscription (in Byzantine Greek) was given by L. Ognenova, 'Nouvelle interprétation de l'inscription

"illyrienne" d'Albanie,' in <u>Bulletin de Correspondance Hellénique</u> 83:
2, 794-99. See also Katičić 1976: 169-70.

[7] Cf. e.g. Carlo de Simone, <u>La lingua messapica: tentativo</u>
<u>di una sintesi</u> (in <u>Le genti non greche della Magna Grecia.</u> Atti dell'
undicesimo convegno di studi sulla Magna Grecia—Taranto 10-15
ottobre 1971 [Naples, 1972]).

[8] For the -<u>apa</u>- names, Kuhn relied essentially on the study
of H. Dittmaier, <u>Das -apa- Problem</u> (Louvain, 1955), whereas he
used the data on European hydronymy compiled by Hans Krahe as they
appear in <u>Beiträge zur Namenforschung</u> for his listings of -<u>st</u>- derivations (cf. Kuhn, in Hachmann and Kossack and Kuhn 1962: 139).

[9] Meid (1964) remains quite restrained in his criticism and
points to the pitfalls of the method: 'Nun sind gerade die Wörter mit
germ. p̱- noch ein verhältnismässig günstiges Forschungsobjekt, da
idg. ḇ ja ein seltener Konsonant war. Bei Wörtern mit andern Ver-
schlusslauten sind die Bedingungen bei weitem nicht so günstig; bei
ihnen muss die Suche nach vorgermanischen Etymologien, die sicher
bald eine Mode werden wird, mit grosser Vorsicht und Behutsamkeit
verfahren, auf dass der Germanistik die Exzesse der Pelasgerforschung
erspart bleiben mögen' (p. 115).

BIBLIOGRAPHY

Benveniste, Emile. 1969. Le vocabulaire des institutions indo-
        européennes. 1. Economie, parenté, société. 2. Pouvoir,
        droit, religion. Paris.
Birkhan, Helmut. 1970. Germanen und Kelten bis zum Ausgang der
        Römerzeit. (Österreichische Akademie der Wissenschaften.
        1. Philosophisch-historische Klasse-Sitzungsberichte, vol.
        272.) Wien-Graz-Köln.
Birnbaum, Henrik, and Jaan Puhvel, eds. 1966. Ancient Indo-
        European Dialects. Berkeley/Los Angeles.
Cardona, George, Henry M. Hoenigswald, and Alfred Senn, eds. 1970.
        Indo-European and Indo-Europeans. Papers presented at the
        3rd Indo-European Conference at the University of Pennsyl-
        vania, Philadelphia.
Chantraine, Pierre. 1968. Dictionnaire étymologique de la langue
        grecque. Histoire des mots. Paris.

Dittmaier, H. 1963. Die westfälischen Namen auf -ei(ey) und -egge. Niederdeutsches Wort 3: 1-14.

Georgiev, Vladimir T. 1966. Introduzione alla Storia delle Lingue Indeuropee. Roma.

Gysseling, M. 1952. Inleiding tot de studie van het oude Belgisch. Mededelingen van de Vereniging voor Naamkunde te Leuven en de Commissie voor Naamkunde te Amsterdam 28: 3-4, 69-76.

Hachmann, Rolf, Georg Kosack, and Hans Kuhn. 1962. Völker zwischen Germanen und Kelten. Neumünster.

Hester, D. A. 1965. 'Pelasgian'—a new Indo-European language? Lingua 13: 4, 335-84.

Katičić, Radoslav. 1962. Die illyrischen Personennamen in ihrem südöstlichen Verbreitungsgebiet. Živa Antika 12.1: 95-120.

_____. 1963. Das mitteldalmatische Namengebiet. Živa Antika 12.2: 255-92.

_____. 1965. Zur Frage der keltischen und pannonischen Namengebiete im römischen Dalmatien. Godišnjak Akademija nauka i umjetnosti Bosne i Hercegovine 3: 53-76.

_____. 1968. Die einheimische Namengebung von Ig. Godišnjak Akademija nauka i umjetnosti Bosne i Hercegovine 6: 61-120.

_____. 1976. Ancient languages of the Balkans. (Trends in Linguistics. State-of-the-Art Reports 4.) The Hague.

Krahe, Hans. 1940. Der Anteil der Illyrier an der Indogermanisierung Europas. Die Welt als Geschichte 6: 54-73.

_____. 1949. Die Indogermanisierung Griechenlands und Italiens. Heidelberg.

_____. 1955. Die Sprache der Illyrier. 1. Die Quellen. Wiesbaden.

_____. 1957. Vorgeschichtliche Sprachbeziehungen von den baltischen Ostseeländern bis zu den Gebieten um den Nordteil der Adria. Akademie der Wissenschaften und Literatur, Abhandlungen der Geistes- und Sozialwissenschaftlichen Klasse. Jahrgang 1957, Nr. 3, pp. 103-21. Wiesbaden.

_____. 1964. Vom Illyrischen zum Alteuropäischen. Methodologische Betrachtungen zur Wandlung des Begriffs 'Illyrisch.' Indogermanische Forschungen 59: 201-13.

Kretschmer, Paul. 1943. Die vorgriechischen Sprach- und Volksschichten. Fortsetzung. Glotta 30: 84-218. (Die illyrische Frage, pp. 99-168.)

Kuhn, Hans. 1959. Vor- und frühgermanische Ortsnamen in Nord-
deutschland und den Niederlanden. Westfälische Forschungen
12: 5-44.

_____. 1961. Anlautend p- im Germanischen. Zeitschrift für Mund-
artforschung 28: 1-31.

Lejeune, Michel. 1974. Manuel de la langue vénète. Heidelberg.

Meid, Wolfgang. 1964. Review of Rolf Hachmann, Georg Kossack,
and Hans Kuhn, Völker zwischen Germanen und Kelten.
Schriftquellen, Bodenfunde und Namengut zur Geschichte des
nördlichen Westdeutschlands um Christi Geburt (Neumünster,
1962). Beiträge zur Namenforschung 15: 104-15.

Neumann, Günter. 1971. Subtrate im Germanischen? (Nachrichten
der Akademie der Wissenschaften in Göttingen. 1. Philo-
logisch-historische Klasse. 1971: 4.) Göttingen.

Pellegrini, G. B., and A. L. Prosdocimi. 1967. La Lingua Venetica.
1. Le iscrizioni. 2. Studi. Firenze/Padova.

Pisani, Vittore. 1938. Il problema illirico. Pannonia 3 (1937): 276-
90 (= Illyrica. Pannonia-könyvtár, 46). Pecs.

Pokorny, Julius. 1938. Zur Urgeschichte der Kelten und Illyrier.
Halle/Saale.

Polomé, Edgar C. 1953. Review of Ernst Schwarz, Goten, Nord-
germanen, Angelsachsen. Studien zur Ausgliederung der
germanischen Sprachen. In Revue Belge de Philologie et
d'Histoire 31: 112-21.

_____. 1957. Germanisch und Venetisch. In Mnēmēs Kharin.
Gedenkschrift Paul Kretschmer. 2.86-98. Vienna/Wiesbaden.

_____. 1966. The position of Illyrian and Venetic. In H. Birnbaum
and J. Puhvel, eds., Ancient Indo-European dialects, pp.
59-76. Berkeley/Los Angeles.

_____. 1967. Swahili language handbook. Washington, D. C.

_____. 1970. Germanic and regional Indo-European (lexicography
and culture). In George Cardona, Henry M. Hoenigswald,
and Alfred Senn, eds., Indo-European and Indo-Europeans,
pp. 55-72. Philadelphia.

_____. 1972. Germanic and the other Indo-European languages.
In Frans van Coetsem and Herbert L. Kufner, eds., Toward
a grammar of Proto-Germanic, pp. 43-69. Tübingen.

_____. 1974. Notes on the Germano-Baltic lexical correspondences.
Journal of Indo-European Studies 2.2: 101-16.

Polomé, Edgar C. 1977. The reconstruction of Proto-Bantu culture from the lexicon. In L'expansion bantoue (Colloques Internationaux du C.N.R.S.—Sciences Humaines), pp. 1-12 (preprint).

Untermann, Jürgen. 1961. Die Venetischen Personennamen. Wiesbaden.

Van Brock, Nadia. 1959. Substitution rituelle. Revue Hittite et Asianique 17: 117-46 (1. tarpalli-, tarpanalli-, tarpassa-, and Gk. therápŏn, pp. 117-26).

Van Coetsem, Frans, and Herbert L. Kufner, eds. 1972. Towards a grammar of Proto-Germanic. Tübingen.

Author's Postscript

The collection of papers in this volume might convey the impression that most of my work of the last two decades has focused on problems of language policy, sociolinguistics, and creolization in Central and East Africa. During the same period, however, I have written papers on Indo-European phonology in connection with the laryngeal theory, on problems of Germanic morphology, on etymology and lexical correspondences between Germanic and the other Indo-European languages, on Germanic religion and its Indo-European background, and on Indic religion and culture. With a dual focus of activity since the fifties, I have been an Africanist and an Indo-Europeanist at the same time, and I feel that each field has enriched the other for me.

Just as the comparison with the Nilotic cattle-herding civilizations helped Bruce Lincoln reconstruct the original cattle cycle in Indo-Iranian mythology,[1] daily contact with the Bantus of Central and East Africa for a number of years has given me an insight into some aspects of daily life and social processes at levels of technical and cultural development comparable to those that we assume for various stages in the growth and expansion of the Indo-European peoples. During four years in Zaire and more than a year and a half in East Africa, with prolonged stays in Uganda (1963) and Tanzania (1969-70), I traveled all over the backcountry to remote settlements, interviewing older people, attending ceremonies, participating in various local activities, and directly observing rites of passage, initiation procedures, the workings of customary law, palavers, rituals, the pervasive influence of magico-religious elements in people's daily existence, and other familiar features of ethnic societies that I had theretofore known only from the anthropological literature. The resulting knowledge of how a pastoral society, a clan of hunter-gatherers, or a subsistence-agriculture community actually lives and operates has enabled me, I hope, to draw a better picture of what Indo-European culture may have been like.

Conversely, following the example of Carl Meinhof, who applies the views of the great German nineteenth-century Indo-Europeanists to the reconstruction of proto-Bantu, I have tried to apply the techniques I learned in my Indo-European work to the study of Bantu. In 1974, attempting to do in a modest way what Emile Benveniste had done for Indo-European culture on the basis of the lexicon, I tentatively sketched what proto-Bantu culture would look like on the basis of Malcolm Guthrie's Comparative Bantu (1967-71). The resulting picture is obviously still quite provisional, partly because of the rapid change in our views on African prehistory, especially as regards the date of the introduction of iron, and partly because Guthrie's materials do not provide a set of neatly defined proto-Bantu forms. The work now going on among the so-called "grassland Bantus" in the hitherto neglected area of the Bantu territory and the additional materials being collected elsewhere (e.g. Bernd Heine's linguistic atlas of Kenya and the word lists of Derek Nurse and T. J. Hinnebusch) may soon require a thorough revision of my reconstruction.

As for the papers collected in this volume, if some of my earlier papers on Lubumbashi Swahili, written a decade or so ago, are somewhat dated, it should be remembered that I was breaking new ground by focusing attention on the creolization of Swahili in a major Central African city. Since then a dissertation has been written on the subject at the University of Nice under Professor Gabriel Manessy; texts in Shaba Swahili have been published and analyzed by Walter Schicho and J. Fabian; and at the Université Nationale du Zaire a number of theses and dissertations have been devoted to various sociolinguistic aspects of the use of Lubumbashi Swahili such as bus drivers' slang and the language of billboards. With the growing interest in creolization, such phenomena are bound to be increasingly studied, not only from a comparative point of view, e.g. with reference to Heine's Pidgin Sprachen im Bantu Bereich (1973), but also for their theoretical implications (see Chapter 11 in this volume).

While attending a workshop at the School of Oriental and African Studies in London in April 1982, I was pleased to notice the con-

tinuing interest in some of the questions I tackled in my papers on
Tanzania and Swahili. In Kenya and Tanzania the position of English
versus Swahili in the educational process will remain a strongly debated issue for a long time to come. But progress in rendering modern terms and concepts in Swahili has been considerable: not only are
new word lists being issued by the language planning authorities (e.g.
in Lugha Yetu by the National Swahili Council), but all institutions
(e.g. airlines, international hotels, restaurants) now provide a Swahili text beside the English, where only English used to be the rule.

In a related area, the joint work of historians, archaeologists,
and linguists has led to a renewed effort to discover where Swahili
originated. Thomas Spear and Derek Nurse would now look for its
origins farther north, in the area of Barawa in southern Somalia,
where a Swahili dialect is still spoken. Obviously there will be much
discussion of this question, as well as of the movements of Swahili
speakers, especially if Gill Shepherd is right in placing them on the
Comoro Islands as early as the ninth or tenth century. In the meantime, we are learning more about East African history and about the
dialects along the coast.[2]

Reflecting on all this, one wonders where we go from here.
My days of fieldwork in Africa are over, but much of the collected
material remains to be pondered, compared, and studied for theoretical implications. I am convinced that as more texts become available
in Lubumbashi Swahili, its great value as a living document of the
process of pidginization and creolization of a Bantu language will be
recognized. I believe also that further study of its morphology and
syntax, and perhaps especially of its verbal system (as suggested by
Schicho's preliminary work on auxiliaries), should be particularly
helpful in determining general trends or universals in creolized languages.

My own work in my riper years, however, will likely focus
more and more on paleoculture and religion, and therefore concentrate
more specifically on Indo-European. The study of the world of Indo-
European culture and religion has been transformed by the pioneering
work of Emile Benveniste and Georges Dumézil. Conducting research
on Vedic gods, on Germanic myths, on divine names, and on symbols
and rituals, I intend to pursue my work not as a disciple of these great

masters, but as an independent thinker intent on retrieving as much
as possible of the ancient culture by combining the data of all discip-
lines, carefully, with sound critical judgment and without prior
thesis or theoretical bias—if I can!

I cannot begin to list all the distinguished scholars to whom
I owe a debt of gratitude, but I would like to mention a few besides
Benveniste and Dumézil who influenced me deeply: Jerzy Kuryłowicz,
Emil Vetter, Karl Kerényi, Franz Altheim, Giacomo Devoto, F. B.
J. Kuiper, Michel Lejeune, Maurice Leroy, and Henri Grégoire. I
also owe much to stimulating discussion with my colleagues here in
the States and in Europe, Africa, and South Asia; and maybe even
more to the exciting challenge of teaching a number of vibrant, young,
inquisitive spirits—my graduate students at the University of Texas
at Austin. Many a time did an idea of mine ripen from a discussion
started in class! To all of them, my thanks. My deepest gratitude
also to my wife and family for their patience with me, and especially
to Barbara for her continued support and encouragement, to say
nothing of invaluable help in editing and proofreading my manuscripts.

Finally, I am honored to be included in this series, and I
want to thank Anwar Dil very heartily indeed for his kindness and
efficiency in putting together this collection. Working with him was
more than gratifying; it was the crowning event of an old friendship.

NOTES

[1] Priests, Warriors & Cattle: A Study in the Ecology of
Religion (Berkeley and Los Angeles: University of California Press,
1981), especially pp. 1-48.
    [2] See especially the provisional report of Derek Nurse, dis-
tributed by the Institute for Swahili Research (Dar es Salaam, 1981),
to be published in Sprache und Geschichte in Afrika, vol. 4 (1982).

Bibliography of Edgar C. Polomé's Works

1943   De Middelnederlandse Bewerking van Liber VIII 'De Pro-
prietatibus Rerum' van Bartholomaeus Anglicus. Vol. 1,
Inleiding en Commentaar, 187 pp.; vol. 2, Tekst, 78 pp.
Brussels. M. A. thesis (unpublished).

1947 a.   Bibliographical article. Introduction à l'étude des langues
germaniques. Revue Belge de Philologie et d'Histoire 25:
985-87.
    b.   Research report. Bijdrage tot de studie van de zogenaamde
Oudnoorse wo-praesentia. Handelingen van het XVIIe
Vlaamse Filologencongres, Leuven, pp. 161-63.

1948 a.   Over de etymologie van Nederlands wouw 'reseda luteola.'
Revue Belge de Philologie et d'Histoire 26: 541-68.
    b.   Review of Zum Sekundärumlaut von germ. a in Bairischen,
by I. Löfstedt. Revue Belge de Philologie et d'Histoire 26:
187-91.
    c.   Review of Syncope of Old English present endings. A dialect
criterion, by J. Hedberg. Revue Belge de Philologie et
d'Histoire 26: 613-14.
    d.   Research report. Un corollaire éventuel de la 'Verschärfung'
dans les dialectes germaniques occidentaux. Revue Belge de
Philologie et d'Histoire 26: 342. [See also 1949a.]

1949 a.   A West-Germanic reflex of the 'Verschärfung.' Language
25 (April): 182-89.
    b.   Review of Handelingen van het XVIIe Vlaamse Filologencon-
gres, together with F. Gorissen. Revue Belge de Philologie
et d'Histoire 27: 425-34.

1949 c. Bibliographical article. Textes allemands du moyen-âge.
Revue Belge de Philologie et d'Histoire 27: 477-78.
 d. Review of Manuel de l'allemand du Moyen-Âge; des origines
au XVe siècle, by A. Jolivet and F. Mossé. Revue Belge
de Philologie et d'Histoire 27: 816-18.
 e. Linguistische Studiën in verband met de Germaanse Anlaut-
groep *hw-. Vol. 1, 40 pp.; vol. 2, 259 pp. Brussels.
Doctoral dissertation (unpublished).

1950 a. Etymologische nota over het woord gaver. Mededelingen
van de Vereniging voor Naamkunde te Leuven 26: 27.
 b. Laryngaaltheorie en Germaanse Verscherping. Handelingen
van de Zuid-Nederlandse Maatschappij voor Taal- en Letterkunde en Geschiedenis 4: 61-75.
 c. Reflexes de laryngales en arménien. Annuaire de l'Institut
de Philologie et d'Histoire Orientales et Slaves 10: 539-69.
[= Mélanges Henri Grégoire 2. Brussels, 1950.]
 d. Review of Deutsche Worbildung, by W. Henzen. Revue Belge
de Philologie et d'Histoire 28: 206-10.
 e. Review of Der Ursprung der indogermanischen Deklination,
by F. Specht. Revue Belge de Philologie et d'Histoire 28:
1104-15.
 f. Review of Vergleichendes und etymologisches Wörterbuch
des Altwestnordischen, by F. Holthausen. Revue Belge de
Philologie et d'Histoire 28: 1162-74.
 g. Review of Grundlegung einer Geschichte der deutschen
Sprache, by T. Frings. Revue Belge de Philologie et
d'Histoire 28: 1174-77.
 h. Research report. L'étymologie du terme germanique
*ansuz 'dieu souverain.' Revue Belge de Philologie et
d'Histoire 28: 1427. [See also 1953a.]

1951 a. Translation into Dutch. Afrikaanse Kunsten en Moderne
Wereld, by Maurice Albert. À l'Enseigne du Chat qui Pêche,
63 pp. Brussels.
 b. Nerthus-Njord. Handelingen van de Zuid-Nederlandse
Maatschappij voor Taal- en Letterkunde en Geschiedenis 5
(1950): 99-124.
 c. Research report. Germaans en Venetisch. Handelingen van
het XIXe Vlaamse Filologencongres: 198-203. Brussels.

1951 d.   Research report. Isoglosses germano-illyriennes. Revue
          Belge de Philologie et d'Histoire 29: 313-14.

      e. Review of Laryngeal before Sonant, by L. Hammerich.
          Revue Belge de Philologie et d'Histoire 29: 157-62.

      f. Review of The Rivalry of Scandinavian and native synonyms
          in Middle-English, by A. Rynell. Revue Belge de Philologie
          et d'Histoire 29: 188-90.

      g. Bibliographical article. Le sens du terme 'deutsch.' Revue
          Belge de Philologie et d'Histoire 29: 882-84.

      h. Review of Dictionary of selected synonyms in the principal
          Indo-European languages, by D. C. Buck. Revue Belge de
          Philologie et d'Histoire 29: 1183-98.

      i. Review of Bijdrage tot de studie van de morphologie van het
          Indo-Europeesch Verbum, by E. Raucq. Revue Belge de
          Philologie et d'Histoire 29: 1199-1205.

      j. Review of Huvudlinjer i nordisk språkhistorie (I), by B.
          Hesselman. Revue Belge de Philologie et d'Histoire 29:
          1246-48.

      k. Review of Saxonica, by A. Rooth. Revue Belge de Philologie
          et d'Histoire 29: 1248-51.

1952 a.   À propos du guerrier de Capestrano. La Nouvelle Clio 3:
          261-70.

      b. Zum heutigen Stand der Laryngaltheorie. Revue Belge de
          Philologie et d'Histoire 30: 444-71, 1041-50.

      c. On the origin of Hittite ḫ. Language 28.4 (Oct.): 444-46.

      d. Review of Phonology of the Middle-English dialect of Sussex,
          by S. Rubin. Revue Belge de Philologie et d'Histoire 30:
          257-59.

      e. Review of Untersuchungen zur westfälischen Sprache des 9.
          Jahrhunderts, by W. Foerste. Revue Belge de Philologie
          et d'Histoire 30: 577-78.

      f. Bibliographical article. Synthetische taalvormen in het
          Nederlands. Revue Belge de Philologie et d'Histoire 30:
          573-74.

1953 a.   L'étymologie du terme germanique *ansuz 'dieu souverain.'
          Etudes Germaniques 8.29 (Jan.): 36-44.

      b. À propos de la 2ᵉ édition de 'Gli antichi Italici' de M. G.
          Devoto. La Nouvelle Clio 4: 130-37.

1953 c. Reflexes de laryngales en arménien: notes complémentaires.
        Annuaire de l'Institut de Philologie et d'Histoire Orientales
        et Slaves 8: 669-71.

   d. Review of Goten, Nord-Germanen, Angelsachsen. Studien
      zur Ausgliederung der germanischen Sprachen, by E. Schwarz.
      Revue Belge de Philologie et d'Histoire 21: 112-21.

   e. Review of Proto-Indo-European phonology, by W. Lehmann.
      Revue Belge de Philologie et d'Histoire 31: 537-44.

   f. Review of Studien zur indogermanischen Grundsprache, by
      W. Brandenstein. Revue Belge de Philologie et d'Histoire
      31: 1050-53.

   g. Review of Nordgermanen und Alemannen. Studien zur ger-
      manischen und frühdeutschen Sprachgeschichte, Stammes-
      und Volkskunde, by P. Maurer. Revue Belge de Philologie
      et d'Histoire 31: 1077-80.

   h. Bibliographical note. Linguistique préhistorique. Revue
      Belge de Philologie et d'Histoire 31: 842-44.

   i. Bibliographical note. Abréviations composées. Revue Belge
      de Philologie et d'Histoire 31: 844-46.

   j. Bibliographical note. Edda poétique. Revue Belge de Phil-
      ologie et d'Histoire 31: 875.

   k. Research report. Notes sur le vocabulaire religieux du
      germanique. Revue Belge de Philologie et d'Histoire 31:
      829. [See also 1954a.]

1954 a. Notes sur le vocabulaire religieux du germanique. I. Runique
        alu. La Nouvelle Clio 5: 40-55.

   b. Notes critiques sur les concordances germano-celtiques.
      Ogam 6.34 (Aug.): 145-64.

   c. La religion germanique primitive, reflet d'une structure
      sociale. Le Flambeau 4: 437-63. Brussels.

   d. À propos de la déesse Nerthus. Latomus 13: 167-200.

   e. Review of Aspects of language, by W. Entwistle. Latomus
      13: 81-82.

   f. Review of Sardische Studien, by J. Hubschmid. Latomus
      13: 82-83.

   g. Review of Zinn and Zink, by H. Flasdieck. Latomus 13:
      83-84.

   h. Review of Satura O. Weinreich. Früchte aus der antiken
      Welt. Latomus 13: 112-14.

1954 i. Review of A concise German etymological dictionary, by O'C. Walshe. Revue Belge de Philologie et d'Histoire 33: 153-55.

j. Review of Holz. Etymologien aus dem Niederwald, by J. Trier. Revue Belge de Philologie et d'Histoire 33: 155-61.

k. Review of Language and history in early Britain, by K. Jackson. Latomus 13: 257-58.

l. Review of The place-names of Oxfordshire I and II, by M. Gelling. Latomus 13: 258-59.

m. Review of Belt and Baltisch. Ostseeische Namenstudien, by J. Svennung. Latomus 13: 259-60.

n. Review of Studies of early British history. Latomus 13: 270-80.

o. Review of Les Dieux des Indo-Européens, by G. Dumézil. Latomus 13: 285-86.

p. Review of Rituels indo-européens à Rome, by G. Dumézil. Latomus 13: 287-90.

q. Review of Liber Pater. Origine et expansion du culte dionysiaque à Rome, by A. Bruhl. Latomus 13: 292-96.

r. Review of Festschrift Franz Dornseiff. Latomus 13: 330-32.

s. Review of Beiträge zur Erforschung des Luwischen, by B. Rosenkranz. Revue Belge de Philologie et d'Histoire 32: 533-35.

t. Review of Gestirnnamen bei den indogermanischen Völkern, by A. Scherer. Revue Belge de Philologie et d'Histoire 32: 535-38.

u. Bibliographical article. Langue et Civilisation. Revue Belge de Philologie et d'Histoire 32: 864-66.

v. Bibliographical article. Linguistique indo-européenne. Revue Belge de Philologie et d'Histoire 32: 866-68.

w. Bibliographical article. Etude statistique de l'apocope en moyen-haut-allemand. Revue Belge de Philologie et d'Histoire 32: 917-18.

x. Bibliographical article. Dialecte alémanique. Revue Belge de Philologie et d'Histoire 32: 918-19.

y. Review of Die Gliederung des indogermanischen Sprachgebiets, by W. Porzig. Latomus 13: 475-80.

z. Review of The category of person in language, by P. Forchheimer. Latomus 13: 481.

1954 aa. Review of Die antike Religion. Entwurf von Grundlinien.
    -and- Apollon. Studien über antike Religion und Humanität,
    by K. Kerényi. Latomus 13: 503-5.
  bb. Review of Die Welt des Märchens, vol. 1, by F. Von der
    Leyen. Latomus 13: 507.

1955 a. Research report. Quelques notes à propos de l'énigmatique
    dieu scandinave Lóðurr. Revue Belge de Philologie et
    d'Histoire 33: 483-94.
  b. Review of Allgemeine und vergleichende Sprachwissenschaft
    - Indogermanistik - Keltologie, by V. Pisani and J. Pokorny.
    Revue Belge de Philologie et d'Histoire 33: 94-96.
  c. Review of Handbuch des Gotischen, by W. Krause. Revue
    Belge de Philologie et d'Histoire 33: 114-17.
  d. Review of Lex Salica. 100-Titel-Text, ed. by K. A. Eck-
    hardt. Latomus 14: 127.
  e. Review of Untersuchungen zur Onomatopoiie. I. Die sprach-
    psychologischen Versuche, by H. Wissemann. Latomus 14:
    132-33.
  f. Review of Das Passiv. Eine Studie zur Geistesgeschichte
    der Kelten, Italiker und Arier, by H. Hartmann. Latomus
    14: 133-34.
  g. Review of Runica manuscripta. The English tradition, by
    R. Derolez. Latomus 14: 139.
  h. Review of The Latin language, by L. R. Palmer. Latomus
    14: 134-35.
  i. Review of Religionen der Griechen, Römer und Germanen,
    by W. Müller and G. Trathnigg. Latomus 14: 149-50.
  j. Review of Ammann-Festgabe. Innsbrucker Beiträge zur
    Kulturwissenschaft. Latomus 14: 154.
  k. Review of Notker III von Sankt-Gallen als Übersetzer und
    Kommentator von Boethius, by I. Schröbler (together with
    J. G. Préaux). Revue Belge de Philologie et d'Histoire 33:
    369-72.
  l. Review of Grabstock, Hacke, und Pflug, by E. Werth.
    Latomus 14: 492-93.
  m. Review of La Saga d'Hadingus, by G. Dumézil. Latomus
    14: 498-99.
  n. Review of Il Mediterraneo, l'Europa, l'Italia durante la Pre-
    istoria, by P. Laviosa-Zambotti. Latomus 14: 499-501.

1955 o. Review of Handbuch der italischen Dialekte. Band I, by E.
Vetter. Revue Belge de Philologie et d'Histoire 33: 634-36.

p. Review of Die Genealogie der Götter in germanischer Religion,
by E. A. Philippson. Revue Belge de Philologie et d'Histoire
33: 703-5.

q. Review of Altgermanische Religionsgeschichte. II, Nach-
römische Zeit. 2. Die Westgermanen, by K. Helm. Revue
Belge de Philologie et d'Histoire 33: 705-10.

r. Review of Sprache und Vorzeit. Europäische Vorgeschichte
nach dem Zeugnis der Sprache, by H. Krahe. Latomus 14:
581-83.

s. Review of Lehnbildungen und Lehnübersetzungen im
Altenglischen, by H. Gneuss. Latomus 14: 583-84.

t. Review of Porphyrios und Empedokles - and - Ein Asiatischer
Staat: Feudalismus unter den Sassaniden und ihren Nachbarn,
Bd. 1, by F. Altheim and R. Stiehl. Latomus 14: 598-601.

u. Review of Essays in the history of religion, by R. Pettazzoni.
Latomus 14: 605-7.

v. Review of Die Welt der Märchen, Bd. 2, by F. Von der Leyen.
Latomus 14: 608.

w. Bibliographical note. Linguistique générale. Revue Belge de
Philologie et d'Histoire 33: 783.

1956 a. Veiovis = Vofiono-?, Hommages à Max Niedermann, Collection. Latomus 23: 274-85.

b. L'origine mythique de l'homme.' Les Cahiers du Libre
Examen 16.1: 48-54. [Reprinted in La Pensée et Les Hommes
4.]

c. Research report. Les inscriptions des casques de Negau et
les Germains des Alpes. Revue Belge de Philologie et
d'Histoire 34: 232-33.

d. Review of Schönfeld's Historische Grammatica van het
Nederlands, by A. Van Loey. Revue Belge de Philologie et
d'Histoire 34: 476-81.

e. Review of Zur grammatikalischen und lexikalischen Bestim-
mung der Luvili-Texte, by H. Otten. Oriens 9: 103-12.

f. Review of Wurd. Das Sakrale in der altgermanischen Poesie,
by L. Mittner. Revue Belge de Philologie et d'Histoire 34:
763-66.

1956 g. Review of Schläuche und Fässer. Wort- und sachgeschicht-
         liche Untersuchungen, by J. Hubschmid. Latomus 15: 622-23.
      h. Review of L'évolution phonétique et les sons du latin ancien
         dans le cadre des langues indo-européennes, by A. Maniet.
         Latomus 15: 624-26.
      i. Axel Svinhufvud, Capitaine de la Force Publique, with J.
         Stengers. Biographie Coloniale Belge 4: col. 859-64.
      j. Review of The Great Mother. Analysis of the archetype, by
         E. Neumann. Latomus 15: 646-47.
      k. Review of Sprachgeschichte und Wortbedeutung. Festschrift
         A. Debrunner. Revue Belge de Philologie et d'Histoire 34:
         896-900.
      l. Bibliographical article. Onomastique préhellénique. Revue
         Belge de Philologie et d'Histoire 34: 906-8.

1954-1956 Dutch radio-course, published in weekly installments by
         the Bulletin of the Belgian State Broadcasting system (Micro-
         Magazine).

1957 a. Germanisch und Venetisch. MNHMHΣ XAPIN. Gedenkschrift
         Paul Kretschmer, vol. 2, pp. 86-97. Vienna, Hollinek/
         Wiesbaden, Harrassowitz.
      b. Review of Economie des changements phonétiques. Traité
         de phonologie diachronique, by A. Martinet. Latomus 16:
         172-73.
      c. Review of Aspects de la fonction guerrière chez les Indo-
         Européens, by G. Dumézil. Latomus 16: 186-88.
      d. Review of The All-Knowing God. Researches into early
         religion and culture, by R. Pettazzoni. Latomus 16: 188-89.
      e. Review of Griechische Mythologie. Ein Handbuch, by J. H.
         Rose. Latomus 16: 190-91.
      f. Review of The mysteries, ed. by J. Campbell. Latomus
         16: 194-96.

1958 a. Research report. Personennamen bei einigen Stämmen in
         Belgisch-Kongo. IV. Internationaler Kongress für Namen-
         forschung, Programmheft, pp. 95-96. Munich.
      b. The organization of education in the Belgian Congo. Lever-
         hulme International Conference on Teacher's Education in
         Africa, Reports; 6 mimeo. pp. Salisbury, S. Rhodesia.

1959 a. Théorie laryngale et germanique. Mélanges de Linguistique et de Philologie. Fernand Mossé in memoriam, pp. 397-402. Paris: Didier.

b. Le Centre Interfacultaire d'anthropologie et de linguistique africaines de l'Université Officielle du Congo Belge et du Ruanda-Urundi à Elisabethville. Orbis 13: 504-9.

c. Rapport sur les recherches linguistiques et ethnographiques au Congo Belge et au Ruanda-Urundi. Bulletin of the International Committee on Urgent Anthropological and Ethnographical Research 2: 103-9.

d. Procédés modernes de classement des données lexicales. Service de Documentation Technique de l'Union Minière du Hart-Katanga. 12 mimeo. pp. Jadotville.

e. Prepublication mimeographed editions of syllabuses. Cours de Linguistique générale, 256 pp. Elisabethville: Université Officielle du Congo. [First draft issued in three parts in 1957, respectively 58, 25, and 16 pp.)

f. Cours de linguistique appliquée aux langues africaines. Vol. 1, Phonétique et Phonologie, 58 pp. Vol. 2, Morphologie, 69 pp. Elisabethville: Université Officielle du Congo. [First draft issued in 1957, 114 pp.]

g. Encyclopedie van de Germaanse filologie. Vol. 1, Taalkundig gedeelte, 185 pp. Elisabethville: Université Officielle du Congo.

1960 Pour la promotion des études onomastiques en Afrique Centrale. Revue Internationale d'Onomastique 12: 40-41.

1961 a. Review of Die Sprache der Illyrier. I, Die Quellen, by H. Krahe. Latomus 20.1 (Jan.-March): 139-45.

b. Review of English place-name elements, by A. H. Smith. Latomus 20.1 (Jan.-March): 145-48.

c. Review of De Origine et Situ Germanorum by Cornelius Tacitus (ed. by M. Scovazzi). Latomus 20.1 (Jan.-March): 134-36.

d. Bibliographical article. Inleiding tot de taalstudie. Revue Belge de Philologie et d'Histoire 39.2: 149-50.

e. Bibliographical article. Origines du langage et multiplicité des langues. Revue Belge de Philologie et d'Histoire 39.1: 179-81.

1961 f. Bibliographical article. Classification morphologique des
         langues. Revue Belge de Philologie et d'Histoire 39.1:
         181-83.
    g.   Bibliographical article. Lexique proto-indo-européen.
         Revue Belge de Philologie et d'Histoire 39.2: 552-54.
    h.   Bibliographical article. Dictionnaire étymologique indo-
         européen. Revue Belge de Philologie et d'Histoire 39.2:
         554-56.
    i.   Bibliographical article. Mode verbal en indo-européen.
         Revue Belge de Philologie et d'Histoire 39.2: 555-57.
    j.   Bibliographical article. Grammaire comparée du hittite.
         Revue Belge de Philologie et d'Histoire 39.2: 557-60.
    k.   Bibliographical article. Onomastique paléo-européenne de
         la Baltique à l'Adriatique. Revue Belge de Philologie et
         d'Histoire 39.2: 560-62.
    l.   Bibliographical article. Religions du monde antique à
         l'avènement du christianisme. Revue Belge de Philologie et
         d'Histoire 39.2: 564-65.
    m.   Bibliographical article. Ethnographie germanique. Revue
         Belge de Philologie et d'Histoire 39.2: 626-29.
    n.   Bibliographical article. Noms des runes. Revue Belge de
         Philologie et d'Histoire 39.2: 610-13.
    o.   Bibliographical article. Dictionnaire du vieil-haut-allemand.
         Revue Belge de Philologie et d'Histoire 39.2: 615-16.
    p.   Review of Grammaire des dialectes Mangbetu et Medje, by
         J. Larochette. African Studies 20.1: 69-77.

1962 a. Les langues indo-européennes dans le milieu méditerranéen.
         Latomus 20.4 (1961, but published in 1962): 806-16.
    b.   Review of Antichi dialetti germanici. Origini e sviluppo, by
         Gemma Manganella (Naples, 1959). Revue Belge de Philol-
         ogie et d'Histoire 40.3: 938-42.
    c.   Bibliographical article. Germaanse etymologiëen. Revue
         Belge de Philologie et d'Histoire 39.3 (1961, but published
         in 1962): 1016-18.
    d.   Bibliographical article. Influence du christianisme sur le
         vocabulaire vieil-haut-allemand. Revue Belge de Philologie
         et d'Histoire 39.3 (1961, but published in 1962): 1019.
    e.   Bibliographical article. Peuple et Langues. Revue Belge de
         Philologie et d'Histoire 40.1: 215-16.

1962 f. Research report. Personennamen bei einigen Stämmen in
         Belgisch-Kongo. Sixth International Congress of Onomastic
         Sciences (Reports of the Congress, vol. 3). [= Studia Ono-
         mastica Monacensia 4: 615-21.]

1963 a. Cultural languages and contact vernaculars in the Republic
         of the Congo. Texas Studies in Literature and Language
         4.4: 499-511. [In this volume, pp. 1-16.]
      b. Bibliographical article. A l'origine des sagas islandaises.
         Revue Belge de Philologie et d'Histoire 41: 997-99.
      c. Review of Kelten und Germanen, by Jan de Vries (Bern,
         1960). Latomus 22: 111-14.
      d. Review of La Saga di Hrafnkell e il Problema delle Saghe
         Islandesi, by Marco Scovazzi (Arona, 1960). Journal of
         English and Germanic Philology 62.2: 472-75.

1964 a. Diachronic development of structural patterns in the German-
         ic conjugation system. Proceedings of the Ninth International
         Congress of Linguistics, pp. 870-80. The Hague: Mouton.
      b. Considerations sur la valeur des données lexicostatistiques.
         Communications et Rapports du Premier Congrès Interna-
         tional de Dialectologie Générale 1: 29-36. Louvain: Centre
         International de Dialectologie Générale.
      c. L'anthroponymie vénète. Latomus, Revue d'Etudes Latines
         23: 788-92.

1965 a. The laryngeal theory so far: A critical bibliographical study.
         Evidence for laryngeals, ed. by W. Winter, pp. 9-78. The
         Hague: Mouton.
      b. Review of Die venetischen Personennamen, by J. Untermann.
         Indogermanische Forschungen 70: 106-9. Wiesbaden: Otto
         Harrassowitz.

1966 a. The position of Venetic and Illyrian. Ancient Indo-European
         dialects, ed. by H. Birnbaum and J. Puhvel, pp. 59-76.
         Los Angeles: University of California Press.
      b. Germanisch und Italisch im Lichte der deskriptiven Sprach-
         betrachtung. Orbis 15: 190-99.
      c. Bibliographical article. Tradition biblique et polygénèse des
         langues. Revue Belge de Philologie et d'Histoire 44: 225-26.

1966 d. Bibliographical article. Les Numéraux Indo-Européens.
         Revue Belge de Philologie et d'Histoire 44: 229-33.
   e. Bibliographical article. Compositie van de Fóstbrœðra Saga.
         Revue Belge de Philologie et d'Histoire 44: 270-71.
   f. Bibliographical article. Oudfries Rudolfsboek. Revue Belge
         de Philologie et d'Histoire 44: 271.
   g. Review of Nederlands Etymologisch Woordenboek. Aflever-
         ing I. A-Dorp, by J. de Vries. Leiden: E. J. Brill (1963).
         Revue Belge de Philologie et d'Histoire 44: 103-14.

1967 a. Swahili language handbook. Washington, D. C., Center for
         Applied Linguistics. 232 pp.
   b. Notes on the reflexes of IE/ms/ in Germanic. Revue Belge
         de Philologie et d'Histoire 45: 800-826.
   c. On the origin of Germanic class III of weak verbs. Beiträge
         zur Indogermanistik und Keltologie, Julius Pokorny zum 80.
         Geburtstag gewidmet, ed. by Wolfgang Meid, pp. 83-92.
         Innsbruck: Sprachwissenschaftliches Institut der Universität
         Innsbruck.
   d. Research report. Geographical differences in lexical usage
         in Swahili. Verhandlungen des zweiten internationalen Dia-
         lektologenkongresses, ed. by L. E. Schmidt, pp. 664-72.
         Wiesbaden: Franz Steiner Verlag.

1968 a. Lubumbashi Swahili. Journal of African Languages 7.1: 14-
         25. [In this volume, pp. 219-35.]
   b. The Indo-European numeral for "five" and Hittite panku-
         "all." Pratidānam. Indian, Iranian and Indo-European stud-
         ies presented to F. B. J. Kuiper, ed. by J. C. Heesterman,
         pp. 98-101. The Hague: Mouton.
   c. The choice of official languages in the Democratic Republic
         of the Congo. Language problems of developing nations, ed.
         by J. A. Fishman, C. A. Ferguson, and J. Das Gupta, pp.
         295-312. New York: Wiley. [In this volume, pp. 17-37.]

1969a.   Some comments on Vǫluspá, stanzas 17-18. Old Norse
         literature and mythology. A symposium, ed. by E. C. Pol-
         omé, pp. 265-90. Austin: University of Texas Press.
   b. Lee M. Hollander: a biographical sketch. Old Norse liter-
         ature and mythology. A symposium, ed. by E. C. Polomé,
         pp. 294-317. Austin: University of Texas Press.

1969 c. Lee M. Hollander: a chronological bibliography. Old Norse
         literature and mythology. A symposium, ed. by E. C. Pol-
         omé, pp. 294-317. Austin: University of Texas Press.
      d. The position of Swahili and other Bantu languages in Katanga.
         Texas Studies in Literature and Language 11.2: 905-13. [In
         this volume, pp. 38-47.]
      e. Das indogermanische Vokalsystem in neuer Sicht? Die
         Sprache 15.2: 175-87. [Reprinted in Robert Schmidt-Brandt,
         Die Entwicklung des indo-germanischen Vokalsystems (2nd
         edition, Heidelberg: Julius Groos, 1973), pp. 167-79.]
      f. (Editor.) Old Norse literature and mythology. A symposium,
         345 pp. Austin: University of Texas Press.
      g. Review of The new comparative mythology, by C. Scott Lit-
         tleton. Berkeley/Los Angeles: University of California
         Press, 1966. Die Sprache 15.2: 190-93.

1970 a. Remarks on the problem of the Germanic 'Verschärfung.'
         Linguistique Contemporaine. Hommage à Eric Buyssens,
         ed. by Jean Diricks and Yvan Lebrun, pp. 177-90. Brussels:
         Editions de l'Institut de Sociologie.
      b. The position of Germanic among West-Indo-European lan-
         guages. Actes du Xe Congrès International des Linguistes
         II, pp. 49-56. Bucarest: Editions de l'Académie de la
         République Socialiste de Roumanie.
      c. Germanic and regional Indo-European (lexicography and
         culture). Indo-European and Indo-Europeans, ed. by G.
         Cardona, H. Hoenigswald, and A. Senn, pp. 55-72. Phila-
         delphia: University of Pennsylvania Press.
      d. The Indo-European component in Germanic religion. Myth
         and law among the Indo-Europeans, ed. by J. Puhvel, pp.
         55-82. Berkeley/Los Angeles: University of California
         Press.

1971 a. Multilingualism in an African urban centre: the Lubumbashi
         case. Language use and social change, ed. by W. H. White-
         ley, pp. 364-75. London: Oxford University Press. [In
         this volume, pp. 48-58.]
      b. The Katanga (Lubumbashi) Swahili creole. Pidginization
         and creolization of languages, ed. by Dell Hymes, pp. 57-
         59. London/New York: Cambridge University Press.

1972 a.   Germanic and the other Indo-European languages. Toward
          a grammar of Proto-Germanic, ed. by Frans Van Coetsem
          and Herbert Kufner, pp. 43-69. Tübingen: Max Niemeyer.
     b.   Reflexes of laryngeals in Indo-Iranian with special reference
          to the problem of the voiceless aspirates. Saga og Språk,
          ed. by John Weinstock, pp. 233-51. Austin: Pemberton
          Press.
     c.   Swahili. - and - Lingua franca. Encyclopaedia Americana
          (latest edition).
     d.   Review of Die gemeinsamen Wurzeln des semitischen und
          indogermanischen Wortschatzes. Versuch einer Etymologie,
          by Linus Brunner. Die Sprache 18.1: 60-61.

1973 a.   Sociolinguistic problems in Tanzania and Zaire. Language
          systems in Africa (= The Conch, Special Issue, Fall, 1972),
          ed. by Sunday O. Anozie, pp. 64-83. New Paltz, N. Y. :
          Conch Magazine Ltd.
     b.   Wilfred H. Whiteley, 1924-1972. Research in African Liter-
          atures 4. 2: 192-93.
     c.   Review of Language and languages in Black Africa, by Pierre
          Alexandre. Evanston, Ill. : Northwestern University Press.
          The Library Journal.
     d.   Review of The philosophical tradition of India, by P. T. Raju.
          University of Pittsburgh Press. The Library Journal.
     e.   Review of Religions of the world, from primitive beliefs to
          modern faiths, by Geoffrey Parrinder. New York: Grosset
          & Dunlap. The Library Journal.
     f.   Review of Tales from Southern Africa, by A. C. Jordan.
          Los Angeles: University of California Press. The Library
          Journal.

1974 a.   Notes on the Germano-Baltic lexical correspondences. A
          critique of Čemodanov's isoglosses. Journal of Indo-Euro-
          pean Studies 2.2: 101-16.
     b.   Approaches to Germanic mythology. Myth in Indo-European
          antiquity, ed. by Gerald J. Larson, C. Scott Littleton, and
          Jean Puhvel, pp. 51-65. Berkeley/Los Angeles/London:
          University of California Press.

1975 a. (Co-editor with Alfred Collins.) Proceedings of the 1974 Annual Meeting of the Southwest Conference on Asian Studies. Austin, Tex.: S.W.C.A.S.

b. (Co-editor with Sirarpi Ohannessian and Charles Ferguson.) Language surveys in developing nations: papers and reports on sociolinguistics survey. Arlington, Va.: Center for Applied Linguistics.

c. Problems and techniques of a sociolinguistically oriented language survey: the case of the Tanzania survey. Language surveys in developing nations: papers and reports on sociolinguistic surveys, ed. by Sirarpi Ohannessian, Charles Ferguson, and Edgar Polomé, pp. 31–50. Arlington, Va.: Center for Applied Linguistics. [In this volume, pp. 59–87.]

d. Old Norse religious terminology in Indo-European perspective. The Nordic Languages and Modern Linguistics 2.13: 654–65, ed. by Karl-Hampus Dahlstedt. Umeå, Sweden: Kunglige Skytteanska Samfundets Handlingar. [In this volume, pp. 285–95.]

e. The reconstruction of the Proto-Bantu culture from the lexicon. Working Papers in Linguistics 19, ed. by Robert Herbert. Columbus, O.: Department of Linguistics. [Reprinted in L'Expansion Bantoue-Actes du Colloque International du CNRS, Viviers (France), 4–16 avril 1977, ed. by Luc Bouquiaux. Paris, SELAF (1980), pp. 779–91.] [See also 1980k.]

f. Iets over Etymologische Woordenboeken. Festschrift for Professor Adolf van Loey, Spel van Zinnen, ed. by R. Jansen-Sieben and S. de Vriendt, pp. 243–49. Brussels: Editions de l'Université de Bruxelles.

g. Linguistic borrowing. Working papers, 1974 Conference, American Council of Teachers of Uncommonly Taught Asian Languages, ed. by Herman van Olphen, pp. 2–14. Austin, Tex.: Center for Asian Studies.

1976 a. (Co-editor with M. A. Jazayery and Werner Winter.) Linguistic and literary studies in honor of Archibald A. Hill. I. General and theoretical linguistics, 448 pp. Lisse, The Netherlands: The Peter de Ridder Press.

1976 b. (Co-editor with Alfred Collins.) Proceedings of the 1975 Annual Meeting of the Southwest Conference on Asian Studies, 201 pp. Austin, Tex.: S. W. C. A. S.

    c. (Co-editor with Herman van Olphen and Andrée Sjoberg.) Proceedings of the Conference on Language Testing and Levels of Proficiency in South Asian Languages, 235 pp. Austin, Tex.: S. A. R. C.

    d. A symposium on the verb in India, Part I. International Journal of Dravidian Linguistics 5.1: 195-201.

    e. Die Stellung des Germanischen innerhalb der indogermanischen Sprachen. Kurzer Ueberblick über einige Probleme. Akten des V. Internationalen Germanisten-Kongresses-Cambridge 1975. Jahrbuch für Internationale Germanistik, A. 2, no. 2, ed. by Forster and Hans-Gert Rolloff, pp. 10-19. Bern: Lang.

1977 a. (Editor.) Proceedings of the 1976 Annual Meeting of the Southwest Conference on Asian Studies, 288 pp. Sherman, Tex.: Austin College Press.

    b. Approaches to the study of Vedic religion. Studies in descriptive and historical linguistics. Festschrift for W. P. Lehmann, ed. by Paul Hopper, pp. 405-15. Amsterdam: Benjamins.

    c. Le vocabulaire proto-bantu et ses implications culturelles. Paleontologia Linguistica, Atti del VI. Convegno Internazionale di Linguisti, pp. 181-201. Brescia, Paideia: Istituto Lombardo-Accademia di Scienze e Lettere.

1978 a. The earliest attestations of Swahili. Indian Linguistics 39: 165-78. [= Professor P. Pandit Memorial Volume.]

    b. A few thoughts about reconstructing Indo-European culture and religion. Journal of the Department of English 14: 45-62. University of Calcutta. [= Suniti Kumar Chatterji Memorial Number.] [In this volume, pp. 296-315.]

    c. (Editor.) Proceedings of the 1977 Annual Meeting of the Southwest Conference on Asian Studies, 219 pp. Austin, Tex.

    d. (Co-editor, with M. A. Jazayery and Werner Winter.) Linguistic and literary studies in honor of Archibald A. Hill. 4 vols. Vol. 1, General and theoretical linguistics, 412 pp.; vol. 2, Descriptive linguistics, 363 pp.; vol. 3, Historical and comparative linguistics, 374 pp.; vol. 4, Linguistics and literature-sociolinguistics and applied linguistics, 392 pp. The Hague-Paris-New York: Mouton, Walter de Gruyter.

1978 e. Review of A bibliography of pidgin and creole language, by J. Reinecke et al. Honolulu: University of Hawaii Press. The South-Central Bulletin 38.2: 45.

f. Report. Working Group 4: Pidgins and creoles. Proceedings of the Twelfth International Congress of Linguistics, 1977, ed. by W. Dressler and W. Meid, pp. 127-30. Innsbruck: Institut für Sprachwissenschaft der Universität.

1979 a. Creolization theory and linguistic prehistory. Studies in diachronic, synchronic, and typological linguistics. Festschrift for Oswald Szemerényi, ed. by Bela Brogyanyi, pp. 679-90. Amsterdam: John Benjamins. [In this volume, pp. 237-48.]

b. Some aspects of the cult of the mother goddess in Western Europe. Vistas and vectors: Essays honoring the memory of Helmut Rehder, ed. by Lee Jennings and G. Schultz-Behrend, pp. 193-208. Austin: University of Texas, Department of Germanic Languages.

c. Tanzanian language policy and Swahili. National language planning and treatment, ed. by Richard Wood, pp. 160-70. [= Word 30.] [In this volume, pp. 88-100.]

d. Foreword. Topics in Pali historical phonology, by Indira Yashwant Junghare, pp. ix-x. Delhi: Motilal Banarsidass.

e. Review of De Taalgebruiker in de mens. Een uitzicht over de taalpsychologie, by G. Kemper. Groningen: Tjeenk-Willink, 1976. Language Problems and Language Planning 3.2: 103.

1980 a. Editor. Man and the ultimate. A symposium, 61 pp. Austin, Tex.: Southwest Branch of the American Oriental Society.

b. (Co-editor with P. C. Hill.) Language in Tanzania, xiii-428 pp. London: Oxford University Press, for International African Institute.

c. Swahili in Tanzania. Language in Tanzania, ed. by Edgar Polomé and P. C. Hill, pp. 79-100. London: Oxford University Press. [In this volume, pp. 189-218.]

1980 d. The languages of Tanzania. Language in Tanzania, ed. by
         Edgar Polomé and P. C. Hill, pp. 1–25. London: Oxford
         University Press.

     e. Tanzania 1970: A sociolinguistic perspective. Language in
         Tanzania, ed. by Edgar Polomé and P. C. Hill, pp. 103–38.
         London: Oxford University Press. [In this volume, pp. 101–
         50.]

     f. Creolization processes and diachronic linguistics. Theoret-
         ical orientations in creole studies, ed. by Albert Valdman
         and Arnold Highfield, pp. 185–202. New York: Academic
         Press. [In this volume, pp. 249–70.]

     g. Armenian and the Proto-Indo-European laryngeals. First
         International Conference on Armenian Linguistics: Proceed-
         ings, ed. by John A. Greppin, pp. 17–34. New York: Cara-
         van Books.

     h. Vedic speculation on the ultimate. Man and the ultimate. A
         symposium, ed. by E. C. Polomé, pp. 39–52. Austin:
         Southwest Branch of the American Oriental Society.

     i. The gods of the Indo-Europeans. The Mankind Quarterly
         21.2 (Winter): 151–64.

     j. Remarques sur quelques isoglosses germano-indo-aryennes.
         Folia Linguistica Historica 1.1: 109–16.

     k. The reconstruction of Proto-Bantu culture from the lexicon.
         L'Expansion Bantoue-Actes du Colloque International du
         CNRS, Viviers (France), 4–16 avril 1977, ed. by Luc Bou-
         quiaux, pp. 779–91. Paris: SELAF. (Slightly revised ver-
         sion of 1975e.) [In this volume, pp. 316–28.]

1981 a. Indo-European verb morphology. An outline of some recent
         views with special regard to Old Indic. Ludwig Sternbach
         Felicitation Volume, pp. 851–61. Lucknow, India: Akhila
         Bharatiya Sanskrit Parishad. [Also in International Journal
         of Dravidian Linguistics 9.1 (Jan.): 158–69.]

     b. Language and dialect. An introduction, with special refer-
         ence to South Asia. Language and dialect in South and South-
         east Asia, ed. by Herman van Olphen, pp. 1–7. Austin, Tex.:
         American Council of Teachers of Uncommonly Taught Asian
         Languages.

     c. Lexical data and cultural contacts: A critique of the study
         of prehistoric isoglosses and borrowings. Logos Semantikos.

III. Semantics, ed. by Wolf Dietrich and Horst Geckeler, pp. 505-13. Berlin: Walter de Gruyter/Madrid: Editorial Gredos. [In this volume, pp. 353-64.]

1981 d. Can graphemic change cause phonemic change? Bono homini Donum. Essays in historical linguistics in memory of J. Alexander Kerns, ed. by Yoël Arbeitman and Allan Bomhard, pp. 881-88. Amsterdam: John Benjamins.

1982 a. (Editor.) The Indo-Europeans in the fourth and third millennia, 186 pp. Ann Arbor, Mich.: Karoma.

b. Preface. The Indo-Europeans in the fourth and third millennia, pp. vii-ix. Ann Arbor, Mich.: Karoma.

c. Indo-European culture, with special attention to religion. The Indo-Europeans in the fourth and third millennia, pp. 156-72. Ann Arbor, Mich.: Karoma. [In this volume, pp. 329-52.]

d. (Editor.) Rural and urban multilingualism, 181 pp. The Hague: Mouton. [= International Journal of the Sociology of Language 34.]

e. Rural versus urban multilingualism in Tanzania: An outline. Rural and urban multilingualism, ed. by E. C. Polomé, pp. 167-81. The Hague: Mouton. [= International Journal of the Sociology of Language 34.]

f. Introduction. Rural and urban multilingualism, ed. by E. C. Polomé, pp. 5-6. The Hague: Mouton. [= International Journal of the Sociology of Language 34.]

g. Sociolinguistically oriented language surveys: Reflections on the survey of language use and language teaching in Eastern Africa. Language in Society 11. 265-83. [In this volume, pp. 151-88.]

h. Creolization and language change. The social context of creolization, ed. by Ellen Woolford and William Washabaugh, pp. 126-36. Ann Arbor, Mich.: Karoma. [In this volume, pp. 271-84.]

i. Author's postscript. [In this volume, pp. 365-68.]

Polomé, Edgar C.   1920-
        Language, society, and paleoculture:
essays by Edgar C. Polomé. Selected and
introduced by Anwar S. Dil. Stanford, California:
Stanford University Press [1982]
        xvi, 388 p.   24cm.
(Language science and national development series,
Linguistic Research Group of Pakistan)
        Includes bibliography.
I. Dil, Anwar S., 1928-   ed.
II. (Series) III. Linguistic Research Group of Pakistan